NORTON ANTHOLOGY OF WESTERN MUSIC

Fourth Edition

VOLUME I

Ancient to Baroque

NORTON ANTHOLOGY OF WESTERN MUSIC

Fourth Edition

EDITED BY

CLAUDE V. PALISCA
Yale University

VOLUME I

Ancient to Baroque

W. W. NORTON & COMPANY · NEW YORK · LONDON

Printed in the United States of America

Editor: Michael Ochs
Project editor: Kathy Talalay
Manufacturing director: Roy Tedoff

The text of this book is composed in Minion
with the display set in Gill Sans
Composition by TSI
Manufacturing by TK
Book design by Mary McDonnell
Cover illustration: Georges Braque. *Musical Instruments* (detail). 1908. Private collection. © 2000 Artists Rights Society (ARS), New York/ADAGP, Paris.

ISBN 0-393-97690-4 (pbk.)

W. W. Norton & Company, Inc., 500 Fifth Avenue, New York, N.Y. 10110
www.wwnorton.com

W. W. Norton & Company Ltd., 10 Coptic Street, London WC1A 1PU

1 2 3 4 5 6 7 8 9 0

CONTENTS

The Beginnings of Polyphony and the Music of the Thirteenth Century

French and Italian Music in the Fourteenth Century

England and the Burgundian Lands in the Fifteenth Century

The Age of the Renaissance: Music of the Low Countries

New Currents in the Sixteenth Century

Church Music of the Late Renaissance and Reformation

Music of the Early Baroque Period

Opera and Vocal Music in the Late Seventeenth Century

Instrumental Music in the Late Baroque Period

Music in the Early Eighteenth Century

Appendixes and Indexes

PREFACE

The title *Norton Anthology of Western Music* (NAWM) needs one important qualifier: it is a *historical* anthology of Western music. There is a wide difference between a historical anthology and one intended to supply music for study and analysis.

Historians cannot confine themselves to studying, in splendid isolation, the great works that are the usual stuff of anthologies. They are interested in products of the imagination, great and small, as they exist on a continuum and in a historical and social context. Just as composers did not create in a musical void, standing aloof from the models of their predecessors and contemporaries, so the historically oriented student and analyst must have access to the primary material in order to establish historical connections. This anthology invites students and teachers to make such connections. It brings together important works and their models—for example, pieces written on a common subject or built according to similar procedures, or influenced by another composer's work.

Composers before 1500 often reworked, adapted, or expanded on earlier compositions, and there are numerous examples of this practice even after that date. Whenever possible in this anthology, I provide the music that served to ignite a composer's imagination. In one notable case a single chant, *Alleluia Pascha nostrum* (NAWM 15), gave rise to a chain of polyphonic accretions. It was elaborated by Léonin in organum purum with clausulae and was refreshed with substitute clausulae by his successors. Anonymous musicians then turned some of the clausulae themselves into motets by fitting them with Latin or French texts or by enhancing them with new voice parts, texted or not. The Alleluia group in this fourth edition has been abridged and conforms with the accompanying recording both in the succession of works and in their manner of notation. (Our Alleluia set, although different in content, format, and realization, is modeled on similar sets based on this chant that were compiled as teaching aids by Richard Crocker and Karl Kroeger. I am indebted to them for the general idea and for certain details.)

Later examples of this process are Du Fay's Mass on the ballade *Se la face ay pale* (NAWM 29); Ockeghem's Mass (NAWM 31) on the tenor of Binchois's rondeau *De plus en plus* (NAWM 30); Josquin's Mass on the hymn *Pange lingua* (NAWM 32); Byrd's *Pavana Lachrymae* (NAWM 46), which is based on Dowland's monodic *Flow, my tears* (NAWM 44); and the Concerto Grosso by Ellen Taaffe Zwilich (NAWM 150), based on a Handel Violin Sonata. In the twentieth century the variation procedure is the structural principle for other excerpts, namely those by Strauss (NAWM 124), Schoenberg (NAWM 136), and Copland (NAWM 143).

Subtler connections may be detected between Musorgsky's song *Okonchen prazdnyi, shumnyi den'* (NAWM 125) and Debussy's *Nuages* (NAWM 128), or between Ravel's minuet from *Le Tombeau de Couperin* (129) and the *Lamentation* by Froberger (NAWM 64) and the harpsichord pieces by Couperin (NAWM 73).

Comparing the same dramatic moments in the legend of Orpheus as realized by Peri and Monteverdi (NAWM 52 and 54), allows us to see the latter's debts to the former.

Some of the selections betray foreign influences—for example, the migration of Italian styles into England, as in Purcell's song from the *Fairy Queen* (NAWM 70), and into Germany, as in the aria from Hasse's *Cleofide* (NAWM 86). Handel's career hit a crisis because of these influences—the popularity of the ballad opera, exemplified by a scene from *The Beggar's Opera* (NAWM 87), and the English audience's rejection of the older type of Italian *opera seria*, as represented by *Giulio Cesare* (NAWM 83), led him to concentrate on the oratorio (*Saul*, NAWM 84). An important stimulus both to Handel and Hasse (NAWM 86) was the new Italian style represented by Pergolesi's *La serva padrona* (NAWM 85).

Several selections document the influence of vernacular and traditional music on art music. Haydn based the finale of his Symphony No. 104 (NAWM 96) on what was probably a Croatian song. Debussy adapted the texture and melodic idiom of a Javanese gamelan to his own orchestral conception (*Nuages*, NAWM 128). Stravinsky simulated folk polyphony in his *Le Sacre du printemps* (NAWM 134). Bartók emulated the styles of Serbo-Croatian *parlando-rubato* chanting and of Bulgarian dance orchestras in his *Music for Strings, Percussion,* and *Celesta* (NAWM 130), and Gunther Schuller caught the flavors of Middle Eastern music in *Arabische Stadt* (NAWM 148b). William Grant Still in his *Afro-American Symphony* (NAWM 144) and Schuller in his *Der Blauteufel* (NAWM 148a) applied elements of blues and jazz.

Some composers are represented by more than one work to permit comparison of early and late styles (for example, Josquin, Monteverdi, Bach, Handel, Vivaldi, Haydn, Beethoven, and Schoenberg) or to show distinct approaches by a single composer to diverse genres (Machaut, Du Fay, Josquin, Victoria, Byrd, Purcell, Buxtehude, Handel, Haydn, Mozart, Beethoven, and Schumann).

A number of the pieces beat new paths in their day, among them Willaert's *Aspro core* from his *Musica nova* (NAWM 37), Viadana's solo concerto *O Domine, Jesu Christe* (NAWM 59), and C. P. E. Bach's sonata (NAWM 91).

Certain pieces won a place because contemporary critics or the composers themselves singled them out. Artusi dismembered Monteverdi's *Cruda Amarilli* (NAWM 53) in his dialogue of 1600, which contains both a critique and a defense of Monteverdi's innovations. Caccini mentioned in the preface to his own *Euridice* that *Vedrò 'l mio sol* (NAWM 51) was one of his pioneering attempts. Cesti's *Intorno all'idol mio* (NAWM 56) was one of the most frequently cited arias of the mid-seventeenth century. Rousseau roundly criticized and d'Alembert carefully analyzed Lully's monologue in *Armide, Enfin il est en ma puissance* (NAWM 68b). Athanasius Kircher praised the scene of Carissimi's *Jephthe* (NAWM 61) as a triumph of the powers of musical expression. The first movement of Beethoven's *Eroica Symphony* (NAWM 103) and the *Danse des adolescentes* in Stravinsky's *Le Sacre du printemps* (NAWM 134) were both objects of critical uproars after their premieres. Shostakovich's opera *Lady Macbeth of Mtsensk* (NAMW 131), after successful performances in Leningrad, Moscow, and in western theaters, was denounced in *Pravda* and subsequently banned in the Soviet Union. The reactions to these compositions are exemplars of "reception history," a field that has recently attracted considerable attention among teachers and historians.

Certain items serve to correct commonplace misconceptions about the history of music. The symphonic movements of Sammartini and Stamitz (NAWM 90 and 92) show that Haydn's was not the only path to the Viennese symphony. The Allegro from Johann Christian Bach's E-flat Harpsichord/Pianoforte Concerto (NAWM 93) testifies to Mozart's dependence on this earlier model in his own Piano Concerto K. 488 (NAWM 99). The movement from Clementi's sonata (NAWM 102) reveals an intense romanticism and creative use of the piano that surpass Beethoven's writing of the same period and probably influenced it.

Women composers are represented across the centuries—in the twelfth century by Hildegard of Bingen and Beatriz de Dia (NAWM 6 and 10); in the seventeenth by Barbara Strozzi (NAWM 57); in the nineteenth by, Clara Wieck Schumann (NAWM 114); and in the twentieth by Sofia Gubaidulina, Amy Cheney Beach, Ruth Crawford Seeger, and Ellen Taaffe Zwilich (NAWM 132, 140, 142, 150).

I have generally aimed to choose superlative creations that represent their makers, genres, or times. Some pieces mark important turning points and shifts of style; others mark historical phenomena that are interesting if not always conducive to creating great music. Still others represent new models of constructive procedures, typical moments in the work of individual composers, or challenging specimens for historical and structural analysis.

The proportion of space assigned to a person or work does not reflect my valuation of the composer's greatness. Regretably, many major figures could not be represented at all. In an anthology of limited size every work chosen excludes another of corresponding length that may be equally worthy. Didactic functionality, historical illumination, and intrinsic musical quality, rather than greatness, genius, or popularity, were the major criteria for selection.

The inclusion of a complete Office (NAWM 4) and a nearly complete Mass (NAWM 3) deserves special comment. I realize that the rituals as represented here have little validity as historical documents of the Middle Ages. It would have been more authentic, perhaps, to present a Mass and Office as practiced in a particular place at a particular moment, say in the twelfth century. Since the Vatican Council, the liturgies printed here are themselves archaic formulas, a circumstance that strengthens the case for their inclusion because opportunities to experience a Vespers service or Mass sung in Latin in their classic formulations are now rare indeed. I decided to reproduce the editions of the modern chant books, with their stylized neumatic notation, even though they are not "urtexts." But these books are the only resources available to many students, and it should be part of their training to become familiar with the editorial conventions of the Solesmes editions.

Many of the recordings that accompany this anthology are new to this edition. I have taken advantage, other factors being equal, of the improved fidelity of digital

recording. I was partly guided in my choices for early music by recent published opinion about performance practices. For the Baroque and early Classic periods, I have favored ensembles that use period instruments. Although the extension of this practice to later music is still controversial, I have included very attractive renditions with period instruments for the symphonies of Beethoven and Berlioz, in part to stimulate discussion and consideration of this option. Users of our recorded anthology should not expect to hear every notated detail, because performers take liberties with written scores. This is particularly true with respect to musica ficta, where the editor may have suggested one solution while the performers chose another, and in periods and genres of music in which artists were expected or chose to improvise and embellish.

Compact-disk track numbers have been added to the scores (in square boxes for the full set of CDs, in diamond-shaped boxes for the shorter set). These numbers are placed not only at the beginning but strategically within selections to aid in study, analysis, and teaching.

Because the Fourth Edition of this anthology, like the Third, contains commentaries and analytical notes following the selections, such discussions are condensed in the Sixth Edition of *A History of Western Music* (HWM). However, more extended treatments of some pieces have been retained in HWM when they clarify some of the general trends and techniques considered under each topic. The selections have been arranged in the order in which they are discussed in HWM rather than by period and genre. An index of references in HWM to numbers of this anthology appears at the back of each volume.

Although this anthology was conceived as a companion to HWM, it also is intended to stand by itself as a collection of music representing major trends, genres, national schools, and historical developments or innovations.

The translations of the poetic and prose texts are my own, except where acknowledged. They are literal to a fault, corresponding to the original line by line, often word for word, with consequent inevitable damage to the English style. In my experience, the musical analyst prefers precise detail of the composer's text to imaginative and evocative locutions. I am indebted to Ann Walters Robertson for helping with some stubborn medieval Latin poems, to Ingeborg Glier for casting light on some impenetrable lines of middle-high German, and to Laurel Fay for help in the English version of Musorgsky's song and the excerpt from Shostakovich's opera.

The Yale Music Library was my indispensable base of operations, and its staff a prime resource for the development of this anthology. I wish to thank particularly the late Harold Samuel, Music Librarian Emeritus; his successor Kendall Crilly; and their associates Kathryn R. Mansi, Suzanne M. Eggleston, and Helen Bartlett. Karl W. Schrom, Record Librarian, was a remarkable fount of knowledge and advice about recorded performances.

The CDs were compiled by Thomas Laskey of SONY Special Products, whom I thank for offering options for some rarely performed works.

This anthology owes very much to Claire Brook, who, as the former music editor of Norton, proposed the idea of an anthology to accompany the Third Edition of Donald J. Grout's *A History of Western Music*. In adjusting the content to the changing needs of the field, I benefited from the advice of Norton's music editor, Michael Ochs, and of those who answered a questionnaire in the spring of 1999.

W. W. Norton and I are grateful to the individuals and publishers cited in the source notes who granted permission to reprint, re-edit, or adapt material under copyright. Where no modern publication is cited, I edited the music from original sources.

Claude V. Palisca
Hamden, Connecticut

RECORDINGS

Recordings accompanying this anthology are available under the titles *Norton Recorded Anthology of Western Music* (12 CDs containing all the pieces in the two volumes) and *Concise Norton Recorded Anthology of Western Music* (4 CDs containing 68 of the pieces in the two volumes). The corresponding CD numbers are indicated in the scores, near the title (in square boxes for the full set of CDs, in diamond-shaped boxes for the shorter set). Track numbers for both sets of CDs are indicated in the scores as follows:

12-CD set (tracks indicated by boxed numbers):

CD 1: NAWM 1–19
CD 2: NAWM 20–38
CD 3: NAWM 39–53
CD 4: NAWM 54–67
CD 5: NAWM 68–80
CD 6: NAWM 81–84
CD 7: NAWM 85–96
CD 8: NAWM 97–104
CD 9: NAWM 105–117
CD 10: NAWM 118–124
CD 11: NAWM 125–138
CD 12: NAWM 139–150

4-CD set (tracks indicated by diamond-shaped boxes):

CD 1: NAWM 1–45
CD 2: NAWM 46–83
CD 3: NAWM 85–119
CD 4: NAWM 121–149

NORTON ANTHOLOGY OF WESTERN MUSIC

Fourth Edition

VOLUME I

Ancient to Baroque

Epitaph of Seikilos CD 1 CD 1

1 1

found in 1st cent C.E.
plucked + voice
syllabic
diatonic tetrachord
monophonic

C Z Z K I Z I
Ὅ – σον ζῇς φαί – νου
K I Z I K O C O Φ
μη – δὲν ὅλ – ως σὺ λυ – ποῦ·
C K Z I K I K C O Φ
πρὸς ὀ – λί – γον ἐσ – τὶ τὸ ζῆν,
C K O I Z K C C C X
τὸ τέ – λος ὁ χρό–νος ἀ – παι – τεῖ.

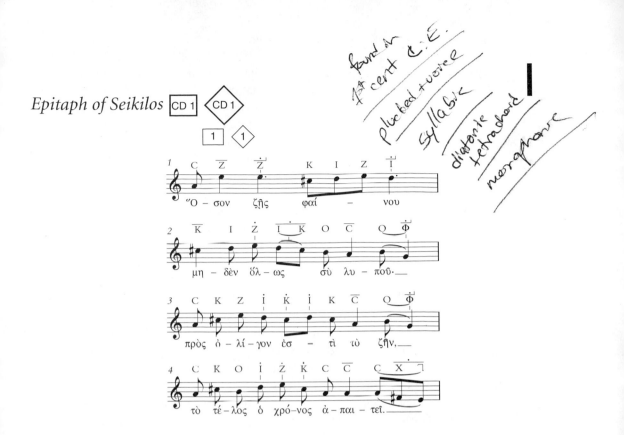

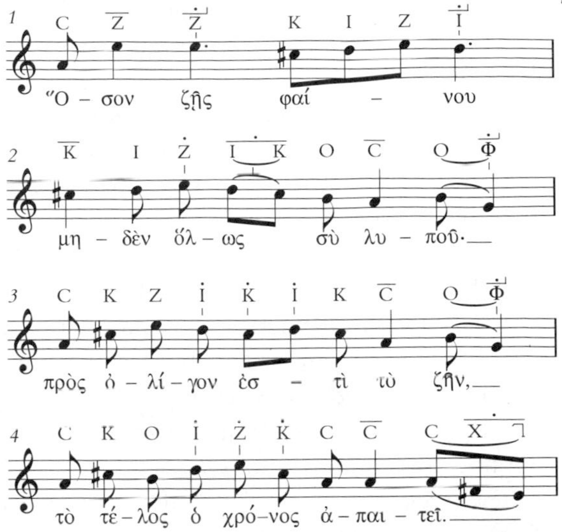

As long as you live, be lighthearted.
Let nothing trouble you.
Life is only too short,
and time takes its toll.

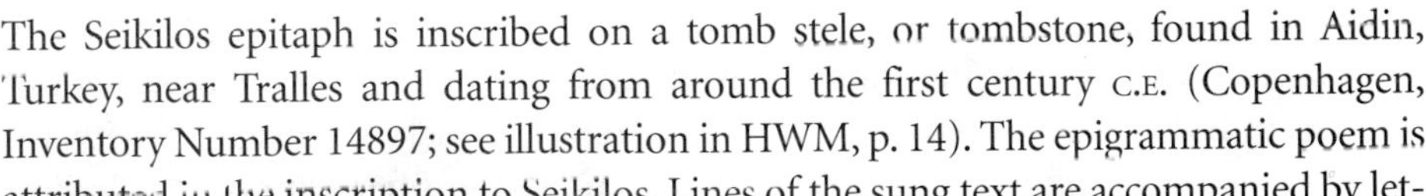

The Seikilos epitaph is inscribed on a tomb stele, or tombstone, found in Aidin, Turkey, near Tralles and dating from around the first century C.E. (Copenhagen, Inventory Number 14897; see illustration in HWM, p. 14). The epigrammatic poem is attributed in the inscription to Seikilos. Lines of the sung text are accompanied by letters representing pitches in the Greek notation and by signs indicating their duration.

It is possible to transcribe the piece by using the notational tables of Alypius and to analyze the song by using criteria from theorists of the time, especially Claudius Ptolemy.

Every note of the octave *e–e′*, with *F* and *C* sharped, is in the song, so that the octave species is unambiguously identifiable as that called Phrygian by Cleonides, equivalent to the *D*-octave on the white keys of a piano. The most prominent notes are *a* and the two boundary notes *e* and *e′*. The note *a* is the most frequent note (eight occurrences), and three of the four phrases begin on it; *e′* is the topmost pitch in all four phrases and occurs six times; *e* is the final note of the piece. Of subsidiary importance are *g*, which closes two of the phrases but is skipped over at the end, and *d′*, which closes one.

The prominence of *a* is significant, because it is the central note or mese of the octave. In the *Problems* attributed to Aristotle that may include writings of others, it is stated: "In all good music *mese* occurs frequently, and all good composers have frequent recourse to *mese*, and, if they leave it, they soon return to it, as they do to no other note."*

The *e–e′* octave with two sharps is a segment of the two-octave scale *B–b′* with two sharps, identified by Alypius as the diatonic Iastian tonos, a lower form of the Phrygian that is also known as Ionian (see analysis of the inscription on facing page). Although the Greeks were not thinking in terms of fixed pitch, this tonos effectively transposes the Greater Perfect System up a whole tone from Alypius's Hypolydian, or in our notation, from *A–a′* to *B–b′*. In terms of Ptolemy's theory, the superimposition of the Phrygian octave species on the Iastian tonos within the central octave of the Greater Pefect System (see Ptolemy's Phrygian tonos in HWM, Example 1.2) explains the alteration of the "natural" Dorian sequence of intervals through the composer's use of raised second (*f* to *f*♯) and sixth (*c* to *c#*) degrees of the scale. Thus, although the sequence of notes in the octave of the composition still extends (in Ptolemy's thetic nomenclature) from hypate meson to nete diezeugmenon and the most important notes in the composition still fall on the fixed pitches of the two tetrachords, the sequence of pitches causes one of the movable notes in each tetrachord (the thetic parhypate meson and the trite diezeugmenon) to occupy a higher position than it would normally have done in the natural sequence of intervals.

So far as the ethos of the song is concerned, it seems to be neither excited nor depressed, but balanced between the two extremes, which is consistent with the Ionian tonos. In terms of Alypius's arrangement of the fifteen tonoi, the Ionian, with proslambanomenos on *B* and mese on *b*, is intermediate between the lowest, Hypodorian, with proslambanomenos on *F* and mese on *f*, and the highest, Hyperlydian, with proslambanomenos on *g* and mese on *g′*. The major thirds would be perceived today, and probably then also, as bright, as would the rising fifth of the opening. The message of the poem is, indeed, optimistic.

The Seikilos song has been of particular interest to historians because of its clear rhythmic notation. The notes without rhythmic markings above the alphabetical signs are worth a unit of duration (*protos chronos*); the horizontal dash indicates a *diseme*, worth two beats, and the horizontal mark with an upward stroke to the right is a *triseme* worth three. Each line has twelve beats.

*Aristotle, *Problems* 19.20 (919a), trans. E. M. Forster in *The Works of Aristotle*, ed. W. D. Ross, Vol. 7, *Problemata* (Oxford: Clarendon Press, 1927).

Analysis of Seikilos Inscription

Thetic names		*Name by function* (Iastian tonos)	*Species* (Phrygian)
fixed nete diezeugmenon	*e′*	paranete diezeugmenon	
			Tone
paranete diezeugm	d	trite diezeugmenon	
			Semitone
trite diezeugmenon	c♯	paramese	
		disjunction	Tone
fixed paramese	b	mese	
disjunction			Tone
fixed mese	a	lichanos meson	
			Tone
lichanos meson	g	parhypate meson	
			Semitone
parhypate meson	f♯	hypate meson	
			Tone
fixed hypate meson	e	lichanos hypaton	

2 EURIPIDES (CA. 485–CA. 406 B.C.E.)

Orestes: Stasimon Chorus CD 1

Fragment, lines 338–44

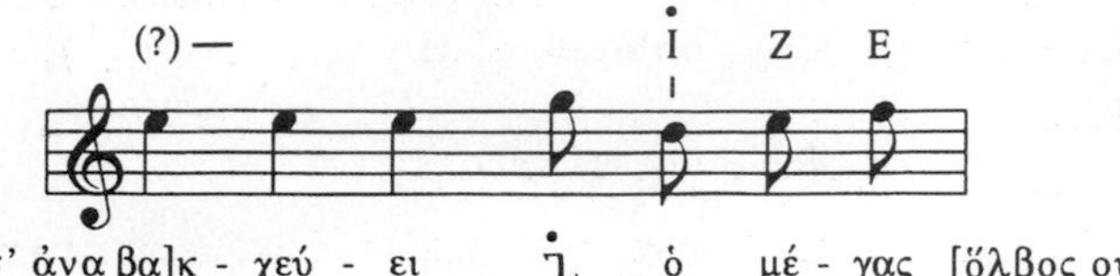

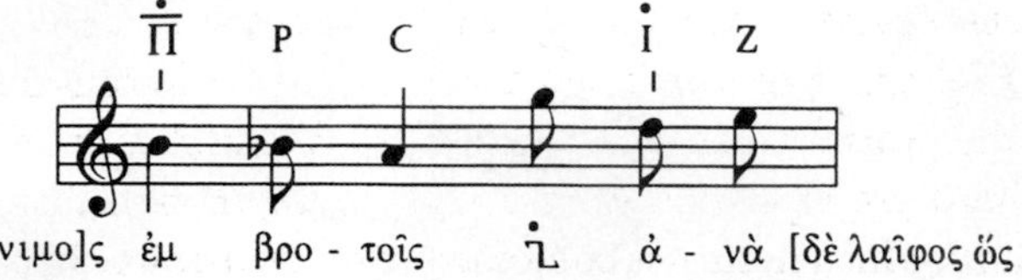

· C P Z

[text uncertain]

You wild goddesses who dart across the skies seeking vengeance for murder, we implore you to free Agamemnon's son from his raging fury. . . . We grieve for this boy. Happiness is brief among mortals. Sorrow and anguish sweep down on it like a swift gust of wind on a sloop, and it sinks under the tossing seas.

Vienna, Österreichische Nationalbibliothek, Papyrus G2315. Reprinted from *Apollo's Lyre: Greek Music and Music Theory in Antiquity and the Middle Ages* by Thomas J. Mathiesen by permission of the University of Nebraska Press. © 1999 by the University of Nebraska Press, p.117. For a detailed analysis, see ibid, pp. 117–20.

This fragment of the chorus from Euripides' *Orestes* is on a papyrus from the third century B.C.E. The tragedy has been dated 408 B.C.E. It is possible that the music was composed by Euripides himself, who was renowned for his musical settings. This chorus is a *stasimon*, an ode sung while the chorus stood still in its place in the *orchestra*, a semicircular rim between the stage and the benches of the spectators.

The papyrus contains seven lines with musical notation, but only the middle of each of the seven lines survives; the beginning and end of each line of text are shown within brackets. Forty-two notes of the piece survive, but because a good many are missing, any performance must be a reconstruction, like that in the recording that accompanies this anthology.

Some of the alphabetical signs are vocal and some instrumental; some are enharmonic (or chromatic) and some diatonic (see the analysis on the following page). This transcription renders the dense intervals as chromatic, but by varying the "shade," these could be converted to the denser enharmonic. The surviving notes fit into the Lydian tonos of Alypius. The three lowest notes of the diezeugmenon tetrachord are separated by the tone of disjunction from the chromatic meson tetrachord, which in turn is conjoined with the diatonic hypaton tetrachord, whose top two notes are used. The piece, therefore, seems to be written in a mixture of the chromatic and diatonic genera. The octave species, or *harmonia*, appears to be Phrygian, but two harmoniae described as dating from the time of Plato by the musical theorist and philosopher Aristides Quintilianus (fourth century C.E.)—his Dorian and Phrygian—almost exactly coincide with the scale that is found here, as the analysis of the *Orestes* Stasimon fragment below shows.

Analysis of *Orestes* Stasimon Fragment

Dynamic names	Phryg. diat.	octave spec.	*Alypius signs for Lydian* enharmonic voc.	inst.	*Aristides Q. harmoniae* Dorian		Phrygian	
					a′	⊖		
							g′	Ⴎ
paranete diezeugmenon	g′			Z	f′	Δ	f′	Δ
trite diezeugmenon	f′	T	E		e′ +	E	e′ +	E
paramese	e′	S	Z		e′	Z	e′	Z
(disjunction)		T						
mese	d′				d′	I	d′	I
lichanos meson chrom.	b	T	Π	Ɔ	a♯	Π	a♯	Π
parhypate meson	b♭	T	P		a +	P	a +	P
hypate meson	a	S	C		a	C	a	C
lichanos hypaton	g	T	Φ		g	Φ	g	Φ
[parhypate hypaton]	[f]	]						
hypate hypaton	e			⅂				

In the stasimon, the women of Argos implore the gods to have mercy on Orestes, who had murdered his mother, Clytemnestra, six days before the play begins. He had plotted with his sister Electra to punish their mother for infidelity to their father, Agamemnon. The chorus begs that Orestes be released from the madness that has overwhelmed him since the murder. The rhythm of the poetry, and therefore of the music, is dominated by the dochmiac foot, which was used in Greek tragedy during passages of intense agitation and grief. The dochmiac consists of three long followed by two short syllables, but often, as here, a long syllable is resolved into two short ones, so that instead of five notes per foot there are six. In the transcription, the feet are separated by vertical bars in the "text rhythm" symbols.

Instrumental notes punctuate the choral singing: *g′* in lines 1 through 4, *f♯′–b* in lines 5 and 6. The hypate meson (*a*) is prominent, in that two of the lines of verse (marked in lines 1 and 3 by the instrumental note *g*) end on *a*, and a number of phrases of the melody are clustered around the paramese *e′*; both *a* and *e* are stable pitches in the Lydian tonos, and they are the lowest steps in the two tetrachords utilized in the piece (see the analysis above).

Gregorian Chant 3

Mass for Christmas Day CD 1 ⟨CD 1⟩

Instructions for Reading Modern Plainchant Notation

One line of the four-line staff is designated by a clef as either middle *C* (𝄡) or the *F* immediately below it (𝄢). These are not absolute but relative pitches. The *neumes*, as the shapes are called, are usually assigned equal durations, although at one time they may have had some temporal significance. Two or more neumes in succession on the same line or space, if on the same syllable, are sung as though tied. Composite neumes, representing two or more pitches, are read from left to right, except for the *podatus* or *pes* (⁝), in which the lower note is sung first. Oblique neumes (⊾) stand for two different pitches. A neume, whether simple or composite, never carries more than one syllable. Flat signs, except in a signature at the beginning of a line, are valid only until the next vertical division line or until the beginning of the next word.

The Vatican editions, such as the *Liber usualis* (*LU*), employ in addition a number of interpretive signs, based on the performance practices of the Benedictine monks of the Solesmes Congregation. A horizontal dash above or below a neume means it is to be slightly lengthened. A vertical stroke above or below a note marks the beginning of a rhythmic unit when this would not otherwise be obvious. A dot after a note doubles its value. Vertical bars of varied lengths show the division of a melody into periods (full bar), phrases (half-bar), and smaller members (a stroke through the uppermost staff-line). The note-like symbol on a space or line at the end of the staff is a *custos* (guard), a guide to lead the reader to the first note on the following line.

An asterisk in the text shows where the chorus takes over from the soloist, and the signs *ij* and *iij* (ditto and double-ditto) indicate that the preceding phrase is to be sung twice or three times.

The music for each of the major feasts of the church calendar has special qualities, and that is true of the Mass for Christmas Day (*in die Natali*). The Proper chants are unique to this day in the church calendar. A variety of Ordinary chants may be used, but they must include the Gloria, which is omitted during certain times in the liturgical year. Beginning in the thirteenth century, Ordinary chants were organized into *cycles*; the Ordinary chants chosen for this anthology are taken from a Mass cycle whose Kyrie-Gloria pair occurs in manuscripts as early as the twelfth century and is numbered V in the *Liber usualis* (pp. 28–31). Neither the chants of the Proper of a given day nor the Ordinary cycle shows any consistency of age or mode. The neumes on the four-line staff indicate relative pitch; the cantor chose a pitch that suited the singers' voices.

a) Introit: *Puer natus est nobis*

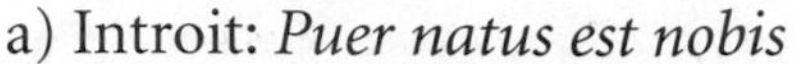

Intr. 7.

PUer * ná- tus est nó- bis, et fí- li- us dá- tus est

nó- bis : cú-jus impé- ri- um super hú- me-rum é-

jus : et vocá- bi-tur nómen é- jus, mágni consí-

li- i Ange- lus. *Ps.* Can-tá-te Dómino cánti-cum nó-

vum : * qui- a mi-rabí- li-a fé- cit. Gló- ri-a Pátri.

E u o u a e.

Puer natus est nobis, et filius datus est nobis:
cujus imperium super humerum ejus:
et vocabitur nomen ejus, magni consili
Angelus.

Ps. Cantate Domino canticum novum: quia
mirabilia fecit.

℣. Gloria Patri, et Filio, et Spiritui Sancto. Sicut
erat in principio, et nunc, et semper, et in
saecula saeculorum.
Amen.

A child is born to us, and a Son is given to us;
whose government is upon His shoulder;
and His Name shall be called the Angel of great
counsel.

Ps. Sing ye to the Lord a new canticle, because He
hath done wonderful things.

℣. Glory be to the Father, and to the Son, and to
the Holy Ghost. As it was in the beginning, is
now, and ever shall be, world without end.
Amen.

The sung portion of the Mass begins with the Introit. The Introit *Puer natus est nobis* was often troped (received added words and music) as a dramatic dialogue (see NAWM 7). Two chant styles may be distinguished in this and other Introits.

Ordinaries from Mass V, *Liber usualis*, pp. 28–31. Propers from *LU*, 408–10.

One style is used to sing the psalm verse (indicated by *Ps.*) and the Gloria Patri, or Lesser Doxology (praise to God), which follows the psalm verse (concerning the Doxology, see below, p. 12). In this recitational manner the melody holds mostly to one pitch—here *D*, the reciting tone of Mode 7, the mode of this Introit—with opening rises and cadential falls, one or two notes per syllable. The other style, more varied and florid, is that of the antiphon—the music preceding the psalm (and normally sung again after the psalm verse). Both the antiphon and the psalm verse end on *G*, the final of Modes 7 and 8. The antiphon shows traces of the reciting tone *C*, which is used in several modes but not in the seventh mode. Like this Introit, many return frequently to the note *C*, even if it is not the reciting tone of the mode.

b) Kyrie

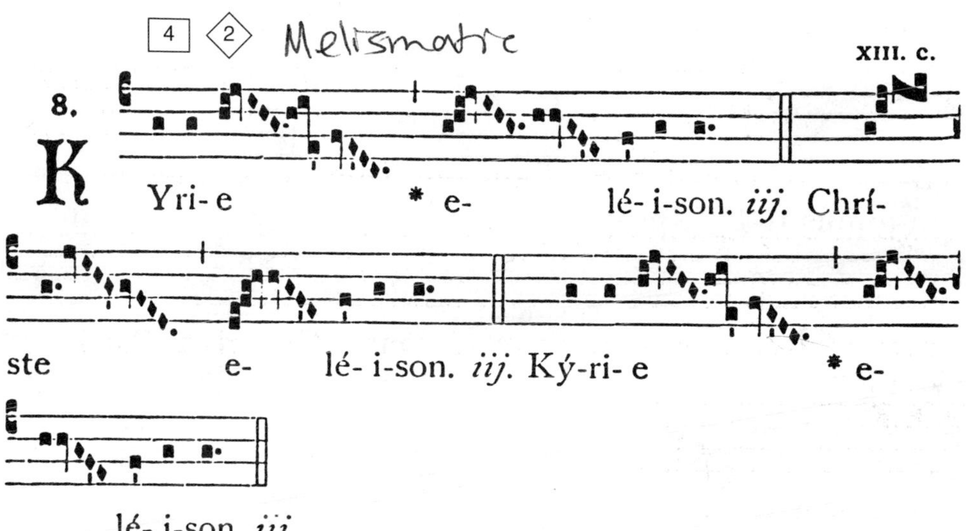

Kyrie eleison. Christe eleison. Kyrie eleison.	Lord have mercy. Christ have mercy. Lord have mercy.

After the Introit the choir chants the Kyrie. Among the musical settings of the Kyrie that may be sung on this Sunday is one known as *Kyrie magnae Deus potentiae*, from the thirteenth century. The invocation "Kyrie eleison" (Lord have mercy) is repeated three times; then "Christe eleison" (Christ have mercy) is repeated three times, after which the threefold Kyrie is sung again. The simplest settings use one melody for all the Kyries and a different melody for all the Christes, and that is the pattern followed here.

This chant is classified as being in Mode 8. It fits the plagal range by extending upward a fifth from the final *g*; it exceeds the downward range by a second to *c*.

c) Gloria

5
XII. c.
8.
GLó-ri- a in excélsis Dé- o. Et in térra pax ho-
mí-ni-bus bónae vo-luntá-tis. Laudámus te. Bene-dí-ci-
mus te. Adorámus te. Glo-ri-fi-cámus te. Grá- ti- as
á-gimus tí-bi propter mágnam gló- ri- am tú- am.
Dó-mi-ne Dé-us Rex caeléstis, Dé-us Pá-ter o-mní-
pot-ens. Dó-mi-ne Fí-li unigéni-te Jé-su Chríste.
Dómine Dé-us A-gnus Dé- i, Fí-li- us Pá- tris. Qui
tól-lis peccáta múndi, mi-se- ré- re nó-bis. Qui tól-
lis peccá-ta múndi, súscipe depre-ca-ti- ónem nó-

stram. Qui sé-des ad déxteram Pátris, mi-se- ré-
re nó-bis. Quó- ni- am tu só-lus sánctus. Tu só- lus Dóminus. Tu só- lus Al- tíssimus, Jé- su Chrí- ste. Cum
Sáncto Spí-ri-tu, in gló-ri- a Dé- i Pá- tris. A-
men.

Gloria in excelsis Deo
Et in terra pax hominibus bonae voluntatis.
Laudamus te. Benedicimus te. Adoramus te.
Glorificamus te.
Gratias agimus tibi propter magnam gloriam tuam.
Domine Deus, Rex caelestis,
Deus Pater omnipotens.
Domine Fili unigenite Jesu Christe.
Domine Deus, Agnus Dei, Filius Patris.
Qui tollis peccata mundi,
miserere nobis.
Qui tollis peccata mundi,
suscipe deprecationem nostram.
Qui sedes ad dexteram Patris,
miserere nobis.
Quoniam tu solus sanctus.
Tu solus Dominus.
Tu solus Altissimus, Jesu Christe.
Cum Sancto Spiritu,
In Gloria Dei Patris. Amen.

Glory be to God on high.
And on earth peace to men of good will.
We praise thee, we bless thee, we adore thee,
we glorify thee.
We give thee thanks for thy great glory.
O Lord God, King of heaven,
God the Father Almighty.
O Lord, the only begotten Son, Jesus Christ.
O Lord God, Lamb of God, Son of the Father.
Thou who takest away the sins of the world,
have mercy on us.
Thou who takest away the sins of the world,
receive our prayer.
Thou who sittest at the right hand of the Father,
have mercy on us.
For thou only art holy,
Thou only art Lord.
Thou only art most high, O Jesus Christ,
With the Holy Ghost,
In the glory of God the Father. Amen.

Because the Gloria, or Greater Doxology, has a relatively long text, most syllables are sung to only one, two, or three notes. This chant, in the eighth mode, holds strictly to its plagal octave between *d* and *d′*. The *Liber usualis* attributes this chant to the twelfth century, and its unusual pattern of melodic repetition suggests a late date. The repeated melodic units are sometimes shorter, sometimes longer than a textual phrase. For example, the melody for "in excelsis Deo" is set to the complete sentence "Benedicimus te," the unpunctuated phrase "agimus tibi," and eight other segments of text. The melodic member first heard at "Laudamus te" serves three other two-word groups, four single words, and the syllable "A" of "A-men." The longest melodic element, first heard at "Et in terra pax hominibus," is split between two sentences at "Adoramus te. Glorificamus te," with the melisma broken up into four syllables. The melody is heard six more times, with the melisma kept intact. The reciting tone *c′*, usually prominent in a wordy text, plays no part in the composition.

After the Gloria a prayer called the Collect is chanted to a very simple formula, practically a monotone. Then the Epistle, one of the letters of the apostle Paul to the Hebrews, is recited, again to a simple formula.

d) Gradual: *Viderunt omnes*

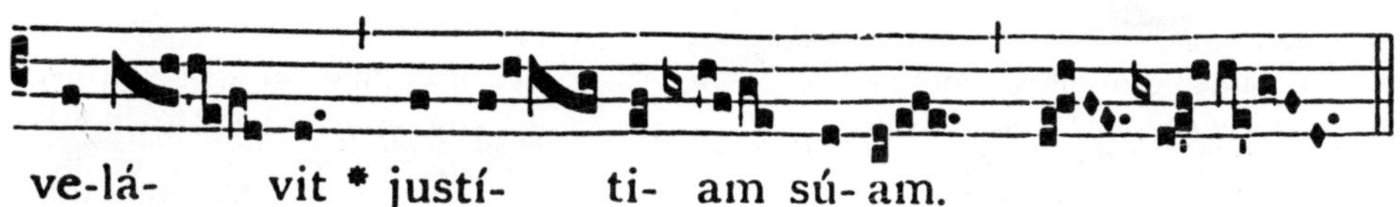
ve-lá- vit * justí- ti- am sú- am.

Viderunt omnes fines terrae salutare Dei nostri: jubilate Deo omnis terra.
℣. Notum fecit Dominus salutare suum: ante conspectum gentium revelavit justitiam suam.

All the ends of the earth have seen the salvation of our God; sing joyfully to God, all the earth.
℣. The Lord hath made known His salvation; He hath revealed His justice in the sight of the Gentiles.

This Gradual exemplifies responsorial psalmody, in which a soloist singing the psalm (Vulgate Ps. 97 [Eng. 98]:3-4, 2) alternates with a choir performing the respond. The extended melismas of *omnes* and *terrae*—typical of Graduals—received polyphonic elaboration in the twelfth century. Unlike the Introit's psalm verse, which was recitational, this verse is extremely ornate, intended as it was for a soloist, although the recitation tone *C* is prominent. Many Graduals exhibit a structure unified by motivic repetition, but this example does not. The fifth mode is frequently used in Graduals, as it is here. Its final is *F*, and the note *B* is sometimes flatted to avoid the melodic tritone.

e) Alleluia

8
2.
ALle-lú-ia. * *ij.* ℣. Dí-
es sancti-ficátus illúxit nó- bis :
ve- ní-te géntes, et adorá-te Dóminum : qui-a hó-di- e descéndit lux má-
gna * su-per tér- ram.

Alleluia. Alleluia. ℣. Dies sanctificatus illuxit nobis: venite gentes, et adorate Dominum: quia hodie descendit lux magna super terram.	Alleluia, alleluia. ℣. A sanctified day hath shone upon us; come ye Gentiles, and adore the Lord; for this day a great light hath descended upon the earth.

During most of the year, the Alleluia, another responsorial chant, follows the Gradual. As in the Gradual, a soloist sang the psalm verse, while the choir responded with "Alleluia"—from the Hebrew "Hallelujah" (praise Yahweh, or Jehovah). The Alleluia for Christmas Day is one of the oldest; it lacks the extended melisma on the final "a" called the *jubilus*. The phrases of this chant end mainly on the final of the second mode, *D*; some of them end on *C* and one on *A*, but none closes on the reciting tone *F*.

f) Credo

9

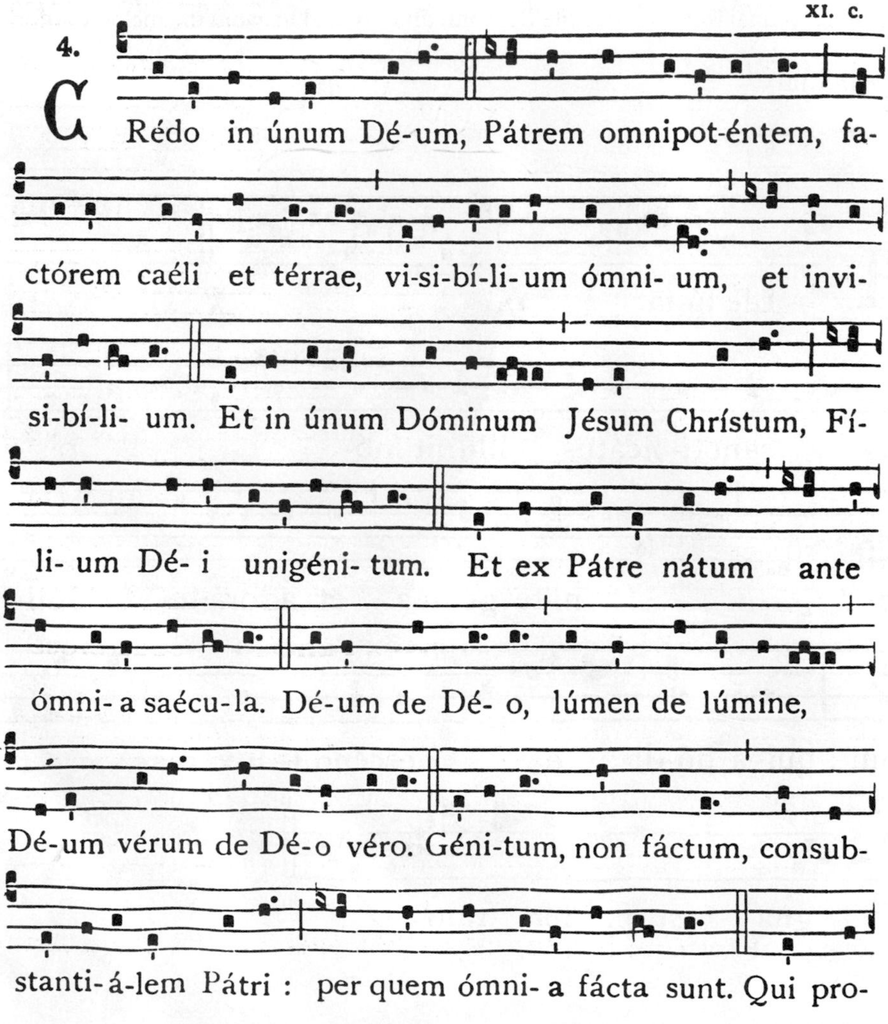

XI. c.

4.

CRédo in únum Dé-um, Pátrem omnipot-éntem, fa-
ctórem caéli et térrae, vi-si-bí-li-um ómni- um, et invi-
si-bí-li- um. Et in únum Dóminum Jésum Chrístum, Fí-
li- um Dé- i unigéni- tum. Et ex Pátre nátum ante
ómni- a saécu-la. Dé-um de Dé- o, lúmen de lúmine,
Dé-um vérum de Dé-o véro. Géni-tum, non fáctum, consub-
stanti-á-lem Pátri : per quem ómni- a fácta sunt. Qui pro-

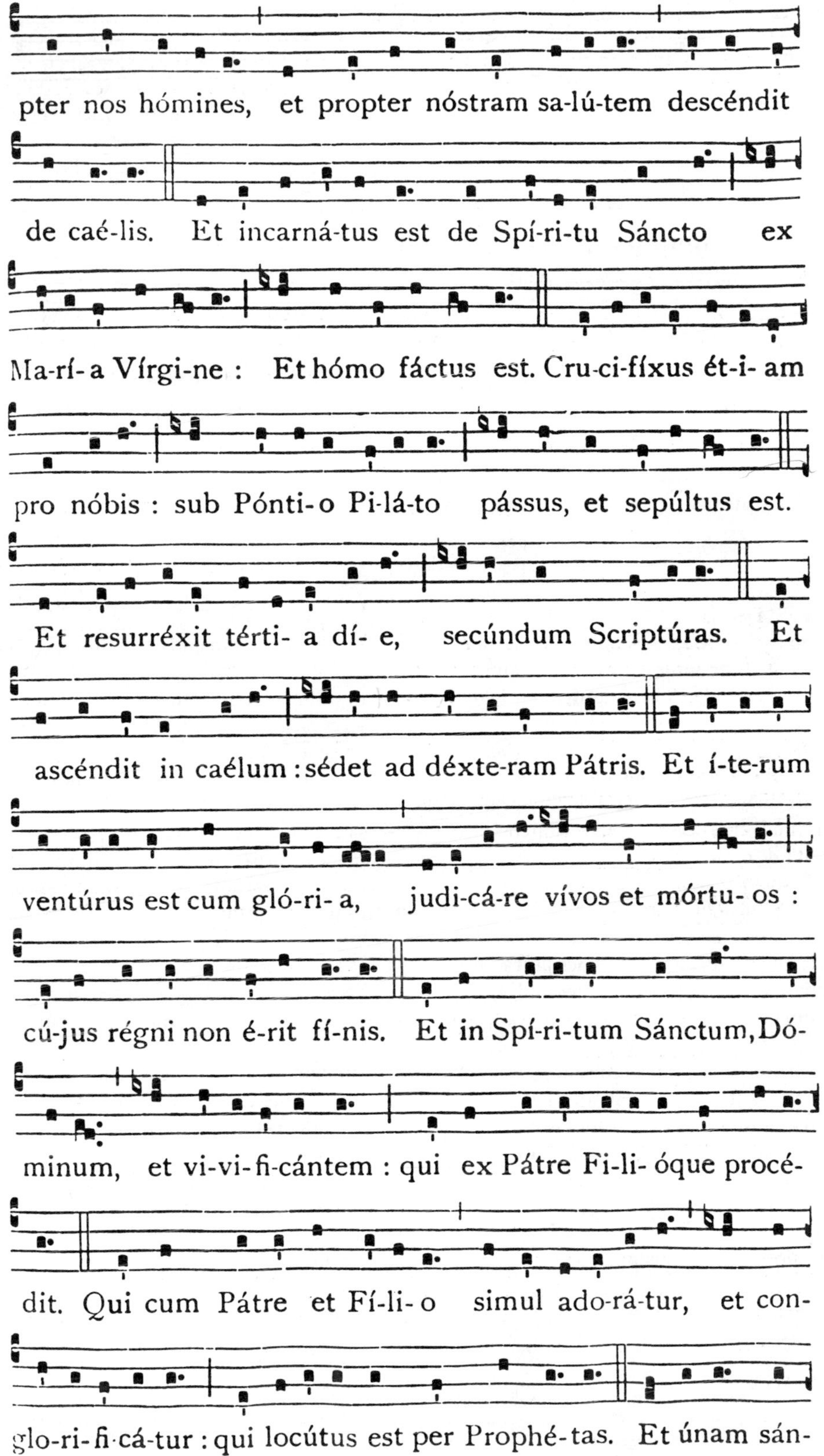
pter nos hómines, et propter nóstram sa-lú-tem descéndit
de caé-lis. Et incarná-tus est de Spí-ri-tu Sáncto ex
Ma-rí- a Vírgi-ne : Et hómo fáctus est. Cru-ci-fíxus ét-i- am
pro nóbis : sub Pónti- o Pi-lá-to pássus, et sepúltus est.
Et resurréxit térti- a dí- e, secúndum Scriptúras. Et
ascéndit in caélum : sédet ad déxte-ram Pátris. Et í-te-rum
ventúrus est cum gló-ri- a, judi-cá-re vívos et mórtu- os :
cú-jus régni non é-rit fí-nis. Et in Spí-ri-tum Sánctum, Dóminum, et vi-vi-fi-cántem : qui ex Pátre Fi-li- óque procé-
dit. Qui cum Pátre et Fí-li- o simul ado-rá-tur, et con-
glo-ri-fi-cá-tur : qui locútus est per Prophé-tas. Et únam sán-

Credo

Credo in unum Deum, Patrem omnipotentem, factorem caeli et terrae, visibilium omnium et invisibilium. Et in unum Dominum Jesum Christum Filium Dei unigenitum. Et ex Patre natum ante omnia saecula. Deum de Deo, lumen de lumine, Deum verum de Deo vero. Genitum, non factum, consubstantialem Patri: per quem omnia facta sunt. Qui propter nos homines et propter nostram salutem descendit de caelis. Et incarnatus est de Spiritu Sancto ex Maria Virgine: et homo factus est. Crucifixus etiam pro nobis: sub Pontio Pilato passus, et sepultus est. Et resurrexit tertia die, secundum Scripturas. Et ascendit in caelum: sedet ad dexteram Patris. Et iterum venturus est cum gloria judicare vivos et mortuos: cujus regni non erit finis. Et in Spiritum Sanctum, Dominum, et vivificantem: qui ex Patre, Filioque procedit. Qui cum Patre, et Filio simul adoratur, et conglorificatur: qui locutus est per Prophetas. Et unam sanctam catholicam et apostolicam Ecclesiam. Confiteor unum baptisma in remissionem peccatorum. Et exspecto resurrectionem mortuorum. Et vitam venturi saeculi. Amen.

I believe in one God, Father Almighty, maker of heaven and earth and of all things visible and invisible. And in one Lord Jesus Christ, the only-begotten Son of God, born of the Father before all ages. God of God, light of light, true God of true God. Begotten, not made, being of one substance with the Father, by whom all things were made. Who for us men and for our salvation came down from heaven. And was made incarnate by the Holy Ghost of the Virgin Mary, and was made man. And was crucified for us under Pontius Pilate. He suffered and was buried. And the third day he rose again according to the Scriptures. And ascended into heaven, and sitteth on the right hand of the Father. And he shall come again with glory to judge the quick and the dead; of whose kingdom there shall be no end. And in the Holy Ghost, Lord and giver of life, who proceedeth from the Father and the Son. Who, together with Father and the Son, is worshiped and glorified; who spoke by the prophets. And one holy, Catholic, and Apostolic Church. I acknowledge one baptism for the remission of sins. And I look for the resurrection of the dead, and the life of the world to come. Amen.

After the Alleluia comes the reading of the Gospel, which is chanted on a simple recitation formula. The priest then intones "Credo in unum Deum" (I believe in one God), and the choir continues from "Patrem omnipotentem" (the Father Almighty) to the end of the Nicene Creed. The Credo, together with the sermon (if any), marks the end of the first main division of the Mass, to be followed by the Eucharist proper.

g) Offertory: *Tui sunt caeli*

Tui sunt caeli, et tua est terra:
orbem terrarum, et plenitudinem ejus tu fundasti: justitia et judicium praeparatio sedis tuae.

Thine are the heavens, and Thine is the earth:
the world and the fullness thereof Thou hast founded; justice and judgment are the preparation of Thy throne.

As the preparation of the bread and wine begins, the Offertory is sung, during which donations to the church are offered. In earlier times this was an occasion for the singing of Psalms; all that survives today is a verse or two, as in the Offertory *Tui sunt caeli.* This Offertory uses verse 11 and half of verse 13 from the Vulgate Ps. 88 (English 89). But the music is not in psalmodic style, and there is no trace of the fourth mode's reciting tone *A*, a note rarely reached in this low-placed plagal melody. Rather, the music is graced by exuberant melismas.

The priest now says various prayers in a speaking voice for the blessing of the elements and vessels of the Eucharist, the reenactment of Christ's last supper. One prayer that is chanted is the Preface, to a formula that is more melodious than the other simple readings.

h) Sanctus

Sanctus, Sanctus, Sanctus Dominus Deus Sabaoth. Pleni sunt caeli et terra gloria tua. Hosanna in excelsis. Benedictus qui venit in nomine Domini. Hosanna in excelsis.	Holy, holy, holy, Lord God of Hosts. The heavens and earth are full of thy glory. Hosanna in the highest. Blessed is he who comes in the name of the Lord. Hosanna in the highest.

The Sanctus ("Holy, holy, holy") and Benedictus ("Blessed is he who comes") are both sung by the choir. In Mass V, a twelfth-century chant, the composer took advantage of the threefold "Sanctus" and the twofold "Hosanna" to achieve a symmetrical form at the beginning and end. The melody, in the fourth mode, rises a sixth above the final *e* but only a second below. It hovers around the reciting tone *a*.

Now the celebrant pronounces the Canon, the prayer consecrating the bread and wine, and the congregation recites the prayer *Pater noster* (the Lord's Prayer, "Our Father, who art in heaven . . .").

i) Agnus Dei

12 3

XII. c.

4\. A - gnus Dé- i, * qui tól- lis pec-cá- ta mún- di : mi-seré- re nó- bis. A- gnus Dé- i, * qui tól- lis pec-cá- ta mún-di : mi-se-ré- re nó- bis. A- gnus Dé- i, * qui tól- lis pec-cá- ta mún-di : dóna nó- bis pá- cem.

Agnus Dei, qui tollis peccata mundi: miserere nobis. Agnus Dei, qui tollis peccata mundi: miserere nobis. Agnus Dei, qui tollis peccata mundi: dona nobis pacem.

Lamb of God, who takest away the sins of the world, have mercy on us. Lamb of God, who takest away the sins of the world, have mercy on us. Lamb of God, who takest away the sins of the world: give us peace.

The cantor and choir sing the Agnus Dei. The text consists of a threefold acclamation, "Lamb of God, who takest away the sins of the world," followed by two identical responses, "have mercy on us," and a final response, "give us peace." Despite the two different responses, the three Agnus periods have the same music. Moreover, the responses echo the music of "qui tollis peccata."

j) Communion: *Viderunt omnes*

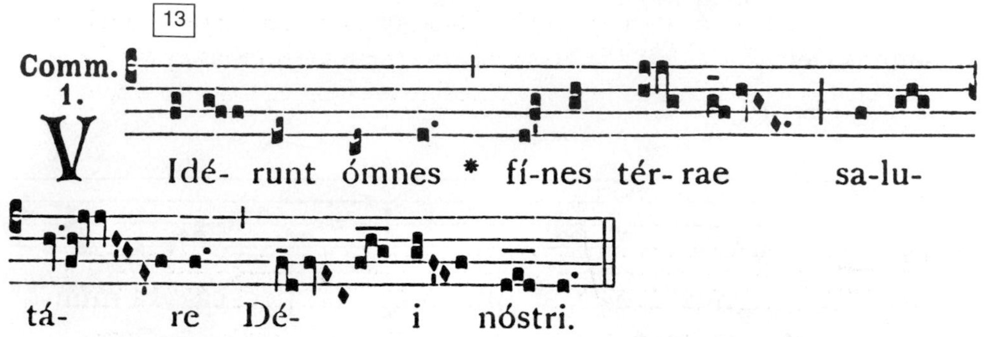
13
Comm.
1.
VIdé- runt ómnes * fí-nes tér- rae sa-lu-
tá- re Dé- i nóstri.

Viderunt omnes fines terrae salutare Dei nostri.	All the ends of the earth have seen the salvation of our God.

After the faithful and celebrants have partaken of the bread and wine, the choir sings the Communion. Originally an antiphon-psalm pair sung during the distribution of the bread and wine, the psalm was dropped by the twelfth century and only the antiphon remained. The text of this unusually short Communion is the same as that beginning the Gradual. The pattern of cadences in the first mode suggests a deliberate search for variety: *D*, *E*, *F*, and *D*.

k) Ite, missa est

8.
I - te, míssa est.
Dé- o grá- ti- as.

Ite, missa est.	Go, the Mass is over.
Deo gratia.	Thanks to God.

This short chant returns to the eighth mode of the Kyrie. The statements are set strophically, with a lengthy melisma on the first word followed by a syllabic cadence. (The "Ite, missa est" is not sung in the recording.)

Gregorian Chant

4

Office of Second Vespers, *Nativity of Our Lord* CD 1 CD 1

Although considerably more ornate than most, the Second Vespers of the feast of the Nativity of Our Lord (December 25) is typical of the Office celebrated at sunset. The service begins with introductory prayers, including the *Pater noster* (the Lord's Prayer) and the *Ave Maria* (Hail Mary).

(The recordings accompanying this anthology contain a sample Antiphon, *Tecum principium*, Psalm 109, *Dixit Dominus*, and the Short Responsory and Verse, *Notum fecit*. The remaining antiphons and psalms are omitted from the record set for reasons of economy.)

a) Verse: *Deus in adjutorium*

℣. DE-us in adjutó-ri- um mé- um inténde. ℟. Dómine ad adju-
vándum me festí-na. Gló-ri- a Pátri, et Fí-li- o, et Spi- rí- tu- i Sáncto. Sic-ut érat in princípi- o, et nunc, et semper, et in saécu-la
saecu-ló-rum. Amen. Alle-lú-ia.

V. Deus, in adjutorium meum intende.
R. Domine, ad adiuvandum me festina.
Gloria Patri, et Filio, et Spiritui Sancto. Sicut erat in principio, et nunc, et semper, et in saecula saeculorum. Amen. Alleluia.

V. O God, come to my assistance.
R. O Lord, make haste to help me.
Glory be to the Father, and to the Son, and to the Holy Ghost. As it was in the beginning, is now and ever shall be, world without end. Amen. Alleluia.

The first verse of Psalm 69, *Deus in adjutorium*, is sung to a special formula somewhat more elaborate than the usual psalm tone.

English translations from *The Saint Andrew Daily Missal*, ed. Dom Gaspar Lefebvre, O.S.B. (New York: Benziger Publishing Co., 1956). Reprinted by permission. The Chapter, Kyrie, *Pater noster*, and Prayer (*Oratio*) have been omitted. Antiphons, Short Responsory and Verse *Notum fecit* from *Antiphonale monasticum*, pp. 245–49. *Deus in adjutorium: Liber usualis (LU)*, p. 112; Psalm 109: *LU*, p. 128, Tone 1g; Psalm 110: *LU*, p. 139, Tone 7a; Psalm 111: *LU*, p. 146, Tone 7d; Psalm 129: *LU*, p. 178, Tone 4A; Magnificat: *LU*, p. 213, Tone 1g[2].

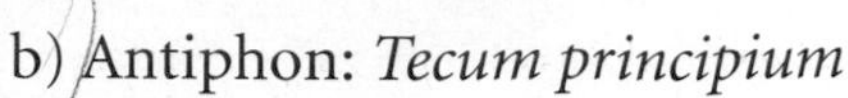

b) Antiphon: *Tecum principium*

14 4

T
ECUM prin-cí- pi- um * in di- e virtú-tis

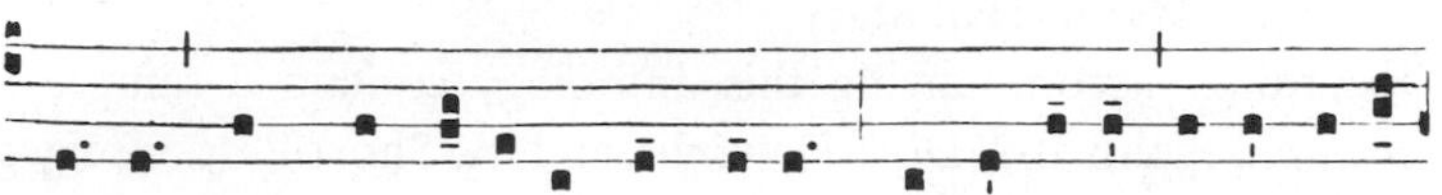
tu- æ, in splendó-ri-bus sanctó-rum, ex ú-te-ro ante lu-cí-

fe-rum gé-nu- i te. E u o u a e.

Tecum principium in die
virtutis tuae in splendoribus
sanctorum, ex utero ante luciferum
genui te.

Thine shall be the dominion in the day
of Thy strength in the brightness
of the Saints, from the womb before the day star
I begot Thee.

c) Psalm 109: *Dixit Dominus*

15 5

Mediant of 2 accents.

g
1. Dí-xit Dóminus Dómino mé- o ; * Séde a déxtris mé- is.

1 Díxit Dóminus **Dó**mino **mé**o:*
Séde a *déxtris* **mé**is.
2 Donec pónam ini**mí**cos **tú**os,*
scabéllum pé*dum tu***ó**rum.
3 Vírgam virtútis túae emíttet Dómi**nus**
ex **Sí**on: * domináre in medio
inimicó*rum tu***ó**rum.
4 Técum princípium in díe virtútis túae
in splendóri**bus** san**ctó**rum:*
ex útero ante lucíferum
*génu***i** te.

The Lord said unto my Lord:
Sit Thou at My right hand.
Until I make Thine enemies
Thy footstool.
The Lord shall send the rod of Thy strength
out of Sion: rule Thou in the midst
of Thine enemies.
Thine shall be the dominion in the day
of Thy power amid the brightness of the
Saints: from the womb, before the day star
have I begotten Thee.

5 Jurávit Dóminus, et non paeni**té**bit **éum**: * Tu es sacérdos in aetérnum secúndum órd*inem Mel***chi**sedech.	The Lord hath sworn, and will not repent: Thou art a Priest for ever after the order of Melchisedech.
6 Dóminus a **déx**tris **túi**s, * confrégit in díe írae *súae* **ré**ges.	The Lord at Thy right hand shall strike through kings in the day of His wrath.
7 Judicábit in natiónibus, im**plé**bit ruínas: * conquassábit cápita in tér*ra mul***tó**rum.	He shall judge among the heathen, He shall fill the places with dead bodies: He shall wound the heads over many countries.
8 De torrénte in **vía bí**bet: * proptérea exal*tábit* **cá**put.	He shall drink of the brook in the way: therefore shall He lift up His head.
9 Glória **Pá**tri, et **Fí**lio, * et Spirí*tui* **Sán**cto.	Glory be to the Father, and to the Son, and to the Holy Ghost.
10 Sicut érat in princípio, et **núnc**, et **sém**per, * et in saécula saecu*lórum*. Amen.	As it was in the beginning, is now, and ever shall be, world without end. Amen.

The first full psalm sung in this Office is Psalm 109, *Dixit Dominus*. It is preceded by the Antiphon *Tecum principium*. Since this antiphon is in the first mode, the psalm tone for this mode is chosen, but provided with an ending on G rather than the final *D*, so that it may lead back easily into the first notes, *F–C*, of the antiphon. This alternate ending is called a *differentia* (difference). The conclusion of the antiphon brings the melody around to the final *D*. After the last verse of the psalm, the Lesser Doxology (from the Greek *doxologia*, a praising), beginning with the words *Gloria Patri* and ending with *saeculorum. Amen*, is sung to the same formula. This Doxology formula is often abbreviated "Euouae," standing for the sound of the vowels in sAEcUlOrUm. AmEn.

d) Antiphon: *Redemptionem misit Dominus*

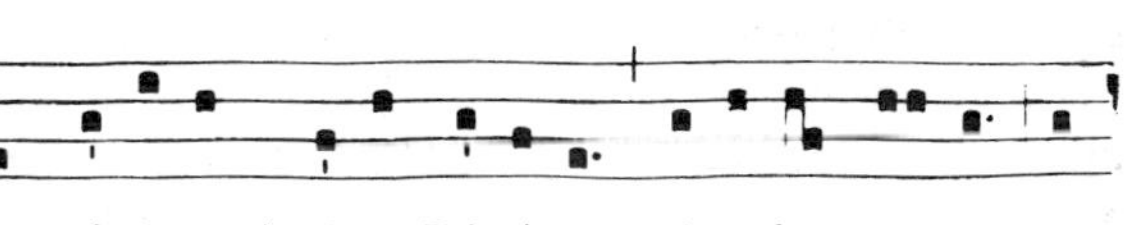

Redemptionem misit Dominus populo suo, mandavit in aeternum testamentum suum.	The Lord hath sent redemption to His people, He hath commanded his convenant for ever.

e) Psalm 110: *Confitebor tibi Domine*

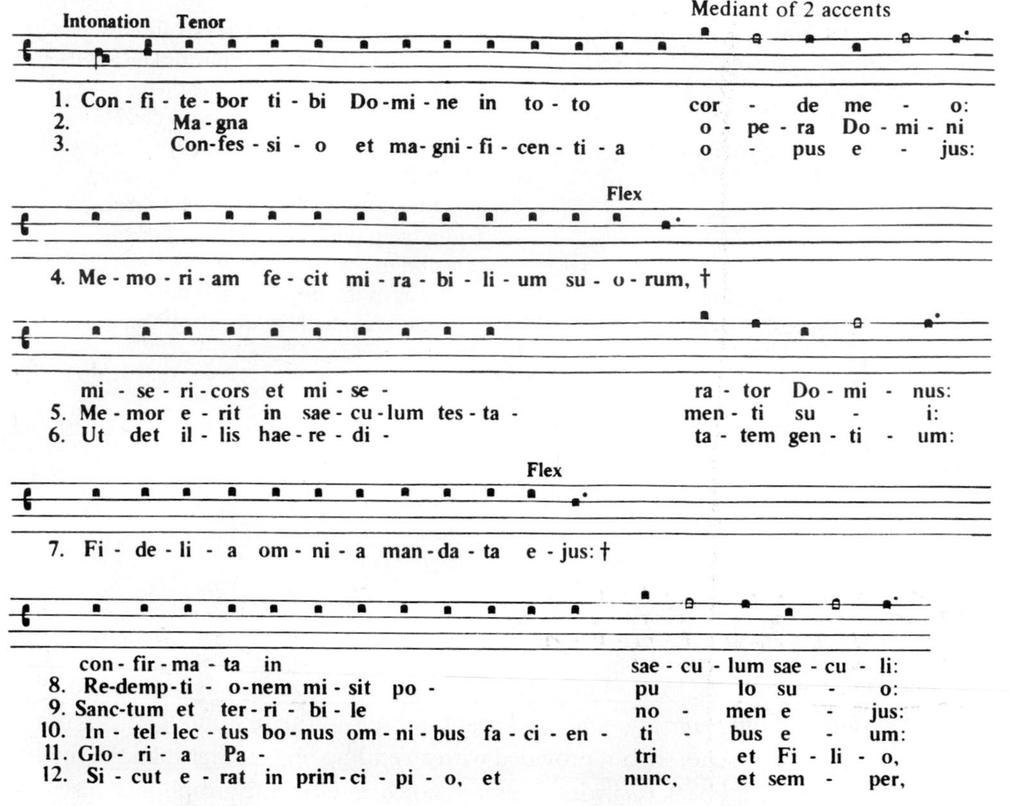

† This symbol in a psalm text calls for a Flex.

* This symbol in a psalm text marks the closing versicle, which is sung to the Tenor followed by the Termination

▫ The hollow note is sung when there are two unaccented syllables after the accented one, as in ***ó-pe-ra Dó-mi-ni.***

1 Confitebor tibi, Domine, in toto **cor**de **me**o: in consilio iustorum, et congre**gátió**ne.	I will praise Thee, O Lord, with my whole heart: in the assembly of the upright, and in the congregation.
2 Magna **ó**pera **Dó**mini: exquisita in omnes volun**tá**tes **é**ius.	The works of the Lord are great, meet to serve for the doing of His will.
3 Confesso et magnificentia **ó**pus **é**ius: et iustitia eius manet in **saé**culum **saé**culi.	His work is honorable and glorious, and His righteousness endureth for ever.
4 Memoriam fecit mirabilium suorum, misericors et mise**rá**tor **Dó**minus: escam dedit **timéntibus** se.	He hath made a memorial of his wonderful works: the Lord is gracious and full of compassion. He hath given meat unto them that fear Him:
5 Memor erit in saeculum testa**mé**nti **súi**: virtutem operum suorum annuntiabit **pó**pulo **sú**o:	He will ever be mindful of His convenant. He will show His people the power of His works:

Tenor — Termination of 2 accents

1 *in con-si - li - o ju - sto-rum, et con-gre - ga - ti - o - ne.
2 *ex - qui - si - ta in om - nes vo - lun - ta - tes e - jus.
3 *et jus - ti - ti - a e - jus ma - net in sae - cu - lum sae - cu - li.

4 *es - cam de - dit ti - men - ti - bus se.
5 *vir - tu - tem o - pe - rum su - o - rum an - nun - ci - a - bit po - pu - lo su o.
6 * o - pe - ra ma - nu - um e - jus ve - ri - tas et ju - di - ci - um.

7 * fac - ta in ve - ri - ta - te et ae - qui - ta - te.
8 *man - da - vit in ae - ter - num te - sta - men - tum su - um.
9 * i - ni - ti - um sa - pi - en - ti - ae ti - mor Do - mi - ni.
10 * lau - da - tio e - jus ma - net in sae - cu - lum sae - cu - li.
11 * et Spi - ri - tu - i San cto.
12 * et in sae - cu - la sae - cu - lo - rum. A - men.

6 Ut det illis haeredi**tá**tem **gén**tium:
opera manuum eius veritas et iu**dí**cium.
7 Fidelia omnia mandata eius:
confirmata in **saé**culum **saé**culi:
facta in veritate et **ae**qui**tá**te.
8 Redemptionem misit **pó**pulo **sú**o:
mandavit in aeternum testa**mén**tum **sú**um.
9 Sanctum et terribile **nó**men **éi**us:
initium sapientiae **tí**mor **Dó**mini.
10 Intellectus bonus omnibus
faci**én**tibus **é**um: laudatio eius manet in
saéculum **saé**culi.
11 Gloria **Pá**tri, et **Fí**lio,
et Spi**rí**tui **Sán**cto.
12 Sicut erat in principio, et **núnc**,
et **sém**per, et in saecula saecu**ló**rum.
Amen.

That He may give them the heritage of the heathen:
The works of His hands are verity and judgment.
All His commandments are sure:
they stand fast for ever and ever,
being done in truth and uprightness.
He sent redemption unto His people:
He hath commanded His convenant for ever.
Holy and terrible is His name.
The fear of the Lord is the beginning of wisdom.
A good understanding have all they that
do His commandments: His praise endureth
for ever.
Glory be to the Father, and to the Son,
and to the Holy Ghost.
As it was in the beginning, is now,
and ever shall be, world without end.
Amen.

Return to Antiphon, *Redemptionem*

Selection e shows how the psalm-tone formula is applied to the singing of a psalm. (See HWM, p. 41, Example 2.3: Outline of the Psalmody of the Office.) There is one tone or formula for each of the eight church modes and an extra one called the *Tonus peregrinus*, or "wandering tone." The formula for the first half of the verse has three components: the *initium*, or intonation (used only in the first verse of the psalm), the reciting tone, or *tenor*, and the *mediatio*, or mediant (semicadence in the middle of the verse). The second half of the verse usually begins on the tenor, which is maintained until the *terminatio*, or final cadence. When the first half of the verse is lengthy, as in verse 4 of this psalm, a *flex* (inflection) serves as a resting point. The mediant and termination are adjusted according to the number of accents of the text, as here in the first verse's mediant of two accents, *cór-de méo*, and the same verse's termination of two accents, *-gá-ti-ó-ne*. The Lesser Doxology usually follows the last verse of the psalm, after which the antiphon is repeated. Originally two choirs alternated in singing the verses of a psalm, a procedure called antiphonal psalmody. Later a soloist chanted the first half of a verse and the choir entered at the asterisk.

f) Antiphon: *Exortum est in tenebris*

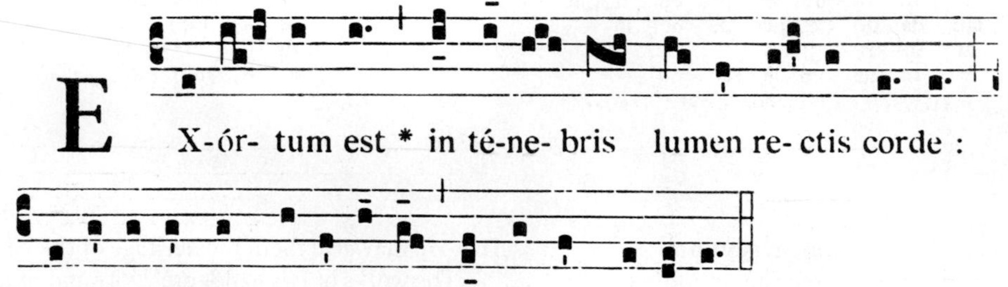

Exortum est in tenebris lumen rectis: misericors, et miserator, et iustus Dominus.	To the true of heart a light is risen in darkness: the Lord is merciful, and compassionate and just.

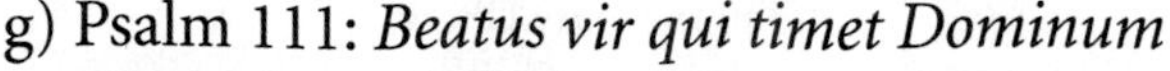

g) Psalm 111: *Beatus vir qui timet Dominum*

1 Beátus vir qui **tí**met **Dó**minum: * in mandátis éjus **vó**let **ní**mis.	Blessed is the man that feareth the Lord, that delighteth greatly in His commandments.
2 Pótens in térra érit **sé**men **é**jus: * generátio rectórum be**ne**dic**é**tur.	His seed shall be mighty upon earth; the generation of the upright shall be blessed.

3 Glória et divítiae in **dó**mo éjus; *
et justítia éjus mánet in **saé**culum **saé**culi.
4 Exórtum est in ténebris **lú**men **réc**tis: *
misericors, et mise**rá**tor,
et **jú**stus.
5 Jucúndus hómo qui miserétur et **cóm**modat,
† dispónet sermónes súos **in judí**cio: *
quia in aetérnum non **com**mo**vé**bitur.
6 In memória aetérna **é**rit **jú**stus: *
ab auditióne mála **non** ti**mé**bit.
7 Parátum cor éjus speráre in Dómino,
† confirmátum**ést** cor éjus: *
non commovébitur donec despíciat
ini**mí**cos **sú**os.
8 Dispérsit, dédit paupéribus:
† justítia éjus mánet in **saé**culum **saé**culi: *
córnu éjus exaltábi**tur** in **gló**ria.
9 Peccátor vidébit, et irascétur,
† déntibus súis frémet **et** ta**bés**cet: *
desidérium pecca**tó**rum períbit.
10 Glória **Pá**tri, et **Fí**lio, *
et Spi**rí**tui **Sán**cto.
11 Sicut érat in princípio, et **núnc,**
et **sém**per, * et in saécula saecu**ló**rum. **A**men.

Glory and riches shall be in his house:
and his righteousness endureth for ever.
Unto the upright there ariseth light in the darkness:
he is gracious, and full of compassion,
and righteousness.
Happy is the man that showeth favor and lendeth;
he will guide his words with discretion:
surely he shall not be moved for ever.
The righteous shall be in everlasting remembrance.
He shall not be afraid of evil tidings.
His heart is ready, trusting in the Lord.
His heart is established,
he shall not be afraid until he see his desire
upon his enemies.
He hath dispersed, he hath given to the poor:
his righteousness endureth for ever:
his horn shall be exalted with honor.
The wicked shall see it, and be grieved;
he shall gnash his teeth, and melt away:
the desire of the wicked shall perish.
Glory be to the Father, and to the Son,
and to the Holy Ghost.
As it was in the beginning, is now,
and ever shall be, world without end. Amen.

Return to Antiphon, *Exortum*

h) Antiphon: *Apud Dominum*

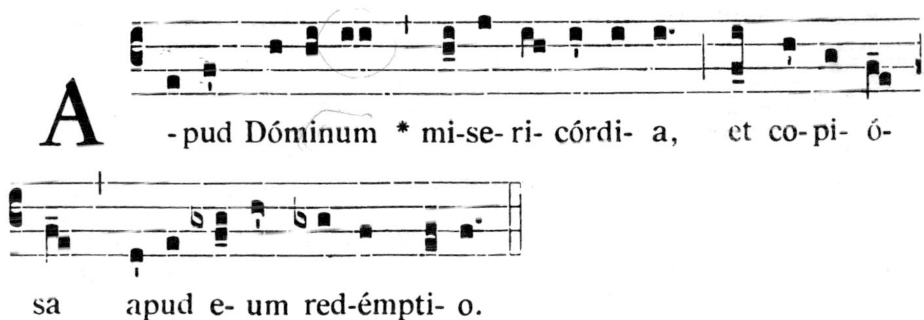
A -pud Dóminum * mi-se- ri- córdi- a, et co-pi- ó-
sa apud e- um red-émpti- o.

Apud Dominum misericordia, et copiosa apud eum redemptio.

With the Lord there is mercy, and with Him plentiful redemption.

i) Psalm 129: *De profundis clamavi ad te*

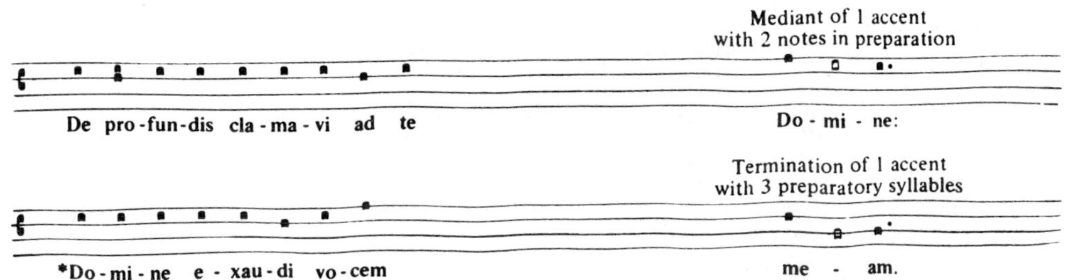
Mediant of 1 accent
with 2 notes in preparation
De pro-fun-dis cla-ma-vi ad te
Do - mi - ne:
Termination of 1 accent
with 3 preparatory syllables
*Do-mi-ne e - xau-di vo-cem
me - am.

1 De profúndis clamávi *ad te* **Dó**mine: * Dómine exáu*di vócem* **mé**am.	Out of the depths I have cried to Thee, O Lord! Lord, hear my voice.
2 Fíant áures túae *inten***dén**tes * in vócem depreca*tiónis* **mé**ae.	Let Thine ears be attentive to the voice of my supplication.
3 Si iniquitátes observá*veris* **Dó**mine: * Dómine, *quis susti***né**bit?	If Thou, Lord, shalt observe iniquities, Lord, who shall endure it?
4 Quia apud te propiti*átio* est: * et propter légem túam sustí*nui te* **Dó**mine.	For with Thee there is merciful forgiveness, and by reason of Thy law I have supported Thee, O Lord.
5 Sustínuit ánima méa in *vérbo* **é**jus: * sperávit ánima *méa in* **Dó**mino.	My soul hath relied on His word: my soul hath hoped in the Lord.
6 A custódia matutína us*que ad* **nóc**tem, * spéret Is*rael in* **Dó**mino.	From the morning watch even until night let Israel hope in the Lord.
7 Quia apud Dóminum mi*seri***cór**dia: * et copiósa apud *éum redém***p**tio.	For with the Lord there is mercy, and with Him plentiful redemption.
8 Et ípse réd*imet* **Is**rael * ex ómnibus iniqui*tátibus* **é**jus.	And He shall redeem Israel, from all his iniquities.
9 Glória Pá*tri, et* **Fí**lio, * et Spi*rítui* **Sán**cto.	Glory be to the Father, and to the Son, and to the Holy Ghost.
10 Sicut érat in princípio, *et nunc, et* **sém**per, * et in saécula sae*culórum.* Amen.	As it was in the beginning, is now, and ever shall be, world without end. Amen.

Return to Antiphon, *Apud Dominum*

Psalms 111 and 129 (g, i), each with its antiphon (f, h) and each in a different mode, are sung in the manner just described. After the psalms have been chanted, a biblical passage called the Chapter is read, on this day verses 1–2 of Hebrews 1.

j) Short Responsory: *Verbum caro*

16
℟. br.
VI
VErbum ca- ro factum est, * Alle- lú- ia, al-
le- lú- ia. Verbum ca- ro factum est, * Alle- lú- ia,
al-le- lú- ia. ℣. Et ha-bi-tá-vit in no- bis.

* Alle- lú-ia. al- le- lú- ia. ℣. Gló-ri- a Patri, et Fí-
li- o, et Spi- rí- tu- i Sancto. Verbum ca- ro factum
est, * Alle- lú- ia, al- le- lú- ia.

R. Verbum caro factum est alleluia, alleluia.
V. Et habitavit in nobis. Alleluia, alleluia.
Gloria Patri, et Filio
et Spiritui Sancto.

R. The Word was made flesh, alleluia, alleluia.
V. And dwelt among us. Alleluia, alleluia.
Glory be to the Father, and to the Son,
and to the Holy Ghost.

The Short Responsory *Verbum caro* is an example of responsorial psalmody, taking the abbreviated form: Respond (choral)—Verse (solo)—Shortened Respond (choral)—Doxology (solo)—Respond (choral). It is called *responsorial* psalmody because a soloist is answered by a choir or congregation.

k) Hymn: *Christe Redemptor omnium*

I
CHriste Red-émptor ómni- um, Ex Patre Patris ú- ni-
ce, So-lus ante prin-cí-pi- um Na-tus in-ef-fa- bí- li- ter.

Christe, Redemptor omnium,
Ex Patre, Patris Unice,
Solus ante principium
Natus ineffabiliter

Jesus! Redeemer of the world!
Who, ere the earliest dawn of light,
Was from eternal ages born,
Immense in glory as in might.

Tu lumen, tu splendor Patris, Tu spes perennis omnium: Intende, quas fundunt preces. Tui per orbem famuli.	Immortal Hope of all mankind In whom the Father's face we see, Hear Thou the prayers Thy people pour This day throughout the world to Thee.
Memento, salutis Auctor, Quod nostri quondam corporis, Ex illibata Virgine Nascendo, formam sumpseris.	Remember, O Creater Lord! That in the Virgin's sacred womb Thou was conceiv'd and of her flesh Didst our mortality assume.
Sic praesens testatur dies, Currens per anni circulum. Quod solus a sede Patris Mundi salus adveneris.	This ever-blest recurring day Its witness bears, that all alone, From Thy own Father's bosom forth, To save the world Thou camest down.
Hunc caelum, terra, hunc mare, Hunc omne, quod in eis est, Auctorem adventus tui Laudans exultat cantico.	O Day! to which the seas and sky, And earth, and heav'n, glad welcome sing; O Day! which heal'd our misery, And brought on earth salvation's King.
Nos quoque, qui sancto tuo, Redempti sanguine sumus, Ob diem natalis tui Hymnum novum concinimus.	We, too, O Lord, who have been cleans'd In Thy own fount of Blood divine, Offer the tribute of sweet song On this blest natal day of Thine.
Gloria tibi, Domine, Qui natus es de Virgine, Cum Patre et Sancto Spiritu In sempiterna saecula. Amen	O Jesu! born of Virgin bright, Immortal glory be to Thee; Praise to the Father infinite And Holy Ghost eternally. Amen.

This hymn hails the arrival of the Savior on this day of his birth. Hymns as a genre are strophic—that is, the number of lines, the syllable count, and the meter of all the stanzas are the same. This hymn has seven stanzas of four lines each, each line containing eight syllables and four iambic feet; there is only occasional rhyme. The poetry imitates that of some hymns ascribed to St. Ambrose (d. 397), who was said to have introduced hymns to the Mass, though recent scholarship is inclined to credit this innovation to Hilary, bishop of Poitiers (ca. 315–366). The singing of "hymns, psalms, and spiritual songs" is mentioned by St. Paul (Col. 3:16; Eph. 5:18–20) and other writers of the first three centuries. The setting of this hymn is simple, with no more than two notes per syllable, and it may have been performed rhythmically rather than with the free durations of prose texts and psalms.

l) Verse: *Notum fecit*

℣. No-tum fe-cit Dómi-nus, alle- lú-ia.

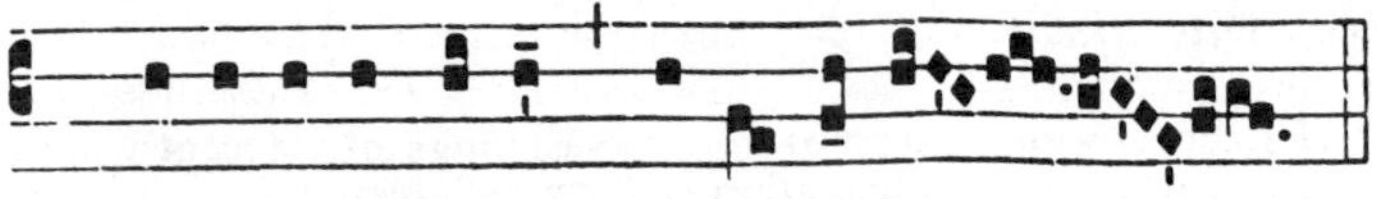
℟. Sa-lu-tá-re su- um, alle- lú- ia.

V.	Notum fecit Dominus, alleluia.	V.	The Lord hath made known, alleluia.
R.	Salutare suum, alleluia.	R.	His salvation, alleluia.

Notum fecit is a responsorial recitation of verse fragments from the Gradual for the Mass of Christmas Day, *Viderunt omnes*, with a florid Alleluia refrain.

m) Antiphon: *Hodie Christus natus est*

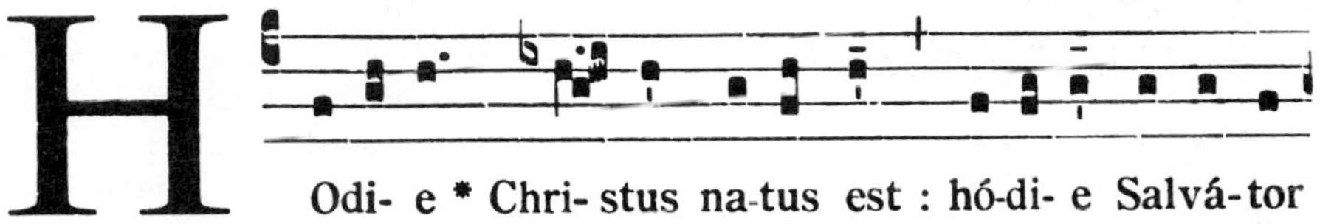
H
Odi- e * Chri- stus na-tus est : hó-di- e Salvá-tor

appá-ru- it : hó-di- e in terra canunt Ange-li, lætán- tur Ar-

chánge- li : hó-di- e exsúl- tant justi, di-céntes : Gló-ri- a

in excélsis De- o, alle- lú- ia.

Hodie Christus natus est: hodie Salvator paruit: hodie in terra canunt Angeli, laetantur Archangeli: hodie exsultant iusti, dicentes: Gloria in excelsis Deo, alleluia.

This day Christ was born: this day the Savior appeared: this day the Angels sing on earth, and the Archangels rejoice: this day the just exult, saying: Glory to God in the highest, alleluia.

n) Canticle: *Magnificat*

Mediant of I accent with 3 preparatory syllables (and an extra note in anticipation of the accent in dactylic cadences).

Endings of I accent with 2 preparatory syllables.

1. Magní- fi-cat * ánima *mé- a* Dóminum.
2. Et exsultávit *spí- ri-tus* mé- us * in Dé- o sa-lu- *tá-ri* mé- o.

1	Magníficat * ánima *méa* **Dó**minum.	My soul doth magnify the Lord.
2	Et exsultávit *spíritus* **mé**us * in Déo salu*tári* **mé**o.	And my spirit hath rejoiced in God my Savior.
3	Quia respéxit humilitátem *ancíllae* **sú**ae: * ecce enim ex hoc beátam me dícent ómnes gener*ati***ó**nes.	For he hath regarded the lowliness of His handmaid: for behold from henceforth all generations shall call me blessed.
4	Quia fécit míhi *mágna qui* **pó**tens est: * et sánctum *nómen* **é**jus.	For He that is mighty hath done great things to me: and holy is His name.
5	Et misericórdia éjus a progéni*e in pro***gé**nies * timén*tibus* **é**um.	And His mercy is from generation unto generations, unto them that fear Him.
6	Fécit poténtiam in *bráchio* **sú**o: * dispérsit supérbos ménte *córdis* **sú**i.	He hath showed strength with His arm: He hath scattered the proud in the imagination of their heart.
7	Depósuit po*téntes de* **sé**de, * et exal*távit* **hú**miles.	He hath put down the mighty from their seat, and hath exalted the humble.
8	Esuriéntes *implévit* **bó**nis: * et dívites dimí*sit in***á**nes.	He hath filled the hungry with good things: and the rich He hath sent empty away.
9	Suscépit Israel *púerum* **sú**um, * recordátus misericór*diae* **sú**ae.	He hath received Israel His servant, being mindful of His mercy.
10	Sicut locútus est *ad pátres* **nó**stros, * Abraham et sémini *éjus in* **saé**cula.	As he spoke to our forefathers, Abraham and to his seed for ever.
11	Glória *Pátri, et* **Fi**lio, * et Spirí*tui* **Sán**cto.	Glory be to the Father, and to the Son, and to the Holy Ghost.
12	Sicut érat in princípio, *et núnc,* *et* **sém**per, * et in saécula saecul*órum.* Amen.	As it was in the beginning, is now, and ever shall be, world without end. Amen.

The Magnificat is the final chant of the Vespers service. Preceded and followed by a timely antiphon, on this occasion *Hodie Christus natus est* (Today Christ is born), it is chanted to a formula very similar to that of the psalms, except that the intonation is sung not only at the outset but at the start of each of the other verses.

Gregorian Chant

Sequence for the Solemn Mass of Easter Day

Victimae paschali laudes CD 1 CD 1

17
6
Seq. 1.
Vic - ti - mae pa - scha - li lau - des *im - mo - lent Chri - sti - a - ni.

2. A - gnus red - e - mit o - ves: Chri - stus in - no - cens Pa - tri re - con - ci - li - a - vit pec - ca - to - res.
3. Mors et vi - ta du - el - o con - fli - xe - re mi - ran - do: dux vi - tae mor - tu - us, re - gnat vi - vus.
4. Dic no - bis Ma - ri - a, quid vi - di - sti in vi - a?
5. An - ge - li - cos te - stes, su - da - ri - um, et ve - stes.
Se - pul - crum Chri - sti vi - ven - tis, et glo - ri - am vi - di re - sur - gen - tis:
Sur - re - xit Chri - stus spes me - a: prae - ce - det su - os in Ga - li - lae - am.
[6. Cre - den - dum est ma - gis so - li Ma - ri - ae ve - ra - ci
7. Sci - mus Chri - stum sur - re - xis - se a mor - tu - is ve - re:
quam Ju - dae - o - rum tur - bae fal - la - ci.]
tu no - bis, vi - ctor Rex, mi - se - re - re. A - men. Al - le - lu - ia.

1 Victimae paschali laudes immolent Christiani.	To the Paschal Victim let Christians offer songs of praise.
2 Agnus redemit oves: Christus innocens Patri reconciliavit peccatores.	The Lamb has redeemed the sheep. Sinless Christ has reconciled sinners to the Father.
3 Mors et vita duelo conflixere mirando: dux vitae mortuus, regnat vivus.	Death and life have engaged in miraculous combat. The leader of life is slain, (yet) living he reigns.
4 Dic nobis Maria, quid vidisti in via? Sepulcrum Christi viventis, et gloriam vidi resurgentis:	Tell us, Mary, what you saw on the way? I saw the sepulchre of the living Christ and the glory of His rising;
5 Angleicos testes, sudarium, et vestes. Surexit Christus spes mea: praecedet suos in Galilaeam.	The angelic witnesses, the shroud and vesture. Christ my hope is risen. He will go before his own into Galilee.

6 [Credendum est magis soli Mariae veraci quam Judaeorum turbae fallaci.]	The truthful Mary alone is more to be believed than the deceitful crowd of Jews.
7 Scimus Christum surrexisse a mortuis vere: tu nobis, victor Rex, miserere	We know that Christ has truly risen from the dead. Thou conqueror and king, have mercy on us.
—Wipo of Burgundy	—Richard Hoppin

Among the many sequences once sung, the celebrated *Victimae paschali laudes* (Praises to the Paschal Victim), is one of only five that are retained in the liturgy and standard modern chant books. It is ascribed to Wipo, chaplain to the Emperor Henry III in the first half of the eleventh century. The classical sequence form of paired strophes is plainly evident, as is the common device of unifying the different melodic segments by similar cadential phrases. Following normal eleventh-century practice, this sequence has an unpaired text at the beginning, but, contrary to the rule, lacks one at the end. Strophe 6, marked by brackets, is omitted in modern chant books, making this sequence conform to the regular pattern.

1) Non-Liturgical - Sacred Music drama

Hildegard of Bingen (1098–1179) 6

Sacred Music Drama: *Ordo virtutum* CD 1 CD 1

In principio omnes

2) Latin Play
3) Bingen was poet and vision seerer

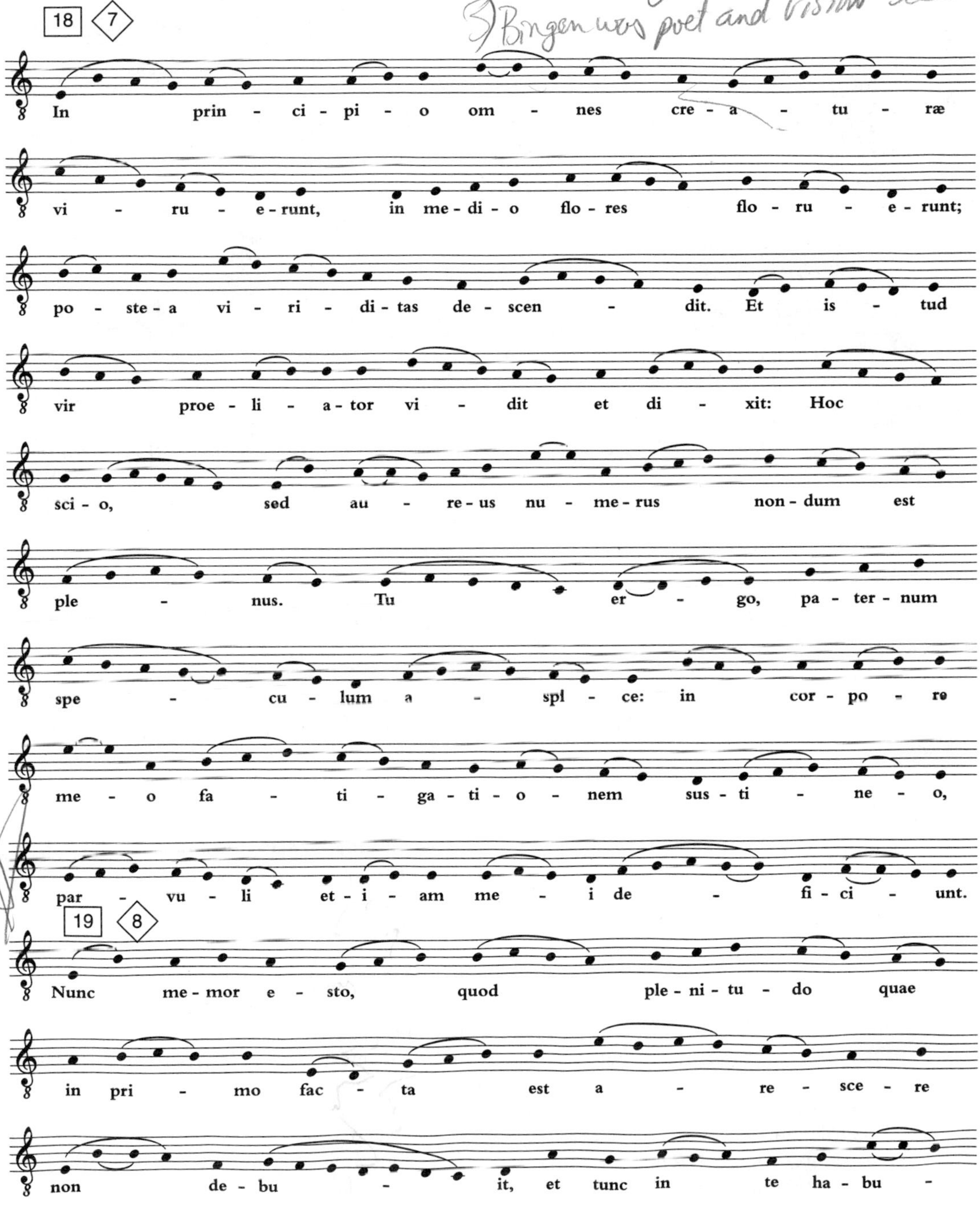

18 7
In prin - ci - pi - o om - nes cre - a - tu - ræ
vi - ru - e - runt, in me - di - o flo - res flo - ru - e - runt;
po - ste - a vi - ri - di - tas de - scen - dit. Et is - tud
vir proe - li - a - tor vi - dit et di - xit: Hoc
sci - o, sed au - re - us nu - me - rus non - dum est
ple - nus. Tu er - go, pa - ter - num
spe - cu - lum a - spi - ce: in cor - po - re
me - o fa - ti - ga - ti - o - nem sus - ti - ne - o,
par - vu - li et - i - am me - i de - fi - ci - unt.
19 8
Nunc me - mor e - sto, quod ple - ni - tu - do quae
in pri - mo fac - ta est a - re - sce - re
non de - bu - it, et tunc in te ha - bu -

is - ti, quod o - cu - lus tu - us num - quam
ce - de - ret us - que dum cor - pus me - um
vi - de - res ple - num gem - ma - rum. Nam me
fa - ti - gat quod om - ni - a mem - bra me - a in ir - ri -
si - o - nem va - dunt. Pa - ter, vi - de, vul - ne - ra me - a
ti - bi o - sten - do. Er - go nunc, om - nes
ho - mi - nes, ge - nu - a ve - stra ad Pa - trem
ve - strum fle - cti - te, ut vo - bis
ma - num su - am por - - -
ri - gat.

VIRTUES

In principio omnes creature viruerunt,
in medio flores floruerunt;
postea viriditas descendit.
Et istud vir proeliator vidit et dixit:
Hoc scio, sed aureus numerus nondum
est plenus. Tu ergo, paternum speculum
aspice: in corpore meo fatigationem
sustineo, parvuli etiam mei deficiunt.
Nunc memor esto, quod plenitudo quae in
primo facta est arescere non debuit, et
tunc in te habuisti quod oculus tuus
numquam cederet usque dum corpus meum
videres plenum gemmarum. Nam me fatigat
quod omnia membra mea in irrisionem
vadunt. Pater, vide, vulnera mea tibi
ostendo.

In the beginning all of creation was
green. In a middle stage the flowers
bloomed. Then greenness declined.
The Fighter [Christ] saw this and said:
"I know this, but the golden number is not
yet attained. You, then, look into the
fatherly mirror. In my body I feel
fatigue, even my little ones weaken.
Be mindful that the fullness that was
first made must not wither, and
make sure that you not turn away your gaze
until you see my body
covered with gems. It wearies me
that all my followers fall into mockery.
Father, behold, I show you my
wounds."

Ergo nunc, omnes homines, genua vestra ad Patrem vestrum flectite, ut vobis manum suam porrigat.	Now, therefore, all humankind, bend your knees before your Father, as he extends his hand to you.

Hildegard, founder and abbess of the convent in Rupertsberg in Germany, was famous for her prophetic powers and revelations. Her most remarkable work, *Scivias* (Know the Ways), is an account of twenty-six visions. Besides writings on natural science and medicine, she left a great quantity of poetry and music.

Her morality play with music, *Ordo virtutum* (The Virtues, ca. 1151), is unusual for its time, because unlike the liturgical dramas such as *Quem quaeritis in praesepe* (NAWM 7), it is not a supplement to the Mass of a certain feast but an independent Latin play, an edifying entertainment for Hildegard's select community of noblewomen. All parts except the Devil are sung in plainchant. The singers represent the Patriarchs and Prophets, sixteen female Virtues (Humility, Love, Obedience, Faith, Hope, Chastity, Innocence, Mercy, etc.), a Happy Soul, an Unhappy Soul, and a Penitent Soul. The Devil, bereft of divine harmony, can only shout and bellow.

The play begins with a chorus of Patriarchs and Prophets who express their wonder at the sight of the richly robed Virtues. Souls in a procession beg the Virtues for divine insight, alternating solos with choral responses. But the Devil tempts the Souls, and one Unhappy Soul succumbs and follows him, only to return later, bedraggled, hurt, and repentant. The Devil tries to reclaim her, but the Virtues, led by Humility, protect her and capture and bind the Devil. Though Victorious, the Virtues lament the spoiling of the green, blossoming paradise and invoke the militant Christ, who urges them to aspire to the goodly fullness of the time of creation.

The final chorus, which serves as an epilogue, consists of four rhymed lines, followed by a prose quotation, and ends with a short prayer. The melody is entirely in Mode 3, keeping mostly to the ambitus of that mode, *d′* to *e″*. It oversteps its upper boundary at "oculus tuus" (your gaze) and "ad Patrem" (to the Father), and its lower boundary at "parvuli" (little ones) and "debuit" (wither), perhaps to emphasize those words. Periods and other strong endings in the text are marked by cadences on the final *E*. The reciting tone of this mode, *C*, plays no part in the structure. Rather the fifth degree, *B*, is the most frequent resting point.

The rhyme of the opening two lines is paralleled by an identical cadence formula in the music, but the next two rhymed lines do not use the same closing pattern, because the second must open the way to Christ's speech. A typical intonation is the rising fifth *e′*–*b′*, which occurs at the beginning, at "sed aureus," "non debuit," "Nam me fatigat," "Pater, vide," "Ergo nunc," and "ut vobis." Hildegard, who was sometimes effusive in her melismas, was here restrained, reserving the longer melismas for particular ideas—for example, "debuit" (wither), "gemmarum" (gems), "flectite" (bend), and the longest, a final flourish, for "porrigat" (extend).

7 Gregorian Chant

Trope: *Quem quaeritis in praesepe* (10th century)

In die natale Domini stacio ad Sanctum Petrum CD 1

In die natale Domini stacio ad Sanctum Petrum

On the day of the nativity of the Lord, at the station of St. Peter

Incipiunt tropus [i.e. tropum] antequam dicatur officium

They begin the trope before the office [i.e. Introit] is said

Transcribed from Paris, Bibliothèque nationale, MS lat. 1118, fols. 8v–9r (MS datable 988–96), by William L. Smoldon in *The Music of the Medieval Church Dramas*, edited by Cynthia Bourgeault. © The Estate of William L. Smoldon, 1980. Used by permission. All rights reserved.

Quem quaeritis in praesepe,
pastores, dicite?

Respondent
Salvatorem, Christum Dominum,
infantem pannis involutum,
secundum sermonem angelicum.

Adest hic parvulus cum Maria,
matre sua, de qua dudum
vaticinando Isaias dixerat propheta:
Ecce virgo concipiet et
pariet filium; et nun euntes
dicite quia natus est.

Respondent
Alleluia, alleluia!
Iam vere scimus Christu natum
in terris, de quo canite omnes
cum propheta dicentes,
PUER NATUS EST NOBIS.

Whom do you seek in the manger,
shepherds, please say?

Our savior, Christ the Lord,
an infant wrapped in cloths,
according to the angelic report.

The infant is attended here by Mary,
his mother, about whom a little while
ago the prophet Isaiah foretold:
behold a virgin will conceive and
give birth to a son; and now as you go
tell that he is born.

Alleluia, alleluia!
Now truly we know that Christ was born
on earth, concerning which sing always
with the prophet, saying:
A SON IS BORN UNTO US.

The rubrics indicate that this dramatic dialogue was performed before the singing of the Introit at the Third Mass of Christmas Day at the altar, which symbolized the Church of Saint Peter.

Certain chants, usually Introits, were extended by a verbal and melodic trope that turned them into little dramatic scenes. Best known is the Easter trope, *Quem quaeritis in sepulcro?*, in which the angels guarding Jesus' tomb ask the two Marys, "Whom do you seek in the sepulchre?" They answer, "Jesus of Nazareth, who was crucified." The angels tell them that he is not there, for he has risen. This genre is sometimes called a liturgical drama.

Quem quaeritis in praesepe is the Christmas version of the dramatic Easter trope. The midwives caring for the Christ child ask the shepherds to tell them whom they seek in the manger. The shepherds answer that they are looking for an infant in swaddling clothes, Christ the Savior, as the angels foretold. The angels explain that the child was born to Mary, a virgin. The shepherds rejoice in the knowledge that they have confirmed the birth of Christ. The Introit, *Puer natus est* (NAWM 3a), is then sung.

There are a number of notable melodic recurrences in this dialogue. The music of the first response (marked "Respondent") parallels that of the midwives, except that its phrase ends a fifth above, because the speech continues. The previous phrases all ended with the same cadence, *G–A–G–F–G*. But the first shepherd's last words, "sermonem angelicum," introduce a new ending formula that will be repeated at "Isaias dixerat propheta" of the second response and "propheta dicentes" of the third. The last four notes of this formula are heard again at the end of the second response at "natus est." Although different characters are singing, the melodic recurrences bestow melodic continuity and unity on the entire composition.

8 ADAM DE LA HALLE (ca. 1237–ca. 1287)

Jeu de Robin et de Marion CD 1

Rondeau: *Robins m'aime*

Robins m'aime,	Robin loves me,
Robins m'a,	Robin has me,
Robins m'a demandée	Robin asked me
Si m'ara.	if he can have me.
Robins m'acata cotele	Robin bought me a skirt
D'escarlate bonne et belle	of scarlet, good and pretty,
Souskanie et chainturele.	a bodice and belt.
Aleuriva!	Hurray!

The most famous of the secular musical plays was *Jeu de Robin et de Marion* by Adam de la Halle, the last and greatest of the trouvères. It is uncertain whether all the songs in this work, dating from about 1284, were written by Adam himself or whether they were popular chansons incorporated into the play. A few of them have polyphonic settings.

Typical of the tuneful songs is *Robins m'aime*, sung by Marion with choral refrains at the opening of the Jeu. It is a monophonic rondeau in the form A B a a b A B (using separate letters for each musical phrase, capitals for choral, lower case for solo performance).

Friedrich Gennrich, *Troubadours, Trouvères, Minne- und Meistergesang* (Cologne, 1951) p. 38.

9

Bernart de Ventadorn (ca. 1150–ca. 1180)

Can vei la lauzeta mover CD 1 CD 1

22 9

1. Can vei la lau - ze - ta mo - ver De joi sas a - las con - tral rai,
Que s'o - blid' e·s lais - sa cha - zer Per la dous - sor c'al cor li vai,
Ai! tans grans en - vey - a m'en ve De cui qu'eu vey - a jau - zi - on,
Me - ra - vil - has ai, car des - se Lo cor de de - zi - rer no·m fon.

Can vei la lauzeta mover	When I see the lark beating
de joi sas alsas contral rai,	its wings joyfully against the sun's rays,
que s'oblid' e • s laissa chazer	which then swoons and swoops down
per la doussor c'al cor li vai,	because of the joy in its heart,
ai! tan grans enveya m'en ve	oh! I feel such jealousy
de cui qu'eu veya jauzion,	for all those who have the joy of love,
meravilhas ai, car desse	that I am astonished
lo cor de dezirer no • m fon.	that my heart does not immediately melt with desire!
Ai, las! tan cuidava saber	Alas! I thought I knew so much
d'amor, e tan petit en sai,	of love, and I know so little;
car eu d'amar no • m posc tener	for I cannot help loving a lady
celeis don ja pro non aurai.	from whom I shall never obtain any favor.
Tout m'a mo cor, e tout m'a me,	She has taken away my heart and myself,
e se mezeis e tot lo mon;	and herself and the whole world;
e can se • m tolc, no • m laisset re	and when she left me, I had nothing left
mas dezirer e cor volon.	but desire and a yearning heart.
Anc non agui de me poder	I have no power over myself,
ni no fui meus de l'or' en sai	and have not had possession of myself
que • m laisset en sos olhs vezer	since the time when she allowed me to look into her eyes,
en un miralh que mout me plai.	in a mirror which I like very much.
Mirahls, pus me mirei en te,	Mirror, since I was reflected in you,
m'an mort li sospir depreon,	deep sighs have killed me,
c'aissi • m perdei com perdet se	for I caused my own ruin, just as
lo bels Narcisus en la fon.	fair Narcissus caused his by looking in the fountain.

Text and translation are from Hendrik van der Werf, *The Chansons of the Troubadours and Trouvères* (Utrecht, 1972), pp. 91–95, where versions of the melody appearing in five different sources are given, showing surprising consistency among readings. The dot splitting two letters of a word, as in e • s, indicates a contraction.

De las domnas me dezesper;
ja mais en lor no • m fiarai;
c'aissi com las solh chaptener,
enaissi las deschaptenrai.
Pois vei c'una pro no m'en te
vas leis que • m destrui e • m confon,
totas las dopt' e las mescre,
car be sai c'atretals se son.

I despair of ladies;
I shall not trust them ever again;
just as I used to defend them,
now I shall condemn them.
Since I see that *one* of them does not help me
against her who is ruining and destroying me
I fear them all and have no faith in them,
for I know they are all the same.

D'aisso's fa be femna parer
ma domna, par qu'e • lh o retrai,
car no vol so c'om deu voler,
e so c'om li devada, fai.
Chazutz sui en mala merce,
et ai be faih co • l fols en pon;
e no sai per que m'esdeve,
mas car trop puyei contra mon.

My lady shows herself to be [merely] a woman
(and that is why I reproach her)
in that she does not want what one should want,
and she does what is forbidden her.
I have fallen out of favor,
and have acted like the fool on the bridge;
and I do not know why this has happened to me,
unless it was because I tried to climb too high.

Merces es perduda, per ver,
et eu non o saubi anc mai,
car cilh qui plus en degr'aver
no • n a ges, et on la querrai?
A! can mal sembla, qui la ve,
qued aquest chaitiu deziron

que ja ses leis non aura be,
laisse morir, que no l'aon!

Mercy is gone, that is sure,
and I never received any of it,
for she who should have the most mercy
has none, and where else should I seek it?
Oh! how difficult it is for a person who sees her
to imagine that she would allow to die this poor
yearning wretch,
and would not help the man
who can have no help but her!

Pus ab midons no • m pot valer
precs ni merces ni • l dreihz qu'eu ai,
ni a leis no ven a plazer
qu'eu l'am, ja mais no • lh o dirai.
Aissi • m part de leis e • m recre;
mort m'a, e per mort h respon,
e van m'en, pus ilh no • m rete,
chaitius, en issilh, no sai on.

Since pleas and mercy and my rights
cannot help me to win my lady,
and since it does not please her
that I love her, I shall speak to her about it no more.
So I am leaving her and her service;
she has killed me, and I reply with death,
and I am going sadly away, since she will not accept
my service, into exile, I do not know where.

Tristans, ges no • m auretz de me,
qu'eu m'en vau, chaitius, no sai on.
De chantar me gic e • m recre,
e de joi d'amor m'escon.

Tristan, you will hear no more of me,
for I am going sadly away, I do not know where,
I am going to stop singing,
and I flee from love and joy.

One of the best-preserved songs by the troubadour Bernart de Ventadorn is a lover's complaint, the main subject of the entire repertory. The song is strophic, each stanza but the last having eight lines rhymed ababcdcd, and each line has eight syllables. The music to which all the stanzas are sung is through-composed, though the seventh line partly repeats the fourth. The melody is clearly in first mode, rising from *d* to *a* in the first phrase and from *a* to d' in the second and third.

10

Beatriz de Dia (d. ca. 1212)

Canso: *A chantar* CD 1

23
1 2 3 4 5 6 7 8 9 10
1. A chan - tar m'es al cor que non deu - ri - e
2. tant mi ran - cun cele a qui sui a - migs,
3. et si l'am mais que nu - le ren qui si - e;
4. non mi val ren bel - tat ni cur - te - si - e
5. ne ma bon - taz ne mon pres ne mon sen;
6. al - tre - si sui en - ga - nade et tra - gi - de
7. qu'e - u - sse fait vers lui de - sa - vi - nen - ce.

A chantar m'es al cor que non deurie
tant mi rancun cele a qui sui amigs,
et si l'am mais que nule ren qui sie;
non mi val ren beltat ni curtesie
ne ma bontaz ne mon pres ne mon sen;
altresi sui enganade et tragide
qu'eusse fait vers lui desavinence.

To sing I must of what I'd rather not,
so much does he of whom I am the lover embitter me;
yet I love him more than anything in the world.
To no avail are my beauty or politeness,
my goodness, or my virtue and good sense.
For I have been cheated and betrayed,
as if I had been disagreeable to him.

In this strophic song, or canso, from the second half of the twelfth century, four distinct melodic components are arranged in the form ABABCDB. All lines but one end on an unaccented syllable, a circumstance emphasized by the triple notes of the penultimate syllable. The melody is clearly in the first mode, with the characteristic

Transcribed by Hendrik van der Werf in *The Extant Troubadour Melodies* (Rochester: Author, 1984), p. 13. Gerald A. Bond, text editor. Used by permission.

fifth, *d´–a´*, and final, *d´*, of this mode displayed in the A and B phrases. As in first-mode plainchant melodies, it descends one note below the final to *c´*. The singer was presumed to vary the melody for each new stanza, holding to the outline of the tune.

A *vida*, or biographical tale, of about a century later tells that "Beatrix, comtessa de Dia, was a beautiful and good woman, the wife of Guillaume de Poitiers. And she was in love with Rambaud d'Orange and made about him many good and beautiful songs." It is not known which parts of this account are legendary and which parts are true.

Hans Sachs (1494–1576)

Nachdem David war redlich und aufrichtig CD 1

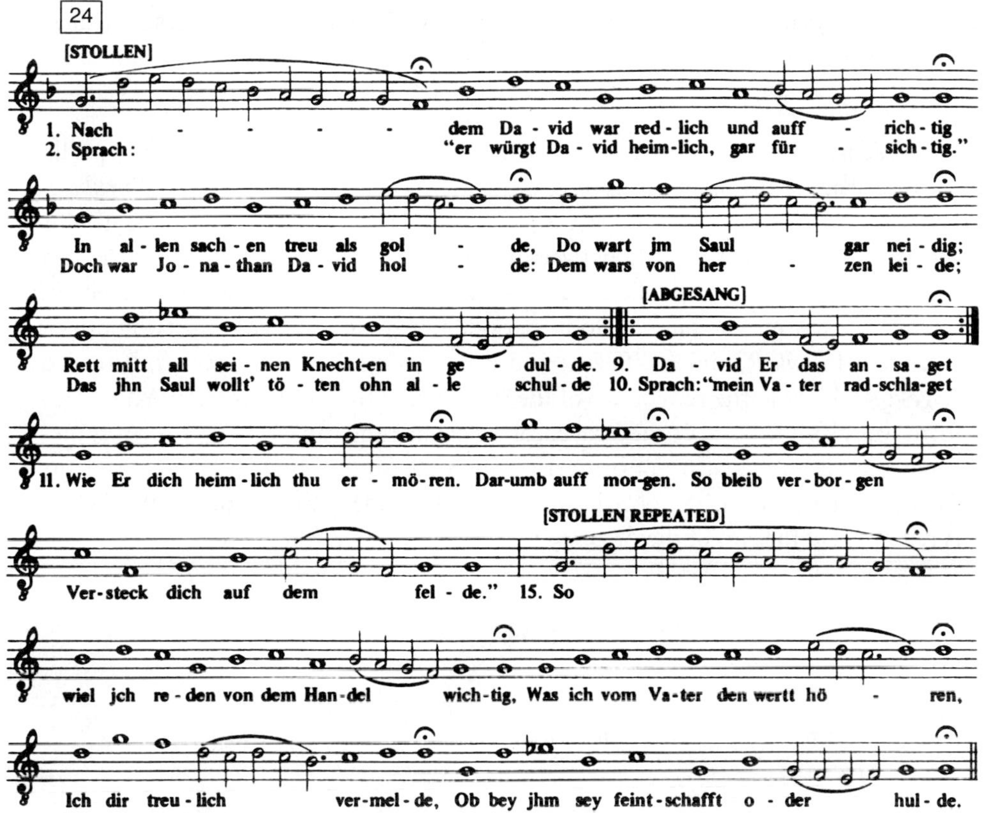

24
[STOLLEN]
1. Nach - - - - dem Da - vid war red - lich und auff - rich - tig
2. Sprach: "er würgt Da - vid heim-lich, gar für - sich - tig."
In al - len sach - en treu als gol - de, Do wart jm Saul gar nei - dig;
Doch war Jo - na - than Da - vid hol - de: Dem wars von her - zen lei - de;
[ABGESANG]
Rett mitt all sei - nen Knecht-en in ge - dul - de. 9. Da - vid Er das an - sa - get
Das jhn Saul wollt' tö - ten ohn al - le schul - de 10. Sprach: "mein Va - ter rad-schla-get
11. Wie Er dich heim - lich thu er - mö - ren. Dar-umb auff mor-gen. So bleib ver - bor - gen
[STOLLEN REPEATED]
Ver - steck dich auf dem fel - de." 15. So
wiel jch re - den von dem Han - del wich - tig, Was ich vom Va - ter den wertt hö - ren,
Ich dir treu - lich ver - mel - de, Ob bey jhm sey feint - schafft o - der hul - de.

Nachdem David war redlich und aufrichtig,
In allen sachen treu als golde,
Do wart jm Saul gar neidig;
Rett mit all seinen knechten in gedulde.
Sprach: "er wurgt David heimlich, gar fürsichtig."
Doch war Jonathan David holde;
Dem wars von herzen leide,
Das jhn Saul wollte töten ohn alle schulde.

David Er das ansaget,
Sprach: "mein Vater radschlaget,
Wie Er dich heimlich thu ermören.

Since David was honest and candid,
in all things true as gold,
so Saul was very jealous of him.
He dealt with all his vassals with patience.
Said he: "He struggled with David secretly, cautiously."
Yet Jonathan was kind to David;
it was painful to his heart
that Saul wanted to kill him [David] without any blame.

Thus he spoke to David:
saying, "My father intimated
how he would stealthily murder you;

Adapted from diplomatic copy in G. Münzer, *Das Singebuch des Adam Puschman* (Leipzig, 1906), p. 80. Notation in whole and half notes, some with dots, is in the original manuscript in Wrocław, Municipal Library. Half notes are meant to go much faster than whole notes. Dotted half notes are somewhat prolonged. Puschamn labels this *Weise*, or melodic formula, "Klingender Ton" (chiming or ringing mode).

Darumb auff morgen,	therefore in the morning
So bleib verborgen,	remain concealed,
Versteck dich auf dem felde."	hide yourself in the field."
So wiel ich reden von dem handel wichtig,	As much as I tell of the affair is important;
Was ich vom Vater den wertt hören,	what I, concerning the father's honor, heard,
Ich dir treu vermelde,	I truthfully impart,
Ob bey ihm sey feintschaft oder hulde.	whether there was hostility in him or kindness.

Hans Sachs, a shoemaker by trade, is the most celebrated of the Meistersinger, partly because Wagner made him a leading character in *Die Meistersinger von Nürnberg.* Of the many fine examples of Sachs's art that survive, one of the most beautiful is this commentary on the strife between David and Saul (1 Samuel 17ff.). It is in a form common in the Minnelied that was taken over by the Meistersinger, called in German *Bar* form. The same melodic period, A, is set to a stanza's first two units of text (called *Stollen*), and a different and usually longer melodic period, B (called *Abgesang*), is set to the remainder of the stanza, resulting in the pattern AAB. This form was also the basis of the Provençal *canzo*; like the canzo, the Bar form sometimes involves a repeat of all or part of the Stollen phrase toward the end of the Abgesang. This is the case in *Nachdem David*, where the entire melody of the Stollen is reiterated at the end of the Abgesang.

12

Istampita Palamento CD 1

Jen ten Bokum, *De Dansen* (Utrecht, 1976), pp. 49–50. Afdeling Muziekwetenschap, Universiteit Utrecht. Facsimile in Gilbert Reaney, ed., *The Manuscript London, British Museum, Additional 29987* (American Institute of Musicology, 1965), fols. 60r–61v.

27
Terça pars
28
Quartta pars
f. 60v.
aperto
1.
chiuso
2.
[fine]

The *istampita* (French: *estampie*; Provençal: *estampida*) was a textless composition perhaps intended for dancing. Its form, which resembles that of the sequence, consists of sections immediately repeated (double versicles), often with open and closed endings.

This istampita has five *partes*. The *prima pars* shows the form most clearly. The same music is heard twice, the first time with an open (*aperto*) ending, the second time with a closed (*chiuso*) ending. The second and third partes use the same two endings and, in addition, borrow the sixteen previous measures from the first pars. The fourth and fifth partes share the same music except for the first eight measures and, of course, the open and closed endings. Some of the later partes borrow material from earlier partes. These borrowings, indicated in the manuscripts and most editions by *signa congruentiae*, have been written out in this transcription to make it easier to follow the recorded performance.

(In two short segments the players in the recording improvise rather than read from the written score: Quarta pars, measures 34–37; Quinta pars, measures 45–52.)

13 Organum: *Alleluia Justus ut palma* CD 1 CD 1

Alleluia Justus ut palma florebit, et sicut cedrus multiplicabitur.	Alleluia. The righteous shall flourish like a palm tree and shall multiply like a cedar.

This organum serves as an example in *Ad organum faciendum*, a treatise on how to make organum. The treatise dates from around 1100 and is housed at the Ambrosian Library in Milan (MS M.17 sup.). An organal voice is set mostly note-against-note above the plainchant Alleluia (but occasionally crossing below). The text of the verse is *Justus ut palma*. The example exhibits both contrary and parallel motion from one interval to the next. There is contrary motion from octaves or unisons to fourths or fifths, particularly at the beginning of a phrase. Within a phrase fourths or fifths or mixtures of these may move in parallel. Particularly at the end of a phrase, a fourth or fifth proceeds to a unison or octave. The composer also discovered that moving from a sixth to an octave or from a third to a unison was an effective cadential device.

Milan, Biblioteca Ambrosiana, MS M. 17 sup., ed. Hans Heinrich Eggebrecht and Frieder Zaminer, *Ad organum faciendum, Lehrschriften der Mehrstimmigkeit in nachguidonischer Zeit* (Mainz, 1970), p. 53.

14

Aquitanian polyphony: *Jubilemus, exultemus* CD 1

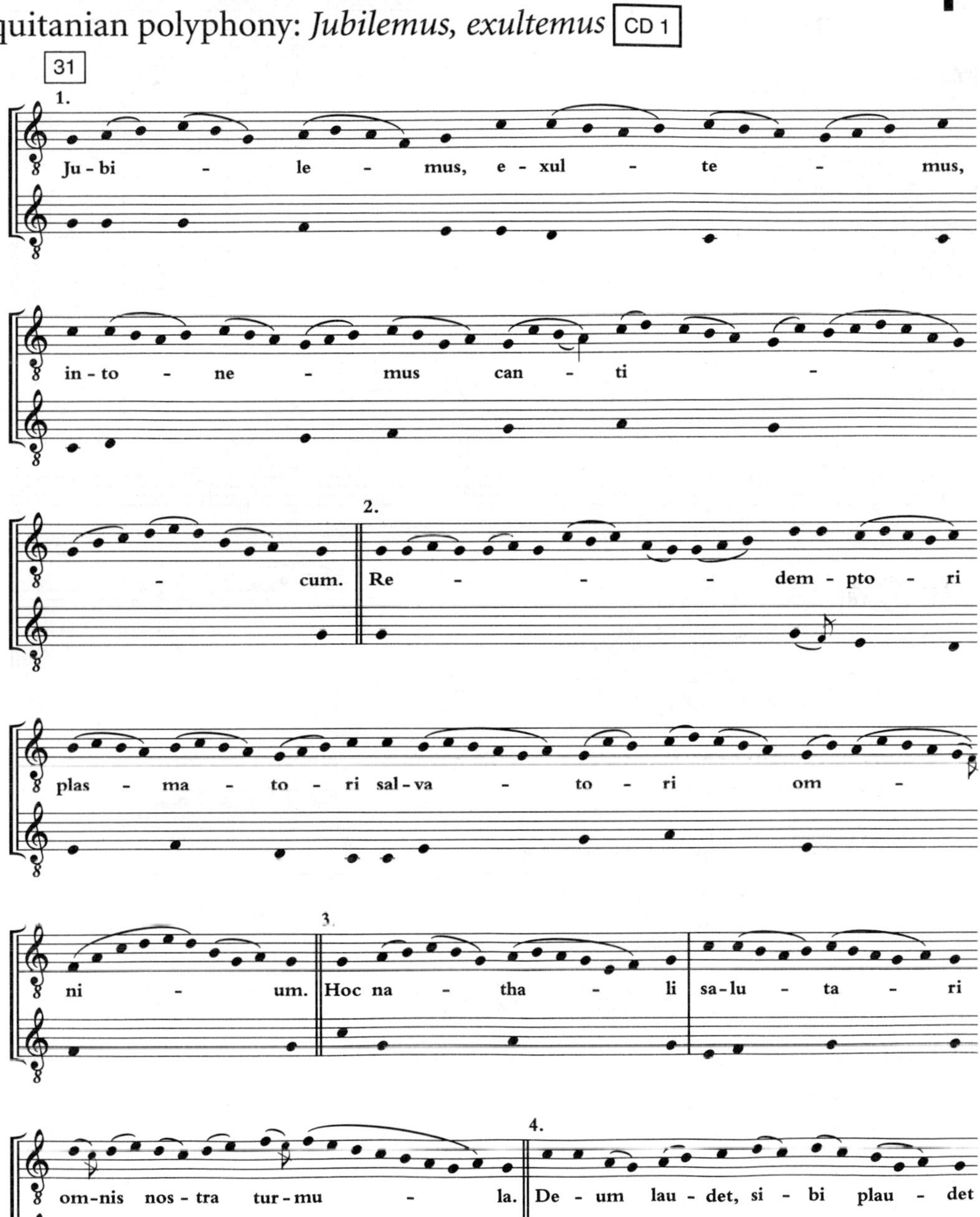

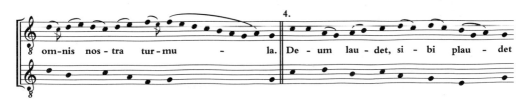

per e - ter - na se - cu - la.
5.
Qui ho - di - e de
Ma - ri - e u - te - ro pro - gre - di - ens.
6.
Ho-mo ve - rus rex at - que
he - rus in ter - ris ap - pa - ru - it.
7.
Tam be - a-tum er - go na - tum cum in - gen - ti gau - di - o.
8.
Con-lau-dan-tes, e-xul - tan - tes be-ne - di - ca-mus Do-mi - no.

Jubilemus exultemus, intonemus canticum	Let us rejoice, sing a song
Redemptori plasmatori, salvatori omnium.	to the redeemer, creator, savior of all.
Hoc nathali salutari omnis nostra turmula	For this blessed birth, let our whole congregation
Deum laudet sibi plaudet per eterna secula.	praise God and eternally applaud.
Qui hodie de Marie utero progrediens	He who today issued from Mary's womb
Homo verus rex atque herus in terris apparuit.	a true man, appeared on earth as a a king and lord.
Tam beatum ergo natum cum ingenti gaudio	In such a blessed birth, then, with boundless delight,
Conlaudantes, exultantes benedicamus Domino.	praising and exulting together, let us bless the Lord.

Paris, Bibliothèque Nationale, fonds latin, fol. 41. For a metrical transcription, see *Saint-Martial Polyphony*, ed. Bryan Gillingham (Henryville, Ottawa, and Binningen: Institute of Mediaeval Music, 1994), pp. 7–9. A facsimile of the page is in Carl Parrish, *The Notation of Polyphonic Music* (New York: Norton, 1957), Plate XXI, and a facsimile of the entire manuscript is published in *Paris, Bibliothèque Nationale, fonds latin 1139 d'après les manuscrits conservés à la Bibliothèque National de Paris*, ed. B. Gillingham (Ottawa: Institute of Mediaeval Music, 1987).

This two-part setting of a rhymed metrical text is from a twelfth-century manuscript associated with the Abbey of St. Martial in Limoges in the Duchy of Aquitaine, now southwest France. The scribe notated the florid upper voice above the slower tenor part in score format, but the text underlay and alignment of the notes are not always clear. Although the poetry has consistent iambic meter, the number of notes in the upper part makes singing the tenor part in first or second rhythmic mode unlikely. Under the circumstances, transcriptions and performances vary and represent interpretations by individual scholars and singers. The upper voice meets the syllabic lower voice at the beginning of a melisma most frequently in perfect consonances—octaves, fifths, and fourths—but also thirds and sixths. Occasionally the composer seems to have purposely chosen a dissonance for variety and spice, as in the first line at "bi" of "jubilemus," "xul" of "exultemus," and "to" of "intonemus," and dissonances generously pepper the melismas. Octaves or unisons between the parts mark the ends of lines. Some lines, for example, line 4, "Deum laudet," suggest a shift to discant style.

15

Alleluia Pascha nostrum

Gregorian Chant and Early Polyphonic Elaborations CD 1

To permit comparison of how plainchant settings were variously embellished in the twelfth and thirteenth centuries, several polyphonic versions of the *Alleluia Pascha nostrum* are given here. Since there is no assurance that any manuscript has the organum and clausulae as Leonin left them, rather than present in notation and recording one of the extant versions, the organum is presented here as it could have been performed in the thirteenth century, when more elaborate settings of certain sections replaced simple organum, just as simple organum replaced sections of plainchant. The series of pieces follows, in performance order. The upper parts of the clausulae on "Nostrum" and on ``la" of the word "immolatus" are not heard in the recording as textless discants but in texted versions as motets. For this reason and to show the derivation of the motets from the clausulae, the duplum or motetus of the motets is printed above the duplum of the clausulae. The *Alleluia Pascha nostrum* is a rare instance among surviving settings that shows such a clear succession of layers of polyphonic embellishment.

a) Plainchant [not performed separately on the recording]

Gordon A. Anderson, *The Latin Compositions in Fascicules VII and VIII of the Notre Dame Manuscript Wolfenbüttel Helmstedt 1099*, Part II, p. 276. Réproduit avec permission de l'institut de musique mediévale, Henriville, Ottawa et Binningen.

b) Léonin (fl. 1163–1190), Organum duplum

Florence, Biblioteca Medicea-Laurenziana, MS Pluteus 29.1, fol. 109; the clausulae are from Anderson, II 25–26.

ia

33

[Chorus]

Al - le - lu - ia.

34

[Soli]

Pas - - - cha no -

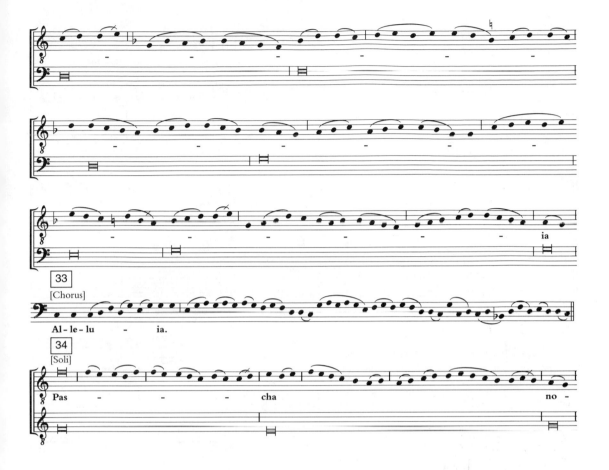

c) Anonymous clausula on *nostrum* (not heard on the recording) [combined in one score with]

d) Texted motet: *Gaudeat devotio fidelium* [The texted duplum of the motet, which is based on the duplum of the clausula, is heard over the *nostrum* tenor.]

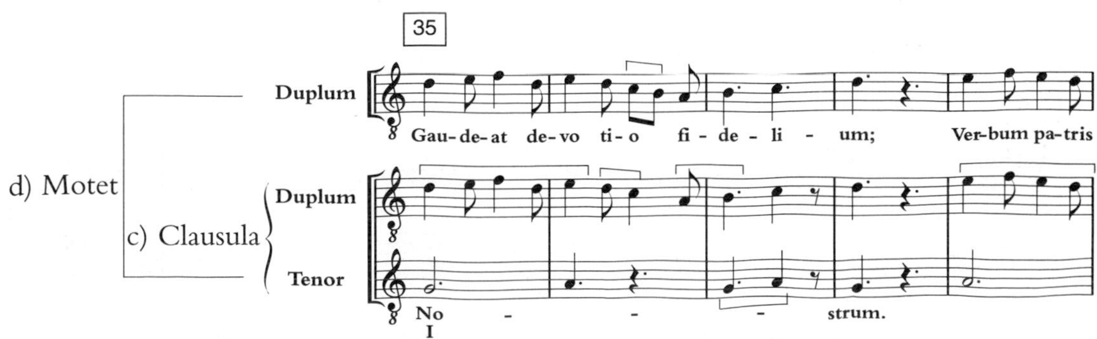

6
in - car - na - tur, No - va pro - les no - bis da - tur Et no - bis - cum con - ver - sa - tur Sa - lus gen - ti -
12
um. Vi - te pan - dit o - sti - um, Dum mor - tis sup - pli - ci - um, Pi - e to - le -
18
rat. Mun - di prin - ceps ex - tur - ba - tur, Dum con - si - de - rat,
II
23
Quod per mor - tem li - be - ra - tur Qui per - i - e - rat, Iu - re su - o sic pri - va - tur,
29
Dum de - si - de - rat Il - lum si - bi sub - de - re, qui nil com - mi - se - rat.

d) Gaudeat devotio fidelium;	Let the devotion of the faithful be raised in rejoicing;
Verbum patris incarnatur,	the word of the father is made flesh,
Nova proles nobis datur	and a new child is given to us,
Et nobis cum conversatur	and He has bestowed Himself upon us.
Salus gentium.	The salvation of the people
Vite pandit ostium,	has opened the gateway of life,
Dum mortis supplicium,	for he in devotion has borne
Pie tolerat.	the punishment of death.
Mundi princeps exturbatur,	Satan was cast down
Dum considerat,	when He stood firm
Quod per morten liberatur	so that through His death
Qui perierat.	he who had perished might be made free;
Iure suo sic privatur,	thus was He stripped of His own devine nature
Dum desiderat	when He chose
Illum sibi subdere, qui nihil commiserat.	to subdue death unto Himself—He who had committed no sin.

[Léonin organum continues]

e) Substitute clausula on la of the word immolatus
[combined in one score with]

f) Motet: *Ave Maria, Fons letitie,* on the same tenor *la*
[The textless clausula is not heard; the almost identical motet is performed on the recording.]

pi - a, Vas mun-di - ti - e, Te vo-ce va-ri - a So-net so-bri - e.
Gens le-ta so-bri - a. Gau-dens va-ri - e Pro - mat ec-cle-si - a
Lau-des Ma-ri - e. So-net in Ma-ri - a Vox ec-cle-si - e. Hec sol-vit
scri-ni-a Y-sa-i - e. Re-se-rans o-sti-a Clau-sa pa-tri-e,
Vi - a dans ex-i-mi-a Re-gem glo-ri - e. Qui so-la gra - ti - a,
-tus

f)	Ave Maria.	Hail Mary,
	Fons letitie,	fount of Joy,
	Virgo pura, pia,	virgin pure and holy,
	Vas munditie,	vessel of chastity,
	Te voce varia	may the joyous people
	Sonet sobrie	sing Thee in various
	Gens leta sobria.	yet restrained voices.
	Gaudens varie	Rejoicing for many blessings,
	Promat ecclesia	let the Church express
	Laudes Marie,	its praise for Mary;
	Vox ecclesie.	and let the voice of the Church
	Sonet in maria.	resound in the sea.
	Hec solvit scrinia	She has fulfilled the prophecies
	Ysaie,	of Isaiah,
	Reserans ostia	unlocking the once-closed
	Clausa patrie,	gates of heaven,
	Via dans eximia	granting access by a wonderful way
	Regem glorie,	to the King of Glory,
	Qui sola gratia,	who by grace alone,
	Plenus gratie,	and full of grace,
	Factus est hostia,	was made sacrifice,
	Finis hostie.	the end of all sacrifice.

—Adapted from ANDERSON, II, 52–53

[Léonin organum continues]

[Chorus]

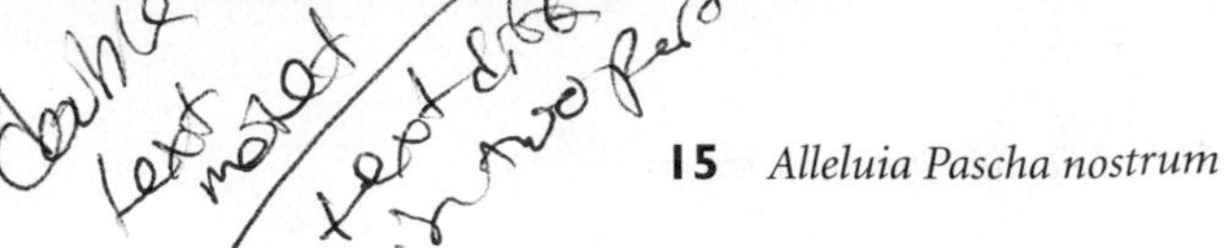

g) Motet: *Salve, salus hominum/O radians stella/nostrum*, a double-texted motet on the tenor *nostrum*.

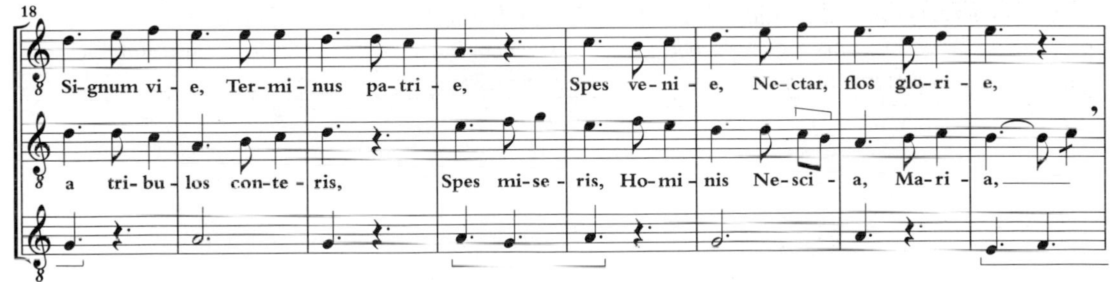

	TRIPLUM
g) Salve, salus hominum, Spes misericordie, Spes venie, Purgatrix criminum, Cecis lumen luminum, Mater prudentie, Signum vie, Terminus patrie, Spes venie, Nectar, flos glorie, Iustitie Sol pie, Clementie Sobrie Ros, virgo munditie.	Hail, safety of men, hope of pity, hope of pardon, cleanser of sins, light of light to the blind, Mother of prudence, sign-post of the way, boundary of Heaven, hope of pardon, nectar, flower of glory, of justice, holy sun, of tranquillity of prudence dew, Virgin of cleanliness! —Adapted from ANDERSON, II, 324.
	DUPLUM
O radians stella pre ceteris, Summi Dei mater et filia, Eximia proles degeneris, Tu generis Mundi letitia, Tu de via tribulos conteris, Spes miseris, Hominis Nescia Maria De lateris luto nos libera, Regenerans genus in posteris regia.	O shining star, outshining all others, Mother and Daughter of the highest God, peerless offspring of a degenerate race, Thou art the joy of the people of the world. Thou turnest away the perils of the way. O hope of wretched humanity; Mary, not knowing [the touch of man], free us from the mire surrounding us, regenerating the human race in thy kingdom for all ages.

When the Alleluia was performed as plainchant, it was sung by a priest, who was joined at certain points by a unison chorus. The priest began by intoning the word "Alleluia," after which the chorus repeated this initial segment of melody. The chorus then continued until the priest intervened with the Verse, a line from one of the psalms. Toward the end of the Verse, the chorus joined in and completed the Verse. The soloist and chorus then repeated the entire Alleluia.

While Léonin set the solo sections polyphonically, comparison of his setting (15b) with the original chant (15a) makes it evident that he expected the sections normally sung by the chorus to remain simple plainsong. The plan of Léonin's organum may be diagrammed as follows:

Soloists	**Chorus**	**Soloists**
Organum duplum (15b)	**Plainchant**	**Organum duplum (15b cont.)**
Alleluia ____	*Alleluia* ____	*Pascha* ____

Soloists (cont.)		
Discant clausula (15c)	**Organum duplum (15b cont.)**	**Substitute clausula (15e)**
no-strum (melisma) ____	*immo-la-* ____	(melisma) *tus* (melisma) *est* ____

Chorus	**Soloists**		**Chorus**
Plainchant	**Org. dupl. (15b cont.)**	**Discant (15b cont.)**	**Plainchant**
Christus. ____	*Alle-* ____	*lu-ia.* ____	

The formal and sonorous contrast already present in the responsorial plainchant performance is thus magnified. The different styles of setting build further contrast into the polyphonic sections. The opening intonation "Alleluia" (15b) resembles the older melismatic or florid organum: the plainsong intonation (transposed down a fifth) is stretched out into unmeasured long notes of indefinite duration to form the tenor; against this a solo voice sings textless melismatic phrases, broken at irregular intervals by cadences and rests. The original notation suggests a free, unmeasured rhythm. The fluid melody—non-periodic and loosely segmented—strongly suggests improvisatory practice. Nevertheless, some scholars have applied the patterns of the rhythmic modes to such passages of organum purum, and their transcriptions are seen in many editions and heard on some recordings. The transcription given here assumes unmeasured rhythm for these passages.

After the chorus responds "Alleluia" in unison, the two-voice solo texture resumes with the psalm verse on the word "Pascha." But beginning with the word "nostrum" a quite different style is heard (15c). The tenor now sings in strictly measured rhythm; the upper voice, which moves in faster notes, likewise assumes the distinctly measured character of discant, the style in which all parts are in measured rhythm. Section 15c constitutes a *clausula*, a closed form in discant style in which a chant melisma is heard twice in the tenor (the two appearances of the tenor are marked by Roman numerals I and II). (See the facsimile in HWM of the page from the Florence manuscript containing this clausula.)

The choice of whether to use organum or discant style was not a matter of caprice. It was based on the general principle that in those portions of the original chant that were syllabic or only slightly florid—where comparatively few notes were sung to a syllable—the organal style with long sustained tones in the tenor was appropriate. In those portions, however, where the original chant was itself highly melismatic, it was necessary for the tenor to move along more quickly, so that the whole piece would not be lengthened unduly. Instead of many notes in the added part to each note in the chant, the discant clausula counterposed two to four notes to each note of a melisma.

In the Florentine source from which 15b, c, and d are taken, this Alleluia has three clausulae: on *nostrum*, as we saw; on *latus* of the word "immolatus"; and on *lu* of the final "Alleluia." Between these clausulae there are contrasting sections in organum purum style. After the last discant section, the chorus closes the piece with the concluding few phrases of the plainsong Alleluia on which the composition is based.

In both organum purum and discant, the attack of a new tenor note is normally accompanied by a consonance in the other parts, the longer such notes by a perfect consonance. At the close of extended sections, such as at *lu* and *ia* of "Alleluia," at *no* of "nostrum," or at *est*, a second may move to a unison or a seventh to an octave in what resembles a modern appoggiatura. The discant sections are additionally organized through rests, which break up the melodies into easily grasped phrases.

Clausulae such as 15c were sometimes converted into motets by the addition of texts in Latin, French, or both. For example, setting a Latin text, *Gaudeat devotio fidelium*, to the duplum turned the clausula on *nostrum* (15c) into a motet (15d).

Similarly, the clausula on *latus* (15e) became a motet in honor of the Virgin, *Ave Maria, Fons letitie* (15f). The brevity of the clausula's musical phrases in the duplum obliged the poet to invent rhyming endings for every second line.

A clausula on *nostrum* different from 15c is behind the duplum of the motet in 15g. This duplum received the text *O radians stella pre ceteris* to form a two-part motet. At a later stage a third part, or triplum, was added, with the text *Salve salus hominum*, making it a three-part motet. The two poetic texts are unrelated to the Alleluia verse but complement each other in that they are addressed to the Virgin. The texts were set to the music, rather than the other way around, so their line lengths are irregular, and the rhyme scheme is extremely simple, alternating two syllables, "is" and "ia" in the duplum, "um" and "ie" in the triplum. The third rhythmic mode of the triplum matches that of the duplum, but the lengths of the phrases are calculated to avoid simultaneous rests. This motet was also converted to secular uses by having a French text substituted for each of the upper parts, namely *Qui d'amors veut bien* in the triplum and *Qui longuement porroit* in the duplum. As in the Latin motet, the two texts reinforced each other and each used only two different rhyming syllables.

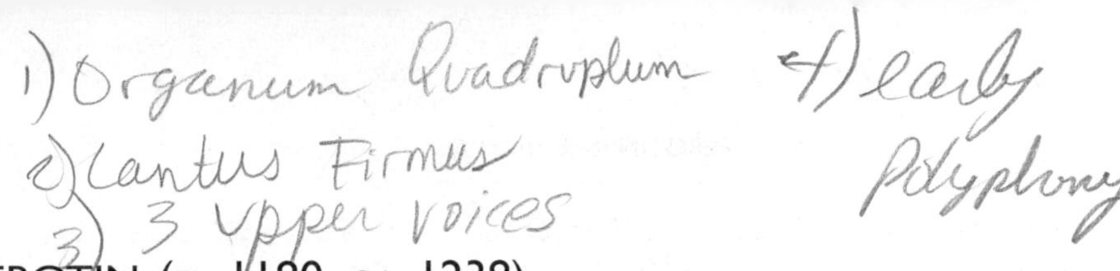

Pérotin (fl. 1180–ca. 1238)

16

Organum quadruplum: *Sederunt* CD 1 CD 1

Gradual for St. Stephen's Day

 For a facsimile of the original notation of the end of the *Sederunt* section, see HWM, p. 83.

25
30
35
40
45
50

55
43
12
60
de -
65
70
75

80

85

90

95
100

105
110
115
120
125

Sederunt principes,	The rulers were seated in council,
et adversum me loquebantur;	and they spoke against me;
et iniqui persecuti sunt me.	and my enemies persecuted me.

—RICHARD HOPPIN

This organum is the music for the intonation (the first word) of the Respond of the Gradual for St. Stephen's Day. It is a portion of a very long composition that must have taken about twenty minutes to perform. Since the text did not provide a means of organizing the music, the composer resorted to abstract, purely musical devices. One of these is voice exchange. In measures 13–18 the duplum and triplum exchange two-measure motives, while the quadruplum sounds the same pattern three times, like an ostinato. The duplum and quadruplum have a similar exchange in measures 24 to 29. Meanwhile there is a more extended line traded between the quadruplum, measures 13–23, and the triplum, measures 24–34. Simultaneously measures 13–23 of the duplum are equivalent to the quadruplum's measures 24–34. In effect, therefore, measures 24–34 sound the same as measures 13–23. The large-scale interchange must have made the music more interesting to the singers, but listeners would simply have heard an eleven-measure section repeated. Shorter voice exchanges occur throughout the "Sederunt" section, and there is also motive repetition within a single voice. Particularly notable are the coupling of phrases that are nearly alike, such as measures 131–134 and 135–138, which exhibit an antecedent-consequent relationship. Johannes de Garlandia, who wrote a treatise on the rhythm of the Notre Dame usage, remarked that complementary phrases of this kind occurred particularly in a style of organum called copula, which he said was intermediate between discant and organum purum. Measures 109–112 and 113–116 are similarly related and, in addition, contain voice exchanges.

17 Conductus: *Ave virgo virginum* CD 1

Ave virgo virginum	Hail, virgin of virgins,
Verbi carnis cella,	shrine of the word made flesh,
In salutem hominum	who for man's salvation
Stillans lac et mella.	drips milk and honey.
Peperisti dominum,	You bore the Lord;
Moysi ficella,	you were a rush-basket for Moses;
O radio	O, from your rays
Sol exit, et luminum	the sun goes forth, and the star
Fontem parit stella.	brings forth a fountain of light.

Florence, Biblioteca Medicea-Laurenziana, MS Pluteus 29.1, fol. 240r–240v.

Ave, plena gratia,	Hail, full of grace,
Caput Zabulonis	chief of Zebulun,
Contrivisti spolia	the spoils of robbers
Reparans predonis.	you restore.
Celi rorans pluvia	Like rain, falling from heaven
Vellus Gedeonis,	on the fleece of Gideon,
O filio	with your son
Tu nos reconcilia,	reunite us,
Mater Salomonis.	O mother of Solomon!
Virgo tu mosayce	You, Virgin,
Rubus visionis,	bramble-bush of the Mosaic vision,
De te fluxit sylice	from you flowed the fountain
Fons redemptionis.	through the rock of redemption.
Quos redemit calice	Those Christ has redeemed through the chalice
Christus passionis,	of his passion,
O gaudio	O, may he clothe them with the joy
Induat glorifice	of his glorious
Resurrectionis	resurrection.

Like so much of the Latin poetry of this period, this thirteenth-century conductus is addressed to the Virgin Mary and was probably used in special devotions and processions. Three strophes are served by the same music, and, besides, the first two couplets have identical music in all parts. Each line occupies two measures of $\frac{6}{8}$ in the transcription, except for the exclamation "O radio!" (O, from your rays), which has only four syllables instead of either seven or six of the rest of the stanza's lines. The short melodic phrases are clearly set off by strokes in the manuscripts, suggesting transcription in either rhythmic mode I or II. The three voices sing the same words at the same time, although only the tenor has text written under it.

18

Motet: *Amours mi font/En mai/Flos Filius eius* CD 1 CD 1

46 14

Tr
fol.153v
1. A-mours mi font souf - frir peine a tort, 2.car ma da - me, qui m'a mort, 3.ne me
M
fol.154
1. En mai, quant rose est flo - ri - e, 2.que j'oi ces oi - siaus chan-ter, 3.moi co-vient par
T
fol.153v
fol.154
FLOS FILIUS EIUS

dai - gne des maus, qu'ai por li, 4.dou - ner con-fort. 5.Et si l'ai toz jours mout bien ser -
dru - e - ri - e 4.joi - e de - me - ner. 5. C'est la fin, je vuoil a - mer; 6.et si

-vi, 6.n'ainc cer - tes ne li men - ti. 7. Ains sui toz a son vo - loir, ne l'en des -
ne croi mi - e, 7.qu'e-le sa - che ja, 8. don[t] vient li maus d'a - mer, 9.qui m'o - cir - ra.

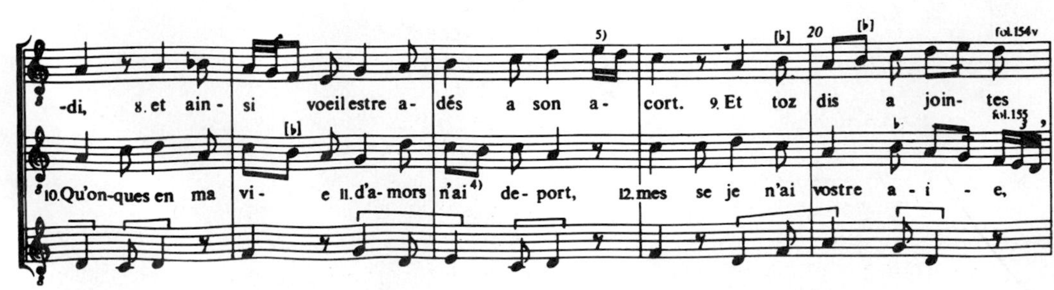
fol.154v
-di, 8. et ain - si voeil estre a - dés a son a - cort. 9. Et toz dis a join - tes
fol.155
10.Qu'on-ques en ma vi - e 11.d'a - mors n'ai de - port, 12.mes se je n'ai vostre a - i - e,

1. Montpellier MS (Mo) has a ligature of 3 breves.
2. Mo has *lei.*
3. Mo has *E*, the correct chant note.
4. Mo has *n'oi.*
5. Mo has a ligature of 2 breves.
6. Mo has *deport.*
7. Mo has a ligature of 3 breves+longa.
8. Mo has *m'eves.*
9. Mo has a longa rest.

TRIPLUM

Amours mi font souffrir peine a tort,
Car ma dame, qui m'a mort,
Ne me daigne des maus, qu'ai por li,
Douner confort.
Et si l'ai toz jours mout bien servi,
N'ainc certes ne li menti.
Ains sui toz a son voloir, ne l'en desdi,
Et ainsi voeil estre adés a son acort.
Et toz dis a jointes mains li cri merci,
Pour Diu, qu'ele le deignast avoir de mi!

Loving makes me wrongly suffer pain,
because my lady, who has killed me,
does not deign while I am in misery
to comfort me.
And if I always served her very well,
I certainly never lied to her.
That I am entirely at her mercy, I don't deny,
and so I wish from now on to be in her good graces,
and every day I clasp my hands and cry for pity,
O Lord, that she grant me mercy.

MOTETUS

En mai, quant rose est florie,
Que j'oi ces oisiaus chanter,
Moi covient par druerie
Joie demener.
C'est la fin, je vuoil amer;
Et si ne croi mie,
Qu'ele sache ja,
Don[t] vient li maus d'amer,
Qui m'ocirra.
Qu'onques en ma vie
D'amors n'ai deport,
Mes se je n'ai vostre aïe,
Vostre amor, vostre confort,
Brunete sans ami,
Vos m'avés mort.

In May, when the rose blooms,
and I hear the birds sing,
I like by whatever means
to strive for joy.
This is it; I want to love.
I don't believe
that she yet knows
where my pains of love come from
that will slay me.
Never in my life
have I known love's pleasure,
but if I don't have your help,
your love, your solace,
brunette without lover,
you will have killed me.

The style of this motet is called *Franconian* after Franco of Cologne, a thirteenth-century composer and theorist who described a notation in which note shapes accurately represented temporal durations and who clarified the rules for consonance and dissonance. All the voices are based on the first rhythmic mode, consisting of a long followed by a breve. In the upper parts both the long and the breve are frequently broken up into shorter notes, a device theorists called *fractio modi* (breaking up of the mode).

A pairing of this tenor with this motetus appears in a clausula in the manuscript Wolfenbüttel 2, so what we have here may be regarded as two compositions in one, a two-part and a three-part motet, and it may be performed either way.

The tenor performs the chant melody of *Flos Filius eius* (see example below) twice (measures 1–12 and 13–25), repeating throughout a rhythmic pattern that occupies two measures of the transcription. Since the music of the motetus originated as a clausula duplum, the French text must have been composed after the music. This accounts for the uneven lengths of poetic lines and the irregular rhyme scheme. The triplum's text and melody are more independent, and its textual-musical lines do not match those of the motetus but sometimes overlap. This feature, together with the breaking up of the rhythmic mode, assures constant animation, and helps to avert the stops and starts found in many motets of this period.

Verse, *Virgo Dei Genitrix*, of the responsory *Stirps Jesse* for the feast of the Blessed Virgin Mary (*Processionale monasticum* [Solesmes: Petrus, 1893], p. 186).

The first and last (sixth) notes of the tenor's modal pattern receive the most perfect consonances—namely, the unison, fifth, and octave—but there are exceptions. Dissonances and imperfect consonances fall mainly on the short notes of the mode or on the second halves of the long notes. The tenor's rhythmic pattern cleverly emphasizes the two most characteristic degrees of the chant's Mode II, the final *D* and the reciting tone *F*. The upper parts share the complementary authentic range of Mode I.

Philippe de Vitry (1291–1361)

19

Motet: *In arboris/Tuba sacre fidei/Virgo sum* CD 1

47

Tu - - - -
In
Virgo sum. Tenor. Nigre notule sunt imperfecte et rube sunt perfecte.
- - - - - - - ba sa-cre fi - de - i pro - pri -
ar - bo - ris em - pi - - ro pro - spe -
A I
- e dic-ta de - i pre-co ar-ca-no-rum in the-a-tris cla-mitat quod ra-ti-o he-si-
- re vir - - gi - ni - tas se - det pu-er - pe -
- tat ba-sis peccato-rum fa - - tendum simpli-ci-ter creden dum-que fir-mi-
- re me - - - di - a - - trix fi - - des In

Philippe de Vitry, *Complete Works*, ed. Leo Schrade, with new intro. and notes by Edward H. Roesner (Monaco: Éditions de l'Oiseau-Lyre, 1984), No. 10, pp. 32–34.

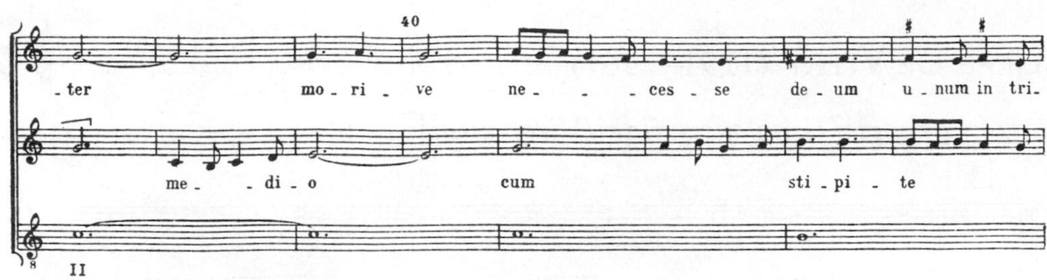
40
-ter mo-ri-ve ne- - - ces-se de-um u-num in tri-
me- -di-o cum sti-pi-te
II

45
50
-bus per- - - so-nis e-qua-li- -bus et tres u-nam es-se
ce- - - - -ca-ta ra- -ti- -o in- - -se-cu-
(3×) 6/8

55
60
vir- - - - -ginem non se-mi-ne vi- -ri set spi-ra-mi-
-ta sep- -tem so- -ro- -ri- - - -
(2×) 6/8
III

65
70
-ne ver-bi con-ce-pis - se ipsem semper vir-gi-nem deum at-que ho-mi-
-bus so- -phis-ma-ta su- - - - -a fo- -ven-ti-

75
80
-nem mun-do pe-pe-ris-se sed trans - na-tu-ra-li - a
-bus hec ut scan- -dat
48
85
90
i - sta cum sint om-ni- -a cre - den - ti - bus vi - ta ne - cis ne - gli-
dum ma- - - - - - -gis ni - ti - tur
B 1
95
100
-gen-ti-bus natu-re quod gressi -bus ra-ti-o po-ti - ta in pre - - mis-sis(?) du-bi-um
de - bi - - li - tas ra - - mo - rum
2
105
gignat et au- -gu - ri - um i-gi-tur ni-te-tur et fi - des per quam vi-
fran-gi - tur Pe - - tat er - go fi - de-
110
115
-a a - pud archana di-a cla-ri-or ha - be - tur semper i - mi - te - tur.
-i dex - - te-ram vel e - ter-num ni - - te-tur per - - pe - ram.
3

Duplum

In arboris empiro prospere
virginitas sedet puerpere
mediatrix fides in medio,
cum stipite cecata ratio
insecuta septem sororibus,
sophismata sua foventibus;
hec ut scandat dum magis nititur
debilitas ramorum frangitur.
Petat ergo fidei dexteram
vel eternum nitetur perperam.

At the top of the tree auspiciously
sits virginity expecting child,
with faith, the midwife, in the middle,
along with the trunk, blind reason,
followed by seven sisters
fostering its sophisms.
Reason strives to climb higher
until the fragile branches break.
Therefore let her seek the right hand of faith
or tread the wrong path forever.

Triplum

Tuba sacre fidei,
proprie dicta Dei.
Preco arcanorum
in theatris clamitat
quod ratio hesitat,
basis peccatorum,
fatendum simpliciter
credendumque firmiter
morive necesse:
Deum unum in tribus
personis equalibus
et tres unum esse;
virginem non semine
viri set spiramine
verbi concepisse;
ipsam semper virginem
Deum atque hominem
mundo peperisse;
sed transnaturalia
ista cum sint omnia
credentibus vita
neces negligentibus,
nature quod gressibus
ratio potita
in premissis dubium
gignat et augurium;
igitur vitetur
et fides per quam via
apud archana dia
clarior habetur,
semper imitetur.

The trumpet of holy faith
is rightly called God's word.
The teller of secrets
proclaims in the theaters
what reason,
the basis of sinners,
hesitates to say simply
and believe firmly
or one must die.
That God is one in three
equal persons;
that the three are one;
that the virgin by no seed
of man but by the breath
of the word conceived;
that she, always a virgin,
gave birth to God and man
in the world.
But since such
supernatural things
are life to those who believe,
death to those who ignore,
let what by natural steps
reason has acquired
from premises beget
doubts and prophesies.
Therefore reason is shunned
and faith, by means of which
secret divine truths
become clearer,
should always be obeyed.

Tenor

Virgo sum.

I am a virgin.

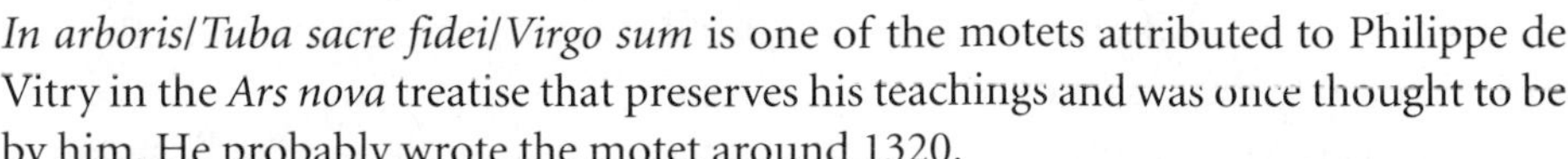

In arboris/Tuba sacre fidei/Virgo sum is one of the motets attributed to Philippe de Vitry in the *Ars nova* treatise that preserves his teachings and was once thought to be by him. He probably wrote the motet around 1320.

The texts of the duplum and triplum are closely related: they both speak of the Virgin Mary and of the need to follow faith rather than reason. These texts also identify with the tenor's plainchant's subject, *Virgo sum* (I am a virgin). Composers strove for this consistency but rarely achieved it in such an obvious way.

The innovation that characterized the music of de Vitry and his contemporaries and led to the label *ars nova* (new art) is the duple division of the larger note values. The long or *modus*, which in Notre Dame polyphony, or *ars antiqua*, was always perfect, that is, divided into three breves, here receives an imperfect division into two breves (dotted half notes in the transcription). The breve, in turn, is divided into two semibreves (dotted quarter notes), making the *tempus* also imperfect. Only the prolation—the division of semibreves into minims—is triple (major prolation; represented in the transcription by three eighth notes). A broader triple organization or *maximodus* of three longs (three measures of the tenor, six of the upper parts) governs the entire work. This large triple may be a symbol of the Trinity (the triple nature of the Christian God—Father, Son, and Holy Spirit), proclaimed in the Triplum's text. The number of measures or breves in each section except the last is divisible by three (12, 24, 24, 24, 12, 12).

The composition is held together by the melody of the lowest part, which consists of two statements (called *colores* from the term used for repetition in classical rhetoric) of the same chant, the second color having note values diminished by half. Each statement of the chant is divided into three segments or *taleae* (cuttings). The first three taleae have identical rhythmic patterns. The second group of three taleae have the same rhythm reduced by half. This kind of organization, called *isorhythm* (same rhythm), evolved from repeating shorter patterns in the tenor parts of thirteenth-century motets.

Because the tenor moves slowly in relation to the more prominent upper parts, most listeners barely notice this organization. However, some in the elite gatherings of clerics and courtiers for which this music was written must have understood the structure and taken delight in it.

Other unifying devices may strike a listener more deeply. Toward the end of each talea three types of intensification occur. After the first three maximodi or six bars of the tenor, the original notes were written in red ink, a sign that the division of the long (dotted whole note) temporarily changed to triple (for example, measures 25–30). In all six taleae, the rhythm of the upper parts as well as the tenor's in this "red" section are isorhythmic—one pattern governing the first color, another the second. Moreover all these "red" sections use a technique called *hocket* (from the

French *hoquet*, meaning "hiccup"), in which the upper voices alternate singing and resting to project a single although choppy melodic line. A long note follows each of the "red" sections, and succeeding this is a proliferation of short notes in both parts until a new talea begins, marked by long notes in the upper parts.

This isorhythmic organization of the tenor part, with the "red" notation marked by half brackets, is readily apparent in the following example:

Apart from the hockets, the three voices are mostly independent of each other. But the first four pitches of the triplum are identical to those of the tenor, a "pre-imitation" of the borrowed melody that was often found in later polyphonic music. The parts meet on the longer notes, with only a few exceptions, on octaves, fifths, fourths, thirds, and sixths. When three voices are singing, they often form triads.

The composer usually observed the accents of the poetic lines in his setting but not the rhythm of speech. The lines of poetry determine the contours and segmentation of the melodies, but neither the rhymes nor the meanings of the lines are reflected in them.

We may conclude that de Vitry aimed for a harmonious, orderly, and lively composition.

GUILLAUME DE MACHAUT (CA. 1300–1377) 20

Rondeau: *Rose, liz, printemps, verdure* CD 2 CD 1

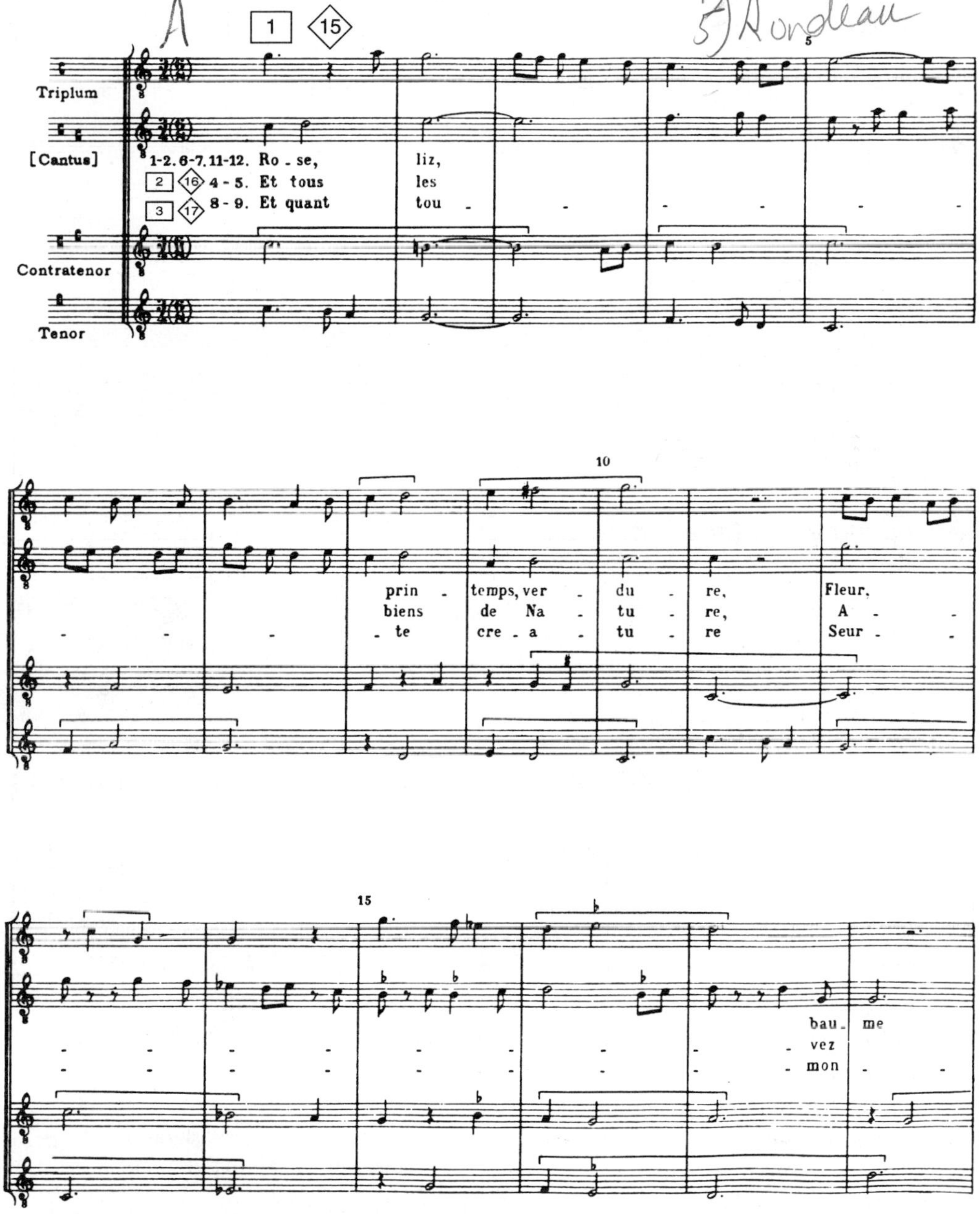

1 15

Triplum

[Cantus]

1-2. 6-7. 11-12. Ro - se, liz,
2 16 4 - 5. Et tous les
3 17 8 - 9. Et quant tou -

Contratenor

Tenor

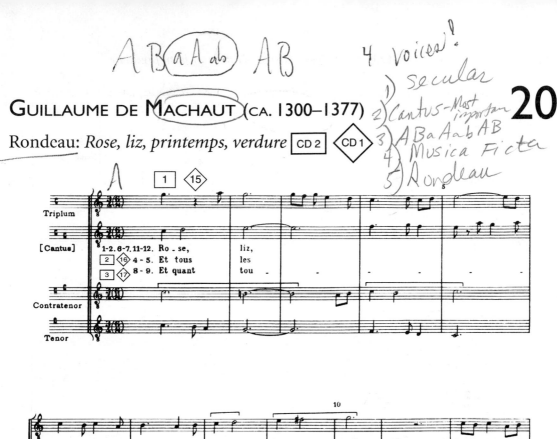

Guillaume de Machaut, *Oeuvres complètes*, Vol. 5, ed. Leo Schrade (Monaco: Éditions de l'Oiseau-Lyre, 1977), pp. 11–12.

Rose, liz, printemps, verdure,	Rose, lily, spring, greenery,
Fleur, baume et tres douce odour,	flower, balm, and the sweetest fragrance,
Belle, passes en doucour,	beautiful lady, you surpass in sweetness.
Et tous les biens de Nature,	And all the gifts of nature
Avez dont je vous aour.	you possess, for which I adore you.
Rose, liz, printemps, verdure,	Rose, lily, spring, greenery,
Fleur, baume et tres douce odour.	flower, balm, and the sweetest fragrance.
Et quant toute creature	And, since beyond any creature's
Seurmonte vostre valour,	your virtue excels,

Bien puis dire et par honour:
Rose, liz, printemps, verdure,
Fleur, baume et tres douce odour,
Belle, passes en doucour.

I can honestly say:
Rose, lily, spring, greenery,
flower, balm, and very sweet fragrance,
beautiful lady, you surpass in sweetness.

The rondeau is a form in which the full refrain, heard at the beginning and the end, contains all the music. In *Rose, liz* the first part of the refrain has two lines and closes without finality on *D*, while the second part has one line and closes on the keytone *C*. The first couplet, of two lines, is set to the music of the first part of the refrain; the second couplet, of three lines, uses all the music. The musical form for the 13 lines is ABaAabAB (capital letters indicate that both the music and the text of the refrain are sung):

Lines of poetry:	1	2	3	4	5	6(1)	7(2)	8	9	10	11(1)	12(2)	13(3)
Rhyme:	a	b	b	a	b	a	b	a	b	b	a	b	b
Sections of music:	A		B	a		A		a		b	A		B

A and B are linked by having similar final rhymes and musical phrases (compare measures 20–25 and 32–36).

As in Machaut's secular songs in general, the music is constructed around a two-voice framework in which the tenor serves as a slower-moving support to the cantus, the only voice provided with a text (although all of the voices may have been sung). The contratenor, in the same range as the tenor, reinforces or complements it, while the triplum shares the upper octave and exchanges motives with the cantus. A diatonic descending-fourth figure dominates the tenor part and at one point is taken up by the triplum (compare tenor, measures 11–12, and triplum, measures 15–16). Thirds and sixths sweeten the harmony along the way but are suppressed at the final note of poetic lines and caesuras, where Machaut preferred the octave and fifth. What may sound like syncopations are really the effect of hemiola, parts simultaneously organized in duple and triple divisions ($\frac{6}{8}$ and $\frac{3}{4}$ in the transcription).

Characteristic of French fourteenth-century secular music is the long melisma at the beginning of lines and sometimes also in the middle. These melismas, occupying as much as four measures, do not fall on important words, nor even necessarily on accented syllables. They have a formal and decorative function and help convey the mood of the text.

21 Guillaume de Machaut

Mass: Agnus Dei

CD 2 CD 1

4 18

Edited by Elizabeth Keitel for "Early Musical Masterworks." For translation of text, see p. 19.

15
mun- - di mi- - - se- - re-
mun- - di mi- se- - re- - - re no- -
mun- di mi- se- re- re no- - -
mun- di mi- se- re- re no- - -

20
5
19
25
re no- bis Ag- - - nus de-
- - - bis Ag- - - - - nus de- -
- bis Ag- - nus de- - -
[2]
- - bis Ag- nus de- - - -

30
- i qui tol- lis
- i qui tol- - - - lis
- i qui tol- - -
- i qui tol- - - lis

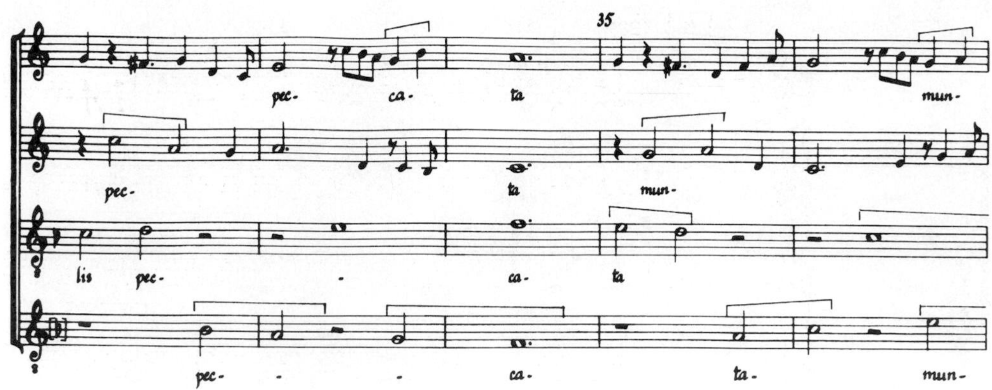
35
pec- ca- ta mun-
pec- ta mun-
lis pec- - ca- ta
pec- - - ca- ta- mun-

40
di mi- - - se- - - -
di mi- se- - - re- - - -
mun- di mi- se- re- re
di mi- se- - re-

45
re- - - re no- - - bis
re no- - - - - - bis
no- - - bis
- re no- - - bis

6
20
50
Ag- - - - nus de- - -
Ag- - - - - - - nus de- - - -
Ag- - nus de- -
Ag- - - - - - nus de-

55
- - i qui tol- -
- - i qui tol- - -
- - i qui tol- - -
- - i qui tol- - - -

- lis pec- - - ca- - -
- lis pec- - ca- -
lis pec- - ca- ta
lis pec- - ca- ta

Machaut's *Messe de Notre Dame* was one of the earliest polyphonic settings of the Ordinary. At least four more or less complete anonymous cycles preceded it, but Machaut's stands out for its spacious dimensions, its control of consonance and dissonance in a four-part texture, and its carefully planned isorhythmic structures. Although it is not unified, as some later Masses, by a single cantus firmus—each movement is based on a different one—there is a unity of approach and style and a tonal focus on *D* and *F* that hold the movements together.

The Kyrie, Sanctus, Agnus Dei, and Ite, missa est are organized by means of isorhythm, a manner of construction Machaut used in his motets. The Agnus Dei is typical of the isorhythmic movements. The tenor melody is taken from the setting of that text in the plainchant Mass numbered XVII in modern chant books (*Liber usualis*, p. 61), though in a slightly different version. The isorhythmic structure begins at the words "qui tollis"—that is, after the intonation of each Agnus (Agnus III repeats Agnus I). Since the "qui tollis" section of the chant is identical in Agnus I and II, the two statements of this constitute the two colores. The first color (Agnus I) has two taleae, each of twelve notes; the second color (Agnus II) has six taleae, each of four notes. The more frequent cadences at the end of the short taleae of Agnus II set it apart and provide contrast with the longer spans of Agnus I (and its repetition in Agnus III). In addition to the tenor, the triplum and contratenor are also wholly or partly isorhythmic.

The two upper parts enliven the rhythm with almost constant syncopation. A characteristic motive outlining a tritone is heard a number of times (measures 2, 5, and 25, and in ornamented form in 19), also in other movements of the Mass.

The occasion for which the work was written must have been one of unusual solemnity and magnificence. On the basis of comparison with datable songs, it seems to be from the early 1360s.

22 Jacopo da Bologna (14th century)

Madrigal: *Fenice fù* CD 2

Fenice fù e vissi pura e morbida,
Et or son trasmutat' in una tortora,
Che volo con amor per le belle ortora
Arbor[e] secho [mai] n'aqua torbida,

A phoenix was I who lived pure and tender
and now am transformed into a turtle-dove
that flies with love through the beautiful orchards, [and]
the dry woods [but] never in muddy waters.

Nino Pirrotta, ed. *Music of Fourteenth-Century Italy* 4: Jacobus de Bononia, Vicentius de Arimino (American Institute of Musicology, 1963), p. 6.

No' me deleta may per questo dubito,	It gives me no pleasure because of this doubt.
Va ne l'astate l'inverno viene subito.	Go in the summer; winter comes quickly.
Tal vissi e tal me vivo e posso scrivere	So I lived and so I live and can write,
C'ha donna non è più chè honesta vivere.	which, for a woman, is no more than to live honestly.

The poem set here has the form typical of the fourteenth-century madrigal: two three-line stanzas followed by a two-line ritornello. Thus the music of the stanza is heard twice, and the ritornello once. The two voices have the same text, and both parts were meant to be sung. In two places (measures 7–9, 24–25) they are in imitation, and in two short passages (measures 9, 16) they indulge in a hocketlike alternation. Otherwise the upper voice is the more florid one, having extended mellifluous runs on the last accented syllable of each line.

The temporal organization is typical of the *ars nova*. The notation of the stanzas divides the breve (half-note of the transcription) into two imperfect (duple) semibreves (quarter notes) and these in turn into two minims (eighth notes), which are further divided into semiminims (sixteenth notes). In the ritornello, the long (represened by a measure of the transcription) is divided into two perfect (triple) breves, each of which may be divided into either three imperfect or two perfect semibreves, which in turn are divided into either two or three minims. The change from duple-duple to duple-triple results in a speeding up of the music. This hierarchy of note values permits much greater variety of rhythm than the mainly triple divisions of the *ars antiqua*. For an exposition of this method of temporal organization, see the extract from Marchetto of Padua, *Pomerium in arte musicae mensuratae* (Garden of Mensural Music) in Strunk (SRrev, pp. 251–61; 2:141–51).

Jacopo's birth and death dates are not known, but between 1346 and 1349 and again in the 1350s his service to the ruling family of Milan, the Visconti, and in between at the court of Mastino II and Alberto della Scala of Verona, is well documented. *Fenice fù* is probably one of his last compositions.

23 Francesco Landini (ca. 1325–1397)

Ballata: *Non avrà ma' pietà* CD 2 CD 1

8 21 & 10 23

Leo Schrade, ed. *Polyphonic Music of the Fourteenth Century*, 4 (Paris: Éditions de l'Oiseau-Lyre, 1958), pp. 144–45.

Non avrà ma' pietà questa mia donna,
Se tu non faj, amore,
Ch'ella sie certa del mio grande ardore.
S'ella sapesse quanta pena i' porto
Per onestà celata nella mente
Sol per la sua bellecça, che conforto
D'altro non prende l'anima dolente,
Forse da lej sarebbono in me spente
Le fiamme che la pare
Di giorno in giorno acrescono 'l dolore.

—B. D'Alessio Donati

She will never have mercy, this lady of mine,
if you do not see to it, love,
that she is certain of my great ardor.
If she knew how much pain I bear—
for honesty's sake concealed in my mind—
only for her beauty, other than which
nothing gives comfort to a grieving soul,
perhaps by her would be extinguished in me
the flames which seem to arouse in
her from day to day more pain.

This ballata is typical of the form adopted by Francesco Landini. A two-line refrain (*ripresa*) is sung both before and after a six-line stanza. The first two pairs of lines in the stanza, which were called *piedi*, have their own musical phrase, while the last pair, the *volta*, uses the same music as the refrain. The form may be represented as follows:

	Ripresa	Stanza (2 piedi + volta)			Ripresa
Lines of poetry:	1 2 3	4 5	6 7	8 9 10	1 2 3
Sections of music:	A	b	b	a	A

Having a melisma on the first as well as the penultimate syllable of a line is characteristic of the Italian style. The end of every line, and often of the first word and of the caesura, is marked by a cadence, usually of the type that has become known as the *Landini cadence*, in which the movement from a major sixth to an octave is ornamented by a lower neighbor leaping up a third in the upper part (see measures 3–4, 5–6, 10–11). Sometimes both the voices that rise to the final chord do so by semitone motion, either written or by musica ficta (feigned or fictitious music)—so called because it is not in the governing mode or scale (*musica vera*), as in measures 3–4—and this form of the cadence is known as the *double leading-tone cadence.*

The use of the open (*verto*) and closed (*chiuso*) endings in the two *piedi*, represented in the transcription by the first and second endings at measure 34, may be traced to the influence of the French virelai.

One of the charms of Landini's music, in addition to the graceful vocal melody, is the sweetness of its harmonies. Gone are the parallel seconds and sevenths that abounded in the thirteenth century, and there are few parallel fifths and octaves. Sonorities containing both the intervals of the third and fifth or of the third and sixth are plentiful, though they are not used to start or end a section or piece.

BAUDE CORDIER (LATE 14TH OR EARLY 15TH CENTURY) 24

Rondeau: *Belle, bonne, sage* CD 2

11

8

1-2.7-8.13-14. Bel-
5-6. De
9-10. car

CONTRATENOR

TENOR

le, bon - ne, sa - ge, plai - sant et gen - -
re - ce - pvoir ce don ne soy - - és len - -
tant vous aim qu'ail - lours n'ay mon en - ten - -

Transcribed by Gilbert Reaney in *Early Fifteenth-Century Music* (American Institute of Musicology, 1955), pp. 9–10. © Hänssler Verlag, D-71087 Holzgerlingen. Used by permission.

21
cy que l'an se re - nou - - vel - - - -
pli, ma doul - ce da - moy - - - sel - - - -
que vous e - stes seu - le cel - - - -

27
le, 3-4.15-16.vous fais le don d'u - ne chan son nou
le,
le 11-12. qui fa - mea- vés que cha - - scun vous ap-

33
- vel - - - - le || de - dans mon
- pel - - - - le:|| flour de beau -

39
cuer qui a vous se - - pre - sen - - - - -
té sur tou - tes ex - - cel - len - - - - -

Belle, bonne, sage, plaisante et gente,
A ce jour cy que l'an se renouvelle
Vous fais le don d'une chanson nouvelle
Dedens mon coeur qui a vous se presente.

De recevoir ce don ne soyes lente,
Je vous suppli, ma douce demoiselle.
Belle bonne sage plaisante et gente,
A ce jour cy que l'an se renouvelle.

Car tant vous aim qu'ailleurs n'aymon entente,
Et sy scay que vous estes seule celle
Qui fame aves que chascun vous appelle:
Flour de beaute sur toutes excellente.

Belle bonne sage plaisante et gente,
A ce jour cy que l'an se renouvelle
Vous fais le don d'une chanson nouvelle
Dedens mon coeur qui a vous se presente.

Fair lady, good, wise, pleasant, and nice,
on this day when the year is renewed
I make a gift of a new song
within my heart which presents itself to you.

Be not slow in accepting this gift,
I beg you, my sweet damsel.
Fair lady, good, wise, pleasant, and nice,
on this day when the year is renewed.

I love you so much that I have lost my senses,
and I know that you alone
have the fame that everyone calls you
flower of beauty surpassing all.

Fair lady, good, wise, pleasant, and nice,
on this day when the year is renewed
I make a gift of a new song
within my heart which presents itself to you.

Baude Cordier's rondeau, *Belle, bonne, sage*, participates half-seriously in the intellectual play of the *ars subtilior* (subtler art) of the late fourteenth century. But this song is not much more subtle in its music than in its heart-shaped graphic presentation. If there is complexity in the music, it lies in the three levels of hemiola. When the composer departed from the regular fast triple division to a slow triple as in the contratenor at measures 7–11 (from $\frac{3}{4}$ to $\frac{3}{2}$ in the transcription), he indicated this with red notes (see the color illustration in HWM, p. 000). He also used red notes when he wanted triple division against the duple values of the $\frac{3}{2}$ sections (measure 8) or when he wanted a duple division in the cantus against the contratenor's $\frac{3}{4}$ (measures 11–12). In the text, in the line "within my heart which presents itself to you," the word "heart" is replaced with a red heart, and, of course, the entire piece is notated in the shape of a heart. An unusual feature of this chanson is the anticipation by the contratenor and tenor of the opening melody of the voice.

25 JOHN DUNSTABLE (CA. 1390–1453)

Motet: *Quam pulchra es* CD 2 CD 1

12 24

Quam pul-cra es et quam de - co - ra, ca - ris - si - ma in de - li -
Quam pul - cra es et quam de - co - ra, ca - ris - si - ma in de - li -
Quam pul - cra es et quam de - co - ra, ca - ris - si - ma in de - li -

8
- ci - is. Sta - tu - ra tu - a as - si - mi - la - ta est pal -
- ci - is. Sta - tu - ra tu - a as - si - mi - la - ta est pal -
- ci - is. Sta - tu - ra tu - a as - si - mi - la - ta est pal -

15
me, et u - be - ra tu - a bo - tris. Ca - put tu - um ut Car - me -
me, et u - be - ra tu - a bo - tris. Ca - put tu - um ut Car - me -
me, et u - be - ra tu - a bo - tris. Ca - put tu - um ut Car - me -

22
lus, col - lum tu - um si - cut tur - ris e - bur - ne -
lus, col - lum tu - um si - cut tur - ris e - bur - ne -
lus, col - lum tu - um si - cut tur - ris e - bur - ne -

Quam pulchra es et quam decora,
carissima in deliciis.
Statuta tua assimilata est palme,
et ubera tua botris.
Caput tuum ut Carmelus,
collum tuum sicut turris eburnea.
Veni, dilecte mi,
egrediamur in agrum,
et videamus si flores fructus parturierunt
si floruerunt mala Punica.
Ibi dabo tibi ubera mea.
Alleluia.

—The Song of Solomon 7:6–12

How fair and pleasant you are,
O loved one in delights.
You are stately as a palm tree,
and your breasts are like its clusters.
Your head crowns you like Carmel;
your neck is like an ivory tower.
Come, my beloved,
let us go forth into the fields,
and see whether the grape blossoms have opened
and the pomegranates are in bloom.
There I will give you my love.
Alleluia.

—Adapted from the Revised Standard Version of the Bible

Dunstable wrote numerous settings of antiphons, hymns, and other liturgical or biblical texts for a three-part ensemble, most of them based on chant melodies. This antiphon, however, is freely composed.

The three voices, similar in character and of nearly equal importance, move mostly in the same rhythm and usually pronounce the same syllables together. The musical texture resembles that of the conductus, and the short melisma at the end of the word "alleluia" conforms with the ornamented conductus style.

The composer, unfettered by a cantus firmus or an isorhythmic scheme, freely determined the form of the music, guided only by the text. Dunstable divided the piece into two sections. Section one (measures 1–38) comprises in shortened form verses 6, 7, 5, 4, and 11 of Chapter 7 of The Song of Solomon; section two, beginning with "et videamus," draws on verse 12, with an added "alleluia." The longer first section is punctuated near the end by sustained notes on the word "veni" (come); its pattern of subdivision is 9 + 9 + 11 + 8 measures, with cadences on *C*, *C*, *D*, and *G*. The second section subdivides symmetrically into 4 + 3 + 6 + 3 + 4 measures, with cadences on *F*, *D*, *C*, *D*, and *C*. The musical subdivisions of the first section correspond to the division of the text into verses; those of section two are less distinct, just as the subdivisions of the text are less clearly marked than in section one, but the "alleluia" is definitely set off by its melisma and the livelier melodic and harmonic rhythm approaching the final cadence.

Not only is the musical form determined by the text, many phrases are molded to the rhythm of the words—for example, in the declamation of "statuta tua assimilata est," "mala Punica," and "ibi dabo tibi." Other notable details are the frequent use of melodic thirds in the topmost voice, the occasional outlining of a triad in the melody (for example, in measures 43, 46, 55), and the passages of fauxbourdon, particularly at the approach to a cadence (as in measures 12–15, 32–34, 44–45, and 52–54).

26

Carol: *Salve, sancta parens* CD 2

Salve, sancta parens,	Hail, holy parent,
Enixa puerpera Regem.	from a woman in labor issued a King.
Salve, porta paradisi,	Hail, gate of paradise,
Felix atque fixa,	happy and firm,
Stella fulgens in sublimi	start shining on high
Sidus enixa.	from which a constellation sprang.

The carol, originally a monophonic dance song with alternating solo and choral portions, had by the fifteenth century become stylized as a setting in two or three (sometimes four) parts. The text was a religious poem in popular style. The carol consisted of a number of stanzas all sung to the same music, and a *burden* (a refrain with its own musical phrase), which was sung at the beginning and then repeated after each stanza.

In this carol, the music for the stanza, marked *verse*, is in free two-part counterpoint. The burden is sung twice: the first time the two parts move mostly in parallel sixths; the second time a middle voice largely parallels the top voice at a fourth below while making a third with the lowest. At the ends of poetic lines, the voices move out from parallel sixths and thirds to octaves and fifths. Measures 16 to 19 illustrate the technique of making such a cadence. This piece reflects the English improvised practice of discant, which tolerated longer successions of parallel sixths (unmediated by perfect consonances) than Continental discant did and tended to put the chant or traditional melody in the top voice.

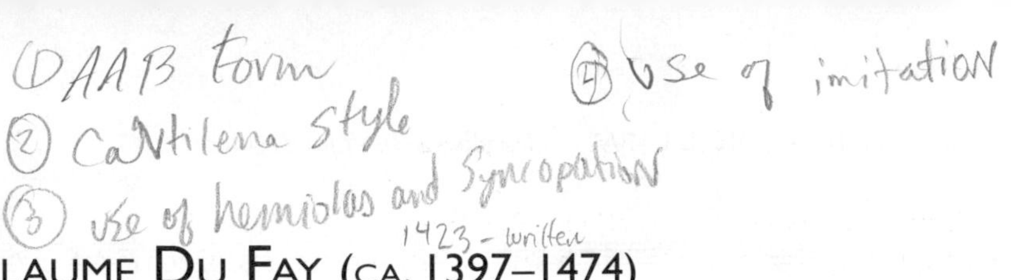

Guillaume Du Fay (ca. 1397–1474)

Ballade: *Resvellies vous et faites chiere lye* CD 2 | 14

A

Contratenor

Tenor

Resvellies vous

Resvellies vous

5

10

1. Res-vel-lies vous et fai - tes chie - re ly - - e Tout a-mou - reux qui gen - ti -
2. Es - ba - tes vous, fu - yes me-ran - co - ly - - e, De bien ser - vir point ne so -

Resvellies vous

15

.S.

20

les - se a - mes
yes ho - dés

.S.

B | 15

25

3. Car au jour d'ui se - ra li es - pou - sés, Par

30

35

grant hon - neur et no - ble sei - gnou - ri - e;

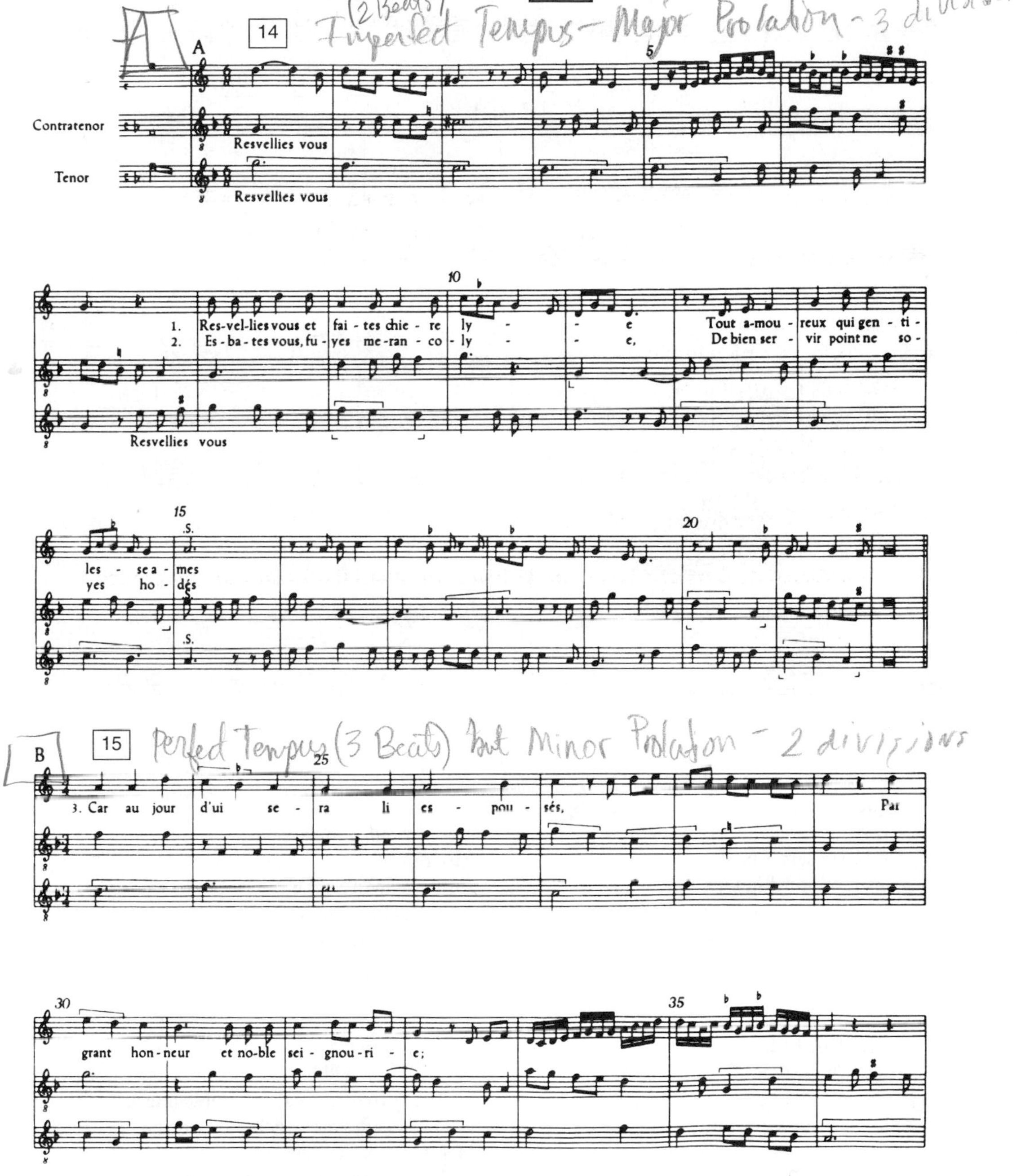

Dufay, *Opera omnia*, Vol. 6, ed. Heinrich Besseler (American Institute of Musicology, 1964), pp. 25–26.

Resvellies vous et faites chiere lye
Tout amoureux qui gentilesse ames
Esbates vous, fuyes merancolye,
De bien servir point ne soyes hodés
Car au jour d'ui sera li espousés,
Par grant honneur et noble seignourie;
Ce vous convient ung chascum faire feste,
Pour bien grignier la belle compagnye;
Charle gentil, c'on dit de Maleteste.

Il a dame belle et bonne choysie,
Dont il sera grandement honnourés;
Car elle vient de tres noble lignie
Et de barons qui sont mult renommés.
Son propre nom est Victoire clamés;
De la colonne vient sa progenie.
C'est bien rayson qu'a vascule requeste
De cette dame mainne bonne vie.
Charle gentil, c'on dit de Maleteste.

Awake and be merry,
lovers all who love gentleness;
frolic and flee melancholy.
Tire not of serving yourself well,
for today will be the nuptials,
with great honor and noble lordship,
and it behooves you, everyone, to celebrate
and join the happy company.
Noble *Charles*, who is named *Malatesta*.

He has chosen a lady, fair and good,
by whom he will be greatly honored,
for she comes from a very noble lineage
of barons who are much renowned.
Her name is Victoria,
and she descends from the Collonas.
It is right, therefore, that his appeal be heard
to live honestly with this lady.
Noble *Charles*, who is named *Malatesta*.

"Awake and be merry," this ballade tells lovers. It was written for the marriage of Carlo Malatesta and Vittoria Colonna, niece of Pope Martin V, in 1423, when Du Fay was serving the ruling family of Rimini and Pesaro. The acclamation "noble Charles," addressed to the bridegroom, is set in block chords with fermatas, while the family name Malatesta gives rise to an orgy of rapid triplets in the superius. The florid treatment at the ends of other lines follows the refined ballade tradition. These passages, with their rapid, angular figurations, seem suited more to instrumental than vocal performance, yet they could easily have been carried off by a trained singer.

This work provides a good example of the treble-dominated style; the two lower parts are less suited to vocal performance, though the players probably joined the soloist in singing "Charle gentil," a passage in the sources where all three parts have text.

The standard AAB musical form of the ballade is heard twice, once for each stanza. The last line of each stanza is a refrain. Hemiola and syncopations abound in both the A and B sections—although the B section begins in a stately syllabic style until the line "Pour bien grignier la belle compagnye," when the superius breaks into a bouncy dance rhythm. Du Fay employed two mensurations in this ballade: in the A and C sections, imperfect tempus with major prolation (the breve, here a dotted half-note, divided into two parts, each containing three semibreves or eighth notes); in the B section, perfect tempus with minor prolation. Both the A and C sections end with the same coda.

An unusual feature of this chanson is the imitation between the superius and the tenor at measures 7–10, involving all three parts at measures 15–19 and 60–64.

28 Guillaume Du Fay

Hymn: *Conditor alme siderum* CD 2

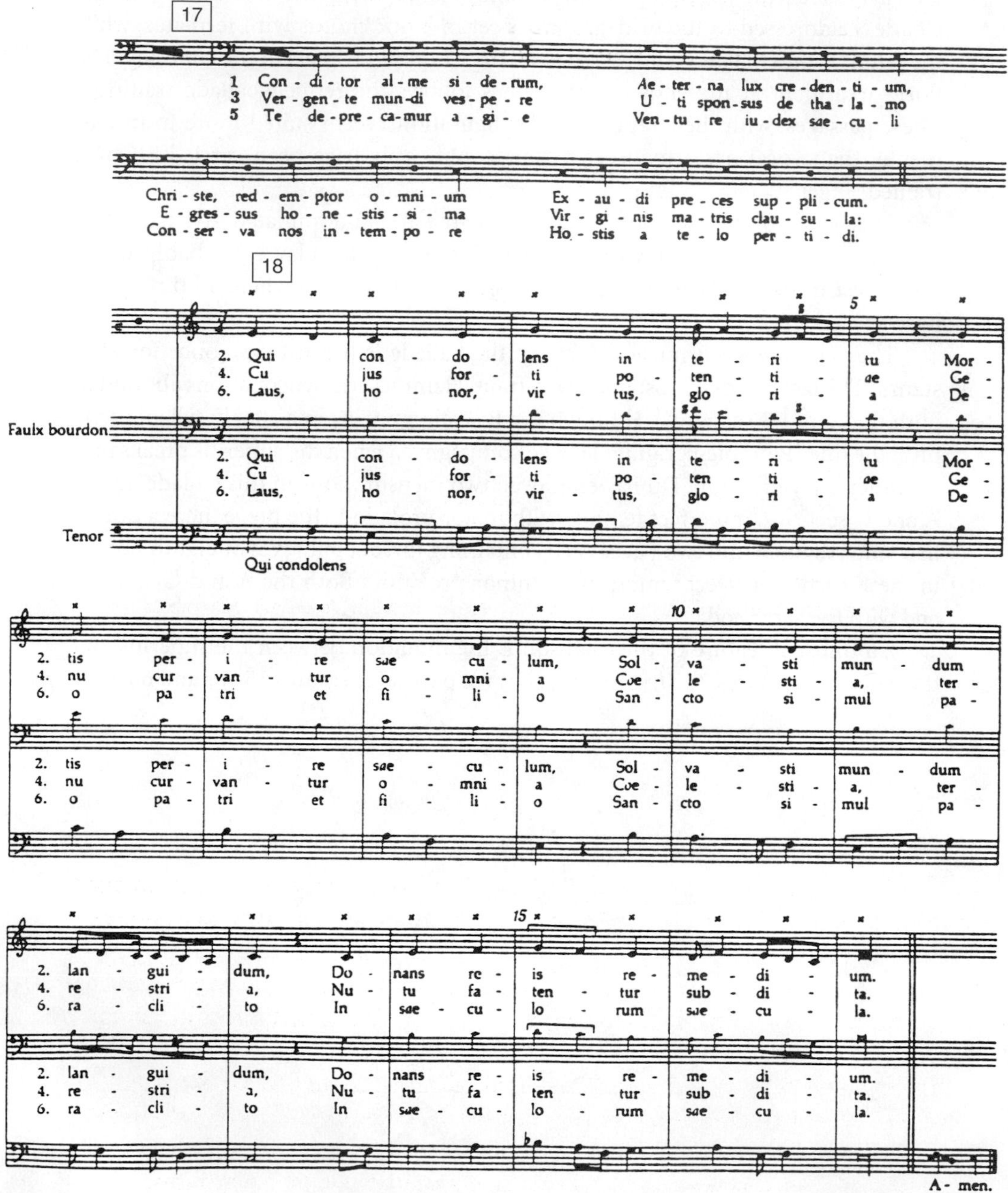

Chant from *Antiphonale*, Appendix, pp. 11–12. Dufay, *Opera omnia*, Vol. 5, ed. Heinrich Besseler (American Institute of Musicology, 1964), p. 39.

Conditor alme siderum, Aeterna lux credentium, Christe redemptor omnium Exaudi preces supplicum.	Bountiful creator of the stars, eternal light of believers, Christ, redeemer of all, hear the prayers of the supplicants.
Qui condolens interitu Mortis perire saeculum, Solvasti mundum languidum, Donans reis remedium:	You who suffer the ruin of death, the perishing of the race, who saved the sick world, bringing the healing balm.
Vergente mundi vespere Uti sponsus de thalamo, Egressus honestissima Virginis matris clausula.	As the world turns toward evening, the bridegroom from his chamber issues forth from the most chaste cloister of the Virgin mother.
Cujus forti potentiae Genu curvantur omnia Coelestia, terrestria, Nutu fatentur subdita.	You, before whose mighty power all bend their knees, celestial, terrestrial, confessing subjection to his command.
Te deprecamur agie Venture judex saeculi Conserva nos in tempore Hostis a telo perfidi.	We entreat you, holy judge of the days to come, save us in time from the weapons of the perfidious.
Laus, honor, virtus, gloria Deo patri, et filio, Sancto simul paraclito in saeculorum saecula.	Praise, honor, courage, glory, to God, the Father, and Son, and also to the Holy Protector, time everlasting, amen.

In performing a plainchant hymn, it was customary for a chorus and soloists to sing alternate stanzas. The poetry was rhymed and followed an accentual meter—here, the iambic—which the plainchant notation reflected in the succession of breve-long neumes. Du Fay wrote polyphonic versions for the even-numbered stanzas in the manner of fauxbourdon. He placed the chant, slightly decorated, in the top voice (the asterisks mark the notes of the chant). Against this voice he wrote a part that began an octave lower and then moved mostly in sixths against the chant. A third voice, represented by the smaller note-heads, was expected to be sung at the interval of a fourth below the chant, producing a succession of third-sixth sonorities, except at cadences, which ended with an octave between the outer voices.

29 Guillaume Du Fay

Se la face ay pale

a) Ballade CD 2 CD 1

Se la face ay pale,	If my face is pale,
La cause est amer,	the cause is love,
Et tant m'est amer	and it is so bitter for me
Amer, qu'en la mer	to love, that in the sea
Me voudroye voir;	I would throw myself.
Or, scet bien de voir	Then would she see—
La belle a qui suis	the fair lady to whom I belong—
Que nul bien avoir	that no joy can I have
Sans elle ne puis.	without her.

Dufay, *Opera omnia,* ed. Heinrich Besseler (American Institute of Musicology, 1951–66), 6:36 (ballade); 3:5–13 (Mass).

b) *Missa Se la face ay pale:* Gloria CD 2 CD 1

For the text of the Gloria, see NAWM 3.

mus te. Glo - ri - fi - ca - - - - mus
ca - - - mus te. Gra -
te. Glo - - - - - - - ri - - - fi - - - - - - -
Glo - ri - - - - - - - - - - - - - - - - - - -

te. Gra - ti - as a - gi - -
ti - as a - gi - mus ti - - bi pro - pter ma - gnam
ca - - - - - - - mus te.
fi - - - - ca - mus te. Gra - ti - as

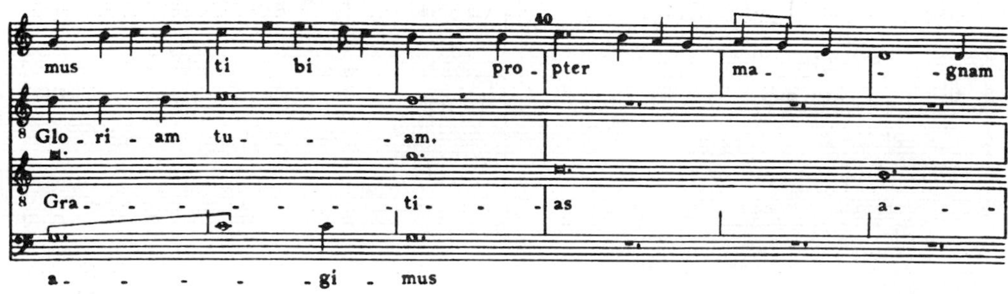
mus ti bi pro - pter ma - - gnam
Glo - ri - am tu - - - am.
Gra - - - - - - - - ti - - as a - - -
a - - - - - - gi - mus

glo - ri - am tu - - - - - am. Do - - - - mi - -
Do - mi - - - - - - - - - - - -
gi - - mus ti - - - bi.
Do - mi - - - - - - - -

50
ne de - - - us, rex cæ - le - stis, de - us
ne de - - - - us, rex cæ - - - - - - le - - - -
Do - - - mi - ne de - us, rex
- - - ne de - - - us, rex cæ - -

55
60
pa - - - ter o - - - mni - - po - - tens.
stis, de - - - us
cæ - - - le - - - - - - stis, de -
le - - - - - - - - - - - - - - - stis,

65
Do - - - mi - - -
pa - - - ter o - - - mni - po - - tens.
us pa - - - ter o - mni - po - tens. Do -
de us pa - - - - - - - - ter o - - mni - po -

70
ne fi - - - - - li
Do - - - - - mi -
mi - - ne fi - - li
tens. Do - mi - - - - - - - -

75
ne fi - - - - - - li u - ni - ge -
- - - - - - - - - - ne fi - - - li u - - ni -

80
u - ni - ge - ni -
- - - - - - - - - - - ni te
Je - - - - - - - su
ge - - - - - - - - - - - - - ni - - te Je - su

85
90
te Je - - su Chri - - -
Je - - - - - - - - - su
Chri - - - - - - - - - - - - ste.
Chri - - - - - - - - ste. Do - -

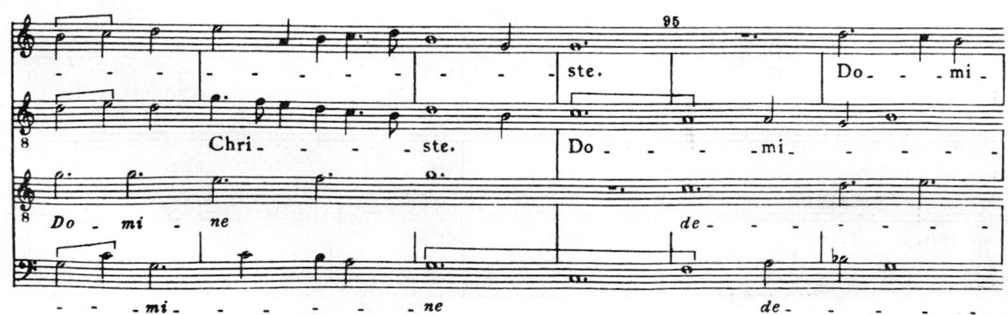
95
- - - - - - - - - - ste. Do - - mi -
Chri - - - - ste. Do - - - - mi - - - - -
Do mi - ne de - - - - - - - -
- - mi - - - - - - - ne de - - - - - -

100
ne de- -us, a- -gnus
ne de- -us, a- -gnus de-
-us, a-
-us, a- -gnus de-

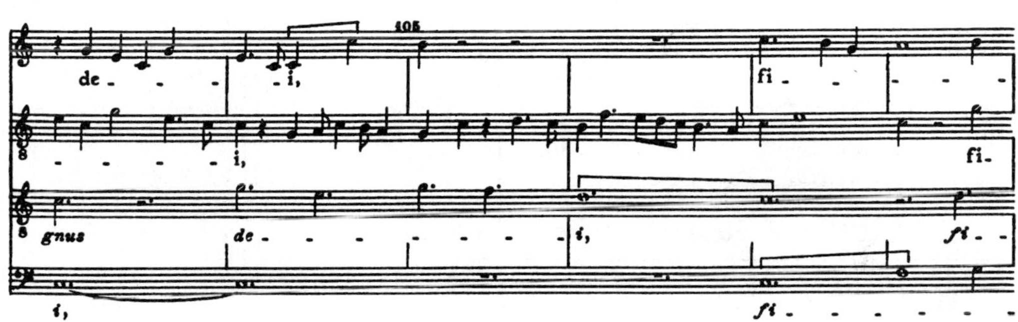
105
de- -i, fi-
-i, fi-
gnus de- -i, fi-
i, fi-

110
-li- -us pa-
li- -us pa-
-li- -us pa-
-li- -us pa-

22 28

115
B
-tris. Qui tol- -lis pec-
-tris, Qui tol-
tris.
-tris.

- ca - ta mun - - - - di, mi - se - re - re no -
- - lis pec - ca - ta mun - - - - di, mi - se -

23 29

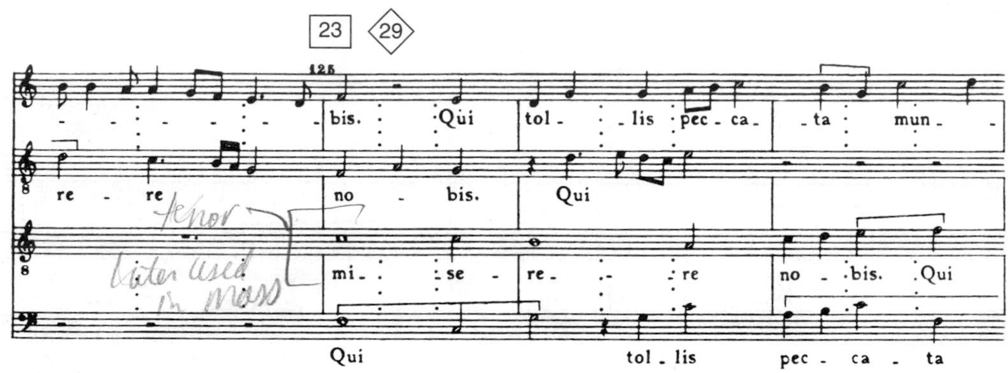
- - - - - - - bis. Qui tol - lis pec - ca - ta mun -
re - re no - bis. Qui
mi - se - re - re no - bis. Qui
Qui tol - lis pec - ca - ta

- - - - - - di, su - sci - pe de - pre - ca - ti -
tol - - lis pec - ca - ta mun - di, su - sci - pe
tol - lis pec - ca - ta mun - di, su - - sci -
mun - - - - - - - - di, su - -

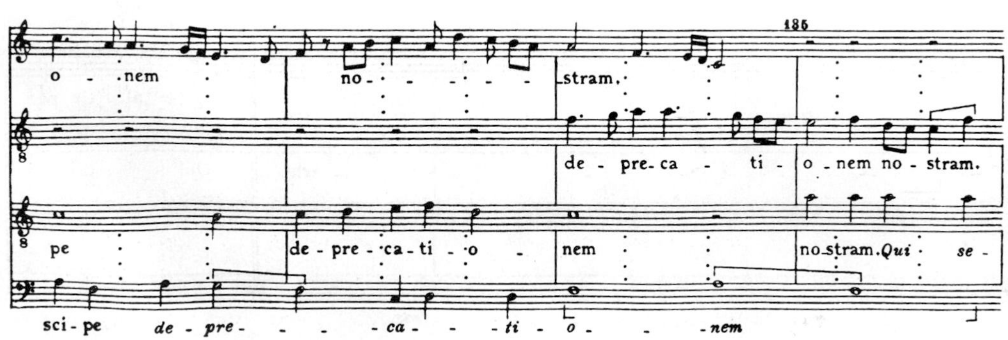
o - nem no - - - - stram.
de - pre - ca - ti - o - nem no - stram.
pe de - pre - ca - ti - o - nem no - stram. Qui se -
sci - pe de - pre - - - ca - - ti - o - - nem

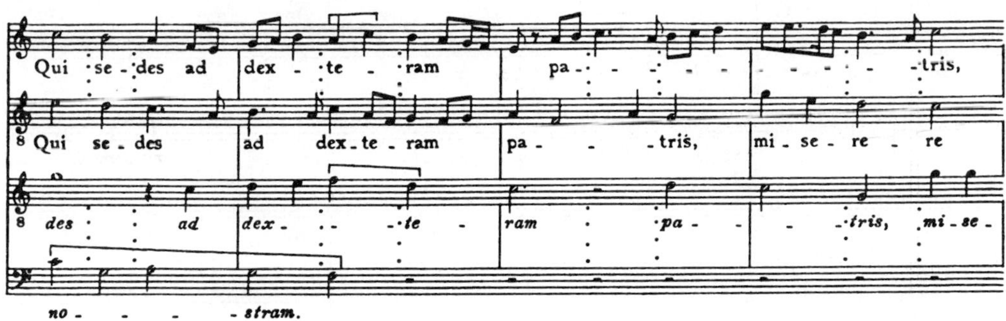
Qui se - des ad dex - te - ram pa - - - - - - - - - tris,
Qui se - des ad dex - te - ram pa - - tris, mi - se - re - re
des ad dex - - te - ram pa - - tris, mi - se -
no - - - - stram.

140
mi - se - re - re - no - - - bis.
no - - bis. Quoni - am tu so - - - - - -
re - re no - - - - - - bis.
mi - - se - - re - re no - bis. Quo - ni - am tu so - - - - -

145
Quo - ni - am tu
- - lus san - - - ctus. Tu so - - lus
Quo - - ni - am
- - lus san - - - - - - - - - - - - - - - - ctus.

150
so - - - lus san - - - ctus. Tu so - - lus do - - mi - nus.
do - - - - - - mi - - - - nus.
tu so - lus san - ctus. Tu so - lus do - - mi - - -
Tu so - - - - lus do - - - mi - nus. Tu so - - -

Tu so - lus al - tis - si - mus,
Tu so - lus al - tis - si - mus,
nus. Tu so - lus al - tis - si - mus, Je -
- lus al - tis - si - mus, Je -

155
Je - su Chri - ste.
Je su Chri - ste.
- su Chri - ste.
- su Chri - ste.

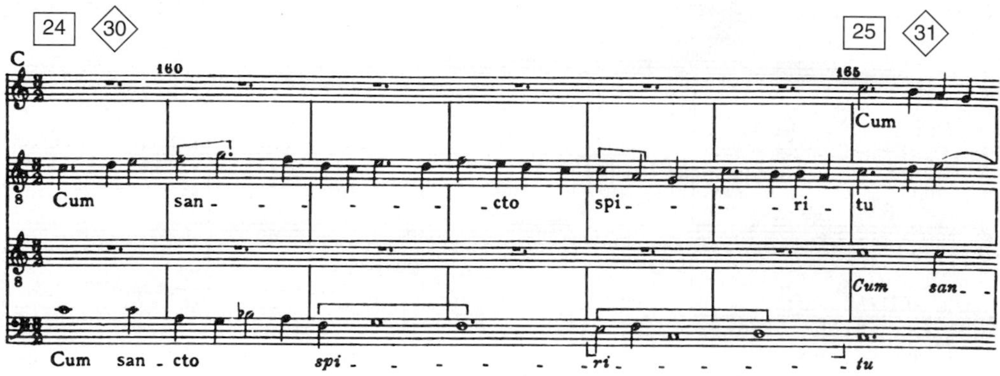
24 30
25 31
C
160
165
Cum
Cum san - cto spi - ri - tu
Cum san -
Cum san - cto spi - ri - tu

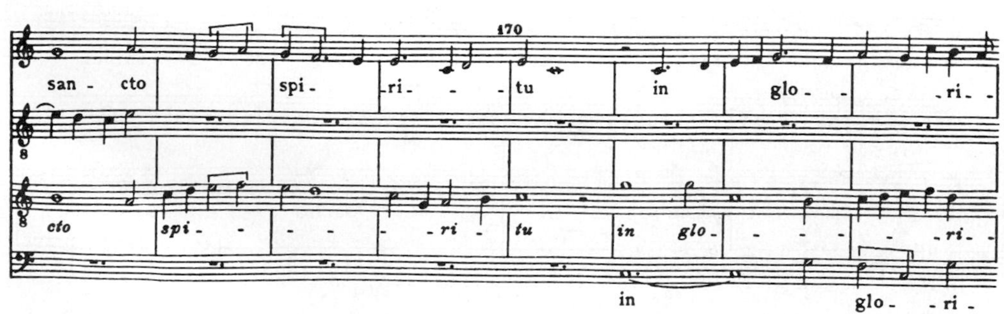
170
san - cto spi - ri - tu in glo - ri -
cto spi - ri tu in glo - ri -
in glo - ri -

For this Mass, perhaps written for a special occasion at the court of Savoy in the 1450s, Du Fay used the tenor of his own ballade, *Se la face ay pale* (NAWM 29a), composed in the 1430s, as a cantus firmus. The chanson, of which only the first of three stanzas is given here, is not in the usual ballade form—AAB—but is through-composed.

In the Mass, Du Fay used the ballade's tenor melody as a cantus firmus, applying mensural proportions so that it is heard at different speeds in the several movements or sections. In the Kyrie, Sanctus, and Agnus the value of each note of the ballade is doubled. In the Gloria and in the Credo the cantus firmus is heard in the tenor three times, first at triple the normal note values, then with doubled note values, and finally at normal note values, so that the melody becomes easily recognizable only when it is heard at its normal pace this third time. As a result, each measure of the tenor corresponds to three measures of the other parts in measures 19–118; to two measures of the other parts in measures 125–158; and to one measure in measures 165–198. Thus the calculated restatement of the tune imposes on the Gloria a form that is further marked by preceding each entrance of the cantus firmus with a duet. The speeding up of the tenor's cantus firmus and the imitation of some of its motives in the other parts contribute to the excitement of the closing Amen.

More immediately evident to the listener than the unity achieved by the threefold statement of the chanson melody in the tenor is the diverse character of the several voices. Each is an independent layer having its own melodic and rhythmic logic and function. The top two voices—the superius and the contratenor altus—have soft melodious contours and occasionally exchange motives, while the contratenor bassus, more angular though still vocal, provides a harmonic foundation.

The most obvious level of temporal organization is the perfect tempus, represented in the transcription by the $\frac{3}{2}$ measures. Each of the three beats within this tempus is divided into two (minor prolation). A broader triple organization is evident in the tenor's perfect modus consisting of three tempora, or three of the modern measures. Interrupting this pattern are an instance of hemiola in measures 19–20 between the superius–contratenor altus and the tenor bassus, and shifts in meter at measures 26, 34, and 36 in the altus, from the prevailing $\frac{3}{2}$ to a compound duple $\frac{6}{4}$.

Besides the repetitions of the ballade tune throughout the Mass, another unifying feature is the so-called *head motive*, or *motto*. Each principal division of a movement begins in the uppermost voice with the motive that in the Gloria is set to the words "Et in terra pax." The motive is alluded to also within movements, as in the Gloria at measures 40, 88, 119, 165, and 184.

Although the ballade is clearly centered on *C*, and many of the internal cadences in the Mass movement also close on this tonality, Dufay left himself free to center the Mass on *F* by putting the tune in the tenor. The choice of *F* as the center permitted greater tonal variety, since *C* remains a focus for some of the subdivisions of the work.

Consonance and dissonance are also under rational control. The stronger lingering dissonances are properly resolved suspensions, as at measures 33, 36, 72, and 81, while other dissonances, mainly between beats, pass quickly. Otherwise, the composer obviously strove to include as many thirds and sixths—along with octaves, fifths, and fourths—among the parts as possible, producing many triads (to use modern terminology) on the beats of the tempus.

Gilles Binchois (ca. 1400–1460)

30

Rondeau: *De plus en plus* CD 2 CD 1

Musikalische Denkmäler 2, *Die Chansons von Gilles Binchois*, ed. Wolfgang Rehm (Mainz: B. Schott's Söhne, 1957).

A	*De plus en plus se renouvelle*	*More and more renews again,*
	Ma doulce dame gente et belle,	*my sweet lady, noble and fair,*
	Ma voulonté de vous veir.	*my wish to see you.*
B	*Ce me fait le tres grant désir*	*It gives me the great desire*
	Que j'ai de vous oir nouvelle.	*I have to hear news of you.*
a	Ne cuidiés pas que je recelle,	Don't heed that I hold back,
	Comme a tous jours vous estes celle	for always you are the one
	Que je veul de tout obeir.	whom I want to follow in every way.
A	*De plus en plus se renouvelle*	*More and more renews again,*
	Ma doulce dame gente et belle,	*my sweet lady, noble and fair,*
	Ma voulonté de vous veir.	*my wish to see you.*
a	Hélas, se vous m'estiés cruelle	Alas, if you were cruel to me,
	J'auvoie au cuer angoisse telle	I'd have such anguish in my heart
	Que je voudroye bien mourir,	that I will want to die.
b	Mais ce seroit sans déservir,	But this would do you no wrong,
	En soustenant vostre querelle.	while supporting your cause.
A	*De plus en plus se renouvelle*	*More and more renews again,*
	Ma doulce dame gente et belle,	*my sweet lady, noble and fair,*
	Ma voulonté de vous veir.	*my wish to see you.*
B	*Ce me fait le tres grant désir*	*It gives me the great desire*
	Que j'ai de vous oir nouvelle.	*I have to hear news of you.*

The poetic form of this rondeau is similar to Machaut's *Rose, liz* except that 1) the rhyme scheme is different and 2) the first part of the refrain consists of three lines, the second part of two. The refrain contains all of the music, which is also set to the words of the couplets. The full refrain text and its music is heard only at the beginning and the end.

Lines of poetry:	**1 2 3 4 5**	**6 7 8**	**9 10 11**	**12 13 14 15 16**	**17 18 19 20 21**
Rhyme:	a a b b a	a a b	a a b	a a b b a	a a b b a
Sections of music:	A B	a	A	a b	A B

The slow-moving tenor part provides a foundation for the faster-moving cantus, which indulges in runs, dotted figures, and syncopations, the two meeting mostly in thirds and sixths. The contratenor, less vocally conceived, supplies the missing note of the triads and enlivens the rhythm. A cadence marks the end of each line of poetry, with the tenor-cantus pair moving from a sixth to an octave or a third to a unison, except in measure 12, where the major third leaves us in suspense, intensified by the rests, as we anticipate the second section of the music. The cadential motion to the octave from the sixth (changed to major when necessary by musica ficta) is usually decorated in the cantus by the third below the last note of the cadence. In most of the cadences syncopation causes a dissonance before the penultimate note in a pattern later called "suspension." The upbeat opening, the relatively full harmony, and the great number of triadic leaps may reflect the influence of English music. At the time Binchois composed this chanson, around 1425, he was probably in the service of the duke of Suffolk.

This chanson is organized through imperfect tempus and major prolation, transcribed as two dotted quarters per measure, usually subdivided into two groups of three eighth notes but often, particularly in the tenor, into three quarter notes (the familiar hemiola effect). Each line occupies four measures in the melismatic first part. The second part of the text is set syllabically until the penultimate syllable, which receives a florid finish harmonized by descending thirds and sixths similar to fauxbourdon. Typical for this period, the length of the two sections is in a simple proportion, 4 : 3, the first section having twelve measures (or breves), the second, nine.

31 Johannes Ockeghem (ca. 1420–1497)

Missa De plus en plus: Kyrie and Agnus Dei CD 2

a) Kyrie

Johannes Ockeghem, *Masses and Mass Sections* 2, ed. Jaap van Benthem (Utrecht: Koninklijke Vereniging voor Nederlandse Muziekgeschiedenis, 1994–2000), pp. 1–3, 31–35. Used by permission.

15
son.
son.
15 16 17
son.
son.
29
Xpri– ste, xpri–
Xpri– ste, xpri–
18 19 20 21 22 23 24
Xpri– ste– ley
Xpri– stc e– ley– son,
25
ste– ley–
ste– ley–
25 26 27 28 29 30
son, xpri– ste ley–
e– ley–
son.
son.
31 32 33 34
son.
–son.

30
Ky– ri– e e– ley–
Ky– ri– e– ley– son, e–
Ky– ri– e e– ley–
Ky– ri– e– ley– son, e– ley–
son, ky– ri–
ley– son, ky– ri–
son, ky– ri–
son, e– ley– son, ky– ri– e–
40
e– ley– son, e–
e– ley– son, e– ley–
e e– ley– son,
ley– son, e– ley– son, e–
45
ley– son.
son, ky– ri– e, ky– ri– e– ley– son.
e– ley– son.
ley– son.

b) Agnus Dei

31
D
Ct
T
Ct2
Ag– nus de–
Ag– nus de–
Ag– nus de–
Ag– nus de– i
(105)
i qui tol–
i qui tol–
i ... pec–
qui tol– lis
(110)
lis pec– ca– ta mun– di:
lis pec– ca– ta mun– di:
ca– ta mun– di, pec–
pec– ca– ta mun–
(115)
First ending
mi– se– re–
mi– se– re–
ca– ta mun– di:
di, mun– di:
20

re no– bis, no– bis,
re no– bis, no–
mi– se– re– re, mi– se–
mi– se– re– re, mi– se– re– re
no– bis.
bis, no– bis.
re– re no– bis.
no– bis, no– bis.
Go to Agnus 2
Second ending
do–
do– na, do–
di: do–
di: do– na, do– na
na no– bis pa–
na no– bis pa–
na no– bis pa– cem,
no– bis, no– bis pa–

130
cem,
pa–
29 30 31 32 33 34 35 36 37 38 39 40 41 42 43 44 45 47 48 49 50
pa–
cem, pa–
cem,
pa–
135
cem.
cem.
51 52 1 2 3 4 5 6 7 8
cem.
cem.
32
Agnus 2
mensuration canon
35
Ag–
nus
de–
i
Ag–
nus
de–
i
40
45
qui
tol–
lis
pec–
qui
tol–
lis
pec–
29
pec–

ca–
ta
mun–
di,
mun–
di:
mi–
se–
re–
re
no–
bis,

Ockeghem probably chose *De plus en plus* as a cantus firmus to pay tribute to Gilles Binchois, with whom he may have studied and on whose death he wrote the lament *Mort tu as navré*. But it is not the attractive and recognizable top voice of the chanson that Ockeghem took but rather the tenor part, which makes an excellent foundation for a composition. The example below presents the tenor part in its original time values, with each note numbered. The black notes indicate a switch to duple division of note values, the breve now worth two semibreves and the semibreve (black whole note), two minims.

Gilles Binchois, *De plus en plus,* Tenor

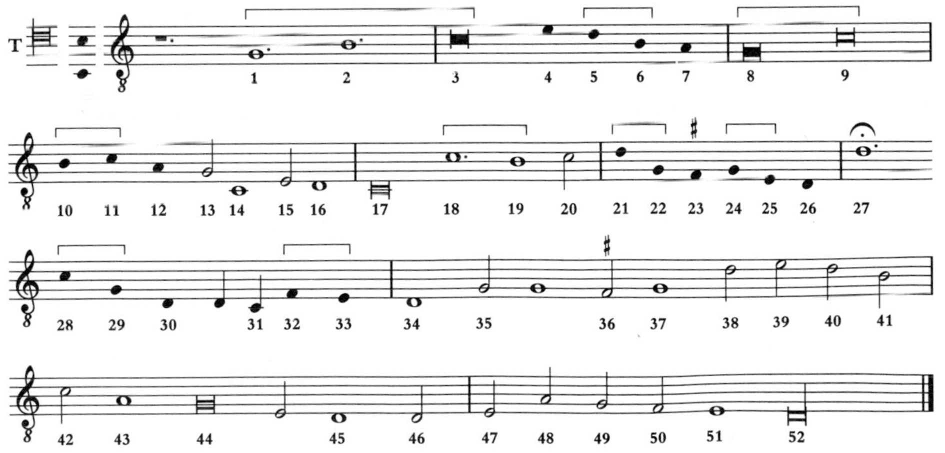

The *Missa De plus en plus* is a "cyclical mass," that is, the Kyrie, Gloria, Credo, Sanctus, and Agnus Dei are all based on the same cantus firmus, the tenor part of the chanson by Binchois. For variety's sake, Ockeghem omits the tenor voice and the cantus firmus in sections of the Sanctus—the Pleni sunt caeli, for three voices, and Benedictus, for two voices. He also reduces the texture to two voices for shorter spans, as in the first Agnus Dei at measures 15–22 and in the second Agnus at measures 31–47. These duets are particularly interesting because they employ imitation, which is otherwise rare in this Mass. The first of these has a short canon at the octave between the two uppermost voices, while the second duet begins with a canon at the octave (the voices start at the same time) but the second voice has doubled note values.

As customary, Ockeghem assigns the cantus firmus to the tenor part. It occasionally invades the other voices, for example, in the first three measures of the Kyrie: notes 1, 2, 5, and 3, in that order, occur in the top voice, a kind of pre-imitation that subsequent composers would do more deliberately. But most of the time the three other parts weave free counterpoints around the tenor. As shown by the numbers above the notes, Ockeghem interpolates many notes in the chanson's tenor in the Kyrie, fewer in the Agnus Dei. After exhausting the fifty-two notes in the Kyrie, the composer returns to the first eight notes of the cantus firmus. The main cadences tend to fall at the ends or beginnings of the chanson's phrases, for instance, in the Kyrie at notes 8, 17, 28, 34, and 52.

The composer achieves a full harmonic sound by including three different consonant pitches in the simultaneous sonorities (forming what we call triads), except in the last chord of an important cadence, which admits only perfect consonances. Where the tenor or the lowest voice descends at a cadence, one or more voices syncopate to cause a suspension. Otherwise, dissonances occur at the semiminim level, while minims, with a few exceptions, are consonant. This gives the work an overwhelmingly euphonius sound. Despite the continuous flow of the meandering voices, the graceful contour of the discantus and the strategically placed cadences provide a clear structure for the listener. Most of the cadences are on *G*, the final of Mode 7, in which the tenor is written; the next most important choice for cadences is *C*.

Josquin des Prez (ca. 1450s–1521) 32

Missa Pange lingua: Kyrie and Credo (*Et incarnatus est* and *Crucifixus*)

a) Kyrie CD 2 CD 1

15
Ky - ri - e e - - le - i-son]e - le - i-son
son, Ky- ri-e e - le - i- son]e - le - i-son
e - - le - i- son]e - le - i-son
i - son, e - le - i - son]e - le- i - son

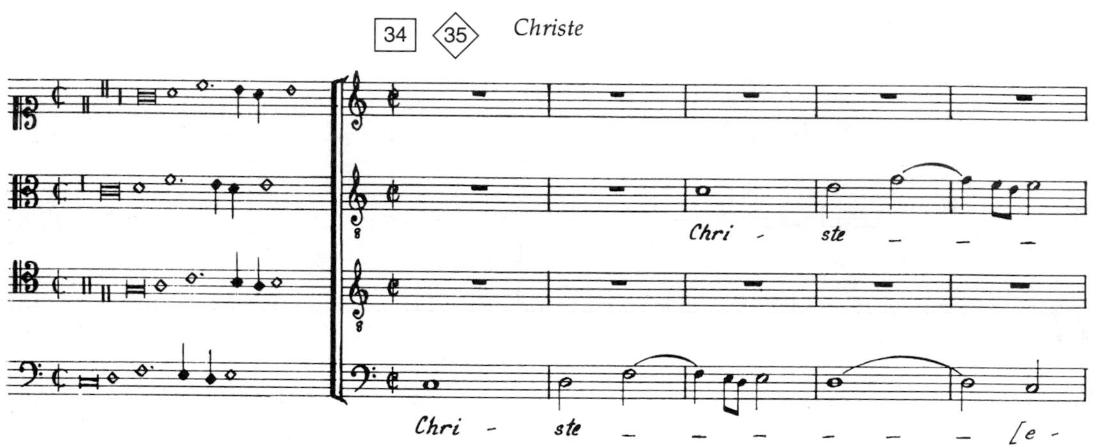
34
35
Christe
Chri - ste
Chri - ste [e -

Chri - ste
[e - le - i - son
Chri - ste
le - i - son

30
35
[e - le - - - - - - - i - son
Chri - -
[e - le - - - - i - son, e - le - - i - son,

40
Chri - ste
ste e - le
Chri -
Chri - ste e - le - i -

45
50
] e - le - i son
- i - son] e - le - i - son
ste e - le - i - son] e - le - i - son.
son e - le - i - son] e - le - i - son

35
36
Kyrie II
55
Ky - ri - e [e - - - - - - le - - - - - - - i -
Ky - ri - e [e - - - - - - - le - i -
Ky - ri - e

60
son, Ky - - ri - e, Ky - ri - e, Ky - ri - e
son, Ky - ri - e, Ky - - ri - e, Ky - - ri -
[e - - - - - - le - i - son, Ky - ri - e, Ky - ri - e, Ky - ri - e
Ky - ri - e [e - - le - i - son, Ky - ri - e

65
70
e - - le - i - son - - -] e - le - i - son - - - - -
e e - le - - - - - - - i - son] e - le - i - son - - -
e - le - - i - son - -] e - le - i - son - - - - - - -
e - - le - - - - - - - - i - son] e - lei - son [e - le - i - son.]

b) Credo CD 2

36
95
Et in - car - na - tus est de spi - ri -
Et in - car - na - tus est de spi - ri -
Et in - car - na - tus est de spi - ri -
Et in - car - na - tus est de spi - ri -

100
tu sanc - to ex Ma - ri - a vir - gi - ne
tu sanc - to ex Ma - ri - a vir - gi - ne
tu sanc - to ex Ma - ri - a vir - gi - ne
tu sanc - to ex Ma - ri - a vir - gi - ne

37
105
110
et ho - mo fac - tus est. Cru - ci -
et ho - mo fac - tus est. Cru - ci - fi - xus
et ho - mo fac - tus est.
et ho - mo fac - tus est.

115
fi - xus e - ti - am _ pro no - bis _ Sub Pon-ti - o Pi - la - to _
e - ti - am _ pro - no - - bis _ _ _ _ _ Sub Pon-ti - o Pi - la -

38
120
125
_ pas - sus, Et se - pul - tus est.
to pas - sus, Et se - pul - tus est. Et re - sur - re - xit ter - ti - a
pas - sus, Et se - pul - tus est. Et re - sur - re - xit ter - - ti -
pas - sus, Et se - pul - tus est. Et re - sur - re - xit ter - ti -

130
se - cun - dum scrip - tu - ras _ _ _. Et a - scen - dit in cae - lum se - det ad
di - e _ _, se - cun - dum scrip - tu - ras. _
a di - e _, se - cun - dum scrip - tu - ras. Et a - scen - dit in cae - lum
a di - e _, se - cun - dum scrip - tu - ras. se - det ad

135
140
dex-te-ram Pa-tris. Et i - te-rum ven-tu-rus est cum glo-ri - a, ju - di - ca -
Et i - te-rum ven-tu-rus est cum glo-ri - a, ju - di - ca -
se - det ad dex - te-ram Pa - tris. Et i - ter-rum ven-tu-rus est cum glo-ri - a, ju - di - ca -
dex - te-ram Pa - tris. Et i - te-rum ven-tu-rus est cum glo-ri - a, ju-di-ca -

145
re vi-vos et mor - tu - os cu - jus re - gni non
re vi-vos et mor - tu - os cu - jus re - gni non
re vi-vos et mor - tu - os cu - jus re - gni non
re vi-vos et mor - tu - os cu - jus re - gni non

150
e - rit fi - nis.
e - rit fi - nis.
e - rit fi - nis.
e - rit fi - nis.

The *Pange lingua* Mass must be one of the last Josquin des Prez composed, since it did not get printed in Petrucci's third collection of Josquin's masses in 1514. It was first published in the anthology *Missae tredecim* (Thirteen Masses) in 1539 and is based on the melody of the hymn *Pange lingua gloriosi* (text by St. Thomas Aquinas), assigned to second Vespers on the feast of Corpus Christi (*Liber usualis* 957). The six strophes are sung to the melody given below with the first strophe.

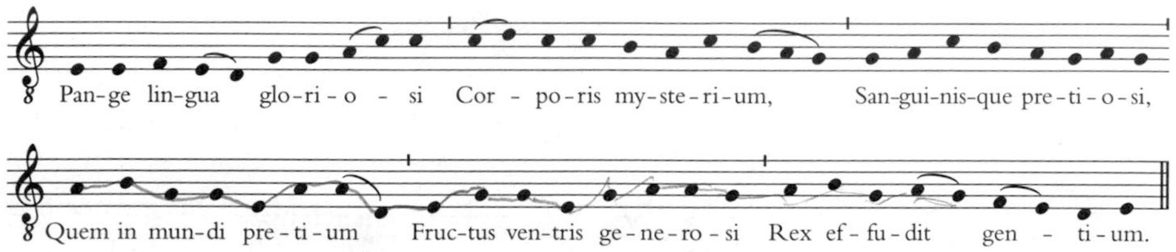
Pan-ge lin-gua glo-ri-o - si Cor - po-ris my-ste-ri-um, San-gui-nis-que pre-ti-o-si,
Quem in mun-di pre-ti-um Fruc-tus ven-tris ge-ne-ro-si Rex ef-fu-dit gen - ti-um.

Pange lingua gloriosi	Sing, tongue, of the glorious
Corporis mysterium,	body's mystery
Sanguinisque pretiosi,	and of the precious blood,
Quem in mundi pretium	ransom of the world, that
Fructus ventris generosi	the fruit of the generous womb,
Rex effudit gentium	the king of all peoples, poured fourth.

Josquin based all the movements of the Mass—though not all its subdivisions—on the hymn melody. Rather than rigidly placing the chant in a single voice, he had all the voices sharing it. Because the hymn is a rhymed poem, its melody is broken into discrete units. These individual phrases of the hymn melody serve as material for motives and subjects that are developed through polyphonic imitation.

The Kyrie follows the hymn most faithfully. The last notes of each poetic line of the hymn determine the modal degrees on which the polyphony reaches cadence, namely *C* (measure 9), *G* (measure 16), *G* (measure 36), *D* (measure 50), *G* (measure 61), and *E* (measure 68). The tenor part takes the lead at the outset in an imitative duet with the bass. The top two voices then repeat this duet an octave higher. The first eight notes of the tenor come from the first phrase of the hymn, after which Josquin meanders between the three *C*'s of the hymn. This technique of elaborating the source melody has been called "paraphrase."

The similarity between the beginnings of the hymn's first and second phrases encouraged Josquin to repeat the rhythm and contour of his first subject in the second statement of "Kyrie eleison," giving this movement a nearly monothematic composition. The march to the cadence on *G* (measures 13–16) builds excitement not only by speeding up the note values but insistently repeating a four-note motive in the tenor.

Josquin worked through the third and fourth phrases of the hymn in the *Christe*, lightening the texture by alternating pairs of voices, each constituting a near canon.

The final Kyrie treats the fifth and sixth phrases of the hymn freely. In contrast to the preceding movements, this one begins with the top pair of voices followed by the lower pair. Then, in a frantic plea for mercy, we hear "Ky-ri-e" three times in a downward sequence of the dotted descending-third figure derived from the hymn's sixth phrase, followed by striking repetitions of a motive that rearranges the triple meter into a compound duple. The motive of the descending thirds returns against the final chord, making this one of Josquin's most dramatic cadential gestures.

The *Et incarnatus est* and *Crucifixus* of the Credo further demonstrate Josquin's attention to text expression. The solemn proclamation "Et incarnatus est"—And he was made incarnate by the Holy Ghost of the Virgin Mary, and was made man—is declaimed in block chords, with the top voice paraphrasing the opening line of the hymn. For the word "Crucifixus," Josquin took advantage of the plaintive semitone motion of the hymn's opening, using the rest of the first and second phrases of the hymn as in the Kyrie but interrupting the imitative texture to break into block chords at the mention of Christ's trial and burial "[sub Pontio Pilato] passus, et sepultus est." Then a lively triple time in minims and close imitations of the descending thirds from the fourth phrase of the hymn mark the words "Et resurrexit tertia die" (And he rose again on the third day).

33 Josquin des Prez

Motet: *De profundis clamavi ad te* CD 2 ◇CD 1

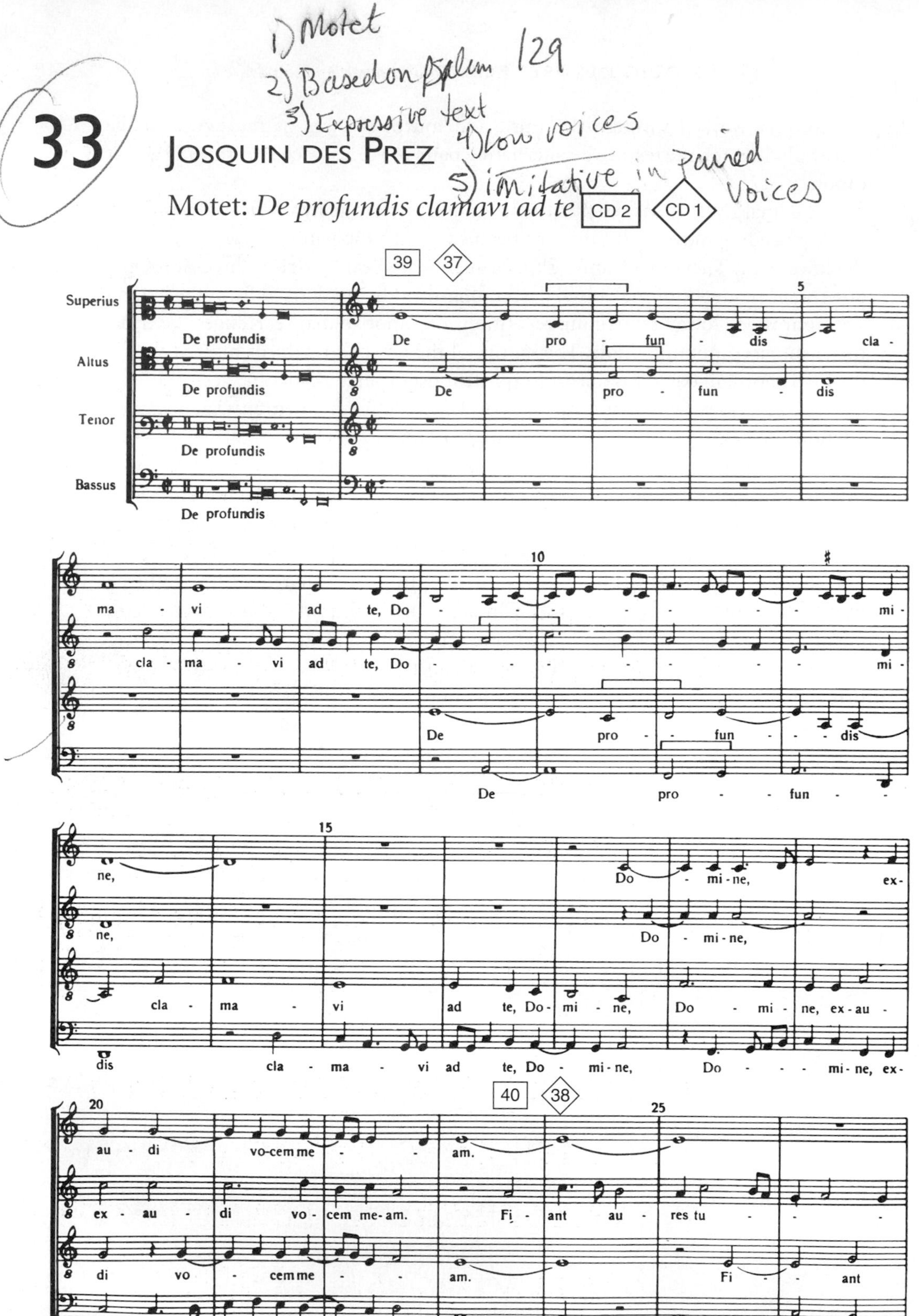

Josquin Desprez, *Werken*, ed. A. Smijers et al (Amsterdam, 1921–), *Motetten*, deel 3, aflevering 35, pp. 20–25. For the text and translation of Psalm 129, see NAWM 4i.

in vo - cem de-
ae in
au - res tu - ae in - ten - den - - tes,
- res tu - - ae in - ten - den - - - - tes,

- pre - ca - ti - o - - nis me - - - - - - ae.
vo - - cem de - pre - ca - ti - o - nis me - - - ae.
in vo - cem de - preca - ti - o - nis me - ae.
in vo - cem de - preca - ti - o - nis me - ae.

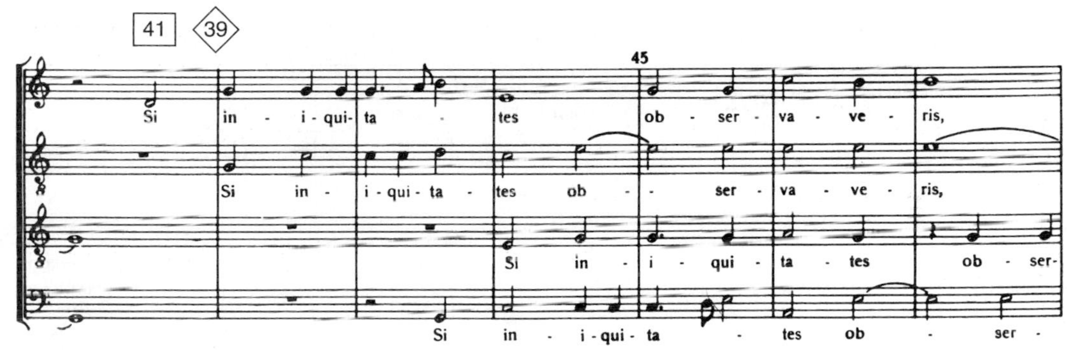
Si in - i - qui - ta - tes ob - ser - va - ve - ris,
Si in - i - qui - ta - tes ob - - ser - va - ve - ris,
Si in - i - qui - ta - tes ob - ser-
Si in - i - qui - ta - tes ob - ser -

Do - mi - ne, Do - mi ne, quis su - sti - ne - -
Do - mi - ne, Do - mi - ne, quis su - sti - ne - -
va - ve - ris, Do - mi - ne,
va - ve - ris, Do - mi - ne,

55
60
bit, quis su - sti - ne - - bit?
bit, su - sti - ne - bit?
Do - mi - ne, quis su - sti - ne - - - bit?
Do - mi - ne, quis su - sti - ne - - - - - - bit?

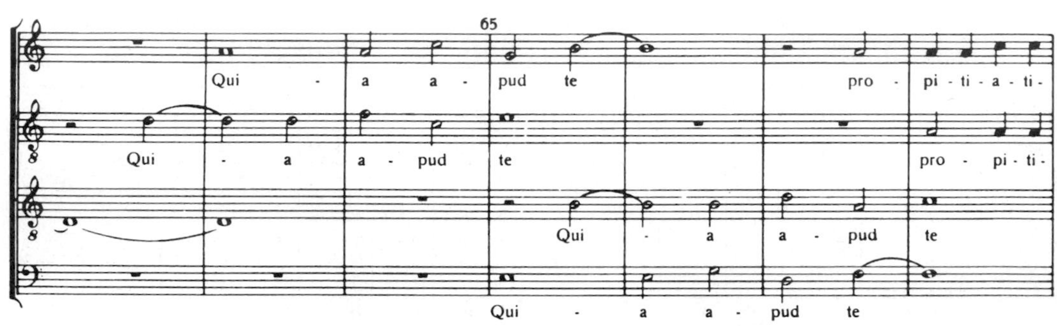
65
Qui - a a - pud te pro - pi - ti - a - ti -
Qui - a a - pud te pro - pi - ti -
Qui - a a - pud te
Qui - a a - pud te

70
75
o est, et prop-ter le - gem tu - am
- a - ti - o est, et prop-ter le-gem tu - am
pro - pi - ti - a - ti - o est, et prop-ter le - gem
pro - pi - ti - a - ti - o est, et prop-ter le-gem

80
su - sti - nu te, Do - mi - ne, Su - sti - nu -
su - sti - nu - i te, Do - mi - ne. Su - sti - nu it a -
tu - am su - sti - nu - i te, Do - mi - ne. Su - sti - nu -
tu - am su - sti - nu - i te, Do - mi -

SECUNDA PARS

115
a a - pud Do-mi - num mi - se - ri - cor - di - a, et co - pi - o - sa
no. mi - se - ri - cor - di - a, et co - pi-
no. Qui - a a - pud Do-mi - num mi - se - ri - cor - di - a,

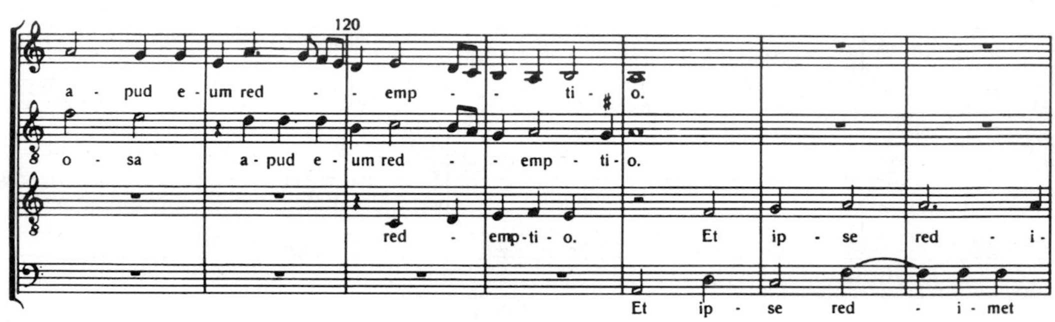
120
a - pud e - um red - - emp - ti - o.
o - sa a - pud e - um red - - emp - ti - o.
red - emp - ti - o. Et ip - se red - i-
Et ip - se red - i - met

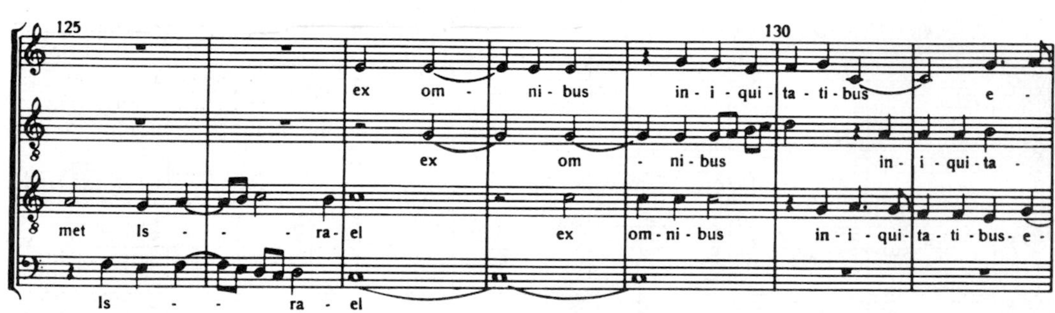
125
130
ex om - ni - bus in - i - qui - ta - ti - bus e -
ex om - ni - bus in - i - qui - ta -
met Is - - ra - el ex om - ni - bus in - i - qui - ta - ti - bus - e -
Is - - ra - el

135
- - jus. et
ti - bus - e - jus. et Spi-
- - jus. Glo - ri - a Pa - tri et Fi - - li - o, et
Glo - ri - a Pa - tri et Fi - - li - o, et

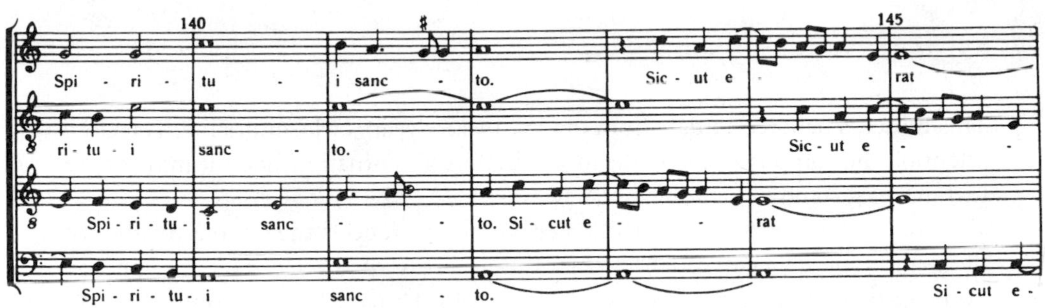
140
145
Spi - ri - tu - i sanc - to. Sic - ut e - - rat
ri - tu - i sanc - to. Sic - ut e - -
Spi - ri - tu - i sanc - - to. Si - cut e - - rat
Spi - ri - tu - i sanc - to. Si - cut e -

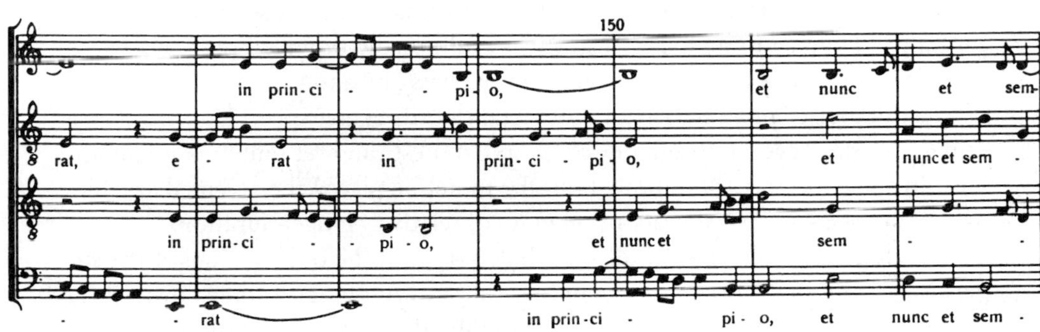
150
in prin - ci - - pi - o, et nunc et sem-
rat, e - rat in prin - ci - pi - o, et nunc et sem -
in prin - ci - - pi - o, et nunc et sem - -
- - rat in prin - ci - pi - o, et nunc et sem -

155
- per, et in sae - cu - la sae - cu -
per, et in sae - cu - la sae - cu - lo - rum.
- per, et in sae - cu - la sae - cu - lo - rum. A - -
per, et in sae - cu - la sae - cu - lo - rum, a - men, sae -

160
165
lo - rum a - men, sae - cu - lo - - rum. A - men.
a - - men, et in sae - cu - la sae - cu - lo - rum. A - men.
- - - - - - - - - men.
- cu - lo - - - rum. A - - - - - - - - men.

This motet is believed to date from the last twenty years of Josquin's life. The close attention the composer paid to the form, rhythm, accentuation, and meaning of the text makes it stand out among his late works.

The construction of the musical periods clearly reflects the double versicles of the psalm. The strongest cadences mark the ending of each verse and the beginning of the next, as at measures 23 (plagal cadence), 40–41, 61–62, 80 (the only Phrygian cadence), 96 (plagal cadence), 111, 122, 133, and 142 (plagal cadence). The prima pars ends on A, the reciting tone of Mode 4 (Hypophrygian), while the *secunda pars* ends on its final, E. This is confirmed as the governing mode of the piece by the plagal range of the tenor and superius, which traditionally provided the framework, and the complementary authentic ranges of the bass and alto.

Josquin seized upon the rhythms of certain words to give speechlike vitality to a number of passages—for example, at "propitiatio est" and "et omnibus iniquitatibus." In these instances and throughout the motet he placed the accented syllables on downbeats, syncopated beats, or on notes of relatively longer duration.

Josquin captured the spirit of the whole psalm in the opening line of the superius. It traces the "Dorian" species of fifth (like our A minor), leaping down a fifth for the word "profundis" and reaching up to the minor sixth above for "clamavi," a perfect image of a soul in despair crying for help, straining to be heard. The other voices imitate the first five pitches and durations exactly.

Indeed, the device of imitation pervades the texture. Each new versicle of text receives its own subject, often stated and imitated in paired voices. The moments of simultaneous declamation are few but carefully chosen: "exaudi vocem meam" (hear my voice, measures 20–24), and "sustinui te, Domine" (I have supported Thee, Lord, measures 76–81).

Heinrich Isaac (ca. 1450–1517) 34

Lied: *Innsbruck, ich muss dich lassen* CD 2

10
hin. Mein Freud ist mir ge - nom - men, die ich nit weiss
hin. Mein Freud ist mir ge- nom - men, die ich nit weiss
hin. Mein Freud ist mir ge - nom - men, die ich nit weiss
hin. Mein Freud ist mir ge - nom - men, die ich nit weiss

be - kom - men, wo ich im E - - lend
be-kom - men, wo ich im E - - lend
be-kom - men, wo ich im E - - lend
be - kom - men, wo ich im E - lend, im E - lend

20
bin, wo ich im E - - lend bin.
bin, wo ich im E - - lend bin.
bin, wo ich im E - - lend bin.
bin, wo ich im E - - lend bin.

Innsbruck, ich muss dich lassen, ich fahr dahin mein Strassen, in fremde Land dahin. Mein Freud is mir genommen, die ich nit weiss bekommen, wo ich im Elend bin.	Innsbruck, I must leave you I am going on my way into a foreign land. My joy is taken from me, I know not how to regain it, while in such misery.
Gross Leid muss ich jetzt tragen, das ich allein tu klagen dem liebsten Buhlen mein. Ach Lieb, nun lass mich Armen im Herzen dein erbarmen, dass ich muss dannen sein.	I must now endure great pain which I confide only to my dearest love. O beloved, find pity in your heart for me, that I must part from you.
Mein Trost ob allen Weiben, dein tu ich ewig bleiben, stet treu, der Ehren fromm. Nun muss dich Gott bewahren, in aller Tugend sparen, bis dass ich wiederkomm.	My comfort above all other women, I shall always be yours, forever faithful in honor true. May the good Lord protect you and keep you in your virtue for me, till I return.

—N. Greenberg and P. Maynard

The polyphonic lied was usually an arrangement of a folk or popular song for four voices, analogous to some of the French chansons. The tune may be in the tenor or treble part and it may or may not use imitation. In the present arrangement, the melody is in the soprano, and, except for some pseudo-imitative entries at the beginning, the other parts harmonize the soprano. A cadence on either *C* or *F* formed with a suspension ends each phrase, followed by a rest, as in the Italian part-songs. This homophonic style looks forward to the texture adopted in the chorale settings arranged for congregational singing. In fact, the melody of this perennial favorite was later adapted to sacred words and became widely known as the chorale *O Welt, ich muss dich lassen* (O world, I now must leave thee).

35 Marco Cara (ca. 1470–ca. 1525)

Frottola: *Io non compro più speranza* CD 2

Note values halved. Notes in the lute part with dots under them are played with an upward stroke. Bars through the lute staves are original. Those between the voice part and lute accompaniment are added by the present editor to show the true metrical organization. Franciscus Bossinensis, ed., *Tenori e contrabassi intabulati col sopran in canto figurato per cantar e somar col lauto, libro primo* (Venice, 1509). Benvenuto Disertori, ed., *Le Frottole per canto e liuto intabulate da Franciscus Bossinensis* (Milan: Ricordi, 1964), pp. 390–91.

	Io non compro più speranza	I'll buy no more hope,
	Ché gli è falsa mercancia	which is fake goods;
	A dar sol attendo via	I can't wait to give away
	Quella poca che m'avanza.	the little that I have left,
	Io non compro più speranza	I'll buy no more hope,
	Ché gli è falsa mercancia.	which is fake goods.
47	Cara un tempo la comprai,	Once I bought it dear;
	Hor la vendo a bon mercato	now I sell it cheap;
	E consiglio ben che mai	and I would advise that never
	Non ne compri un sventurato	should the wretched buy it;
	Ma più presto nel suo stato	rather let them in their condition
	Se ne resti con costanza.	remain in constancy.
48	Io non . . .	I'll buy . . .
49	El sperare è come el sogno	To hope is like a dream
	Che per più riesce in nulla,	that mostly results in nothing,
	El sperar è proprio il bisogno	and hoping is the craving need
	De chi al vento si trastulla,	of him who plays with the wind.
	El sperare sovente anulla	Hoping often annihilates
	Chi continua la sua danza.	the one who continues its dance.
50	Io non . . .	I'll buy . . .

This lighthearted complaint of a disappointed lover appeared in Petrucci's first book of frottole (Venice, 1504). The barring in four beats of the lute tablature obscures the dance rhythm of six beats to the measure, as marked off by the bars inserted between the voice and the lute parts. These six beats are organized now in duple groups, now in triple, producing the hemiola so characteristic of the canzonets popular throughout the century and later adopted in seventeenth-century monody. The harmonization consists almost entirely of root chords, a style that was to have a far-reaching effect on music produced in Italy in the sixteenth century by both native composers and foreigners.

Although the term "frottola" is applied to musical settings of various types of popular poetry, this song manifests the poetic and musical form of the frottola proper, also called *barzelletta*. The poem consists of a four-line *ripresa*, whose first two lines return as a refrain, and a six-line *stanza*, consisting of two two-line *piedi* (literally, feet) and a two-line *volta* (a turning back). The music is coordinated with this poetic structure through the following scheme:

Music mm.	Poetic lines	Rhyme	Poetic form
1–3	Io non compro più speranza	a	—Ripresa
4–6	Ché gli è falsa mercancia	b	
7–9	A dar sol attendo via	b	
10–12	Quella poca che m'avanza.	a	
13–15	Io non compro più speranza	a	—Refrain
16–27	Ché gli è falsa mercancia.	b	
	Stanza 1		
1–3	Cara un tempo la comprai	c	—Piede
4–6	Hor la vendo a bon mercato	d	
1–3	E consiglio ben che mai	c	—Piede
4–6	Non ne compri un sventurato	d	
7–9	Ma più presto nel suo stato	d	—Volta
10–12	Se ne resti con costanza.	a	
13–15	Io non compro più speranza	a	—Refrain
16–27	Ché gli è falsa mercancia.	b	

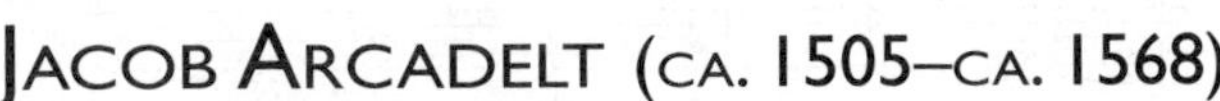

Jacob Arcadelt (ca. 1505–ca. 1568)

Madrigal: *Il bianco e dolce cigno* CD 2 CD 1

51 41

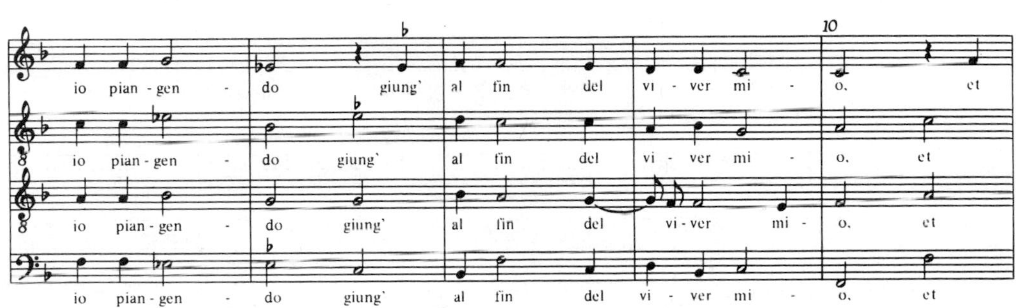

Note values halved. *Il primo libro di Madrigali d'Archadelt a quatro con nuova gionta impressi* (Venice, 1539); first edition lost but probably from 1538. Arcadelt, *Opera omnia*, ed. Albert Seay (American Institute of Musicology, 1970), 2:38–40.

52
42
a - - - - to. mor - te che nel mo - ri - re,
ro be - a - - - - - to, mor - te che nel mo - ri - re,
ro, et io mo - ro be - a - to, mor - te che nel mo - ri - re,
et io mo - ro be - a - - - to, mor - te che nel mo - ri - re,
m'em - pie di gio - ia tutt' e di de - si - re, se nel mo - rir'
m'em - pie di gio - ia tutt' e di de - si - re, se nel mo - rir'
m'em - pie di gio - ia tutt' e di de - si - re, se nel mo - rir'
m'em - pie di gio - ia tutt' e di de - si - re, se nel mo - rir'
al - tro do - lor non sen - to, di mil - le
al - tro do - lor non sen - to, di mil - le mort' il dì, di mil - le
al - tro do - lor non sen - to, di mil - le mort' il dì, di mil - le
al - tro do - lor non sen - to, di mil - le mort' il dì,
mort' il dì sa - rei con - ten - to, di mil - le mort' il dì sa -
mort' il dì, di mil - le mort' il dì, di mil - le mort' il dì,
mort' il dì sa - rei con - ten - to, di mil - le mort' il dì, di mil - le mort' il dì sa -
sa - rei con - ten - to, di mil - le mort' il dì sa -
rei con - ten - to.
di mil - le mort' il dì sa - rei con - ten - - - to.
rei con - ten - to, di mil - le mort' il di sa - rei con - ten - to.
rei con - ten - to, di mil - le mort' il dì, sa - rei con - ten - to.

Il bianco e dolce cigno	The white and sweet swan
Cantando more. Et io	dies singing. And I,
Piangendo giung' al fin del viver mio.	weeping, come to the end of my life.
Stran' e diversa sorte,	Strange and different fate—
Ch'ei more sconsolato,	it dies disconsolate,
Et io moro beato.	and I die happy—
Morte che nel morire,	a death that in dying
M'empie di gioia tutt'e di desire.	fills me fully with joy and desire.
Se nel morir' altro dolor non sento,	If when I die I feel no other pain,
Di mille mort' il dì sarei contento.	then I would be content to die a
—Alfonso d'Avalos	thousand deaths a day.

Dating from the mid-1530s this is the most famous of the early madrigals and was reprinted many times. Its mainly homophonic motion and square rhythms ally it to the chanson and frottola. But the first three lines do not follow the structure of the poem, as was customary in those genres. The first cadence falls in the middle of the second line, completing the thought and the sentence, and the end of that line runs into the third, observing the verse's enjambment. Thus the composer not only preserves the syntax and meaning but underscores the word "more" (dies) with a dissonant suspension. At "Et io piangendo" (And I weeping), he marks the sharp contrast between the swan's song and the lover's tears with an excursion into the *E*♭-harmony. The juxtaposition of the major triads on *F* and *E*♭, causing a false relation between *A* and *E*♭ (measure 6), becomes a metaphor for death; this same relation exists in transposition between the triads on *B*♭ and *C* at "morire" in measure 26, and at "morir" in measure 31.

Although Arcadelt indulges in some moments of imitation, he saves full use of this device to illustrate "di mille mort' il dì" (a thousand deaths a day), when we hear twelve single or paired entries of the lilting motive of contentment that reminds us that "death" here has a double meaning.

37 Adrian Willaert (ca. 1490–1562)

Madrigal: *Aspro core e selvaggio* CD 2

Willaert, *Musica nova* (Venice, 1559). Willaert, *Opera omnia*, Vol. 13, ed. Hermann Zenck and Walter Gerstenberg (American Institute of Musicology, 1966), pp. 54–60.

25
Se ___ l'im-pre - so ri - gor gran tem-po du - ra, Ha - vran di me po - co ho-no - ra - ta
ra, Se l'im - pre - so ri - gor gran tem - po du - ra,
ra, Se l'im - pre - so ri - gor gran tem - - po du - ra, se ___ l'im-pre -
gu - ra, Se l'im - pre - so ri -
ra, Se l'im - pre - so ri - gor gran tem - po du - ra, se l'im-pre-
ra, Se l'im -

30
spo - glia, ha - vran di me po-co ho-no-ra - ta spo -
gran tem-po du - ra, Ha-vran di me po-co ho-no - ra - - ta spo -
so ri - gor gran tem-po du - ra, Ha - vran di me po - co ho-no- ra-ta spo - glia:
gor gran tem-po du - ra, gran tem-po du - ra, Ha-vran di me po - co ho-no
so ri-gor gran tem - po du - - - ra, Ha-vran di me po-co ho-no-
pre - so ri - gor gran tem-po du - ra, Ha-vran di me po-co ho-no - ra-ta spo -

55
35
40
- - glia: Ché quan - do na-sce e mor ___ fior, her - ba, e
- - glia: Ché quan - do na sce e mor fior, her-ba, e fo -
Ché quan-do na-sce e mor ___ fior, her-ba, e fo - - glia, fior, her - ba, e
ra - ta spo - glia: Ché quan - do na-sce e mor fior, her-ba, e fo - - glia, fior ___, her -
ra - ta spo - glia: Ché quan - do na-sce e mor fior, her-ba, e fo - glia,
glia: Ché quan - do na-sce e mor fior, her-ba, e fo - glia, fior,

45
fo - - glia, Quan - do è'l dì chia - ro, e quan-do è not-te o-
- glia, Quan - do è'l dì chia - - ro, e quan-do è not - te o - scu -
fo - glia, fior, her-ba, e fo-glia, Quan - do è'l dì chia - - - ro,
- ba, e fo - glia, Quan - do è'l dì chia - ro, quan-do è'l dì chia - ro,
fior, her-ba, e fo - glia, Quan-do è'l dì chia - ro, e quan-do è not-te o-scu-
her-ba, e fo - glia, Quan-do è'l dì chia - ro, e quan-do è not-te o-scu-

50
55
scu - ra, Pian - - go ad o - gni hor, pian - go ad o - gni hor,
- ra, Pian - go ad o - gni hor, pian - go ad o - gni hor,
e quan-do è not-te o-scu ra, Pian - go ad o - gni hor, pian-go ad o-gni hor,
e quan-do è not - te o - scu - - ra, Pian - go ad o - gni hor
- ra, Pian - go ad o - gni hor, pian - go ad o - gni hor, pian - go ad o-gni hor
- ra, e quan-do è not-te o-scu - ra, Pian - go ad o - gni hor, pian -

60
pian - go ad o - gni hor. Ben hò di mia ven - tu - ra,
pian - go ad o - gni hor. Ben hò di mia ven-tu - ra, ben hò di mia
pian - go ad o-gni hor. Ben hò di mia ven - tu - - ra,
, pian - go ad o - gni hor. Ben hò di mia ven-
, pian - go ad o - gni hor. Ben hò di mia ven - tu - - ra, ben hò di
go ad o-gni hor, pian - go ad o - gni hor. Ben hò di mia ven-

Di Ma-don - na e d'A-mo-re on- de mi do - glia,
ven-tu - ra, Di Ma-don -
Di Ma-don - na e d'A-mo - re on-de mi do-glia, on - de mi do -
tu - - ra, ben hò di mia ven-tu - ra, Di Ma-don - na e d'A-mo-re on- de mi do -
mia ven-tu - ra, Di Ma-don - na e d'A-mo-re on- de mi do - glia,
tu - ra, Di Ma - don - na e d'A-mo-re on-de mi do - glia, on - de mi do -

di Ma - don - na e d'A- mo-re on-de mi do - glia, on - de mi do - glia.
na e d'Amor, di Ma-don - na e d'A-mo-re on de mi do - glia
glia, di Ma-don - na e d'A- mor, di Ma-don- na e d'A-mo-re on- de mi do - glia.
- glia, on - de mi do - glia, di Ma- don - na e d'A - mo - re on - de mi do - glia.
di Ma - don - na e d'A- mo - re on - de mi do - glia, on - de mi do - glia.
glia, di Ma - don - na e d'A - mo - re on - de mi do - glia, on-de mi do - glia.

56

Vi - vo sol, vi - vo sol di spe -
Vi - vo sol di spe-ran - za, vi - vo sol
Vi - vo sol di spe - ran - za, vi - vo sol di spe - ran - za, ri - membran -
Vi - vo sol, vi - vo sol, vi - vo sol di spe -
Vi - vo sol, vi - vo sol di spe - ran - za, vi - vo sol,
Vi - vo sol di spe-ran - za, vi -

ran - za, ri - mem-bran - do, Che po-co hu-mor, che po-co hu-mor già per con - ti - nua
di spe-ran - za, ri-mem-bran - do, Che po-co hu-mor già per con - ti-nua pro - va, che po-co hu-
do, ri - mem-bran - do, Che po-co hu-mor già per con - ti-nua pro -
ran - za, ri - mem-bran - do, Che po - co hu-mor già per con-ti-nua pro - va
vi - vo sol di spe-ran - za, ri - mem-bran - do, Che po-co hu-mor già per con-ti-nua
- vo sol di spe-ran - za, vi-vo sol di spe - ran-za, ri - mem-bran - do, Che po-co hu-

pro - - - va Con - su - mar vi - di mar - mi e pie - tre
mor già per con - ti-nua pro - va Con - su-mar vi - di mar-mi e
va Con - su - mar vi - di mar-mi e pie - - tre sal - de, con - su-mar
già per con-ti - nua pro - - - va Con - su-mar vi - di mar - mi e
pro - va, già per con-ti-nua pro - va Con - su-mar vi - di,
mor già per con - ti-nua pro - va, già per con-ti-nua pro - va

57

sal - de. Non è sì du - ro cor,
pie-tre sal - de, con - su-mar vi - di mar - mi e pie-tre sal - de. Non è sì du - ro
vi - di mar - mi e pie - tre sal - de. Non è sì du - ro cor,
pie-tre sal - - de. Non è sì du -
con - su-mar vi - di mar-mi e pie-tre sal - - de. Non è sì
Con - su-mar vi - di mar-mi e pie - tre sal - de. Non è sì

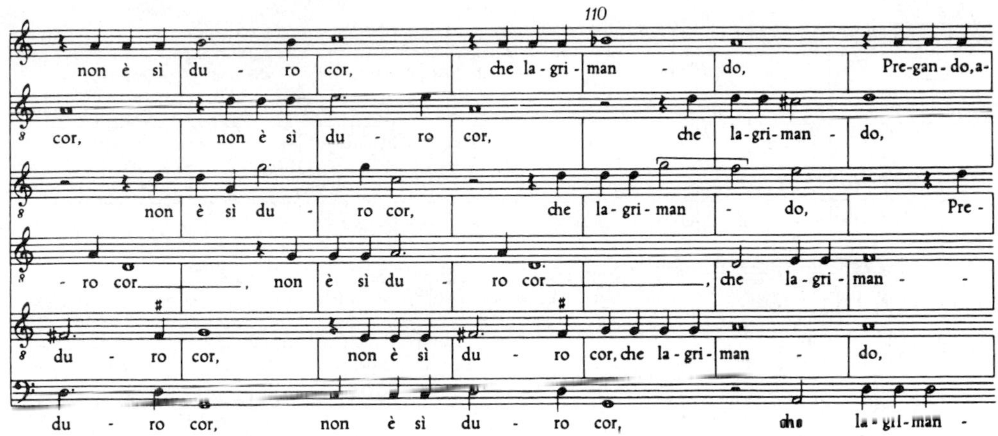
110
non è sì du - ro cor, che la - gri - man - do, Pre-gan - do,a-
cor, non è sì du - ro cor, che la-gri-man - do,
non è sì du - ro cor, che la - gri - man - do, Pre -
- ro cor, non è sì du - ro cor, che la - gri - man - -
du - ro cor, non è sì du - ro cor, che la - gri - man - do,
du - ro cor, non è sì du - ro cor, che la - gri - man -

115
man - - do, tal -
Pre - gan-do, a-man - do, pre - gan-do, a -
gan - do, a-man - - do, tal hor non si smo - - - -
do, Pre - gan - do, a - man - - do, tal - hor non si smo -
Pre gan-do, a - man - - do, tal - hor non si smo - va, non
do, Pre - gan-do, a-man - - do, tal - hor non si smo - va,

120
hor non si smo - - - - va, Né sì fred - do vo - ler
man - do, tal - hor non si smo - va, Né sì fred - do vo - ler,
va . Né sì fred-do vo - ler, né sì fred - do vo -
va, tal - hor non si smo - - - va, Né sì fred - do vo - ler, che
si smo - va, Né sì fred - do vo - ler, che non si
tal - hor non si smo - va, Né sì fred - do vo - ler,

Aspro core e selvaggio, e cruda voglia
In dolce, umile, angelica figura,
Se l'impreso rigor gran tempo dura,
Avran di me poco honorata spoglia:
Che, quando nasce e mor fior, erba e foglia,
Quando è 'l dí chiaro e quando è notte oscura,
Piango ad ogni hor. Ben ho di mia ventura,
Di madonna e d'Amore onde mi doglia.
Vivo sol di speranza, rimenbrando,
Che poco humor già per continua prova
Consumar vidi marmi e pietre salde.

Non è sí duro cor, che lagrimando,
Pregando, amando, talhor non si smova,
Né sì freddo voler, che non si scalde.

—Francesco Petrarca

Harsh heart and savage, and a cruel will
in a sweet, humble, angelic face,
if this adopted severity persist for long,
they will get from me spoils of little honor;
for when flower, grass, and leaf are born and die,
when it is shining day and when it is dark night,
I weep at every hour. Well may I grieve,
for my luck, my lady and my love.
I live by hope alone, remembering
that by continuous drops
I have seen little liquid consume marble and
solid stones.
There is no heart so hard that weeping,
begging, loving sooner or later does not move,
nor so cold a resolve that it cannot be warmed.

This setting of a sonnet by Petrarch that Willaert probably composed in the mid-1540s was one of the pioneering works that helped to set the trend toward faithful text declamation and vivid expression. The composer probably knew the analysis Pietro Bembo had published in 1525 that demonstrated how Petrarch carefully suited the sound of the words to two worlds of feeling, the *grave* (serious, majestic) and the *piacevole* (charming, sweet). In the beginning of the sonnet, Petrarch expressed Madonna Laura's "harsh and savage heart" in a *grave* line, filled with double consonants and clipped, harsh sounds; he then described her "sweet, humble, angelic face" in a contrasting *piacevole* line made up of liquid, resonant, and sweet sounds.

Willaert's setting seems almost to grow out of Bembo's theory. For the first line (measures 1–10), Willaert lingered on the rawer consonances, emphasizing major sixths and thirds, including parallel major thirds, and favoring melodic motion in whole steps and major thirds. For the second line, he chose the sweeter consonances of minor thirds and minor sixths (realized through accidental flats), melodic motion by semitones and minor thirds, and simulated triple time to match Petrarch's deliberate arrangement of accented syllables. It is interesting that his pupil Zarlino counseled precisely these devices for attaining these emotional effects (see vignette in HWM, p. 186),* with the exception of parallel major thirds, of which he disapproved. For the first line Willaert gained a crude effect by repeatedly sliding from the major sixth to the fifth instead of resolving it to the octave, as was normally expected at this time.

Purely musical imagery provides contrasts in the line "Quando è 'l di chiaro" (when it is shining day) and "e quando è notte oscura" (and when it is dark night): in the first phrase, the parts ascend toward a clear C-major chord, while for the second the soprano drops an octave and descends through a *B*♭ to a dark A-minor chord. Another musical shift differentiates between the hard heart (harsher major intervals) and the softening effect of tears (softer minor intervals) in measures 103 to 114. Willaert rendered the repeated weeping described in the half-line—"piango ad ogni hor" (I weep at every hour, measures 50–58)—by imitating or reworking sixteen times the motive introduced by the soprano.

The composer divided the fourteen lines of the sonnet into two sections, similar to the two *partes* of longer motets, the first setting the *ottava* or first eight lines, the second the *sestina* or final six lines. The first section ends on the fifth degree of the mode, the second on the final. Willaert was careful to devise his scheme of cadences according to the grammatical units of the poem. The first full cadence occurs at measure 36, coinciding with the text's colon (then equivalent to our modern semicolon). He avoided a cadence where the punctuation did not call for a stop.

* Zarlino, *The Art of Counterpoint*, Ch. 57, pp. 177–78; *Le institutioni harmoniche*, Book IV, Ch. 32, SRrev, pp. 457–60; 3:179–82, where this and four other madrigals from *Musica nova* are cited as models for the expression of various moods.

38 Cipriano de Rore (1516–1565)

Madrigal: *Da le belle contrade d'oriente* CD 2 CD 1

Rore, *Opera omnia*, ed. Bernhard Meier (American Institute of Musicology, 1969), pp. 96–99. © Hänssler Verlag, D=71087 Holzgerlingen. Used by permission.

20
pia - cer che non ca - pe hu - ma - - na men - te,
cer che non ca - - - pe hu - ma - na men - - te, Quan - do sen -
pia - cer che non ca - pe hu - ma - na men - - - - - - te, Quan - do sen -
cer che non ca - - pe hu - ma - - na men - - - - te, Quan - do sen -
cer che non ca - pe hu - ma - - na men - te, Quan - do sen -
25
59
44
Spe - ran - za del mio cor, dol - ce
tii do - po un so - spir ar - den - te: Spe - ran - za del mio cor, dol -
tii do - po un so - spir ar - den - te: Spe - ran - za del mio cor, dol -
tii do - po un so - spir ar - den - te: Spe - ran - za del mio cor,
tii do - po un so - spir ar - den - te: Spe - ran - - za del mio cor, dol -
30
de - si - - o, Te'n vai, hai - me, so - la mi la - sci, a -
- ce de - si - o, Te'n vai, hai - me, te'n vai, hai - me, a - di - o.
ce de - si - o, Te'n vai, hai - me, a - di - o.
Te'n vai, hai - me, a -
ce de - si - o, Te'n vai, hai - me, hai - me, a - di - o.
35
40
di - o. Che sa - rà qui di me scu - ra e do - len - - te?
Che sa - rà qui di me scu - ra e do - len - te?
Che sa - rà qui di me scu - ra e do - len - te?
di - o. Che sa - rà qui di me scu - ra e do - len - te?

60
45
Ahi cru - do A - mor, ahi cru - do A - mor, ben son du - bio - se e
Ahi cru - do A - mor, ahi cru - do A - mor, ben son du - bio - se e
Ahi cru - do A - mor, ahi cru - do A - mor, ben son du - bio - se e
Ahi cru - do A - mor,
Ahi cru - do A - mor, ben son du - bio - se e
cor - te Le tue dol - cez - ze, poi - ch'an - cor ti go - di Che l'e - stre -
cor - te Le tue dol - cez - ze, poi - ch'an - cor ti go - di Che l'e - stre - - -
cor - te Le tue dol - cez - ze, poi - ch'an - cor ti go - di Che l'e - stre - mo pia -
Che l'e - stre - mo pia -
cor - te Le tue dol - cez - ze, poi - ch'an - cor ti go - di Che l'e - stre - mo pia -
mo pia - cer fi - ni - sca in pian - to. Nè po - ten -
mo pia - cer fi - ni - sca in pian - - to. Nè po - ten - do dir più, nè po - ten -
cer fi - ni - sca in pian - - to. Nè po -
cer fi - ni - sca in pian - - to. Nè po - ten - do dir più,
cer fi - ni - sca in pian - - to. Nè po - ten - do dir più, nè po - ten -
do dir più, cin - se - me for - te, cin - se - me for - te, I - te - ran - do gl'am - ples - si,
do dir più, cin - se - me for - te, cin - se - me for - te, I - te - ran - do gl'am -
ten - do dir più, cin - se - me for - te, cin - se - me for - te, I - te -
cin - se - me for - te, cin - se - me for - te, I - te - ran - do gl'am - ples - si in tanti no -
do dir più, cin - se - me for - te, cin - se - me for - te, I - te - ran - do gl'am - ples - si,

Da le belle contrade d'oriente
Chiar' e licta s'ergea Ciprigna, ed io
Fruiva in braccio al divin idol mio
Quel piacer che non cape' humana mente,
Quando senti dopp'un sospir ardente:
"Speranza del mio cor, dolce desio,
T'en vai, haimè! Sola mi lasci! Adio!
Che sarà qui di me scur' e dolente?
Ahi crud' amor! Ben son dubbios' e corte
Le tue dolcezze, poi ch'anchor ti godi,
Che l'estremo piacer finisc' in pianto."
Ne potendo dir più cinseme forte
Iterando gl'ampless' in tanti nodi,
Che giamai ne fer più l'edro o l'acanto.

—Anonymous

From the fair regions of the East,
clear and bright rose Venus, and I
enjoyed in the arms of my idol
the pleasure that no human mind can understand,
when I heard after a burning sigh:
"Hope of my heart, sweet desire,
you're leaving me, alas, all alone! Farewell!
What will become of me, gloomy and sad?
O cruel love! Much too tentative and brief are
your sweet caresses. Besides, you even take delight
in seeing this extreme pleasure end in tears."
Unable to say more, she held me tight,
repeating her embraces in many coils,
more than ever heather or acanthus made.

Da le belle contrade d'oriente represents the second generation of the madrigal, when five and six parts were common. The extended range suits this sonnet particularly well, since the ensemble divides easily into two personae in the second quatrain, when the woman's speech is distinguished from the narrating poet's (measures 25–56). Rore has the two sopranos form a duet, while the other voices accompany or echo them. The woman's first phrase, "Speranza del mio cor" (Hope of my heart), brightly climbs the circle of fiths in major triads; then the line ominously descends in minor chords to a deceptive cadence, after which she exclaims "T'en vai, haimè!" (You're leaving me, alas!), interrupted by sighs marked by rests and a plaintive chromatic inflection on "lasci!" The octave (the first eight lines) of the sonnet ends in an ambiguous cadence.

The woman's speech continues in the sestet (the last six lines), as her complaint turns to irony, reflected in the harmony and rhythm of the popular dance song, marked by mixed triple and duple time, parallel fifths, and cross-relations. After a plagal cadence and a moment of silence, two basses resume the narration. Now Rore indulges in graphic musical images sometimes called "madrigalisms." Close entrances of the motive "cinseme forte" describe "held me tight," multiple repetitions and semiminim runs represent the coils of embraces that are like the climbing vines of heather or acanthus.

Although the madrigal is anchored in what we call *F* major, along the way it dwells on *C* major, *D* minor, and *C* minor, and resorts to chords as distant from *F* as *E* major and *D♭* major. Monteverdi must have had compositions such as this in mind when he credited Rore with starting a "seconda pratica," a new harmonic practice in which the text rules over the musical composition, free of the restrictions of strict modal counterpoint.

Luca Marenzio (1553–1599)

39

Madrigal: *Solo e pensoso* CD 3

Luca Marenzio, *Il nono libro de madrigali a 5 voci* (Venice: Gardano, 1599). *Music and Patronage in Sixteenth Century Mantua*, ed. Iain Fenlon (Cambridge: Cambridge University Press, 1982), 2:99–105. Reprinted with the permission of Cambridge University Press.

9
C
- ti cam - - pi Vò' mi - -
A
- - pi Vò' mi - su - ran - do Vò' mi -
T
Vò' mi - su - ran - do a pas - si tar - - - di e
Q
- pi Vò' mi - su - ran - do a pas - si tar -
B
- pi Vò' mi - su - ran - do a pas - si tar - di e
14
C
- su - - ran - do a pas - si tar -
A
- su - - ran - do a pas - si tar -
T
len - - ti Vò' mi - su - ran - - do
Q
- di e len - ti a pas - si tar
B
len - - ti Vò' mi - su - ran - do a pas -
20
C
- di e len - - ti
A
- - di e len - - - - ti
T
a pas - si tar - di e len - - ti
Q
- di e len - - ti
B
- si tar - - di e len - - ti

25
2
C
E gl'oc - chi por - to per fug-gir in - ten - ti
A
E gl'oc - chi por - to per fug-gir in - ten - ti
T
E gl'oc - chi por - to per fug - gir in - ten -
Q
E gl'oc - chi por - to per fug-gir in - ten -
B
E gl'oc - chi por -
29
C
E gl'oc - chi por - to per fug - gir in - ten - -
A
E gl'oc - chi por - to per fug-gir in-ten - -
T
- ti E gl'oc - chi por - to per fug- gir in - ten - -
Q
- - ti
B
- to per fug-gir in - ten - ti
33
C
- ti Do - ve ve - stig - gio hu-man
A
- ti Do - ve ve - stig -
T
- ti Do - ve ve - stig - gio hu - man
Q
Do - ve ve - stig - gio hu-man
B
Do - ve ve - stig - gio hu-man

37
C
Do - ve ve - stig - gio hu-man l'a - - re - na stam -
A
- gio hu-man l'a - re -
T
Do - ve ve - stig - gio hu -
Q
Do - ve ve - stig - gio hu-man l'a -
B
Do - ve ve - stig - gio hu-man l'a - - re - na stam -
41
3
C
- pi l'a - re - na stam - pi Al - - tro
A
- na l'a - re - na stam - pi Al - - tro
T
- man l'a - re - na stam - - pi Al - - tro
Q
- re - na stam - - pi Al - - tro
B
- pi l'a - re - na stam - - pi Al - - tro
46
C
scher - - mo non tro - vo che mi scam - - -
A
scher - - mo non tro - vo che mi
T
scher - - mo non tro - vo
Q
scher - - mo non tro - - vo
B
scher - - mo non tro - vo

50
C - - - - pi
A scam - - - pi
T non tro - vo
Q non tro - vo che mi scam - -
B non tro - vo che mi
54
C Dal ma - ni - fe -
A Dal ma - ni
T Dal ma - ni
Q - - - - pi Dal ma - ni -
B scam - - - pi Dal ma - ni -
58
C sto ac - cor - - ger de le gen - - -
A - fe - - sto ac - - cor - ger de le gen - -
T - fe - - sto ac - - cor - ger de le gen - -
Q - fe - - sto ac - cor - - ger de le gen - -
B - fe - - sto ac - cor - - ger de le gen - -

62
4
C - ti Per - che ne - gli at - ti d'al - le - grez - za spen - ti
A - ti Per - che ne - gli at - ti d'al - le - grez - za spen - ti
T - ti Per - che ne - gli at - ti d'al - le - grez - za spen - ti
Q - ti
B - ti
66
C Per - che Per - che ne -
A Per - che Per - che ne -
T Per - che ne - gli at - ti d'al - le - grez - za spen - ti
Q Per - che ne - gli at - ti d'al - le - grez - za spen - ti Per - che ne -
B Di fuor si leg - ge co - m'io den-tro a -
70
C - gli at - ti d'al - le - grez - za spen - ti Per - che
A - gli at - ti d'al - le - grez - za spen - ti d'al -
T Di fuor si leg - ge com'io dentro a -
Q - gli at - ti Per - che ne - gli at - ti d'al - le - grez -
B - vam - pi Per - che ne - gli at - ti d'al - le - grez -

74
C
Di fuor si leg - ge
A
- le - grez - za spen - ti Per - che ne - gli at - ti d'al - le - grez -
T
vam - - pi Per - che ne - gli at - ti d'al - le - grez -
Q
- za spen - ti
B
- za spen - ti co - m'io
77
C
Per - che ne - gli at - ti d'al - le - grez - za spen - ti
A
- za spen - ti co - m'io den - tro avam - pi
T
- za spen - ti Di fuor si leg - ge
Q
Di fuor Di fuor si
B
den - tr'a - vam - pi Di
81
C
Di fuor si leg - - ge
A
Per - che ne - gl'at - ti d'al - le - grez - za spen -
T
co - m'io dentro a - vam - pi
Q
leg - - ge co - me io den - tr'a - vam - - - -
B
fuor si leg - - ge co - m'io den - tr'a - vam -

84
C
co-m'io den-tr'a-vam - pi co-m'io den-tr'a-vam - - pi.
A
- ti co-m'io den-tr'a-vam - - - - pi.
T
co-m'io den-tr'a - vam - - - - pi.
Q
- pi co-m'io den-tr'a - vam - - pi.
B
- pi co-m'io den-tr'a-vam - - - - pi.
88
5
C
Si ch'io mi cre - d'ho-mai che mon -
A
Si ch'io mi cre - d'ho - mai che mon - ti e piag -
T
Si ch'io mi cre - d'ho - mai che mon - - ti e
Q
B
92
C
- ti e piag - ge E fiu - - mi
A
- - ge E fiu - -
T
piag - ge E fiu - - - mi e
Q
E fiu - - - mi E
B
E fiu - mi e sel - - -

96
C
E fiu - - mi e sel - - - - -
A
- - mi e sel - ve sap - - - pian
T
sel - ve e sel - -
Q
fiu - mi e sel - - ve sap -
B
- ve E fiu - - - mi e sel - -
100
C
- ve sap - pian di che tem - - - pre
A
sap - pian di che tem - - - pre
T
- - ve sap - pian di che
Q
- pian di che tem - - pre *Sap* -
B
- - ve sap - pian di che tem - pre Sia
103
C
sap - pian di che tem - - pre *sap* -
A
sap - pian di che tem - - pre *sap* -
T
tem - pre *sap - pian di che tem - pre*
Q
- *pian di che tem - pre* Sap - pian di che
B
la mia vi - - ta Sia la

106
C
- pian di che tem - pre Sia la mia vi - ta
A
- pian di che tem - pre Sia la mia vi - ta
T
Sia la mia vi - ta
Q
tem - - - pre
B
mia vi - ta
110
C
ch'è ce - la - ta al - tru - i Ma pur sì a
A
ch'è ce - la - ta al - tru - i Ma pur sì a -
T
ch'è ce - la - ta al - tru - i Ma pur sì a -
Q
Ma pur sì a - spre vie
B
Ma pur sì a -
116
C
- spre vie ne sì sel - vag - ge
A
- spre vie ne sì sel - vag - ge
T
- spre vie ne sì sel - vag - ge
Q
ne sì sel - vag - ge Cer - car non
B
- spre vie ne sì sel - vag - ge Cer - car non

123
C
ch'A - mor non ven - ga sem - pre Ra - gio-nan - do con me - co Cer -
A
Cer - car non sò Cer - car non sò Cer - car non sò
T
Cer - car non sò ch'A - mor non ven - ga sem - pre Ra -
Q
sò Cer - car non sò Cer - car non sò ch'A -
B
sò ch'A - mor non ven - ga sem - pre Ra - gio-nan - do con
127
C
- car non sò Cer - car non sò et io con lu -
A
ch'A - mor non ven - ga sem - pre Ra - gio - nan - do con me -
T
- gio-nan - do Cer - car non sò ch'A - mor non
Q
- mor non ven - ga sem - pre Ra - gio - nan - do con me - co
B
me - co Cer - car non sò Cer - car non sò
131
C
- i Cer - car non sò et io con lu - - -
A
- co et io con lu - i Cer - car non
T
ven - ga sem - pre Ra - gio-nan - do con me - co
Q
Cer - car non sò et io con lu -
B
Cer - car non sò

Solo e pensoso i più deserti campi
Vo misurando a passi tardi e lenti;
E gl'occhi porto, per fuggire, intenti,
Dove vestigio uman l'arena stampi.
Altro scherno non trovo che mi scampi
Dal manifesto accorger de le genti;
Perchè negli atti d'allegrezza spenti
Di fuor si legge com'io dentro avampi:
Si ch'io mi credo homai che monti e piagge
E fiumi e selve sappian di che tempre
Sia la mia vita, ch'è celata altrui.
Ma pur sì aspre vie nè sì selvagge
Cercar non sò, ch'Amor non venga sempre
Ragionando con meco, et io con lui.

—Francesco Petrarca

Alone and pensive, the deserted fields
I measure with deliberate and slow steps,
and my eyes I hold in readiness to flee
from a place marked by human footsteps.
I find no other defense to save me
from the peering eyes of people.
Because when laughter and cheer are spent
my flame within can be read outside.
So I've come to believe that mountains and beaches
and rivers and woods know of what fibers,
hidden from others, is made my life.
Yet paths neither so rough nor wild
can I find where Cupid does not seek me
to debate with me and I with him.

This setting of Petrarch's sonnet is one of Marenzio's most celebrated madrigals. It is a masterpiece of sensitive musical imagery, harmonic refinement, and deft counterpoint. The chromatic scale in the topmost voice, rising deliberately one half-step per measure from *g′* to *a″* and returning to *d″*, represents the poet's measured pace as he wanders pensively in the deserted fields. The other voices' descending arpeggios paint a forbidding, desolate landscape.

The jagged melodic subject imitated by all the voices in measures 25–33 describes the poet's darting eyes as he looks for a hiding place—he fears that his eyes will reveal his inner fire. He feels safe among the mountains, beaches, rivers, and woods, which already know him. These surroundings are depicted musically: the mountains by a series of leaps (measures 88–92), the flowing rivers by eighth-note runs spanning a seventh passed from voice to voice (measures 93–100). When the poet complains that he cannot find turf rough enough to discourage Cupid from following him, Marenzio has the voices stumble over each other in syncopations, suspensions, and cross-relations (measures 111–21). A subject that gallops headlong down an octave in dotted notes tells us that Cupid is in hot pursuit, while two of the voices keep repeating "cercar non sò" (I cannot find).

Despite the chromaticism, the madrigal is clearly in the G-mode, with a cadence on the fifth degree at the end of the eighth line.

1) chromaticism for expression
2) avoids traditional cadences
3) Imitative Entrances

40 Carlo Gesualdo (ca. 1561–1613)

Madrigal: *"Io parto" e non più dissi* CD 3

6
che il do - lo - re, che il
„Io par - to" e non più dis - si, che il do - lo - re
„Io par - to" e non più dis - si, che il do - lo - re,
„Io par - to" e non più dis - si, che il
„Io par - to" e non più dis - si, che il do -

6
do - lo - re Pri - vò di vi - ta il
Pri - vò di vi - ta il co -
che il do - lo - re Pri - vò di vi - ta il co -
do - lo - re Pri - vò di vi - ta il co -
lo - re Pri - vò di vi - ta il

11
co - - re. Al-lor, al-lor pro-rup - pein pian- - -to,
- - re. Al - lor, al-lor pro - rup-pein pian -
- - re. Al-lor, al-lor pro-rup - pein pian - to, pro -
- - re. Al-lor, al-lor pro - rup -
co - - re. Al-lor, al-lor pro -

7
15
pro-rup - pein pian - to e dis - se Clo - ri Con in - - ter -
to e dis - se Clo - ri
rup-pein pian- - -to e dis - se Clo - ri Con in -
- - - pein pian - to e dis - se Clo - ri Con in - -
rup - - pein pian - to e dis- - -se Clo - ri

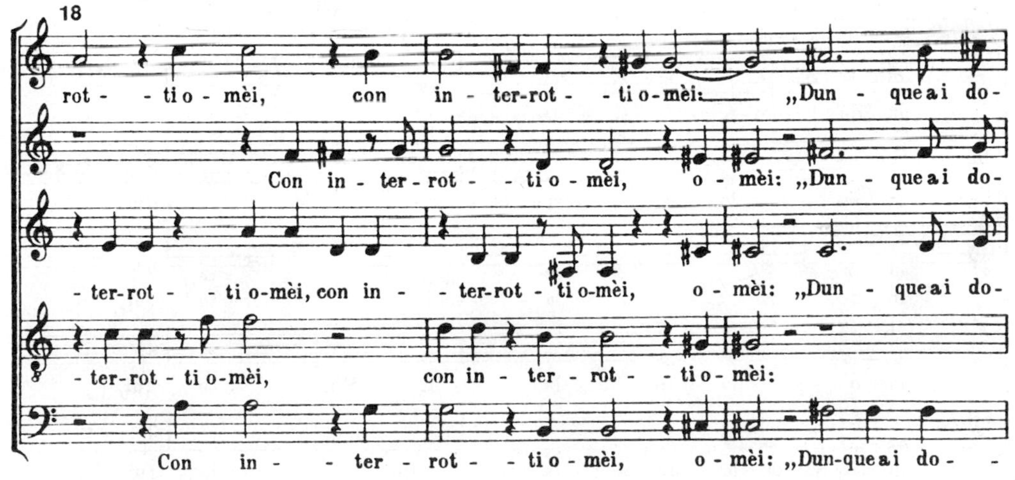
18
rot - - ti o - mèi, con in - ter-rot - - ti o-mèi: „Dun - que ai do -
Con in - ter - rot - - ti o - mèi, o - mèi: „Dun - que ai do -
- ter-rot - - ti o-mèi, con in - - ter-rot - ti o-mèi, o - mèi: „Dun - que ai do -
- ter-rot - ti o-mèi, con in - ter - rot - - ti o - mèi:
Con in - - ter - rot - - ti o - mèi, o - mèi: „Dun-que ai do - -

21
lo - ri Io re - sto. Ah, non fia ma - - i
lo - ri Io re - sto, ai do - lo - ri Io re - sto. Ah, non fia ma -
lo - ri Io re - sto, ai do - lo - ri Io re - sto. Ah, non fia
ai do - lo - ri Io re - sto. non fia ma - i
lo - ri Io re - sto, ai do - lo - ri Io re - sto. Ah,

24
Ch'io non lan - guis - ca
i Ch'io non lan - guis - - - ca, ch'io non lan - guis - ca
mai Ch'io non lan - guis - - ca, ch'io non lan - guis - ca
Ch'io non lan - guis - ca
non fia ma - i Ch'io non lan - guis - - - - - ca

26
8
(♭)
in do - lo - ro - - si la - - i." vi - vo
in do - - lo - ro - - si la - - i." Mor - to fui, vi -
in do - lo - ro - - si la - - i." Mor - to fui,
in do - - lo - ro - si la - - i." Mor - - to fui,
in do - lo - ro - si la - - i." Mor - to fui,

30
son, vi - vo son, vi-vo son, chei spir - ti spen- - - ti,
vo son, vi - vo son, vi - vo son,chei spir - ti spen- - - ti, chei spir -
vi - vo son, vi - vo son, vi-vo son, chei spir - ti spen -
vi - vo son, vi - vo son, chei spir - ti
vi - vo son, vi - vo son, chei spir -

34
chei spir - ti spen- - ti, spen -
ti, chei spir - ti spen- - ti, chei spir - ti spen- - -
- ti chei spir - ti spen - ti, spen- - ti
spen- - ti, chei spir-ti spen- - - - ti
ti spen - ti spen- - - - ti

37
ti Tor - naro in vi - ta, tor - naro in vi - ta a sì pie - to-si ac-cen - ti,
ti Tor - naro in vi - ta, tor - naro in vi - ta a sì pie - to-si ac-cen - ti,
Tor - naro in vi - ta, tor - naro in vi - ta a sì pie - to-si ac-cen - ti,
Tor-naro in vi - ta a sì pie - to-si ac-cen - ti,
Tor - naro in vi - ta, tor - naro in vi - ta

"Io parto" e non più dissi che il dolore
Privò di vita il core.
Allor proruppe in pianto e dissi Clori
Con interrotti omèi:
"Dunque ai dolori io resto. Ah, non fia mai
Ch'io non languisca in dolorosi lai."
Morto fui, vivo son che i spirti spenti
tornaro in vita a sì pietosi accenti.

"I depart." I said no more, for grief
robbed my heart of life.
Then Clori broke out in tears and said,
with interrupted cries of "Alas":
"Hence I remain in pain. Ah, may I never
cease to pine away in painful lays."
Dead I was, now I am alive, for my spent spirits
returned to life at the sound of such pitiable accents.

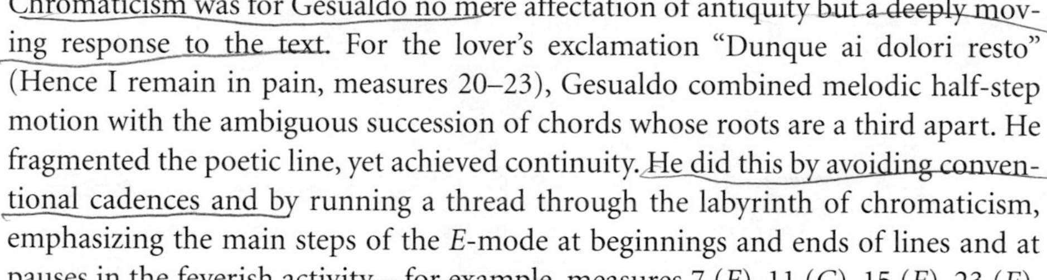

Chromaticism was for Gesualdo no mere affectation of antiquity but a deeply moving response to the text. For the lover's exclamation "Dunque ai dolori resto" (Hence I remain in pain, measures 20–23), Gesualdo combined melodic half-step motion with the ambiguous succession of chords whose roots are a third apart. He fragmented the poetic line, yet achieved continuity. He did this by avoiding conventional cadences and by running a thread through the labyrinth of chromaticism, emphasizing the main steps of the *E*-mode at beginnings and ends of lines and at pauses in the feverish activity—for example, measures 7 (*E*), 11 (*G*), 15 (*E*), 23 (*E*), 25 (*B*), 29 (*E*), and, of course, at the end (*E*).

The listener's attention nevertheless is drawn from this consistent structure to details. For instance, three distinct musical ideas make up the first line: the recitational "Io parto," a chromatic rise to a half-cadence for the speaker's admission that he said no more, and, third, an expression of pain through a descending line and a suspension, immediately intensified by a repetition a semitone higher that alters the descending whole steps to half steps (measure 6). Similarly, the second line is split into two: the simple recitation "Privò," and the descending imitative entries representing a heart breaking. When Clori speaks (measure 20), the three upper parts declaim against the bass, as the three lower parts had done for the opening male exclamation. The music of the penultimate line (measures 28 to 37) contains three separate images: of death, through a chromatic succession of sustained chords; of renewed life, through rapid motion, close imitation, and syncopation; and of exhaustion ("spirti spenti"—spent spirits), through an erratic subject whose descending imitations portray lassitude while the upward imitations suggest a gasping for air. In the final line Gesualdo indulges in a pun, setting the word "accenti" with ornamental runs of the kind that when improvised were called *accenti*.

Although first published in 1611, this madrigal may have been composed in the late 1590s.

41 Claudin de Sermisy (ca. 1490–1562)

Chanson: *Tant que vivray* CD 3 CD 1

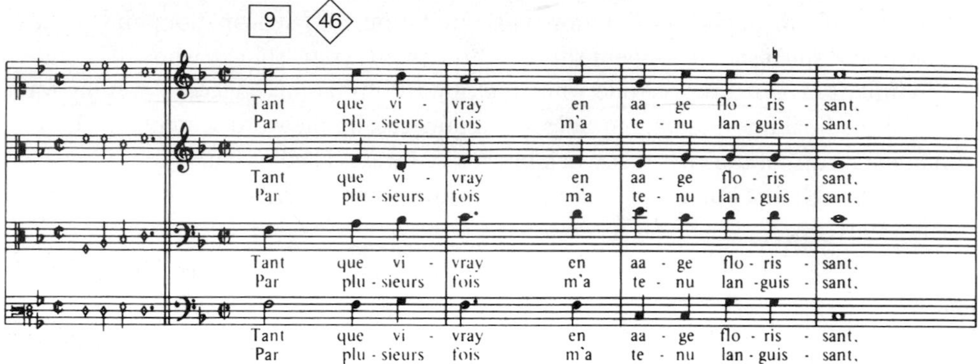
9
46
Tant que vi - vray en aa - ge flo - ris - sant.
Par plu - sieurs fois m'a te - nu lan - guis - sant.
Tant que vi - vray en aa - ge flo - ris - sant.
Par plu - sieurs fois m'a te - nu lan - guis - sant.
Tant que vi - vray en aa - ge flo - ris - sant.
Par plu - sieurs fois m'a te - nu lan -guis - sant.
Tant que vi - vray en aa - ge flo - ris - sant.
Par plu - sieurs fois m'a te - nu lan - guis - sant.

5
Je ser - vi - ray d'a - mours le roy puis - sant En fais en
Mais a - pres deul m'a faict re - jo - ys - sant Car j'ay l'a -
Je ser - vi - ray d'a - mours le roy puis - sant En fais en
Mais a - pres deul m'a faict re - jo - ys - sant Car j'ay l'a -
Je ser - vi - ray d'a - mour le roy puis - sant En fais en
Mais a - pres deul m'a faict re - jo - ys - sant Car j'ay l'a -
Je ser - vi - ray d'a - mour le roy puis - sant En fais en
Mais a - pres deul m'a faict re. - jo - ys - sant Car j'ay l'a -

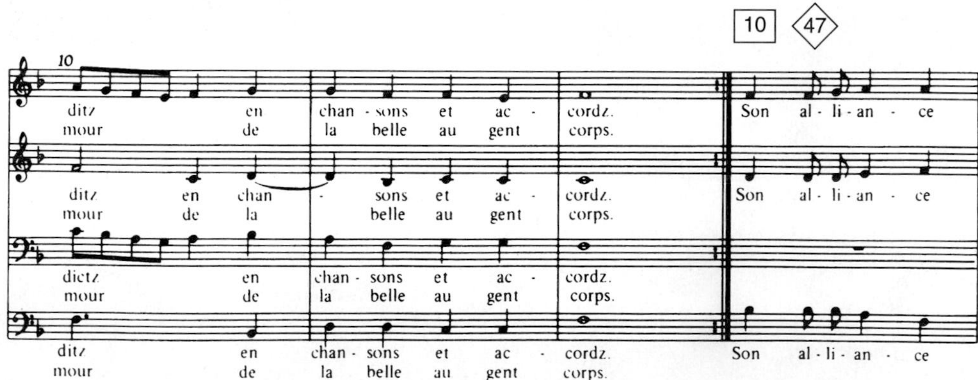
10
47
10
ditz en chan - sons et ac - cordz. Son al - li - an - ce
mour de la belle au gent corps.
ditz en chan - sons et ac - cordz. Son al - li - an - ce
mour de la belle au gent corps.
dictz en chan - sons et ac - cordz.
mour de la belle au gent corps.
ditz en chan - sons et ac - cordz. Son al - li - an - ce
mour de la belle au gent corps.

Claudin de Sermisy, *Collected Works*, Vol. 1, Chansons, ed. Gaston Allaire and Isabelle Cazeaux (American Institute of Musicology, 1974), pp. 99–100.

Tant que vivray en aage florissant,
Je serviray d'amours le roy puissant
En fais en ditz en chansons et accordz.
Par plusieurs fois m'a tenu languissant,
Mais apres deul m'a faict rejoyssant
Car j'ay l'amour de la belle au gent corps.

Son alliance
C'est ma fiance,
Son cueur est mien,
Le mien est sien.
Fy de tristesse,
Vive lyesse,
Puisqu'en amour a tant de bien.

As long as I am able-bodied,
I shall serve the potent king of love
through deeds, words, songs, and harmonies.
Many times he made me languish,
but after mourning, he let me rejoice,
because I have the love of the fair lady with the lovely body.

Her alliance
is my betrothal.
Her heart is mine,
mine is hers.
Shun sorrow.
Live in merriment,
because there is so much good in love.

Quand je la veulx servir et honorer,	When I want to serve and honor her,
Quand par escriptz veulx son nom decorer,	when I want to adorn her name with words,
Quand je la veoy et visite souvent,	when I see and visit her often,
Ses envieux n'en font que murmurer;	those jealous of her do nothing but whisper;
Mais nostre amour n'en scauroit moins durer;	but our love would not last any less,
Autant ou plus en emporte le vent,	however far the wind carries the rumors.
Maulgré envie,	Despite jealousy,
Toute ma vie,	all my life,
Je l'aymeray	I will love her
Et chanteray;	and sing of her;
C'est la premiere,	She is the first,
C'est la derniere	she is the last
Que j'ay servie	that I have served
Et serviray.	and will serve.
—Clément Marot	

This song belongs to the type usually known as the "Parisian chanson." Its lively, syllabic, mostly homophonic setting is true to this type. As in the frottola, the melody is in the top voice, and the harmony consists of thirds and fifths with only an occasional sixth. At the cadences, in place of a suspension, the note that becomes a dissonance (for example, the *c*″ in measure 3), is repercussed on the strong beat, giving an "appoggiatura" effect. The end of each line of text corresponds with a relatively long note or with repeated notes, thereby emphasizing the form of the poetry.

Again as in the frottola, the composer did not set out to illustrate the text in detail but to capture the good cheer and optimism of the poem. In any case, the strophic form does not lend itself to more specific expression.

Claude Le Jeune (1528–1600) 42

Chanson: *Revecy venir du printans* CD 3

Le Printemps (Paris: Ballard, 1603), ed. Henry Expert in *Les maîtres musiciens de la Renaissance française*, 12 (Paris: Alphonse Leduc, 1900), pp. 11–27.

[1] CHANT à 2

12
Dessus
Le cou _ rant des eaus re _ cher _ chant
Haute-Contre
Le cou _ rant des eaus re _ cher _ chant

Le ca _ nal d'é té s'é _ clair _ cît:
Le ca _ nal d'é té s'é _ clair _ cît:

Et la mer cal _ me de ces flots
Et la mer cal _ me de ces flots

A _ mo _ lit le tris _ te cour _ rous:
A _ mo _ lit le tris _ te cour _ rous:

Le Ca _ nard s'e _ gay _ e plon _ jant,
Le Ca _ nard s'e _ gay _ e plon _ jant,

Et se la _ ve coint de _ dans l'eau:
Et se la _ ve coint de _ dans l'eau:

Et la grû' qui four _ che son vol
Et la grû' qui four _ che son vol

Re _ tra _ ver _ se l'air et s'en va.
Re _ tra _ ver _ se l'air et s'en va

RECHANT à 5

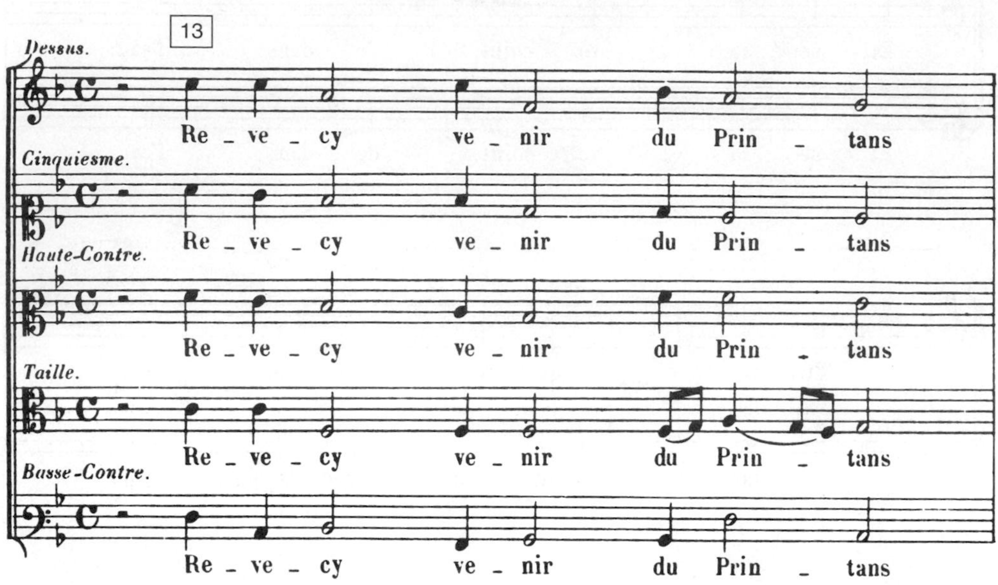
13
Dessus.
Re - ve - cy ve - nir du Prin - tans
Cinquiesme.
Re - ve - cy ve - nir du Prin - tans
Haute-Contre.
Re - ve - cy ve - nir du Prin - tans
Taille.
Re - ve - cy ve - nir du Prin - tans
Basse-Contre.
Re - ve - cy ve - nir du Prin - tans

L'a - mou - reuz' et bel - le sai - zon.
L'a - mou - reuz' et bel - le sai - zon.
L'a - mou - reuz' et bel - le sai - zon.
L'a - mou - reuz' et bel - le sai - zon.
L'a - mou - reuz' et bel - le sai - zon.

[2] CHANT à 3

14
Dessus
Le So - leil é - clai - re lui - zant
Cinquiesme
Le So - leil é - clai - re lui - zant
Taille
Le So - leil é - clai - re lui - zant

D'u - ne plus sé - rei - ne clair - té:
D'u - ne plus sé - rei - ne clair - té:
D'u - ne plus sé - rei - ne clair - té:

Du nu - a - ge l'om - bre s'en - fuit,
Du nu - a - ge l'om - bre s'en - fuit,
Du nu - a - ge l'om - bre s'en - fuit,

Qui se ioû' et court et noir - cît
Qui se ioû' et court et noir - cît
Qui se ioû' et court et noir - cît
Et fo - retz et champs et cou - taus.
Et fo - retz et champs et cou - taus.
Et fo - retz et champs et cou - taus.
Le la - beur hu - main re - ver - dît,
Le la - beur hu - main re - ver - dît,
Le la - beur hu - main re - ver - dît,
Et la prê' dé - cou - vre ses fleurs.
Et la prê' dé - cou - vre ses fleurs.
Et la prê' dé - cou - vre ses fleurs.

RECHANT à 5

15
Dessus
Re - ve - cy ve - nir du Prin - tans
Cinquiesme
Re - ve - cy ve - nir du Prin - tans
Haute-Contre
Re - ve - cy ve - nir du Prin - tans
Taille
Re - ve - cy ve - nir du Prin tans
Basse-Contre
Re - ve - cy ve - nir du Prin - tans

L'a - mou - reuz' et bel - le sai - zon.
L'a mou - reuz' et bel - le sai - zon.
L'a - mou - reuz' et bel - le sai - zon.
L'a - mou - reuz' et bel - le sai zon.
L'a - mou - reuz' et bel - le sai - zon.

[3] CHANT à 4

16
Dessus
De Ve _ nus le filz Cu _ pi _ don
Haute-Contre
De Ve _ nus le filz Cu _ pi _ don
Taille
De Ve _ nus le filz Cu _ pi _ don
Basse-Contre
De Ve _ nus le filz Cu _ pi _ don
L'u _ ni _ vers se _ mant de ses trais,
L'u _ ni _ vers se _ mant de ses trais,
L'u _ ni _ vers se _ mant de ses trais,
L'u _ ni _ vers se _ mant de ses trais,
De sa flam _ me va ré _ chau _ fér,
De sa flam _ me va ré _ chau _ fér,
De sa flam _ me va ré _ chau _ fér,
De sa flam _ me va ré _ chau _ fér,

A - ni - maus, qui vo - let en l'air,
A - ni - maus, qui vo - let en l'air,
A - ni - maus, qui vo - let en l'air,
A - ni - maus, qui vo - let en l'air,

A - ni - maus, qui ram - pet au chams,
A - ni - maus, qui ram - pet au chams,
A - ni - maus, qui ram - pet au chams,
A - ni - maus, qui ram - pet au chams,

A - ni - maus, qui na - get auz eaus.
A - ni - maus, qui na - get auz eaus.
A - ni - maus, qui na - get auz eaus.
A - ni - maus, qui na - get auz eaus.

Ce qui mes - me - ment ne sent pas,
Ce qui mes - me - ment ne sent pas,
Ce qui mes - me - ment ne sent pas,
Ce qui mes - me - ment ne sent pas,

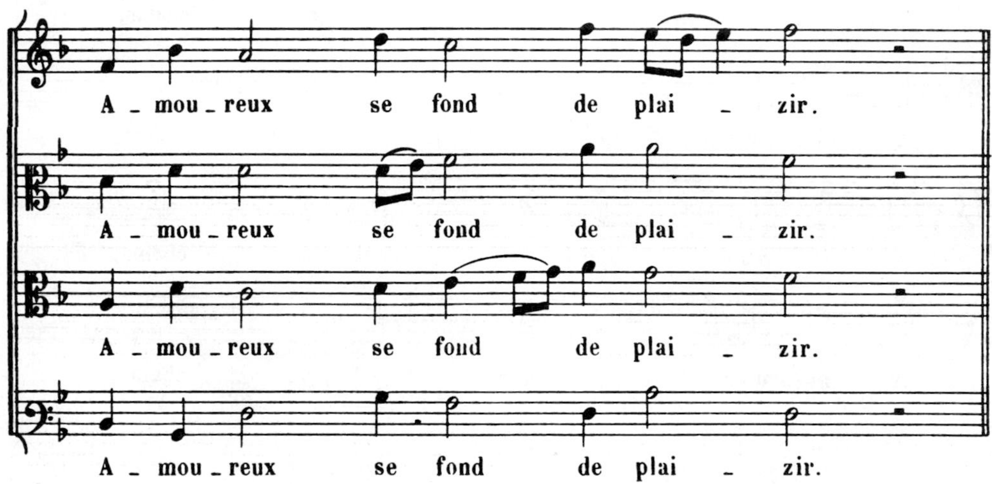
A - mou - reux se fond de plai - zir.
A - mou - reux se fond de plai - zir.
A - mou - reux se fond de plai - zir.
A - mou - reux se fond de plai - zir.

CE RESTE est à 5

(*) Dans l'original, par erreur: Les é _ bas et

19
Tou _ te cho _ se rit de plai _ zir:
Tou _ te cho _ se rit de plai _ zir:
Tou _ te cho _ se rit de plai _ zir:
Tou _ te cho _ se rit de plai _ zir:
Tou _ te cho _ se rit de plai _ zir:

Sé _ le _ bron la gay _ e sai _ zon,
Sé _ le _ bron la gay _ e sai _ zon,
Sé _ le _ bron la gay _ e sai _ zon,
Sé _ le _ bron la gay _ e sai _ on,
(*)
Sé _ le _ bron la gay _ e sai _ zon,

(*) Dans l'orig.

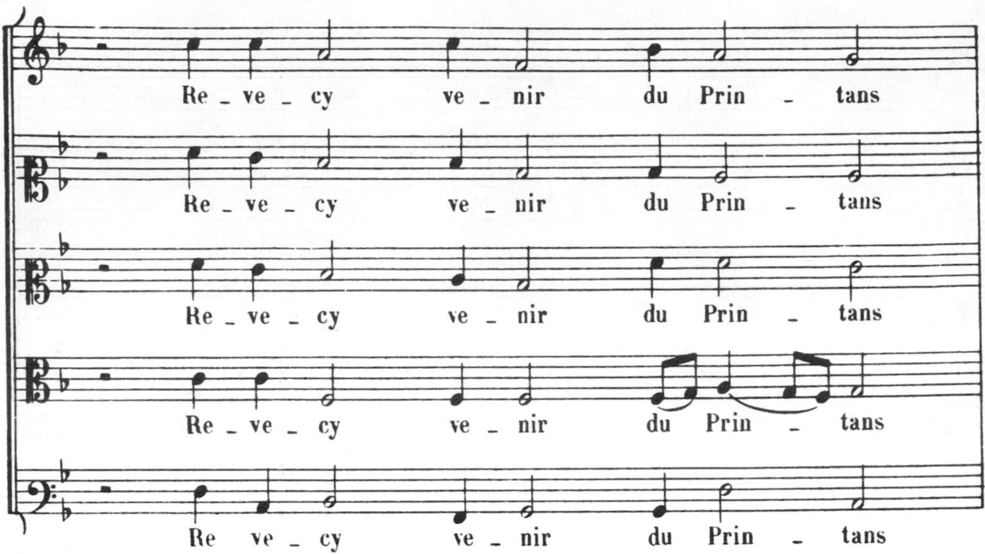
Re _ ve _ cy ve _ nir du Prin _ tans
Re _ ve _ cy ve _ nir du Prin _ tans
Re _ ve _ cy ve _ nir du Prin _ tans
Re _ ve _ cy ve _ nir du Prin _ tans
Re ve _ cy ve _ nir du Prin _ tans

L'a _ mou _ reuz' et bel _ le sai _ zon.
L'a _ mou _ reuz' et bel _ le sai _ zon.
L'a _ mou _ reuz' et bel _ le sai _ zon.
L'a _ mou _ reuz' et bel _ le sai _ zon.
L'a _ mou _ reuz' et bel _ le sai _ zon.

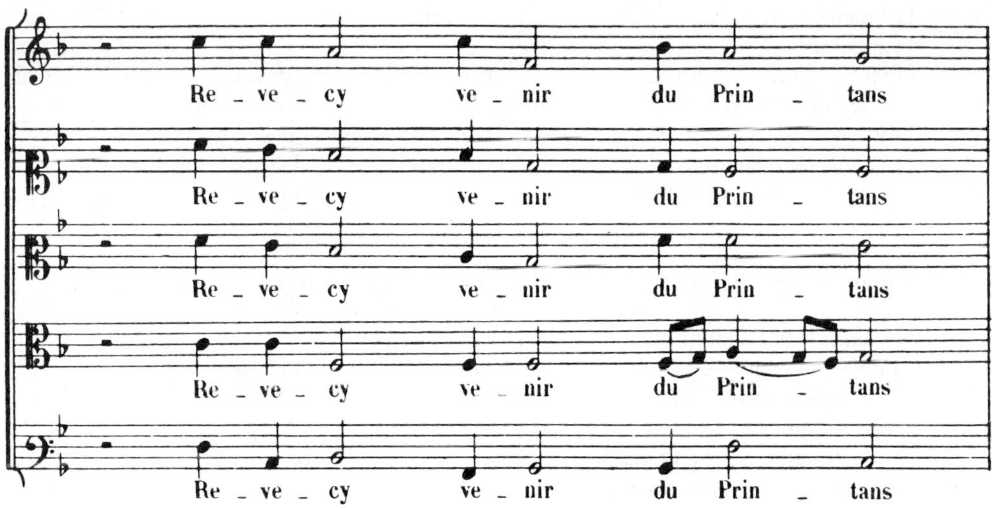

Revecy venir du Printans L'amoureuz' et belle saizon.	Here again comes the Spring, the amorous and fair season.
Le courant des eaus recherchant Le canal d'été s'éclaircît: Et la mer calme de ces flots Amolit le triste courrous: Le Canard s'egaye plonjant, Et se lave coint dedans l'eau; Et la grû' qui fourche son vol Retraverse l'air et s'en va.	The currents of water that seek the canal in summer become clearer; and the calm sea the waves' sad anger soothes. The duck, elated, dives and washes itself quietly in the water. And the crane that branches off in flight recrosses the air and flies away.
Revecy venir du Printans L'amoureuz' et belle saizon.	Here again comes the Spring, the amorous and fair season.

Le Soleil éclaire luizant	The sun shines brightly
D'une plus séreine clairté:	with a calmer light.
Du nuage l'ombre s'enfuit,	The shadow of the cloud vanishes
Qui se ioû' et court et noircît.	from him who sports and runs and darkens.
Et foretz et champs et coutaus	Forests and fields and slopes
Le labeur humain reverdît,	human labor makes green again,
Et la prê' découvre ses fleurs.	and the prairie unveils its flowers.
Revecy venir du Printans	Here again comes the Spring,
L'amoureuz' et belle saizon.	the amorous and fair season.
De Venus le filz Cupidon	Cupid, the son of Venus
L'univers semant de ses trais,	seeding the universe with his arrows,
De sa flamme va réchaufér,	with his flame he will rekindle
Animaus, qui volet en l'air,	animals that fly in the air,
Animaus, qui rampet au chams,	animals that crawl in the fields,
Animaus, qui naget auz eaus.	animals that swim in the seas.
Ce qui mesmement ne sent pas,	Even those that feel not,
Amoureux se fond de plaizir.	in love they melt in pleasure.
Revecy venir du Printans	Here again comes the Spring,
L'amoureuz' et belle saizon.	the amorous and fair season.
Rion aussi nous: et cherchon	Let us, too, laugh, and let us seek
Les ébas et ieus du Printans:	the sports and games of Spring:
Toute chose rit de plaizir:	everything smiles with pleasure;
Sélebron la gaye saizon,	let us celebrate the merry season.
Revency venir du Printans	Here again comes the Spring,
L'amoureuz' et belle saizon.	the amorous and fair season.
Revency venir . . .	Here again comes . . .

The poets of the Académie de Poésie et de Musique (Academy of Poetry and Music), founded in 1570 under the patronage of King Charles IX, wrote strophic French verses in ancient classical meters (*vers mesurés à l'antique*), substituting for the modern stress accent the ancient Greek and Latin quantities of long and short syllables. Since the French language lacked any consistent distinction between long and short vowels, the theorists of *vers mesuré* worked out a system in which syllables were assigned long and short values, and composers set them accordingly.

In this poem the following pattern is used almost throughout: ⏑⏑– ⏑– ⏑––. In terms of quarter notes, this results in the pattern 2 3 3 2 2, which is identical to a popular hemiola rhythm used by Cara in his frottole and Monteverdi in his canzonets (see NAWM 35 and 54b). The refrain, or *rechant*, is for five voices, whereas the strophes, or chants, are for successively two, three, four, and five voices. Melismas, ordinarily of no more than four notes, relieve the uniformity of rhythm and add lightness and charm to the individual parts.

Thomas Weelkes (ca. 1575–1623) 43

Madrigal: *O Care, thou wilt despatch me* CD 3 CD 1

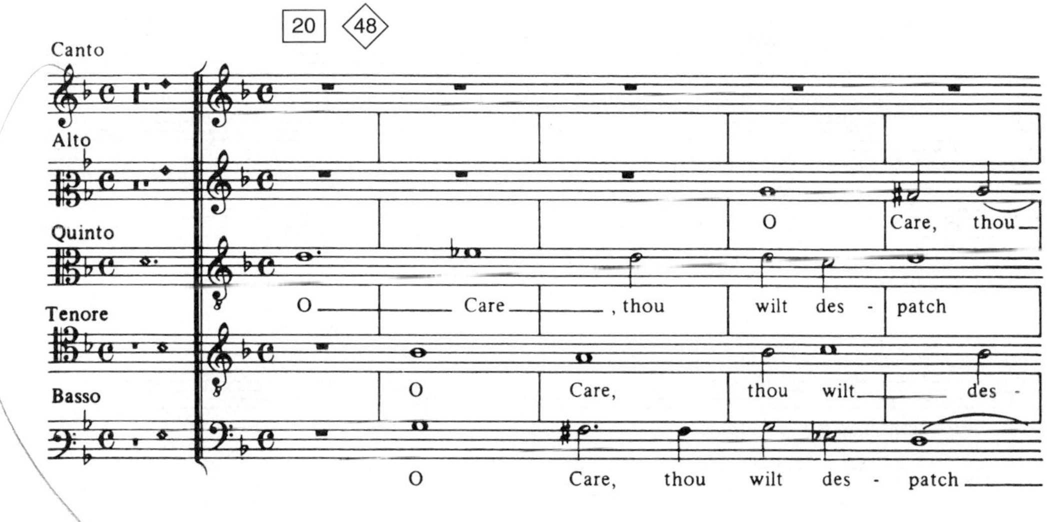

Ed. Nigel Davison in John Wilbye et al., *Neun englische Madrigale zu 5 und 6 Stimmen, Das Chorwerk* 132:37–44 (Wolfenbüttel: Möseler Verlag, 1983).

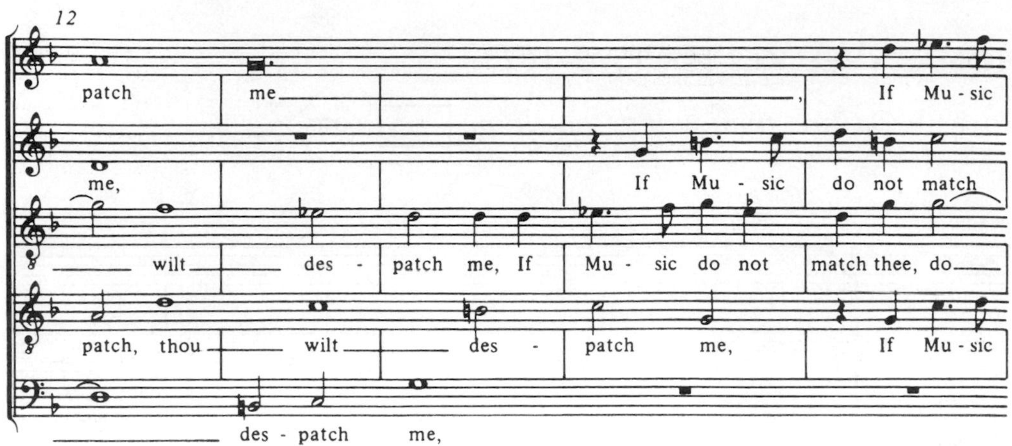
12
patch me, If Mu - sic
me, If Mu - sic do not match
wilt des - patch me, If Mu - sic do not match thee, do
patch, thou wilt des - patch me, If Mu - sic
des - patch me,

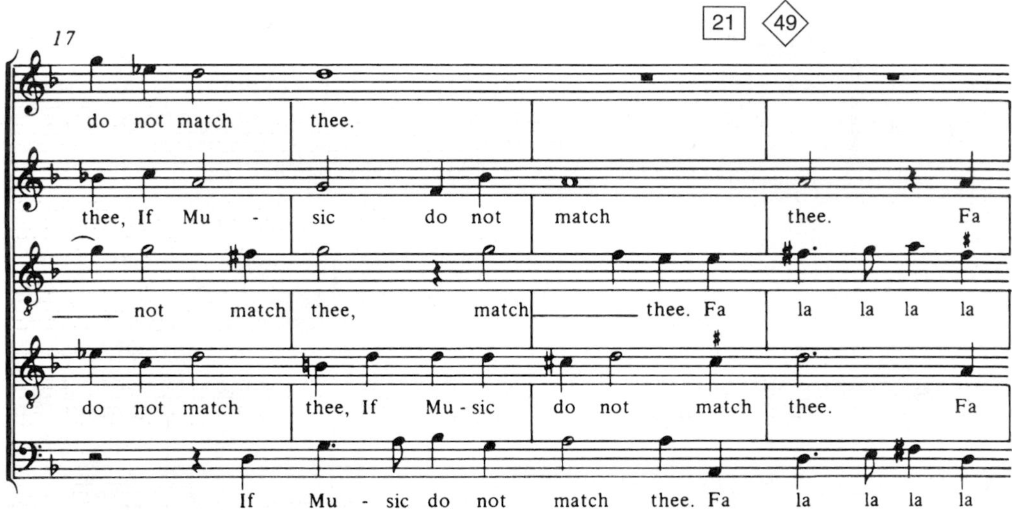
21
49
17
do not match thee.
thee, If Mu - sic do not match thee. Fa
not match thee, match thee. Fa la la la la
do not match thee, If Mu - sic do not match thee. Fa
If Mu - sic do not match thee. Fa la la la la

21
Fa la la la la la la. So dead-
la la la la la la la la la la. So
la la la la la la la la la. So
la la la la la la. Fa la la la
la. Fa la la la la la la.

26
- - ly dost thou sting me, So dead - ly
dead - ly dost thou sting, so dead - ly
dead - ly dost thou sting, so dead - -
So dead - ly,
So dead - - - ly

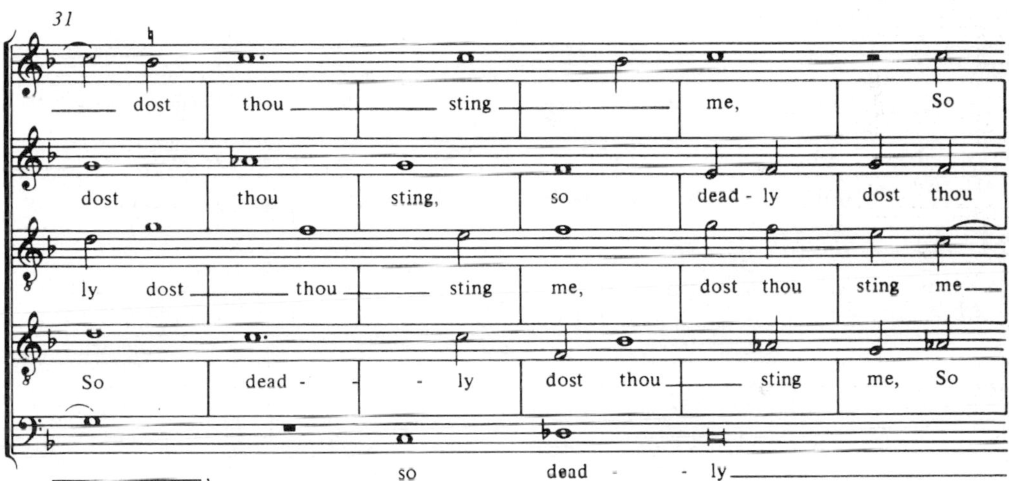
31
dost thou sting me, So
dost thou sting, so dead - ly dost thou
ly dost thou sting me, dost thou sting me
So dead - - ly dost thou sting me, So
, so dead - - ly

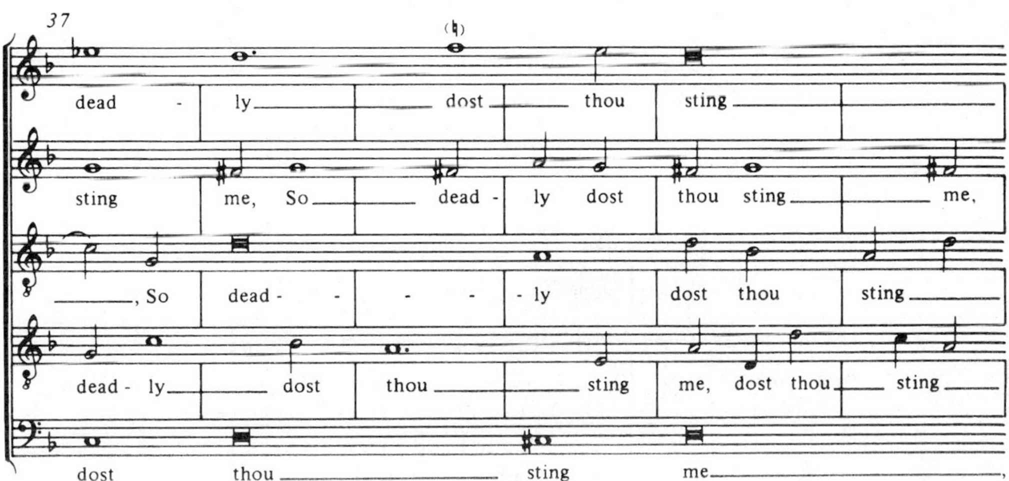
37
dead - ly dost thou sting
sting me, So dead - ly dost thou sting me,
, So dead - - - - ly dost thou sting
dead - ly dost thou sting me, dost thou sting
dost thou sting me ,

43
me, Mirth on - ly help can bring me, Mirth on - ly help can
sting me, Mirth on - ly help can bring me,
me, Mirth on - ly help can bring me, Mirth
(♭)
me, Mirth on - ly help can bring
Mirth on - ly help can bring me

46
bring, Mirth on - ly help can bring me, Mirth on - ly help can bring
Mirth on - ly help can bring me, Mirth on - ly help can bring, mirth
on - ly help can bring me, can bring me,
me, Mirth on - ly help can bring me,
, Mirth on - ly help can bring me, Mirth

49
me, Mirth on - ly help can bring me. Fa la la la la
on - ly help can bring me, Mirth on - ly help can bring me. Fa
Mirth on-ly help can bring me, can bring me.
Mirth on-ly help can bring me. Fa la la la la la. Fa
on - ly help can bring me. Fa la la la la la la

52
la la. Fa la la la la la.
la la la la la. Fa la la la la la la la la la la la la la.
Fa la la la la la la la.
la la la la la la. Fa la la la la la la la la.
la la la.

56 22 50
(Second part)
Hence Care, thou art too cru -
Hence Care, thou art too cru - -
Hence Care, thou art too, too
Hence Care, thou art too cru - -
Hence Care, thou art too cru - - el,

63
- - el, thou art too cru -
el, thou art too cru - - el,
cru - - el, thou art too cru - -
el, Hence Care, thou art too, too cru - el, thou
Hence Care, thou art

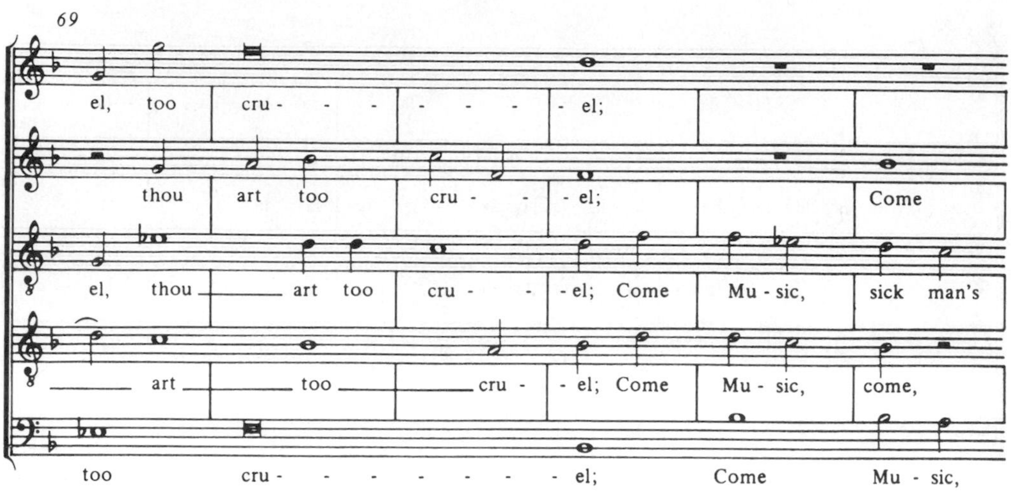
69
el, too cru- - - - - - - - el;
thou art too cru - - - el; Come
el, thou art too cru - - - el; Come Mu - sic, sick man's
art too cru - - el; Come Mu - sic, come,
too cru- - - - - - - - - el; Come Mu - sic,

75
Come Mu - sic, sick man's Jew - el, sick man's Jew - - - -
Mu - sic, come Mu - sic, sick man's Jew - - -
Jew - - el, Come Mu - sic, sick man's Jew - - el.
come Mu - - sic, sick man's Jew - -
sick man's Jew - - el, sick man's Jew - - - -

82
23
51
el. Fa la la la la la. Fa la la la la la. Fa
el. Fa la la la la la la la. Fa la la la la.
Fa la la la la la. Fa la la la. Fa la la la la
el. Fa la la la la la. Fa la la la la la la la la la la.
el. Fa la la la la la la la. Fa la la

85
la la la la la la la la la la la la
Fa la la la la la . His
la. Fa la la la la la la la la la la. His
Fa la la la la la la la. His force had
la la la la la la

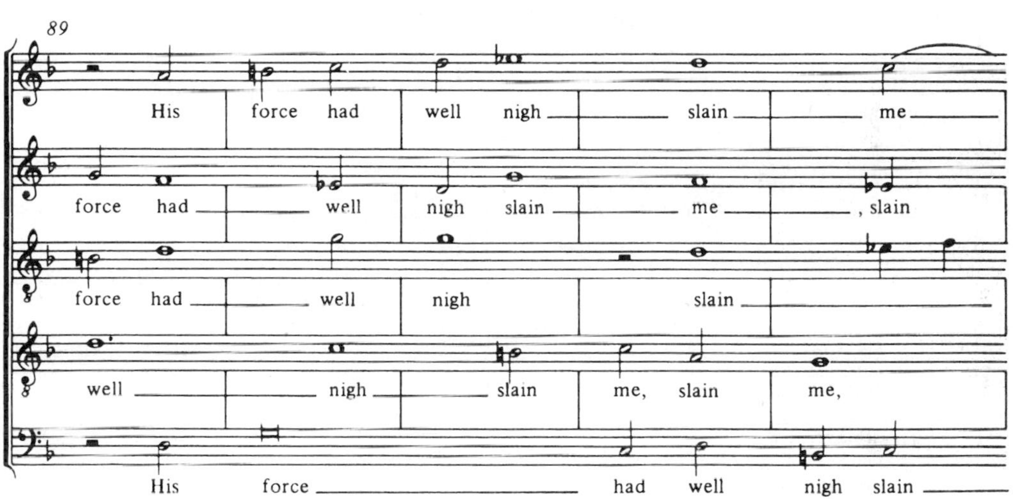
89
His force had well nigh slain me
force had well nigh slain me , slain
force had well nigh slain
well nigh slain me, slain me,
His force had well nigh slain

94
, His force had well nigh slain
me, His force had well nigh slain
me, His force had well nigh slain
His force had well nigh slain
me, had well nigh slain

99
me: But thou must now sus-tain me, But thou must now sus - tain
me: But thou must now sus - tain me, But
me: But thou must now sus-tain
me: But thou must now sus - tain me, sus - tain
me:

103
me, But thou must now sus - tain
thou must now sus - tain me, sus - - tain me, But thou must
me, But thou must now sus - tain me,
me, But thou must now sus-tain me.
But thou must now sus - tain me

107
me, now sus - tain me. Fa la la la la
now sus - tain me. Fa la la
now sus - tain me. Fa la la la la la la
Fa la la la la la la
Fa la la la la la la la

The presence of the syllables "fa-la" in this madrigal is deceptive, for the composer treats the first line of each tercet with extreme seriousness. Particularly notable is the opening, with its learned imitations in both direct and contrary motion and the chain of suspensions (including a diminished seventh at measure 3) to convey the poet's complaint. Weelkes evaded a resolution of this series of dissonances by turning away from the major triad on *G* in measure 7: the soprano moves to make a minor sixth with the bass, causing a diminished fourth with the tenor. He intensified the subsequent chain of suspensions by preparing two of the dissonances with a fourth. Weelkes's harmony is as intense and wry as Rore's or Gesualdo's, but the overall effect is one of suave vocality and broadly sweeping momentum. He achieved a smooth progression to the gleeful fa-las of the third line by introducing their music as early as the second line, producing the pattern ABB CDD.

44 John Dowland (1562–1626)

Air: *Flow, my tears* CD 3 CD 1

Dowland, *Second Booke of Songes* (London, 1600). *The English Lute Songs*, Series 1, ed. Edmund H. Fellowes, revised by Thurston Dart, 5–6. © 1922, 1969 Stainer & Bell Ltd. pp. 4–6. Reproduced by permission.

10
- ty is fled; And tears and sighs and groans my wea - ry
- tune is thrown; And fear and grief and pain for my de -
days, my wea - ry days Of all joys have de - priv - ed.
- serts, for my de-serts Are my hopes, since hope is gone.
26
54
16
Hark! you sha - dows that in dark - - - ness

Among Dowland's songs best known to Elizabethans, *Flow, my tears*, from his *Second Booke of Ayres* of 1600, spawned a whole series of variations and arrangements with titles such as *Pavana Lachrymae* by William Byrd (NAWM 46). Most of Dowland's airs are strophic; this one is a compromise between strophic and through-composed. The first two stanzas are sung to the first strain; the next two to the second strain; and the final stanza has its own music; therefore musically the form is AABBCC. Thus it duplicates the pattern of the pavane, and it may have been conceived as a dance-song.

Clearly, concrete painting or expression of individual words and phrases is not possible under the circumstances, but Dowland captures the dark mood that pervades all five stanzas, particularly through the downward diatonic motion from *C* to *G*♯, which dominates each of the strains. One can speak in this music of modern tonalities. The first strain is in A minor, the second modulates from the relative major, C, to the dominant of A minor, and the third strain returns to A minor.

Pierre Attaingnant (ca. 1494–ca. 1551) **45**

Danseries a 4 Parties, Second Livre CD 3 CD 1

a) Basse danse (No. 1)

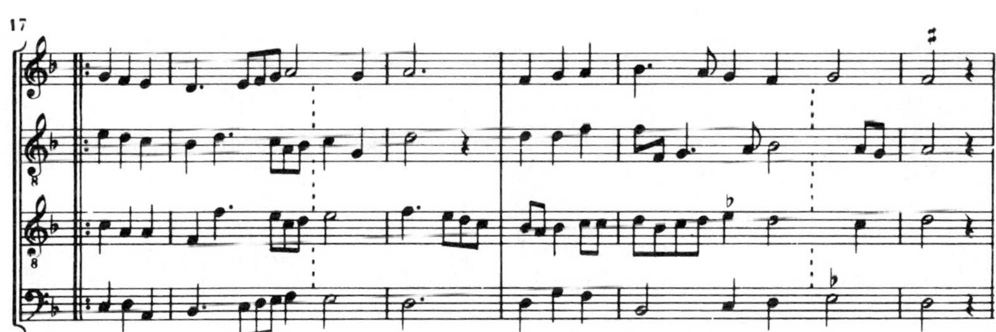

Note values reduced by half. Barlines through the entire brace mark the *quaternions* of the choreography; triple-time measures are set off by barlines through the staff; after every seventh minim of a *quaternion* a broken line appears. *Danseries a 4 parties, Second livre* (Paris, 1547), ed. Raymond Meylan (Paris: Heugel & Cie., ©1969), pp. 1, 38–39.

b) Branle gay: *Que je chatoulle ta fossette* (No. 36)

28 56

9

17

Attaingnant was not a composer but an editor and printer who issued many collections of chansons and of dance music. The *basse danse* reached the height of popularity in the fifteenth century. By the time Attaingnant's collection was published in 1547, it had almost disappeared. In the basse danse of NAWM 45a, the pattern of beats, 3 4 2 3, is repeated throughout, while there is little melodic repetition.

One of the basic steps of the basse danse was the *branle*, a side step with a swaying shift of weight from the right to the left foot. The branle later became an independent dance and several varieties emerged. The *branle double* and *branle simple* were duple, while the *branle gay* was triple. The branle gay in NAWM 45b is consistently triple and is made up of a limited number of melodic four-measure phrases, some of which are inconclusive, others cadential, allowing for various antecedent-consequent combinations. The distribution of these phrases takes the overall shape of an A B A' form (A = measures 1–12; B = measures 13–28; A′ = 29–48). Branles were often identified by the text that was sung to the top line, in this case *Que je chatoulle ta fossette.*

William Byrd (1543–1623)

Pavana Lachrymae CD 3 CD 2

29 1

4

9

Rep.

16

The Fitzwilliam Virginal Book, ed. J. A. Fuller Maitland and W. Barclay Squire (Leipzig: Breitkopf & Härtel, 1899), 2:42–46.

20
26
30
2
2
32

Rep.
44
48
55
31
3

60
66
Rep.
72

Several composers wrote variations on John Dowland's air, *Flow, my tears*, among them Dowland himself. This song has the typical form of a pavane, which consists of three strains, each immediately repeated. Two measures of Byrd's keyboard arrangement are equal to one of Dowland's lute-and-voice original. Byrd added a variation after each strain. In the first statement of each strain Byrd retained the outline of the tune in the right hand while adding short accompanimental motives or decorative turns, figurations, and scale work imitated between the hands. In each of the variations, marked "Rep." in the score, the relationship to Dowland's model is more subtle. There are rhythmic displacements and the melody is less obvious, but the harmony is retained and the melody can usually be traced in some part of the texture. At the words "And tears and sighs and groans" (NAWM 44, measures 11–12), where Dowland imitated the melody in his lute accompaniment, Byrd followed his example (measures 32–33).

47 Giovanni da Palestrina (1525/26–1594)

Pope Marcellus Mass

a) Credo CD 3

Missarum Liber secundus (Rome, 1567). *Opere complete di Giovanni Pierluigi da Palestrina*, ed. Raffaele Casimiri (Rome: Edizione Fratelli-Scalera), 4 (1939): 177–87, 194–96. Reprinted by permission of the Istituto Italiano per la Storia della Musica, Rome. For a translation of the Credo, see NAWM 3.

15
bí - li - um. Et...... in u - num Dó-mi - num, *et in u - num Dó - mi-num* Je -
Et...... in u - num Dó - mi - num
- li - um. Et in u - num Dó - mi-num Je -
Et...... in u - num Dó - mi - num, *et in u - num Dó - mi-num* Je -
Et...... in u - num Dó - mi - num
bí - li - um. Et in u - num Dó - mi-num Je -
20
- sum Chri - stum, Et...... ex Pa-tre na - tum an -
Fí - li-um De-i u-ni - gé-ni-tum. Et ex Pa-tre na - tum an -
- sum Chri - stum, Fí - li-um De-i u - ni - gé-ni-tum.
- sum Chri - stum, Et...... ex Pa-tre na - tum an -
Fí - li-um De-i u - ni - gé-ni-tum. Et...... ex Pa-tre na - tum
- sum Chri - stum. Et...... ex Pa-tre na tum an
25
30
- te ó-mni - a sæ - cu - la. Deum de De - o, De - um
- te ó-mni - a sæ - cu-la. De - um de De - o, lu - men de lú-mi - ne, De - um
De - um de De - o, lu - men de lú-mi - ne,
- te ó-mni - a sæ - cu - la. lu - men de lú-mi - ne, De - um
De - um de De - o, De - um
- te ó-mni - a sæ - cu - la. lu - men de lú-mi - ne,

35
ve - rum, *De - um ve - rum* de De-o ve- - - ro. Gé-
ve - rum de De-o ve- - ro. Gé-
De - um ve - rum de De-o ve- - ro. Gé-
ve - rum, *De - um ve - rum* de De-o ve - ro, *de De-o ve- - - ro.*
ve - rum de De-o ve - ro. Gé -
De - um ve - rum de De-o ve- - - ro.

40
45
- ni-tum, non fa - ctum, con - sub-stan-ti - á - lem Pa - tri: per quem ó-mni-a
- ni-tum, non fa - ctum, per quem ó-mni-a
- ni-tum, non fa - ctum, con - sub-stan-ti - á - lem Pa - tri: per quem ó-mni-a
con - sub-stan-ti - á - lem per quem ó-mni-a fa -
- ni-tum, non fa - ctum, per quem ó-mni-a
con - sub-stan-ti - á - lem Pa - tri: per quem ó-mni-a

50
fa - cta sunt. et pro-pter no-stram sa-
fa - cta sunt. et pro-pter no-stram sa-
fa - cta sunt. Qui pro-pter nos hó- - mi - nes, et pro-pter no-stram sa-
- cta sunt. Qui pro-pter nos hó- - mi - nes,
fa - cta sunt. Qui pro-pter nos hó- - mi - nes,
fa - cta sunt. et pro-pter no-stram sa-

55
- lú - tem de - scén - dit de cæ - lis.
lú - tem de-scén-dit de cæ - lis, de - scén - dit de cæ - lis.
- lú - tem de - scén-dit de... cæ - lis.
de - scén - dit de cæ - lis, de-scén-dit de... cæ - lis.
de - scén - dit de cæ - lis.
- lú - tem de - scén - dit de cæ - lis.

33
60
65
Et in - car - ná - tus est de Spí - ri - tu San - cto, ex Ma -
Et in - car - ná - tus est de Spí - ri - tu San - cto, ex Ma -
Et in - car - ná - tus est de Spí - ri - tu San - cto, ex Ma -
Et in - car - ná - tus est ex Ma -
Et in - car - ná - tus est ex Ma -
Et in - car - ná - tus est de Spí - ri - tu San - cto,

70
rí - a Vír - gi - ne: et... ho - mo fa - - ctus... est.
rí - a Vír - gi - ne: et ho - mo fa - ctus est.
rí - a Vír - gi - ne: et... ho - mo... fa - ctus est.
rí - a Vír - gi - ne: et ho - mo fa - - ctus... est.
rí - a Vír - gi - ne: et ho - mo fa - ctus est.
et... ho - mo fa - ctus... est.

34
75
CANTUS
ALTUS
TENOR I.
BASSUS
sub Pón-ti -
é - ti - am pro no - bis, sub Pón-ti -
Cru - ci - fí - xus é - ti - am pro no - bis,
Cru - ci - fí - xus é - ti - am pro no - bis,

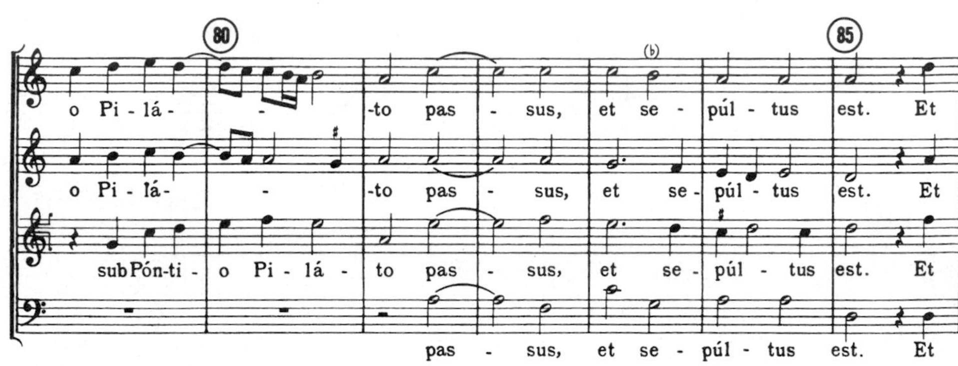
80
85
o Pi - lá - -to pas - sus, et se - púl - tus est. Et
o Pi - lá - -to pas - sus, et se - púl - tus est. Et
sub Pón-ti - o Pi - lá - to pas - sus, et se - púl - tus est. Et
pas - sus, et se - púl - tus est. Et

90
re-sur-ré - xit tér - ti - a di - e
re-sur-ré - xit tér - ti - a di - e
re-sur-ré - xit tér - ti - a di - e se-cún-dum Scri - ptú - -ras.
re-sur-ré - xit se-cún-dum Scri - ptú - -ras.

35
95
Et a - scén-dit in cae - lum, se-det ad déx - te-ram Pa - -
Et a - scén-dit in cae - lum, se-det ad déx - te-ram Pa - -
Et a - scén-dit in cae - lum, se - det ad déx - te-ram Pa - -
Et a - scén - dit in cae - lum,

100
tris. cum gló - ri - a ju - di - cá - re vi-
tris. Et í - te - rum ven - tú - rus est cum gló - ri - a ju - di - cá - re vi-
tris. Et í - te - rum ven - tú - rus est vi-
Et í - te - rum ven - tú - rus est ju - di - cá - re vi-
105
vos et mór - tu - os:
vos et mór - tu - os: cu - jus re - gni non e - rit fi-
vos et mór - tu - os: cu - jus re - gni non e - rit fi-
vos et mór - tu - os: cu - jus re - gni non e - rit fi - nis,
110
115
cu - jus re - gni non e - rit fi - nis, non e - rit fi - nis.
nis, cu - jus re - gni non e - rit fi - nis, non e - rit fi - nis.
nis, cu - jus re - gni non e - rit fi - -nis.
cu - jus re - gni non e - rit fi - -nis.
36
120
CANTUS
ALTUS
TENOR I.
TENOR II.
BASSUS I.
BASSUS II.
Et in Spí - ri - tum San - ctum, Dó - mi - num,
Et in Spí - ri - tum San - ctum, Dó - mi - num, et vi-
Et in Spí - ri - tum San - ctum, Dó - mi - num, et vi-
Et in Spí - ri - tum San - ctum, Dó - mi - num, et vi
San - ctum, Dó - mi - num,
Et in Spí - ri - tum et vi-

125
et vi - vi - fi - cán - tem: qui ex
vi - fi - cán - tem, et vi - vi - fi - cán - tem: qui ex
vi - fi - cán - tem: qui ex
vi - fi - cán - tem, et vi - vi - fi - cán - tem: qui ex Pa -
et vi - vi - fi - cán - tem: qui ex
vi - fi - cán - tem: qui
130
Pa - tre Fi - li - ó - que pro - cé - dit. Qui cum Pa -
Pa - tre Fi - li - ó-que pro - cé - dit. Qui cum
Pa - tre Fi - li - ó - que Qui oum Pa -
- tre Fi - li - ó - que pro - cé - dit. Qui
Pa - tre Fi - li - ó - que pro - cé - dit.
ex Pa - tre Fi - li - ó -[que] Qui cum Pa -
135
tre et con -
Pa - tre et Fí-li - o si - mul ad - o - rá - tur,
tre et Fí - li - o si - mul ad - o - rá - tur, et con -
cum Pa - tre et Fí - li - o si - mul ad - o - rá - tur, et con-glo -
si - mul ad - o - rá - tur,
- tre et Fí-li - o et con -

140
- glo - ri - fi - cá - tur: qui loco-cú-tus est per Pro - phé - - - -
qui lo - cú - tus est per Pro - phé - - -
- glo - ri - fi - cá - tur: qui lo - cú - tus est per Pro- - phé -
ri - fi - cá - tur: qui lo - cú - tus est per Pro - phé - - - -
qui lo - cú - tus est per Pro - phé - tas.
- glo - ri - fi - cá - tur: qui lo - cú - tus est per Pro - phé - - -

145
150
tas. Et u - nam san - ctam ca - thó - li - cam et a - po -
tas. Et u - nam san - ctam ca - thó - li - cam et a - po - stó - li -
tas. Et u - nam san - ctam ca - thó - li - cam et a - po - stó - li -
tas. Et u - nam san - ctam ca - thó - li - cam et a - po -
Et u - nam san - ctam ca - thó li - cam
tas. et a - po - stó - li -

155
stó - li - cam Ec - clé - si - am. Con - fí - te - or u - num ba -
cam Ec - clé - si - am. Con - fí - te - or
cam Ec - clé - si - am. Con - fí - te - or u - num ba -
stó - li - cam Ec - clé - si - am. Con - fí - te - or u - num ba - ptí -
Con - fí - te - or u - num ba -
cam Ec - clé - si - am. Con - fí - te - or

160
ptí- - sma in re-mis-si- ó- - - -
u - num ba - ptí - sma in re-mis-si - ó - nem
ptí- - sma in re - mis - si- ó- - - -
- - sma in re - mis - si - ó-nem pec- - ca
ptí- - sma in re-mis-si - ó - nem
u - num ba - ptí - sma in re - mis - si -

165
nem pec - ca - tó- - - - rum. Et ex- -
pec - ca - tó- - - - rum. Et ex- -
nem pec - ca - tó- - rum, pec - ca - tó - rum. Et ex - spé -
- tó - rum, pec - ca - tó- - rum. Et ex- -
pec - ca - tó- - - - rum.
ó - nem pec - ca - tó- - -rum. Et ex - spé -

170
spe - cto, *et* ex - *spé* - *cto* re - sur - re-cti - ó - nem, *re - sur-*
spé - cto, *et* ex-*spé*- - *cto* re - sur -
cto, *et* ex - *spé* - *cto* re - sur - re-cti - ó - nem
spé - cto, *et* ex-*spé* - *cto* re-sur - re-cti - ó - nem, *re-sur* -
Et ex - spé- - - cto re - sur -
- - -cto, *et* ex-*spé* - *cto* re - sur - re-cti - ó - nem

175
re-cti-ó - nem mor - tu-ó- - -rum. Et vi- -
re-cti-ó- - - nem mor - tu-ó- - -rum. Et
mor - tu-ó- - - rum. Et vi - tam ven-
re-cti-ó - nem mor - tu-ó - rum, mor-tu-ó - rum. Et
re-cti-ó - nem Et vi -
mor - tu - ó- - - - -rum.

180
tam ven-tú - ri saé- - -cu - li, et vi - tam ven-tú-ri
vi - tam ven - tú - ri, et vi - tam ven-tú- - - ri saé -
tú- - -ri saé - cu- li, et vi - tam ven- tú - ri saé-
vi - tam ven - tú - ri saé - cu- li, et vi - tam ven- tú - ri saé-
tam ven-tú - ri saé- - -cu - li.
Et vi - tam ven-tú - ri saé -

185
190
saé-cu-li. A- - -men, a- - -men,
cu - li. A- - - -men, a- -
- -cu - li. A- - - -men, a- -
-cu-li. A - men, a- - -men, a- -
A- - -men, a- - - -
- -cu - li. A- - -men, a - men,

For a translation of the Agnus Dei, see NAWM 3.

15
De- - - -i, qui tol - lis pec - cá -
- - - -i, qui tol - lis pec-
De- - - - -i,] qui tol - lis,
A - gnus De- - - -i, qui tol - lis pec-cá - ta mun -
- - - -i, qui tol - lis pec - cá -
gnus De- - - -i,

20
ta mun- - -di, qui tol - lis pec - cá-ta mun -
cá-ta mun - di, qui tol - lis, qui
qui tol - lis pec- - - cá-ta mun - di,
- - - -di, qui tol - lispec - cá-ta mun- - -
ta mun- - -di, mun - di,
qui tol - lis pec - cá - ta mun- - -di,

25
di, qui tol-lis pec - cá - ta mun- - - -di,
tol - lis pec - cá-ta mun- - -di, qui tol - lis pec-
qui tol - lis pec - cá - ta mun di, qui tol-lis
- - - -di, qui tol - lis pec-
qui tol - lis pec - cá - ta mun- - - -di, qui
pec - cá - ta mun - di, qui tol -

30
35
qui tol - lis pec - cá - ta mun - di: mi - se-ré -
- cá - ta mun - - - - - di: mi - se - ré - re no-
pec - cá - ta mun - - di: mi - se-
- cá - ta mun - - - - di:
tol - lis pec - cá - ta mun - - di: mi - se-ré -
lis pec - cá - ta mun - - - - - di:
40
re no- - - - bis, mi - se - ré - re, mi - se-
- - - - bis, mi - se-ré-re no- -
ré - re no - bis, mi - se - ré - re no- - - - -
mi - se - ré - re no- - bis,
re no- - - - bis, mi-
mi - se-ré - re no- - -
45
ré - re no- - - - bis, mi - se - ré - re
bis, mi-se-ré - re no-bis, mi - se - ré - re no- -
- - - - bis, mi - se - ré - re no - bis, mi - se-
mi - se - ré - re no - - bis, mi - se-ré - re no-bis,
- se - ré - re no- - - bis, mi-
bis, mi - se-ré - re no -

The relation of this Mass to Pope Marcellus II, who reigned for twenty days in 1555, is uncertain. It is also not clear how the Mass relates to the reforms of the Council of Trent (1545–63), in which the use of polyphony in the church was discussed and deplored by some religious leaders. However, by adopting a transparent style of writing in this Mass, Palestrina countered the criticism that the text in much sacred polyphony could not be heard or understood.

The Credo is always a challenge to a composer because of the importance and length of the text. In this setting, Palestrina abandoned imitation for the sake of clear diction as well as brevity. The voices pronounce a given phrase, not in the staggered manner of imitative polyphony but simultaneously, etching the text in the hearer's consciousness. Palestrina could have employed *falsobordone*—a method that accomplishes this easily and that was used to harmonize the psalm tones in Italian and Spanish churches—as he did in his own *Improperia*. But he avoided its monotony by breaking up the six-voice choir into smaller groups, each with its particular tone color. He reserved the full six voices for climactic or particularly significant words, such as "per quem omnia facta sunt" (by whom all things were made) or "Et incarnatus est" (And was made incarnate). Other texts are sung by three, four, or five voices. Thus some voices do not sing some portions of the text, because there is very little of the usual imitation or repetition.

The section that begins at measure 13 illustrates this flexible approach to musical textures. The group C-A-TII-BI is answered by the group C-TI-TII-BII singing the same words, "Et in unum Dominum." Each group pronounces a segment of text in speech rhythm and has its own cadence, in both cases a weak one based on the major sixth-to-octave succession. The "Filium Dei unigenitum" (only-begotten Son of God) is sung by a trio, symbolizing the three-in-one essence of the Trinity, but the texture is now different—it is fauxbourdon resurrected. Fauxbourdon was frowned upon by Willaert's school as crude and uncouth, but Palestrina applied it to great effect here and elsewhere in the Credo. With its sixths and thirds, it provides relief from the almost constant fifth-third combinations, and it also evokes an aura of a distant, more devout age. Palestrina conserved forward motion by postponing closure. At measure 27 there is a perfect cadence, but it is weakened by the third in the top voice. A truly final cadence is reserved for the end of the next five-voice section, at the phrase "de Deo vero" (measure 38).

Palestrina also avoided monotony by rhythmic means. Accented syllables may occur on any of the beats, and only after a cadence is the normal alternation of down- and upbeat restored. For example, in the section "Et in unum Dominum" the listener hears the following alternation of triple, duple, and single beat units: 3 2 2 3 3 3 3 1 3 2 2.

The text of the Agnus Dei presents a different challenge. It has few words, which must be stretched out to produce a piece of sufficient weight to close the Mass. The composer has ample time for leisurely fugal expositions and development of motives. Palestrina seized the opportunity to indulge in his customary imitative style. Each of the six voices has a chance to sing the opening subject in a fugal exposition that lasts fifteen measures. "Qui tollis peccata mundi" is treated with closer imitations (later fittingly called *stretto,* which means "tight"). Voices sometimes enter only a quarter note apart (minims in the original notation). Each voice places accented syllables on different beats, spinning out its line at its own pace. In plainchant, the Agnus is sung three times; the last time, the phrase "dona nobis pacem" replaces "miserere nobis." In Palestrina's Mass, the first two statements are combined in Agnus Dei I; the third statement, Agnus Dei II (omitted in this anthology), is scored for seven voices.

Tomás Luis de Victoria (1548–1611) 48

O magnum mysterium CD 3

a) Motet

Motet from Victoria, *Motectae* (Venice, 1572), ed. Higini Anglès, in Victoria, *Opera omnia* (Barcelona: Instituto español de musicología, 1965–68), Monumentos de la música española, 26:7–9; Mass from Victoria, *Missae . . . liber secundus* (Rome, 1592), ed. Felipe Pedrell, Victoria, *Werke* (Leipzig: Breitkopf & Härtel, 1902–13), 2:6–9. Reproduced by permission of C.S.I.C.

20
le sa _ cra_men _ tum, ut a _ ni _ ma_li _ a vi _ de_rent Do_mi _
le sa _ cra _ men _ tum, ut a _ ni _ ma_li _ a vi _ de_rent Do_mi _
le sa_cra _ men _ tum, ut a _ ni_ma_li _ a, ut a _ ni _ ma_li _ a vi _ de_rent Do_mi _
le sa_cra _ men_ tum, ut a _ ni_ma_li _ a vi _ de_rent Do_mi _

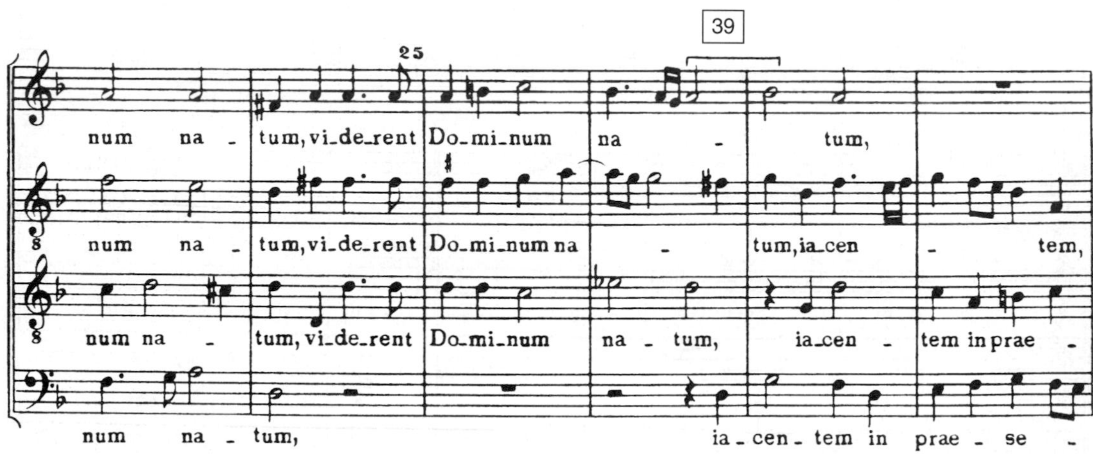
25
39
num na _ tum, vi_de_rent Do_mi_num na _ tum,
num na _ tum, vi_de_rent Do_mi_num na _ tum, ia_cen _ tem,
num na _ tum, vi_de_rent Do_mi_num na _ tum, ia_cen _ tem in prae _
num na _ tum, ia _ cen _ tem in prae _ se _

30
35
ia_cen _ tem in prae _ se _ pi _ o, ia_cen _
ia _ cen _ tem in prae _ se _ pi _ o, ia _ cen _ tem in
se _ _ pi _ o, ia _ cen _ tem in prae_se _ pi _
_ pi _ o, ia _ cen _ tem in prae _ se _ pi _

40
40
tem in prae - se - - pi - o. O be - a - ta
prae - se - - pi - o. O be - a - ta
o, in prae - se - - pi - o. O be - a - ta
o, in prae - ce - - pi - o. O be - a - ta

45
Vir - - go, cu - ius vis - ce - ra me - ru - e -
Vir - - go, cu - ius vi - sce - ra me - ru - e -
Vir - - go, cu - ius vi - sce - ra me - ru - e -
Vir - - go, cu - ius vi - sce - ra me - ru - e -

50
runt por - ta - re Do - mi - num Ie - sum Chri - stum. Al - le - lu -
runt por - ta - re Do - mi - num Ie - sum Chri - stum. Al - le - lu -
runt por - ta - re Do - mi - num Ie - sum Chri - stum. Al - le - lu -
runt Ie - sum Chri - stum.

O magnum mysterium, et admirabile
sacramentum, ut animalia
viderent Dominum natum,
iacentem in praesepio.
O beata Virgo,
cuius viscera meruerunt portare
Dominum Iesum Christum. Alleluia.

O great mystery and awesome
sacrament, that the animals
should see the Lord, newly born,
lying in the manger.
O blessed Virigin,
whose womb was worthy of bearing
the Lord Jesus Christ. Alleluia.

b) Mass: Kyrie

For the text of the Kyrie, see NAWM 3.

Like most of Victoria's Masses, this is based on one of his motets, *O magnum mysterium*, which was written for the feast of the Circumcision on January 1. The motet exploits a variety of textures and motives to express successively the mystery, wonder, and joy of the Christmas season.

The motet's fugal opening—paired entrances at the lower fifth, octave, and twelfth—is in strict Palestrina style, except for an expressive license in the subject, which, after an upward leap of a fifth, presses on in the same direction. The composer then turned to a declamatory delivery of the words "ut animalia viderent Dominum natum" (that the animals should see the Lord newly born), resuming the imitative method in the final clause of the sentence, "iacentem in praesepio" (lying in the manger). After a half-measure of silence, the entire choir solemnly exclaims, "O beata Virgo" (O blessed Virgin), the outer voices weaving a florid garland around the slower inner voices as they simultaneously pronounce "Virgo." A faster euphoric, triple-time, homophonic section articulates the exclamation "Alleluia," which continues to be reiterated in a melismatic coda that reverts to duple time.

In the Kyrie, Victoria reworked two of the motet's points of imitation. He converted the opening of the motet into a double fugue, using two related subjects fashioned from the motet's single subject. The Mass preserves the device of paired entrances and the harmonic relations between the voices. The Christe, as in other imitation Masses, utilizes a freely invented subject. On its return, the "Kyrie" borrows the music of the motet's "iacentem in praesepio" (measures 29–38), reworking the entrances and the counterpoint. Like Palestrina, Victoria strove for complete triadic harmony, although he preferred to end the Kyrie sections with the sound of the perfect consonances.

Orlando di Lasso (1532–1594)

49

Motet: *Tristis est anima mea* CD 3 CD 2

43 5

Cantus
Tri- stis ___

Altus 1
Tri- - stis ___ est ___ a- ni- ma

Altus 2
Tri- - stis ___ est a- ni- ma me- - a,

Tenor
Tri- stis est ___ a- ni- ma me- a, ⟨tri- - stis ___

Bassus
Tri- - stis ___ est a- ni- ma me- a, ___

"Tristis est anima mea," pp. 89–92 in Orlando di Lasso, *The Complete Motets* 4: Motets for Six Voices from *Primus liber concentuum sacrorum* (Paris, 1564); Motets for Four to Ten Voices from *Modulorum secundum volumen* (Paris, 1565), edited by Peter Bergquist, Recent Researches in the Music of the Renaissance, Vol. 105 (Madison, Wisc.: A-R Editions, Inc., 1996). Used by permission.

44
6
mor- tem: su- - sti- ne-
-que ad mor- tem: su- - sti- ne- te hic, ⟨su- sti-
_ ad mor- tem:⟩ su- - sti- ne- te hic, ⟨su- sti- ne-
ad mor- tem:⟩ su- sti- ne- te ___ hic, et vi- gi-
mor- tem: su- - sti- ne- te hic,
19
-te hic, et vi- gi- la- te me- cum, et vi- gi- la- te
-ne- te hic,⟩ et vi- gi- la- - te me- cum, et vi- gi-
- te hic,⟩ et vi- gi- la- te me- - cum, et vi- gi-
-la- te me- cum, et vi- gi- la- te me- cum, ___
et vi- gi- la- - te me- - cum, et vi-
45
7
24
me- - - - cum: ___
-la- te me- - cum, et ⟨vi- gi- la- te me- cum:⟩ nunc vi-
-la- te me- cum, et ⟨vi- gi- la- te me- - cum:⟩ nunc vi-
___ et ⟨vi- gi- la- te me- - cum:⟩ nunc vi-
- gi- la- - te me- cum: nunc vi-

29
nunc vi- de- bi- tis, nunc vi de bi tis tur-
-de- bi- tis, nunc vi- de- bi- tis, ⟨nunc vi- de- bi- tis⟩ tur-
-de- bi- tis, nunc vi- de- bi- tis, ⟨nunc vi- de- bi- tis⟩ tur-
-de- bi- tis, nunc vi- de- bi- tis, ⟨nunc vi- de- bi- tis⟩ tur-
-de- bi- tis, ⟨nunc vi- de- bi- tis⟩ tur- bam,
35
-bam, quae cir cum da bit me, ⟨quae cir- cum- da- bit me:⟩
-bam, quae cir- cum- da- bit me, quae cir- cum- da- bit
-bam, quae cir- cum- da- bit me, ⟨quae cir- cum- da- bit me,⟩ quae
-bam, quae cir- cum- da- bit me, quae cir- cum- da bit me, ⟨quae cir- cum-
quae cir- cum- da- bit me, quae ⟨cir- cum- da- bit me,⟩ quae cir- cum- da- bit me,
46
8
40
vos fu- gam ca- pi- e- tis, vos fu- gam
me: vos fu- gam ca- pi- e-
cir- cum- da- bit me: vos fu- gam ca- pi- e-
-da- bit me,⟩ quae cir- cum- da- bit me: vos fu- gam ca- pi-
⟨quae cir- cum- da- bit me:⟩ vos fu- gam ca- pi- e- tis,

45
ca- pi- e- tis, ⟨vos fu- gam ca- pi- e- tis,⟩ et e- go va- dam
-tis, vos ⟨fu- gam ca- pi- e- tis,⟩ et e- go va- dam
-tis, vos ⟨fu- gam ca- pi- e- tis,⟩ et e- go va- dam
-e- tis, vos ⟨fu- gam ca- pi- e- - tis,⟩ et e- go va- dam
⟨vos fu- gam ca- pi- e- - tis,⟩ et e- go va- dam
51
im- mo- la- ri, et e- go va- dam im- - mo- la- - ri, ⟨et
im- mo- la- ri, et e- go va- dam im- - mo- la- ri, et ⟨e-
im- mo- la- - ri, et e- go va- dam im- mo- - la- ri, ⟨et
im- mo- la- ri, et e- go va- dam im- - mo- la- ri, et
im- mo- la- ri, ⟨et
57
e- go va- dam im- - mo- la- ri⟩ pro vo- bis.
- go va- dam im- - mo- la- ri⟩ pro vo- bis.
e- go va- dam im- mo- la- ri⟩ pro vo- bis.
⟨e- go va- dam im- - mo- la- ri⟩ pro vo- bis.
e- go va- dam im- - mo- la- ri⟩ pro vo- bis.

Tristis est anima mea usque ad mortem: sustinete hic et vigilate mecum: nunc videbitis turbam, quae circumdabit me: vos fugam capietis, et ego vadam immolari pro vobis.	Sad is my soul, even unto death; abide here and watch with me; soon you will see the crowd that will encircle me; you will take flight, and I shall go to be sacrificed for you.

This setting of the Respond for Maundy Thursday was published in 1565 and again in the *Magnus opus musicum*, a collection of Lasso's motets issued posthumously in 1604 by his sons. The text is based on the words of Jesus before he was crucified, as reported by Matthew (26:38) and Mark (14:34).

Lasso was famous in his own time for his forceful and imaginative projection of his texts. *Tristis est anima mea* is one of his most deeply moving and vivid settings. The descending-semitone motive, first heard in the bass on "Tristis" (sad) dominates the first nine measures. A consonant suspension in the first two measures prepares the more pungent dissonant suspension in the alto and the unusual suspension in the soprano, which resolves on the downbeat instead of the upbeat. This use of the suspension to achieve emotional tension rather than to prepare a cadence had become common in the mid-century madrigal but was still rare in sacred music. The word "mortem" (death) is underscored with a plagal cadence ending on a hollow chord lacking a third.

The next phrase of the text is split into two units because of their different connotations. "Sustinete" is interpreted not only in the sense of "abide" but also "hold up," for the harmony rises with hesitation in a series of fifths, sixths, and thirds among the parts. The fast motion at "vigilate" (watch out), on the other hand, suggests wakefulness (Jesus reproached his disciples several times for falling asleep on their watch). Lasso avoided a proper cadence at the end of this section (measure 27) to open the way for the declamatory proclamation "nunc videbis" (soon you will see), repeated with increasing fervor at a higher pitch and with fuller sound.

Lasso now resorted to madrigalistic word-painting for "circumdabit me" (will encircle me), illustrated by a circular melodic figure imitated in all the parts, and for "vos fugam capietis" (you will take flight), portrayed by a fugal stretto in which the subject takes off eleven times (like the eleven disciples who ran away when the twelfth, Judas, joined the angry crowd that beat and captured Jesus). Once again Lasso avoided a cadence, impatient to proclaim, note-against-note in all the voices, "et ego vadam immolari pro vobis" (and I shall go to be sacrificed for you).

To end the motet (measure 60), the composer returned to imitation, by both direct and contrary motion, stepping up the pace to the semiminim level (eighth notes in the transcription), over a pedal point, as if to suggest a sprinkling of grains of wheat (*mola*) over the sacrificial victim (the original meaning of *immolare*). Fittingly, this surge of activity leads to the only really full cadence in the work, marking the only period in the Latin text. Thus the words of the respond stimulated not only the rhythms, accents, and contours of the musical motives but the composer's every gesture: harmonic effects, textures, constructive devices such as suspensions and fugal imitation, the weight and placement of cadences, and, of course, clever allusions.

William Byrd

Full Anthem: *Sing joyfully unto God* CD 3 CD 2

The Byrd Edition, Vol. II: *The English Anthems*, ed. Craig Monson (London: Stainer & Bell Ltd., 1983), pp. 82–90. ©1983 Stainer & Bell Ltd. Reproduced by permission. The pitch has been transposed up a major third from C to E♭ to conform with how, it is believed, the original scheme of clefs was read.

10
48
10
- to God our strength, our strength. Sing loud, sing
strength, un - to God our strength. Sing loud, sing loud
Sing loud, sing
our strength, un - to God our strength. Sing loud, un -
strength, our strength, our strength. Sing loud, sing loud,
Sing loud, sing
15
loud, sing loud un - to the God of Ja -
un - to the God of Ja - - - cob, un - to the God of Ja - - -
loud un - to the God of Ja - cob, un-to the God of Ja -
- to the God of Ja - cob, un - to the God of Ja - - - -
un - to the God of Ja - - - cob, the God of Ja -
loud un - to the God of Ja - cob, un - to the God of Ja -

49
11
- cob. Take the song, and bring forth —
- cob. Take the song, and — bring - forth the
- cob. Take the song, the — song, the song, and bring
- cob. Take the song, take the song, the song,
- cob. Take the song, take the song, the — song, and bring forth —
- cob. Take the song, take the song,
20
— the tim - brel, the plea-sant harp
tim brel, and bring forth — the tim - brel, the plea-sant
forth the tim - brel, and bring forth the tim - brel, the tim - -
and bring forth the tim - - - brel,
— the tim - brel, and bring forth the tim - brel, the
and bring forth — the tim - brel,

25
and the vi - - ol,
harp, the plea-sant harp and the vi -
-brel, the plea-sant harp and the vi - ol,
the plea-sant harp and the vi - ol, the plea - sant harp,
plea-sant harp and the vi - ol, the plea - sant
the plea - sant harp, the plea-sant harp and the vi - ol, and the
30
the plea-sant harp and the vi - ol, and the vi - - ol.
-ol and the vi - - ol. Blow the trum-pet
the vi - ol, and the vi - - - - ol.
the plea-sant harp and the vi - - - ol. Blow the trum-pet
harp, the plea-sant harp and the vi - ol. Blow the trum-pet
vi - ol, and the vi - ol. Blow the trum-pet

Blow the trum-pet in the new moon, in the new moon, in the new
in the new moon, in the new moon, in the new moon,
Blow the trum-pet in the new moon, blow the trum-pet in the new
in the new moon, in the new moon, blow the trum-pet in the new moon,
in the new moon, blow ___ the trum-pet in the new moon, in the new
in the new moon, blow the trum-pet in the new moon, ___
35
moon, blow the trum-pet in the new moon, in the new moon,
blow the trum-pet in the new moon, in the new moon,
moon, blow the trum-pet in the new moon,
blow the trum-pet in the new moon, blow the trum - pet in ___ the new moon,
moon, blow the trum-pet in the new moon, in ___ the new moon, —
blow the trum-pet in the new moon, blow the trum - pet in the new moon, —

40
ev'n in the time ap - point -
ev'n in the time ap - point - ed, ap - point - ed, ev'n in the time ap -
ev'n in the time ap - point-ed, ev'n in the time ap -
ev'n in the time ap-point - - - ed, ev'n in the
ev'n in the time ap - point - - ed, ev'n in the time ap -
ev'n in the time ap - point - - - - ed,
45
- - - ed, and at our feast day, our feast
- point - ed, and at our feast day, and
- point - - - - - - ed, and at our feast
time ap-point - ed, and at our feast day, and
- point - ed, and at our feast day,
ev'n in the time ap - point - ed, and at our

50
50
12
day, and at our feast day. For
at our feast day, and at our feast day.
day, our feast day, and at our feast day. For
at our feast day, and at our feast day. For
and at our feast day, our feast day. For
feast day, and at our feast day. For
this is a sta-tute for Is - ra - el, and a
For this is a sta-tute for Is - ra - el,
this is a sta - tute for Is - ra - el,
this is a sta-tute for Is - ra - el, and a law
this, for this is a sta-tute for Is - ra - el,
this is a sta - tute for Is - ra - el, and a

55
law of the God of Ja - cob, of ___ Ja - - - - cob,
of the God ___ of Ja - cob,
and a law of the
of the God of Ja - - - cob,
and ___ a law of the God ___
and a law of the God of Ja - cob,
law of the God of Ja - cob, of Ja - cob, and a law of the
60
of the God of Ja - - - cob,
and a law of the God of Ja - - - - cob,
God of Ja - cob,
and a law of the
___ of Ja - - cob, of the God of ___ Ja - cob,
and a law of the God ___ of Ja - - cob, of the God ___
God of Ja - cob, of Ja - - cob,
of the God of

65
and a law of the God of Ja - - cob, and a
of the God of Ja - - - - - cob, and a
God of Ja - cob, and a law of the God of Ja - - -
and a law of the God of Ja - cob, of Ja - cob,
of Ja - - cob, Ja - cob, and a law of the God of Ja -
Ja - cob, of the God of Ja - cob, and a law
70
law of the God of Ja - - - - - - - - cob.
law of the God of Ja - - - - - cob.
- cob, of the God of Ja - - - - - cob.
and a law of the God of Ja - - - - - - cob.
- cob, of the God of Ja - - cob.
of the God of Ja - - - - - cob.

This setting of the first four verses of Psalm 81 was one of the most popular of Byrd's anthems. It belongs to the category of full anthem, which is the English equivalent of a choral motet, as opposed to the verse anthem, which was scored for soloists with instrumental accompaniment. Some of the sources for the full anthems include an organ accompaniment, but it is probably not by Byrd.

A comparison with the compositional methods of Palestrina, Lasso, and Victoria helps isolate the traits that are distinctively Byrd's. Cadences are more frequent, imitation is almost constant but freer, homophony is rare, and the voice lines are more angular and energetic.

The cadences, limited to the tonic and dominant (apart from one on the dominant of the dominant in measure 23), make the structure clear and anchor the work solidly in the major mode. The opening point of imitation, involving only four of the six parts, treats the subject freely, answering the rising fifth with a second, fourth, and octave. Vigorous leaps, which Byrd and Lasso used more often than the other two composers, bring to life texts such as "Sing loud" (measures 10ff.) or "Take the song, and bring forth the timbrel" (tenor, measures 16ff.). A line made up almost entirely of leaps—even two successive rising fourths (the bass at measure 14)—is not unusual. A conspicuous evocation of the text stands out in the fanfares at "Blow the trumpet in the new moon" (measures 30–38). Homophonic texture is infrequent. The vertical harmony at measures 50–54 must have been inspired by the text "For this is a statute." Similarly, the music on the final line, "and a law of the God of Jacob," illustrates the idea of rule through a long fugal section.

Byrd paid close attention to the rhythm of the words as well as their meaning. Unstressed syllables are pronounced or begin on weak beats. Stressed syllables fall on the down- or upbeat of the *alla breve* measure (whole notes of the transcription) or are accented by syncopation.

GIULIO CACCINI (CA. 1550–1618)

51

Madrigal: *Vedrò 'l mio sol* CD 3

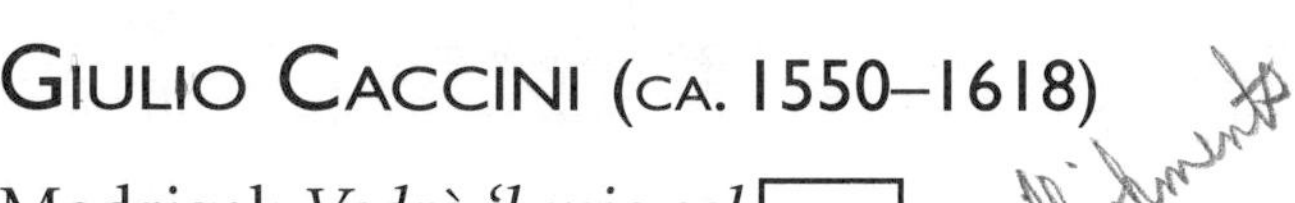

Le nuove musiche (Florence, 1602). H. Wiley Hitchcock, ed., *Giulio Caccini: Le nuove musiche* in Recent Researches in the Music of the Baroque Era, Vol. 9 (Madison, Wisc.: A-R Editions, Inc., 1970), pp. 81–85. Reprinted by permission. Abbreviations used in the score—*senza mis.*: *senza misura*, freely, without beating the measure; *escl.*: *esclamazione*, a decrescendo after attacking a note, followed by a sforzando.

15
[escl]
[tr]
O mia lu- ce, o mia gio- ia, O mia lu- ce, o mia gio-
[senza mis.]
20
[tr] [rit.]
ia, Ben più m'è dol- c'il tor- men- tar per vu- i Che'l gio- ir per al- tru-
52
[a tempo]
25 [escl]
i. Ma sen- za mor- te io non po- trò sof- fri- re Un sì lun-
30
- go mar- ti- re; E s'io mor- rò, mor- rà mia spe- me an-

35 [senza mis.]
co- ra Di ve- der mai d'un sì bel dì, di ve- der mai d'un sì bel
[a tempo]
40
[tr]
dì l'au- ro- ra, d'un sì bel dì l'au- ro- ra.
45
O mia lu- ce,o mia gio - ia, O mia
[tr]
[senza mis.]
50
lu- ce,o mia gio- ia, Ben più m'è dol- c'il tor- men- tar per vu-

53
[rit.]
[tr]
[a tempo]
55
i Che'l gio- ir per al- tru- i. Ma sen- za mor-te io non po-
6
11
10
14
trò sof- fri- re Un sì lun- go mar-
60
ti - re; E s'io morrò, morrà mia spe- me an- co-
[tr]
11
10
[senza mis.]
65
[a tempo]
ra Di ve- der mai d'un sì bel dì, di ve- der mai d'un sì bel dì l'au- ro-

Vedrò 'l mio sol, vedrò prima ch'io muoia	I'll see my sun; before I die.
Quel sospirato giorno	I'll see that wished-for day,
Che faccia 'l vostro raggio à me ritorno.	when your ray returns to me.
O mia luce, o mia gioia,	O my light, O my joy,
Ben più m'è dolc' il tormentar per vui	much sweeter is my torment for you
Che 'l gioir per altrui.	than delight in others.
Ma senza morte io non potrò soffrire	But without death I cannot suffer
Un sì lungo martire;	such a long martyrdom.
E s'io morrò, morrà mia speme ancora	And if I die, will die my hope
Di veder mai d'un sì bel dì l'aurora.	to see ever again the dawn of such a beautiful day.
—Giovanni Battista or Alessandro Guarini	

Caccini boasted in his foreword to *Le nuove musiche* that this madrigal was among those received "with loving applause" in Bardi's Camerata around 1590. Each line of poetry is set as a separate phrase, ending either in a cadence or in a sustained note or pair of notes. This convention (and the many repeated notes in speech rhythm) was characteristic of the airs improvised on melodic formulas throughout the sixteenth century. At a number of the cadences, Caccini wrote out the embellishments that singers customarily added, for example at the words "muoia" (measure 7) and "aurora" (measures 70–72). Caccini, himself a singer, indicated the ornaments because he did not trust others to improvise appropriately. Other refinements that Caccini considered essential to performance—although not always indicated in the score—are crescendos and decrescendos, trills and turns (called *gruppi* or *groppi*), rapid repetitions of the same pitch (called *trilli*), *esclamazioni*—decrescendo after attacking a note, then sforzando—and departures from strict observance of the printed note values, or what we call *tempo rubato*. He described these and gave examples of some of them in his foreword. The editor of *Vedrò 'l mio sol* has suggested the placement of some of these effects in brackets.

For emotional effect, Caccini borrows from oratory the device of heightened repetition, as in measures 35–37 and 43–48. He repeats the text and music of the last lines, as was customary in the polyphonic madrigal. However, he forsakes contrapuntal part-writing for a simple chordal accompaniment cued by a figured bass, in order that the words and melody will hit the listener with full force. Hardly a trace of modality remains in this tonally organized song in G major, with modulations to the dominant and relative minor.

Jacopo Peri (1561–1633)

52

Le musiche sopra l'Euridice CD 3

a) Prologue, Tragedy: *Io, che d'alti sospir*

PROLOGUE: TRAGEDY

1. Io, che d'alti sospir vaga e di pianti,
   Spars' or di doglia, hor di minaccie il volto,
   Fei negl'ampi teatri al popol folto
   Scolorir di pietà volti e sembianti.

   I, who with deep sighs and tears am smitten,
   my face, covered now with grief, now with menace,
   once in ample theatres crowded with people
   made their faces turn pale with pity.

2. Non sangue sparso d'innocenti vene,
   Non ciglia spente di tiranno insano,
   Spettacolo infelice al guardo umano,
   Canto su meste e lagrimose scene.

   Not of blood spilled from innocent veins,
   nor of eyes put out by an insane tyrant,
   but of a spectacle unhappy to human sight,
   do I sing on this sad and tearful stage.

3. Lungi via, lungi pur da' regi tetti
   Simulacri funesti, ombre d'affanni:
   Ecco i mesti coturni e i foschi panni
   Cangio, e desto ne i cor più dolci affetti.

   Stay far from under this royal roof,
   dismal images, shadows of anguish.
   Behold, the gloomy buskins and the dark rags
   I transform, and awaken in the hearts sweeter
   affections.

Note values reduced by half. Original barring retained. Time signatures added by the editor are in brackets; editorial accidentals are above the staff. In the Prologue, the composer intended that rhythmic adjustments be made in the strophes. Peri, *Le musiche sopra l'Euridice* (Florence, 1601), pp. 2, 11–12, 14–17.

4. Hor s'avverrà che le cangiate forme
Non senza alto stupor la terra ammiri.

Tal ch'ogni alma gentil ch'Apollo inspiri
Del mio novo cammin calpesti l'orme,

Now, if it should happen that the changed forms
not without great amazement the world should admire,
so that every gentle genius whom Apollo inspires
takes up the tracks of my new path,

5. Vostro, Regina, fia cotanto alloro,
Qual forse anco non colse Atene, o Roma,
Fregio non vil su l'onorata chioma,
Fronda Febea fra due corone d'oro.

Yours, Queen, will be so much laurel
that perhaps not even Athens or Rome won more,
no mean ornament on the honored head,
a leafy branch of Phoebus between two crowns.

6. Tal per voi torno, e con sereno aspetto
Ne' reali Imenei m'adorno anch'io,
E su corde più liete il canto mio
Tempro, al nobile cor dolce diletto.

Thus for you I return, and with a serene countenance
at this royal wedding I too adorn myself,
and with happier notes my song
I temper, for the noble heart's sweet delight.

7. Mentre Senna real prepara intanto
Alto diadema, onde il bel crin si fregi

E i manti e' seggi de gl'antichi regi,
Del Tracio Orfeo date l'orecchie al canto.

Meanwhile the royal Seine prepares
a lofty diadem with which the beautiful hair to crown
and the cloaks and thrones of ancient kings;
to the song of the Thracian Orpheus, lend your ears.

b) Tirsi: *Nel pur ardor*

TIRSI

Nel pur ardor della più bella stella
Aurea facella di bel foc'accendi,
E qui discendi su l'aurate piume,
Giocondo Nume, e di celeste fiamma
L'anime infiamma.

With the pure flame of the brightest star
light the golden torch with beautiful fire
and here descend on golden wings,
O happy god, and with celestial fire
the souls inflame.

Lieto Imeneo d'alta dolcezza un nembo
Trabocca in grembo a' fortunati amanti
E tra bei canti di soavi amori
Sveglia nei cori una dolce aura, un riso
Di Paradiso.

Happy Hymen, let your shower of lofty sweetness
overflow into the breasts of the fortunate lovers
and, amidst pretty songs of delightful loves,
stir in their hearts a gentle breeze, a smile
of Paradise.

c) Dafne: *Per quel vago boschetto*
Arcetro: *Che narri, ohimè*
Orfeo: *Non piango e non sospiro*

piè sul ver - de pra - to, Quand'ahi ria sor - te a - cer - ba! An-gue cru-do, e spie-
25
ta - to, Che ce-la - to gia-cea tra' fio - ri e l'er - ba, Pun - se-le il piè con si ma-
li - gno den - te, Ch'im-pa-li - dì re-pen - te Co-me rag- gio di sol che nu - be a
30
dom bri E dal pro-fon-do co-re Con un so-spir mor-ta - le Si spa-ven-to-so ohi-mè so-spin-se
35
fuo - re. Che, qua-si a-ves - se l'a - le, Giun-se o-gni Nin - fa al do-lo-ro - so suo - no, Et

el - la in ab-ban-do - no Tut-ta la - scios - si all' or nel-l'al - trui brac - cia. Spar-gea il bel vol -
to, e le do-ra - te chio-me Un su-dor viè più fred-d'as-sai che giac - cio. In - di s'u-dio'l tuo
no-me Tra le-lab-bra so-nar fred-d'e' tre-man-ti E, vol - ti gl'oc - chi al cie - lo, Sco-lo -
ri - to il bel vol-to, e' bei sem-bian-ti, Res-tò tan - ta bel-lez-za im - mo - bil gie
58
ARCETRO
lo. Che nar - ri, ohi - mè, che sen - to? Mi - se-ra Nin - fa, e

ORFEO
più mi - se-ro a-man - te, Spet - ta - col di mi - se - ria e di tor - men - to! Non
pian - go e non sos - pi - ro, O mia ca - ra Eu - ri - di - ce, Ché sos - pi - rar,
ché la - cri - mar non pos - so. Ca - da - ve-ro in - fe - li - ce, O mio co - re o mia
spe - me, o pa - ce, o vi - ta! Ohi - mè, chi mi t'ha tol - to, Chi mi t'ha
tol - to, o - hi - mè! do - ve sei gi - ta?

DAFNE

Per quel vago boschetto,	In the beautiful thicket,
Ove, rigando i fiori,	where, watering the flowers,
Lento trascorre il fonte degl'allori,	slowly courses the spring of the laurel,
Prendea dolce diletto	she took sweet delight
Con le compagne sue la bella sposa,	with her companions—the beautiful bride—
Chi violetta o rosa	as some picked violets, others roses,
Per far ghirland' al crine	to make garlands for their hair,
Togliea dal prato o dall'acute spine,	in the meadow or among the sharp thorns.
E qual posand' il fianco	Another, lying on her side
Su la fiorita sponda	on the flowered bank,
Dolce cantava al mormorar dell' onda;	sang sweetly to the murmur of the waves.
Ma la bella Euridice	But the lovely Eurydice
Movea danzando il piè sul verde prato	dancingly moved her feet on the green grass
Quand'ahi ria sorte acerba,	when—O bitter, angry fate!—
Angue crudo e spietato	a snake, cruel and merciless,
Che celato giacea tra fiori e l'erba	that lay hidden among flowers and grass
Punsele il piè con si maligno dente,	bit her foot with such an evil tooth
Ch'impalidì repente	that she suddenly became pale
Come raggio di sol che nube adombri.	like a ray of sunshine that a cloud darkens.
El dal profondo core,	And from the depths of her heart,
Con un sospir mortale,	a mortal sigh,
Si spaventoso ohimè sospinse fuore,	so frightful, alas, flew forth,
Che, quasi avesse l'ale,	almost as if it had wings;
Giunse ogni Ninfa al doloroso suono.	every nymph rushed to the painful sound.
Et ella in abbandono	And she, fainting,
Tutta lasciossi all'or nell'altrui braccia.	let herself fall in another's arms.
Spargea il bel volto e le dorate chiome	Then spread over her beautiful face and her golden tresses
Un sudor viè più fredd'assai che giaccio.	a sweat colder by far than ice.

Indi s'udio 'l tuo nome Tra le labbra sonar fredd'e' tremanti E volti gl'occhi al cielo, Scolorito il bel volto e' bei sembianti, Restò tanta bellezza immobil gielo.	And then was heard your name, sounding between her lips, cold and trembling, and her eyes turned to heaven, her beautiful face and mien discolored, this great beauty was transformed to motionless ice.
	ARCETRO
Che narri, ohimè, che sento? Misera Ninfa, e più misero amante, Spettacol di miseria e di tormento!	What do you relate, alas, what do I hear? Wretched nymph, and more unhappy lover, spectacle of sorrow and of torment!
	ORFEO
Non piango e non sospiro, O mia cara Euridice, Ché sospirar, ché lacrimar non posso. Cadavero infelice, O mio core, o mia speme, o pace, o vita! Ohimè, chi mi t'ha tolto, Chi mi t'ha tolto, ohimè! dove sei gita? Tosto vedrai ch'in vano Non chiamasti morendo il tuo consorte. Non son, non son lontano: Io vengo, o cara vita, o cara morte. —Ottavio Rinuccini	I do not weep, nor do I sigh, O my dear Eurydice, for I am unable to sigh, to weep. Unhappy corpse, O my heart, O my hope, O peace, O life! Alas, who has taken you from me? Who has taken you away, alas? Where have you gone? Soon you will see that not in vain did you, dying, call your spouse. I am not far away; I come, O dear life, O dear death.

Euridice, on a text by Ottavio Rinuccini (1562–1621), with music by Jacopo Peri, is the earliest opera to survive in a complete score. It was produced for the wedding in 1600 of Henry IV of France and Maria de' Medici in Florence (though the music for some of the parts was then replaced by Caccini's version) and published the following year.

The three excerpts from Peri's *Euridice* illustrate three styles of monody found in this work. Only one of the styles is truly new. The Prologue (a) is modeled on the strophic aria for singing verses as practiced throughout the sixteenth century. Each line of verse is sung to a melodic scheme that consists of a repeated pitch and a cadential pattern ending in two sustained notes. A ritornello separates the strophes.

Tirsi's song (b) is also a kind of aria, but it is markedly rhythmic and tuneful, and the cadences at the ends of lines are harmonically stronger, being mostly dominant–tonic. It is framed by a "symphony" that despite its brevity is the longest purely instrumental interlude in the score.

Finally, Dafne's speech and the reactions to it of Arcetro and Orfeo (c) are true examples of the new recitative. The chords specified by the basso continuo and its figures have no rhythmic profile or formal plan and are there only to support the voice's recitation, which is free to imitate the rhythms of speech. The voice returns frequently to pitches consonant with the harmony on the main accents of the poetic line, but it wanders from the chordal tones of the accompaniment on syllables that would not be sustained in a spoken recitation. Only some line endings are marked by cadences; many are elided.

In the midst of preparations for the wedding of the legendary musician Orfeo and the nymph Euridice, Dafne reports that Euridice, while picking flowers to make a garland for her hair, was bitten by a snake and died. There is a natural progression in Dafne's speech; at first it is emotionally neutral, consonant, and slow-changing harmonically. As she tells of Euridice's fatal snakebite, it becomes more excited, with more dissonances, sudden changes of harmony, and fewer cadences, and the bass moves more quickly.

The responses to the news by Arcetro and Orfeo are also in the new recitative style but made more lyrical by the melodic construction with quasi-repetitions and sequences.

53

Claudio Monteverdi (1567–1643)

Madrigal: *Cruda Amarilli* CD 3 CD 2

ahi las - so
las - - so
las - - so Che col no-me anco - ra D'a-mar
las - so Che col no-m'anco - ra D'a-mar ahi
las - - so Che col no-m'anco - ra D'a-mar ahi

18
ahi las - so a-ma - ra - men-te a-ma - ra - men-te in-
ahi las - so a-ma - ra - men-te a-ma - ra - men - te in-
las - - - so a - ma - ra - men - te in -

61
15
A - ma - ril - li A - - ma - ril - li
A - ma - ril - li A - ma - ril - - li
- se - - gni A - ma - - ril-li A - - ma - ril - li
- se - - gni A - ma - ril - li A - - ma - ril - li
- se - - gni A - ma - ril - li

62
16
30
del can - di - do li - gu - stro Più can - di - da e più bel - la
del can - di - do li - gu - stro Più can - di - da e più bel - la Ma del -
del can - di - do li - gu - stro Più can - di - da e più bel - la
(♯)
del can - di - do li - gu - stro Più can - di - da e più bel - la Ma del - l'A - spi - do
Ma de l'Aspi - do sor - do E più sor - da
- l'a - spi - do sor - do E più sor - da e
Ma del - l'A - spi - do sor - - do E più sor - da
sor - - - - do E più sor - da
Ma del - l'A - spido sor - - do E più sor - da
63
17
41
e più fe - ra e più fu - ga - ce e più fu - ga - ce
più fe - ra e più fu - ga - ce e più fu - ga - ce Poi che col
e più fe - ra e più fu - ga - ce e più fu - ga - ce Poi che col dir t'of -
e più fe - ra e più fu - ga - ce e più fu - ga - ce
e più fe - ra e più fu - ga - ce e più fu - ga - ce Poi che col dir t'of -

1) Nell'originale:

Cruda Amarilli che col nome ancora
D'amar, ahi lasso, amaramente insegni.
Amarilli del candido ligustro,
Più candida e più bella,
Ma dell'aspido sordo
E più sorda e più fera e più fugace.
Poi che col dir t'offendo
I mi morò tacendo.
—Giovanni Battista Guarini

Cruel Amaryllis, who with your name
to love, alas, bitterly you teach.
Amaryllis, more than the white privet
pure, and more beautiful,
but deafer than the asp,
and fiercer and more elusive.
Since telling I offend you,
I shall die in silence.

The text of this madrigal, a speech from Giovanni Battista Guarini's *Il pastor fido*, is one of eleven in Monteverdi's fifth book of madrigals (1605) that are drawn from this pastoral verse play. Here, in the second scene from the first act, Mirtillo complains that Amaryllis is spurning his love. The speech begins with a pun on the name Amarilli, whose stem "amar" can be a contraction either of "amare" (to love) or "amaro" (bitter). With her name, Mirtillo protests, Amaryllis teaches how to love bitterly. Monteverdi seized the bitter mood of the opening words "Cruda Amarilli" with the canto's suspended seventh against the bass; this resolves in an even more biting dissonance, a minor ninth. The same pattern is then repeated a fourth higher. But then, echoing the text's sardonic humor, Monteverdi lightens the mood by setting the next half-line in a dancelike dotted rhythm that takes us without a pause into the next line, which mixes the jeering laughter of sixteenth notes with the crudest dissonances of the piece.

This madrigal was already in circulation in 1598, the date of an imaginary dialogue in which these violations of the contrapuntal rules for the treatment of dissonance were criticized in Giovanni Maria Artusi's *L'Artusi overo delle imperfettioni*

*SRrev, p. 528: 4: 20.

della moderna musica (The Artusi, or Imperfections of Modern Music) of 1600. One interlocutor in the dialogue particularly objected to measures 12–14, which he quoted,* pointing out that the soprano part in measure 13 failed to agree with the bass. The *A*, a ninth, appears out of nowhere and leaps to a seventh, *F*. The other interlocutor in the dialogue defends the passage, arguing that if one imagines a *G* on the first beat of the soprano part, the figure is like an *accento*, an improvised embellishment common at this time, replacing the stepwise motion *G–F–E* with *G–A–F–E*. Such written-out embellishments, or diminutions, as they were called, also season the harmony with runs in measure 12. The grating dissonances of measure 2 can also be explained as the diminution of the leaps *D–B* and *B–G* in the upper parts. Although some of Monteverdi's dissonances may thus be rationalized as embellishments, their real motivation was to convey through harmony, rather than through the graphic images of some earlier madrigals, the meaning and feeling of the poet's message. In his preface to the fifth book of madrigals of 1605, in which this composition was published, Monteverdi called his approach a second practice (*seconda pratica*) that set composers free to violate, for the sake of expressing a text, some of the strict rules of the first practice taught in the manuals on counterpoint.

Cruda Amarilli typifies the flexible, animated, evocative, and variegated style of Monteverdi's polyphonic madrigals. It is rich in musical invention, humorous yet sensitive, and audacious yet perfectly logical in its harmonies.

CLAUDIO MONTEVERDI

54

L'Orfeo

a) Prologue, La Musica: *Dal mio Permesso* CD 4

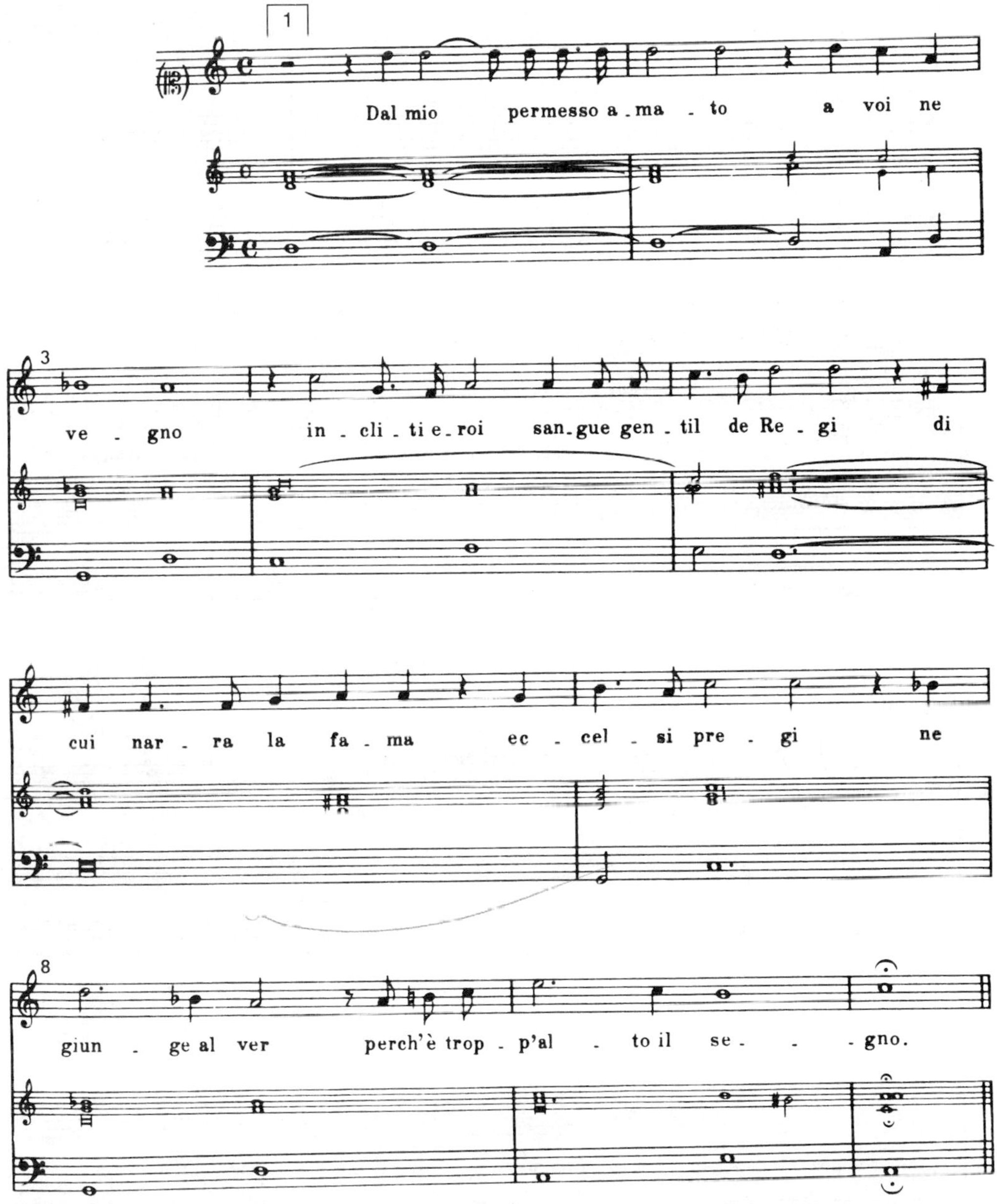

1
Dal mio permesso a - ma - to a voi ne
3
ve - gno in - cli - ti e - roi san - gue gen - til de Re - gi di
cui nar - ra la fa - ma ec - cel - si pre - gi ne
8
giun - ge al ver perch'è trop - p'al - to il se - - - gno.

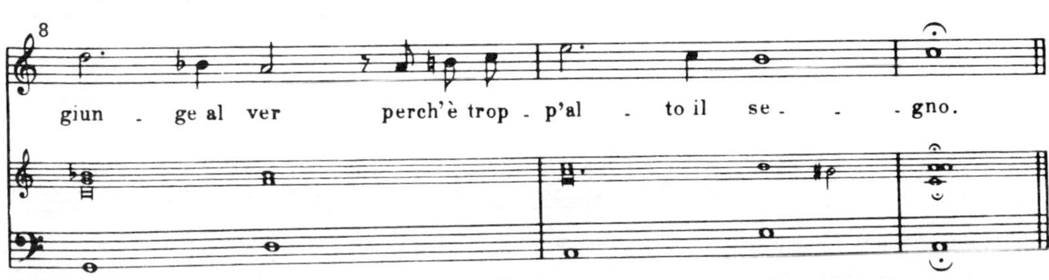

Ritornello
11

14
2
Io la mu_si_ca son ch'ai dol_ci ac_cen_ - _ti so far tranquil_lo
p

o_gni tur_ba - to co - re et hor di no_bi - l'i - ra et hor d'a_

19
_mo_re pos - - - - s'in - fiammar le più ge_la - te men - ti.

Ritornello

3
25
Io su ce-te-ra d'or cantan-do so - glio mor-tal o-rec-chio

lu-sin-gar ta-l'ho - ra e in que - sta gui - sa a l'ar-mo-

30
-nia so-no-ra de la li - ra del ciel più l'al - me in-vo - glio,

Ritornello

36
4
Quin - ci a dir - vi d'Orfeo de - sio mi spro - - - na, d'Or - feo che tras - se
p

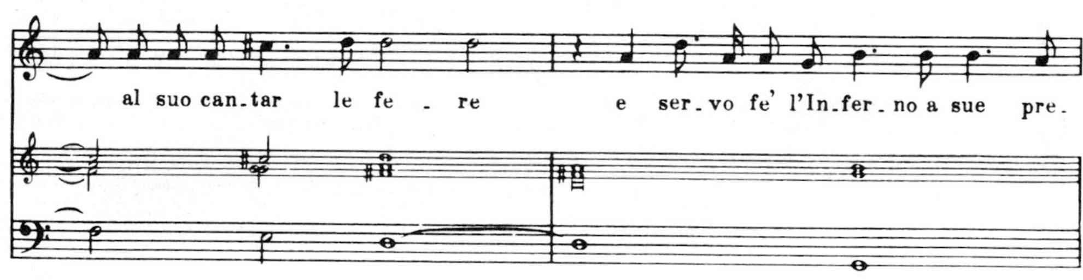
al suo can - tar le fe - re e ser - vo fe' l'In - fer - no a sue pre -

41
- ghie - re Glo - ria immortal di Pin - do e d'E - li - co - na.

Ritornello

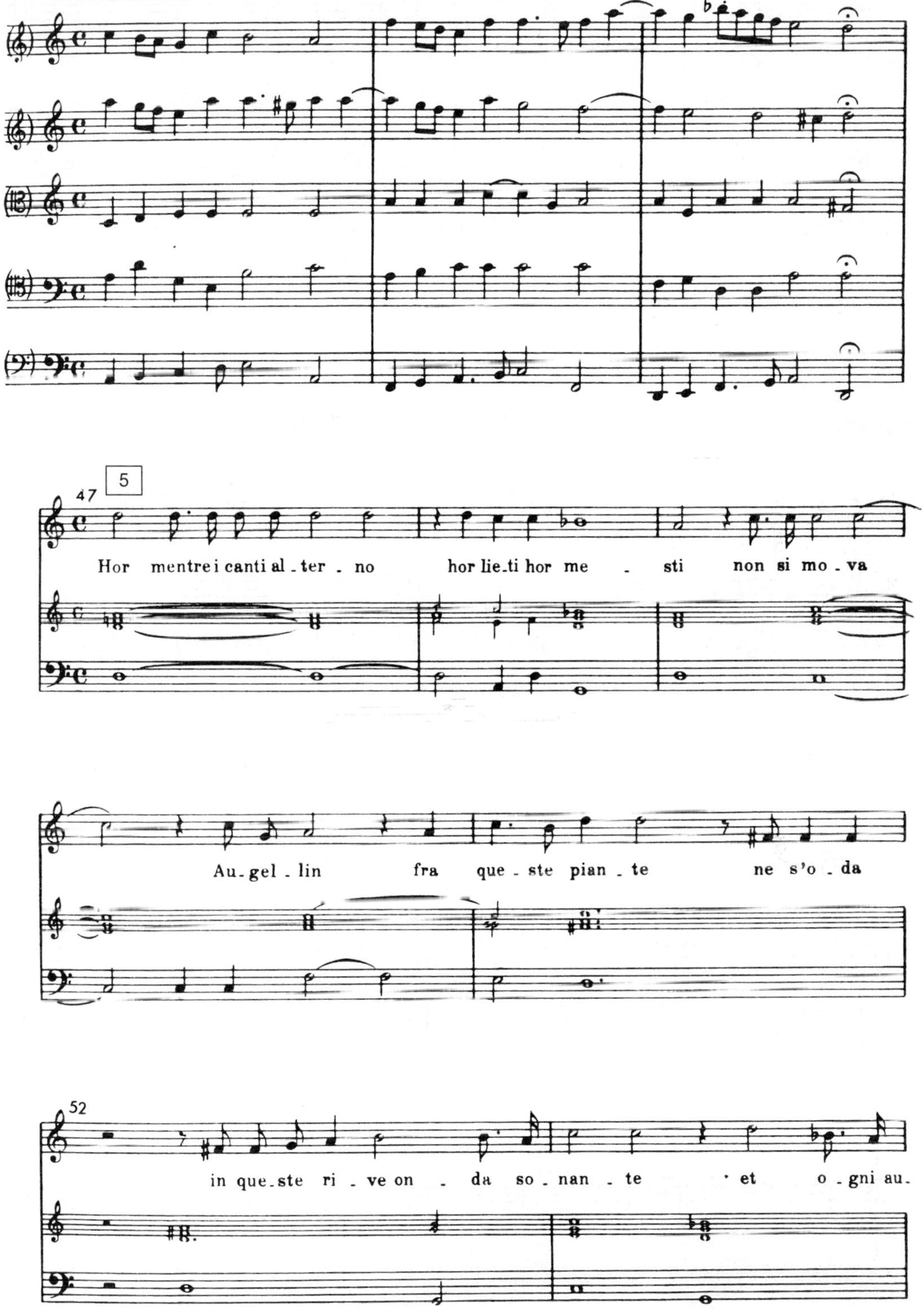

5

47

Hor mentre i canti al - ter - no hor lie - ti hor me - sti non si mo - va

Au - gel - lin fra que - ste pian - te ne s'o - da

52
in que - ste ri - ve on - da so - nan - te et o - gni au -

54
-ret - ta in suo cam-min s'ar-re - - - sti.

Ritornello
6

58

MUSIC

Dal mio Permesso amato a voi ne vegno,
Incliti Eroi, sangue gentil de' Regi
Di cui narra la Fama eccelsi pregi,
Ne giunge al ver perch'è tropp'alto il segno.

From my beloved Permessus I come to you,
Illustrious heroes, noble blood of kings,
of whom Fame relates their lofty worth,
yet falls short of the truth because the standard
is too high.

Io la Musica son, ch'ai dolci accenti
So far tranquillo ogni turbato core,
Et hor di nobil' ira et hor d'amore
Poss' infiammar le più gelate menti.

I am Music, who, through sweet accents
know how to quiet every troubled heart,
now with noble ire and now with love,
I can inflame the most frozen spirtits.

Io su cetera d'òr cantando soglio
Mortal orecchio lusingar tal'hora
E in questa guisa a l'armonia sonora
De la lira del ciel più l'alme invoglio.

I, on a kithara of gold am used to singing,
charming mortal ears on occasion,
and in this guise to the sonorous harmony
of the heavenly lyre, the spirits beguile.

Quinci a dirvi d'Orfeo desio mi sprona,
D'Orfeo che trasse al suo cantar le fere
E servo fè l'Inferno a sue preghiere
Gloria immortal di Pindo e d'Elicona.

Hence to tell you of Orpheus the desire spurs me:
of Orpheus, who with his singing attracted the beasts,
and made a servant of Hell with his pleas,
immortal glory of Pindus and Helicon.

Hor mentre i canti alterno hor lieti, hor mesti,
Non si mova augellin fra queste piante,
Ne s'oda in queste rive onda sonante,
Et ogni auretta in suo cammin s'arresti.

Now while I alternate happy and sad songs,
not a bird moves among these trees,
nor is heard on these shores a resounding wave,
and every little breeze arrests its course.

b) Act II, Orfeo: *Vi ricorda* (excerpt) CD 4 CD 2

3
ORFEO
8
19
Vi ri - cor - da o bo - schi ombro - si Vi ri - cor - da o boschi om -
7
- bro - si de'miei lungh'aspri tor - menti quando i sassi ai miei la - men - ti rispondean fat - ti pie -

ORPHEUS

Vi ricorda, o boschi ombrosi,
de' miei lungh' aspri tormenti,
quando i sassi ai miei lamenti
rispondean, fatti pietosi?

Do you recall, o shady woods,
my long, bitter torments,
when the stones to my laments
replied, pitiable deeds?

c) Messenger: *In un fiorito prato*
Orfeo: *Tu se' morta*
Chorus: *Ahi caso acerbo*

8
-ra fra l'erbe asco-so, le pun-se un piè con ve-le-no-so den-te.
10
21
Ed ec-co imman-ti-nente sco-lo-rir-si il bel vi-so
3 4 3
12
e nei suoi lumi sparir que lam-pi ond'ella al sol fea scor-no al-
-l'hor noi tut-te sbi-got-ti-te e me-ste le fummo intor-no ri-chia-
17
-mar tentando li spir-ti in lei smarri-ti con l'onda fresca e con possen-ti carmi, ma

nul-la val-sè ahi las - sa ch'el-la i langui-di lu - mi alquan-to apren -
22
- do e te chiamando Orfe - o, Or - fe - o Do-po un gra - ve so -
- spi - ro spi - rò fra queste braccia ed io ri-ma - si piena il cor di pie -
(♮)
11
22
28
- ta - de e di spa-ven - to.
PASTORE
Ahi ca-so acer-bo ahi fat'empio e crude - le, Ahi
PASTORE
12
23
stel-le ingiu-rio - se, ahi ciel a-va - ro.
A l'a-ma -
p

34
-ra novel-la rassembral'infeli - ce un mu-to sas-so che per trop-po do-lor non
può do-ler-si; Ahi ben havrebbeuncordi Tigre o d'Orsa chi non sentis-se
40
del tuo mal pie-ta-te, pri-vo d'ogni tuo ben mi-se-ro a-man-te.
ORFEO 13 24
Tu se' mor-ta se' mor-ta mia vi-
Un organo di legno e un chitarone
-ta ed io respi--ro, tu se' da me par-ti-ta,

se' da me par_ti _ ta per mai più, mai più non torna _ re ed io ri_man _
51
_ go, no, no, che se i ver_si al_cu_na co _ sa pon _ no,
n'andrò si _ cu _ ro a più profon _ di a _ bis _ si e in _ te _ ne _ ri _ to il
55
cor del Re de l'om_bre me _ co trar_rot _ ti a ri_ve_der le
stel _ le, O se ciò ne_ghe _ rammi em _ pio de_sti _ no,

59
ri_marrò te_co in compagnia di mor_te a dio ter_ra
a dio cie_lo e So_le, a Di_o.
14
25
Ahi ca_so a_cer_bo, Ahi fat'em_pio e cru_de_le, Ahi stel_le ingiu_rio_
Ahi ca_so a_cer_bo, Ahi fat'empio e cru_de_le, Ahi stel_le ingiu_rio_
Ahi ca_so a_cer_bo, Ahi fa_t'em_pio e cru_de_le, Ahi stel_le ingiu_rio_
Ahi ca_so a_cer_bo, Ahi fa_t'em_pio e cru_de_le, Ahi stel_le ingiu_rio_
Ahi ca_so a_cer_bo, Ahi fa_t'em_pio e cru_de_le, Ahi stel_le ingiu_rio_
5
15
26
_se ahi cie_lo a_va_ro. Non si fidi huom mor_ta_le
_se ah cie_lo ava_ro. Non si fi_di huom mor_ta_le
_se ahi ciel a_va_ro. Non si fi_di huom mor_ta_le
_se ahi ciel_a_va_ro. Non si fi_di huom mor_ta_le Di ben ca_
_se ahi cie_lo a_va_ro. Non si fi_di huom mor_ta_le

MESSENGER

In un fiorito prato	In a flowered meadow
Con l'altre sue compagne	with her companions
Giva cogliendo fiori	she was going about gathering flowers
Per farne una ghirlanda a le sue chiome,	to make a garland for her hair,
Quand'angue insidioso,	when a treacherous serpent
Ch'era fra l'erbe ascoso,	that was hidden in the grass
Le punse un piè con velenoso dente:	bit her foot with venomous tooth:
Ed ecco immantinente	then at once
Scolorirsi il bel viso e nei suoi lumi	her face became pale, and in her eyes
Sparir que lampi, ond'ella al sol fea scorno.	those lamps that vied with the sun grew dim.
All'hor noi tutte sbigottite e meste	Then we all, frightened and sad,
Le fummo intorno, richiamar tentando	gathered around calling, tempting
Li spirti in lei smarriti	the spirits that were smothered in her
Con l'onda fresca e con possenti carmi;	with fresh water and powerful songs.
Ma nulla valse, ahi lassa!	But nothing helped, alas,
Ch'ella i languidi lumi alquanto aprendo,	for she, opening her languid eyes slightly,

E te chiamando Orfeo, Dopo un grave sospiro Spirò fra queste braccia, ed io rimasi Piena il cor di pietade e di spavento.	called to you, Orpheus, and, after a deep sigh, expired in these arms, and I remained with heart full of pity and terror.
	SHEPHERD
Ahi caso acerbo, ahi fat' empio e crudele! Ahi stelle ingiuriose, ahi cielo avaro!	Ah, bitter event, ah, wicked fate and cruel! Ah, malicious stars, ah, greedy heavens!
A l'amara novella rassembra l'infelice un muto sasso, che per troppo dolor non può dolersi. Ahi ben havrebbe un cor di Tigre o d'Orsa Chi non sentisse del tuo mal pietate, Privo d'ogni tuo ben, misero amante!	The bitter news has turned the unfortunate one into a mute stone; from too much pain, he can feel no pain. Ah, he must have the heart of a tiger or a bear who did not feel pity for your loss, as you are bereft of your dear one, wretched lover.
	ORPHEUS
Tu se' morta, mia vita, ed io respiro? Tu se' da me partita Per mai più non tornare, ed io rimango? No, che se i versi alcuna cosa ponno, N'andrò sicuro a' più profondi abissi, E intenerito il cor del Re de l'Ombre	You are dead, my life, and I still breathe? You have departed from me, never to return, and I remain? No, for if verses have any power I shall go safely to the most profound abyss, and having softened the heart of the King of the Shades
Meco trarrotti a riveder le stelle, O se ciò negherammi empio destino Rimarrò teco in compagnia di morte, A dio terra, a dio cielo, e sole, a dio.	I shall bring you back to see the stars once again, and if this is denied me by wicked fate, I shall remain with you in the company of death. Farewell earth, farewell sky and sun, farewell.
	CHORUS
Ahi caso acerbo, ahi fat'empio e crudele! Ahi stelle ingiuriose, ahi cielo avaro! Non si fidi huom mortale Di ben caduco e frale Che tosto fugge, e spesso A gran salita il precipizio è presso. —ALESSANDRO STRIGGIO	Ah, bitter event, ah, wicked fate and cruel! Ah, malicious stars, ah greedy heavens! Trust not, mortal man, in goods fleeting and frail, for they easily slip away, and often after a steep ascent the precipice is near.

Monteverdi's *Orfeo* was first performed in 1607 for the Accademia degli Invaghiti in Mantua. Alessandro Striggio (ca. 1573–1630), son of a Florentine musician and composer, expanded the story told by Rinuccini into a five-act play.

It is instructive to consider three sections from *Orfeo* that are more or less parallel to those selected from *Euridice*: the Prologue (a), Orfeo's song (b), the Messenger's narration of Euridice's death, and the reactions of the shepherds, Orfeo, and the chorus (c). It is immediately obvious that the whole is very much expanded. The ritornello for the Prologue is carefully scored, and although the

Prologue itself is patterned on the air for singing poetry, Monteverdi wrote out each strophe, varying the melody while leaving the harmony intact, a technique practiced in the sixteenth century in the improvised singing of poetry.

Orfeo's strophic canzonet, *Vi ricorda o boschi ombrosi* (b), resembles in spirit Peri's aria for Tirsi, but the ritornello is worked out in five-part counterpoint. Again the idiom is a traditional one: the hemiola rhythm is the same as that in Cara's frottola *Io non compro più speranza* (NAWM 35), and the harmonization with root-position chords is also similar.

As in Peri's work, the most modern style is reserved for dramatic dialogue and impassioned speeches. In the Messagera's (messenger's) speech, *In un fiorito prato* (c), Monteverdi imitated the recitative style developed by Peri, but he shaped the melodic contour and the harmonic movement along broader lines. In Orfeo's lament, which follows, Monteverdi attained a new height of lyricism that leaves the first monodic experiments far behind. In the passage that begins "Tu se' morta," each phrase of music, like each phrase of text, builds upon what precedes and intensifies it through pitch and rhythm. When necessary for this process, Monteverdi repeated words and phrases and by this and harmonic means linked the fragments of recitative into coherent arches of melody. Particularly notable is the setting of the last line, "a dio terra" (measures 6–64). Here the rhythmic parallelism, the chromaticism, the rising pitch to the climax on "e sole," and the leap down to a free seventh against the bass convey the depth of Orfeo's grief.

For the first section of the chorus, Monteverdi put the recitative line of the first Pastore (shepherd, measures 28–33), with slight rhythmic modifications, in the bass and built the other four parts on it. As in the *kommos* of the Greek theater, which was a lament by the chorus in dialogue with one or more characters on stage, the chorus joins Orfeo and the shepherds in bemoaning Euridice's death. Then, in the second section (after the double bar), the chorus assumes its usual function, offering moralizing reflections on the stage action. Humankind, it sings, should not trust in the goods and pleasures of the world, for they are elusive and pass quickly. Monteverdi here resorted to the word-painting of the polyphonic madrigal—tenors and basses leap a minor sixth for "a gran salita" (a steep ascent); all the voices speed up for the idea of flight at "che tosto fugge" and leap down sixths at "il precipizio."

55 Claudio Monteverdi

L'incoronazione di Poppea

Act I, Scene 3 CD 4

16
255 POPPEA
Signor, signor deh, non parti - re sostien che queste bracciati circondino il
260
col - lo come le tue bel lez - ze cir - con - da - no il cor mi - o.
264 POPPEA
Non par - tir, non partir, Si -
NERONE
Poppe - a la - sia ch'io par - ta.

Tutte le opere di Claudio Monteverdi, ed. G. Francesco Malipiero (© Copyright 1929 by Universal Edition A. G., Vienna), 13:29–35. Copyright renewed. All rights reserved. Used by permission of European American Music Distributors Corp. Sole U.S. Agent for Universal Edition. Vienna.

268
POPPEA
-gnor deh non parti - re, ap-pe-na spunta l'al-ba e tu che se-i l'incarna-to mio
272
so-le la mia pal-pa-bil lu-ce, e l'amo-ro-so dì, de la mia vi ta
276
vuoi si repen-te far da me da me da me da me par-ti - - -ta?
280
Deh non dir di par - tir che di vo-ce si a - ma - ra un so-lo accen-to A -
p
283
- - hi pe-rir A - hi spi-rar quest'al-ma io sen - to.

17
288 NERONE
La no-bil-tà de nasci - men - ti tuo-i non permette che Roma sappia che siamo u-
292 POPPEA
In sin che, in sin che
NERONE
-ni - ti in sin ch'Ot - ta - via
296
Non ri-ma - ne, non ri-ma - ne.
In sin ch'Otta-via non ri - man'es-clu - sa
300
Van-ne van-ne ben
In sin ch'Ottavia non ri- mane es-clu-sa col re - pudio da me.
p
mp

304 POPPEA
mi_o ben mi_o, Vanne vanne ben mi_o ben mi_o, van_ne ben mi_ _ _o.
f
p
18
310 Ritornello
mf
320 NERONE
In un so_spir, sospir che vien dal pro_fon_do del cor In un so_
p
324
_spir, sospir che vien sospir che vien dal pro_fon_do del cor in_cludo un
329
ba_cio o ca_ra, ca_ra et un a Di_ _ _o Si ri_ve_

332
-drembento-sto si si si ri-vedrem Si ri-vedrem ben to-sto I - do-lo
f
336
mi - o si ri-ve - drembento-sto i- - - - -do-lo mi - o
mf
early aria
340 POPPEA
19
Si - gnor sem-pre mi
344
ve-di,sempresem - pre sem-pre mi ve-di an - zi mai non mi ve -
348
-di si - gnor sem - pre mi ve di sempre sem - - -pre sem-pre mi

352
ve_di an - zi mai non mi ve- - di per_chè
355
s'è ver che nel tuo cor io si_a en - tra'l tuo
358
(♯)
sen cela - ta non posso non pos_so non pos_so da tuoi lumi es - ser mi_ra -
361
-ta non posso non posso non posso da tuoi lumi es - ser mi_ra - ta.
366
20
NERONE
A_do_ra_ti miei ra - i deh resta_temi ho_ma - - i deh resta_temi homa -
p

371
_i rimanti o mia Poppe _ a, cor, vezzo, e lu_ce e lu_ce mi _ a.
374 POPPEA
Deh, non dir di par _ tir, che di vo_ce si a _ ma _ ra un so_lo accento Ahi
377
pe _ rir, ahi mancar que _ st'al _ ma sen_ _ _to.
381 NERONE
Non te _ mer non te _ mer non te _ mer tu stai me_co stai me_co a tutte
386
l'ho _ re splendor negl'occhi e

POPPEA

Signor, deh non partire,
Sostien, che queste braccia
Ti circondino il collo,
Come le tue bellezze
Circondano il cor mio,

Sir, please don't go.
Allow these arms
to encircle your neck,
as your beauty
encircles my heart.

NERO

Poppea, lascia ch 'io parta.

Poppea, let me go.

POPPEA

Non partir, Signor, deh non partire
Appena spunta l'alba, et tu che sei
L'incarnato mio Sole,
La mia palpabil luce,
E l'amoroso dì de la mia vita,
Vuoi sì repente far da me partita!

Don't leave, Sir, please don't go.
The dawn is barely breaking, and you, who are
my incarnated Sun,
my light made palpable,
the loving day of my life,
want to part from me so quickly.

Deh non dir
Di partir,
Che di voce sì amara a un solo accento
Ahi, perir, ahi spirar quest'alma io sento.

Please, don't say
that you're leaving.
It is such a bitter word that from one hint of it,
ah, I feel my soul dying, expiring.

NERO

La nobiltà de nascimenti tuoi
Non permette che Roma
Sappia che siamo uniti.
In sin ch'Ottavia non riman' esclusa
Col repudio da me: Vanne, ben mio;
In un sospir, che vien
Dal profondo del cor
Includo un bacio, o cara et un' a Dio,
Si rivedrem ben tosto, Idolo mio.

The nobility of your birth
does not permit that Rome
should know that we are together,
until Ottavia is set aside,
repudiated by me. Go, my dear;
within a sigh that rises
from the depths of my heart
I enclose a kiss, dearest, and a farewell.
We shall see each other soon, my idol.

POPPEA

Signor, sempre mi vedi,
Anzi mai non mi vedi.
Perchè s'è ver, che nel tuo cor io sia
Entr' al tuo sen celata
Non posso da' tuoi lumi esser mirata.

My lord, you see me constantly;
rather, you never see me.
Because, if it's true that I am in your heart,
hidden in your breast,
I cannot by your eyes be viewed.

NERO

Adorati miei rai, Deh restate homai Rimanti, o mia Poppea, Cor, vezzo, e luce mia.	My adored rays, please stay, then; remain, O my Poppea, my heart, my charm, my light.

POPPEA

Deh non dir....	Please don't say...

NERO

Non temer, tu stai meco a tutte l'hore, Splendor negl'occhi, e deità nel core. —Giovanni Francesco Busenello	Do not fear; stay with me for all time, splendor of my eyes, goddess of my heart.

Monteverdi wrote this opera in his seventy-fourth year on a libretto by Giovanni Francesco Busenello (1598–1659) for performance in Venice in 1642. The love scene between Nero and Poppea in Act I, Scene 3, passes through various levels of recitative, from speechlike unmeasured passages with few cadences, through a style not unlike the Prologue of *Orfeo*, to measured arioso. The aria passages are similarly varied in their degrees of formal organization and lyricism. Monteverdi sometimes turned to aria style even when the poet did not provide strophic or other closed verse forms.

For example, the composer interrupted Nero's recitative with a short triple-time flowing melody for the half-line "Vanne, ben mio." The poet obviously intended the lines "in un sospir che vien/ dal profondo del cor"—of six syllables each (instead of the usual seven or eleven)—to be set as an aria passage, prompting Monteverdi to state a triple-meter harmonic pattern twice, with a slightly different melody each time. But though Poppea's speech, *Signor, sempre mi vedi,* is in *versi sciolti* (blank verse), Monteverdi chose to set it in a similar way, as a two-strophe variation on a harmonic pattern, this time in duple meter. But the poet's more lyrical speech for Poppea, *Deh non dir*, he set as recitative.

Monteverdi dealt very freely with the libretto's formal structure. Content rather than poetic form, and the urge to heighten emotional expression rather than the desire to charm and dazzle, determined the shifts from recitative to aria and back, and from one level of speech-song to another.

Marc' Antonio Cesti (1623–1669)

56

Orontea: Act II, Scene 17

Intorno all'idol mio CD 4

21
Oron.

In — tor — no all' i — dol mi — o, Spi — ra — te_, pur — spi — ra — te___

Edited by William Holmes (Wellesley: Wellesley Edition, No. 11, 1973), pp. 158–62.

15
Au — re ___, au — re ___ so — a — vi e gra —— te ______, E __ nel-le guan — ce e —

20
— let — te Ba —— cia —— te-lo per me ___, cor — te — si, cor —— te — si au —— ret ——— te _
♯6

25
30
______. E nel-le guan-ce e — let — te Ba — cia —— te —lo per me ___, ba — cia —— te-lo per
6

35
me__, cor — te — si, cor — te — si au — ret — te__.

40
♯ 6 6 ♯6 5 6 6
3 ♯4

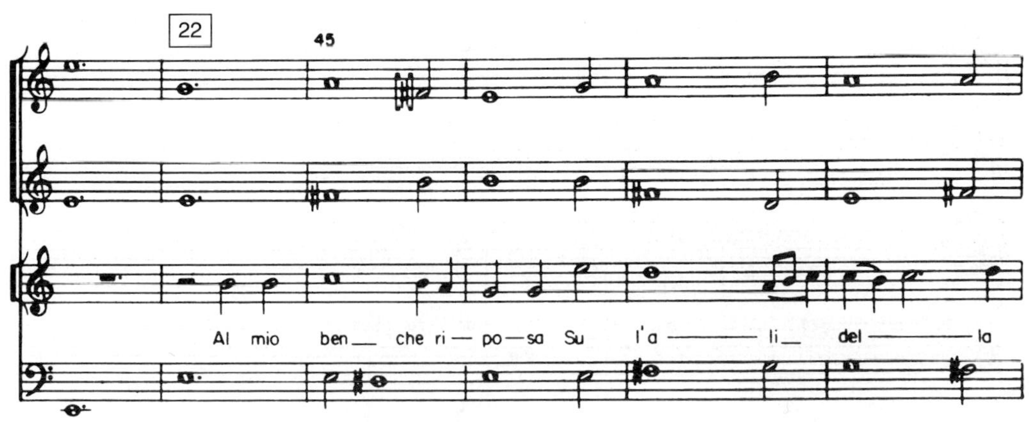
22
45
Al mio ben__ che ri — po — sa Su l'a — li__ del — la

50
quie-te___ Gra—ti___, gra—ti_____ so—gni as-si——ste——— te ________, E'l

55
60
mio racchiu—so ar—do—re Sve—la——te-li per me__, lar ———————————— ve d'a—

65
-mo———— re ___. E'l mio racchiu—so ar—do—re Sve—— la——te-li per me___, sve—
6 ♭ ♭

ORONTEA

Intorno all'idol mio
Spirate, pur spirate
Aure soavi e grate
E nelle guance elette
Baciatelo per me, cortesi aurette.

Al mio ben che riposa
Su l'ali della quiete
Grati sogni assistete,
E'l mio racchiuso ardore
Svelateli per me, larve d'amore.
—GIACINTO ANDREA CICOGNINI

Around my idol
breathe, just breathe,
breezes sweet and pleasant,
and on the favored cheeks
kiss him for me, gentle breezes.

To my darling, who sleeps
on the wings of calm,
happy dreams induce;
and my covert ardor
unveil to him, phantoms of love.

Cesti's *Orontea*, with a libretto by Giacinto Andrea Cicognini, was first produced in Venice in 1649 and became one of the most frequently performed operas of the mid-1600s both in Italy and abroad.

In the previous scene, Orontea, unmarried queen of Egypt, who has been reluctant to acknowledge her love for the painter Alidoro, discovers him painting a portrait of a rival lady of the court and realizes she is about to lose him. She resolves to marry him; in this aria, as she watches him sleeping, she confesses her love.

Orontea's big scene shows how elaborate the aria had become by mid-century. The two violins play throughout, not merely in ritornellos before and after the singer's strophes. The form is the familiar strophic one, though the music makes some adjustments to the new text of the second strophe. The dimensions are generous, and throughout we hear the new bel canto vocal idiom of smooth, mainly diatonic line and easy rhythms that are grateful to the singer. The expressive leap down of a diminished seventh (measure 23) and the unprepared seventh in the following measure stand out (the passage is heard in the opening ritornello and several more times later).

Barbara Strozzi (1619–after 1667)

57

Cantata: *Lagrime mie* CD 4

From Barbara Strozzi, *Diporti di Euterpe overo Cantate & ariette a voce sola*, Op. 7 (Venice: Alessandro Magni, 1659), ed. in Carol MacClintock, *The Solo Song 1580–1730*, © 1973 by W. W. Norton & Company, Inc., pp. 81–88, corrected by reference to the 1659 edition. Used by permission of W. W. Norton & Company, Inc. Half-brackets indicate colored notation for hemiola

15
-re, Che mi to-glie'l re - spi-ro e op-pri - me il co - - - - -
- - - re; Che mi to-glie'l re - spi-ro e op-pri - me il co - -
4 3
20
24
[Arioso]
- - - - - - - - - re. Li - dia, che tant' a -
4 3
25
-do - - - ro,___ Per-chè un guar-do pie-to - - - - so, ahi-

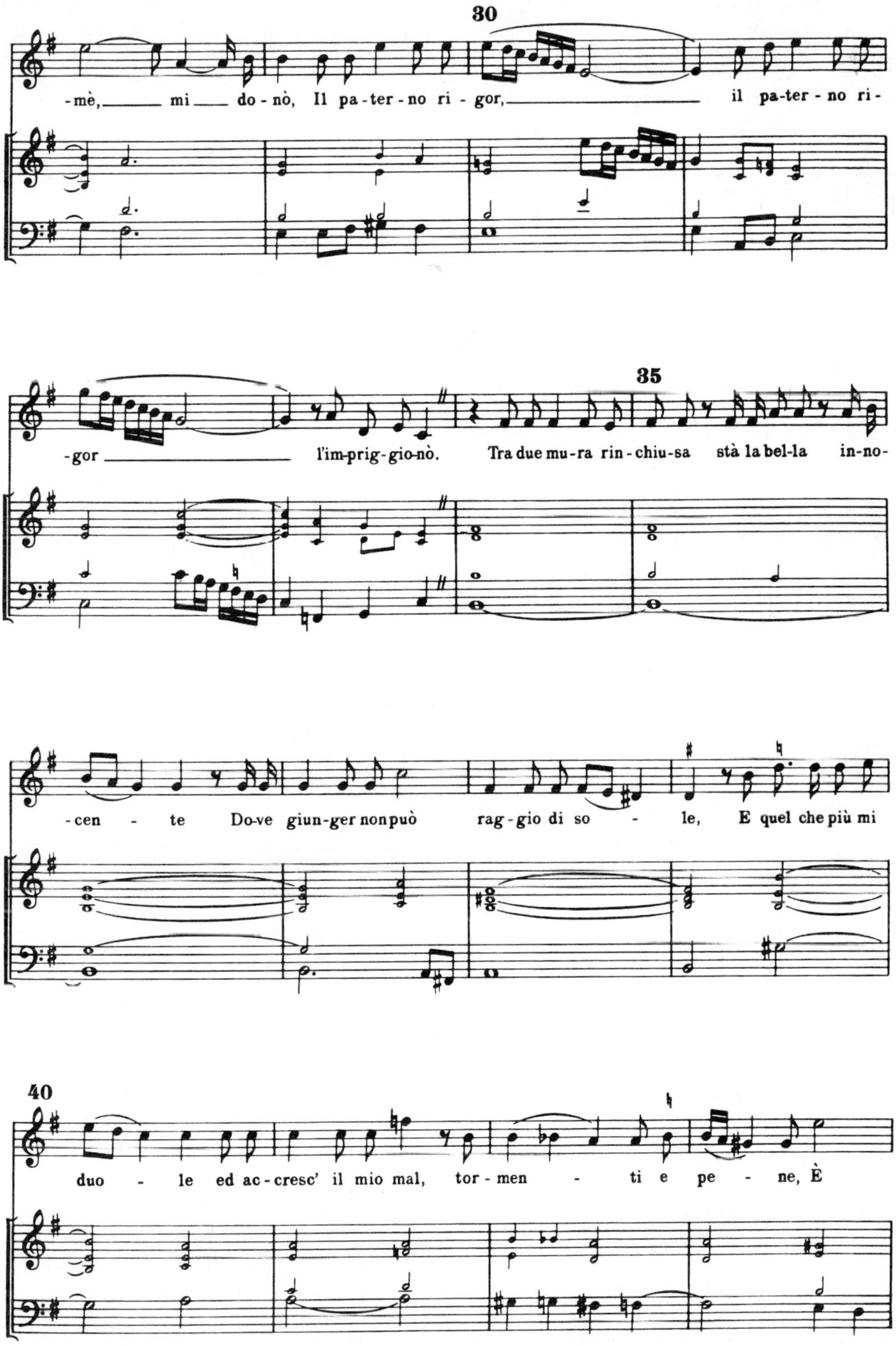

30

-mè, mi dono, Il pa-ter-no ri-gor, il pa-ter-no ri-

35

-gor l'im-prig-gio-nò. Tra due mu-ra rin-chiu-sa stà la bel-la in-no-

-cen - te Do-ve giun-ger non può rag-gio di so - le, E quel che più mi

40
duo - le ed ac-cresc' il mio mal, tor-men - ti e pe - ne, È

45
che per mia ca-gio-ne, per mia ca - gio-ne pro-va ma - le il mi-o be -

25
50
- ne.
E voi lu - mi do - len - ti, do -

55
-len - ti, e voi lu - mi do - len - ti, do - len - ti, non pian -

60
-ge

[Tempo I°]
65
- - te! La - - - - - - - - gri-me

70
mi - e, à che, à che vi trat-te-ne - te?

26
Aria
1. Li-dia,ahi-me, veg-go man-car-mi, Li-dia,ahi-mè, veg-go man-car - mi. L'i-dol
2. Se la mor-te m'è gra-di-ta, se la mor-te m'è gra-di - ta, Or che

75
mio, che tan to a do - - - - - ro, Stà co - lei tra du-ri mar-mi per cui
son pri-vo di spe - - - - - ne, Dhè to-glie-te-mi la vi-ta (Ve ne

80
spi-ro, per cui spi - ro E pur non mo - - ro. Stà co-lei tra du-ri
pre-go, ve ne pre - go) a - spre mi-e pe - - ne. Dhè to-glie-te-mi la

mar-mi, per cui spi-ro, per cui spi - ro E pur non mo - - - - ro.
vi-ta, (ve ne pre-go, ve ne pre - go) a - spre mie pe - - - - ne.

85
1.
85
2.

Adagio
90
Ma ben m'ac-cor-go, che per tor-men-tar - - mi mag - gior - men -

- te, La sor - te mi nie-ga an-co la mor - te, mi nie-ga an - co, mi

95
27
nie-ga an-co la mor - te. Se dun - qu'è ve - ro, o Di -

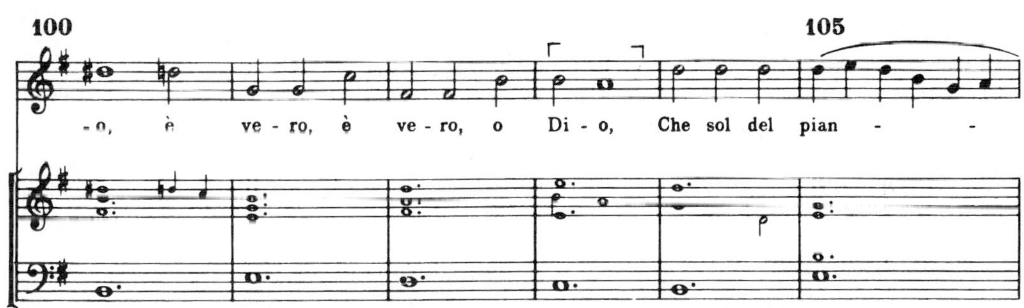
100
105
- o, è ve - ro, è ve - ro, o Di - o, Che sol del pian - -

110
- to, del pian - - - to, del pian - - - to mi -

Lagrime mie, à che vi trattenete,
Perchè non isfogate il fier' dolore,
Chi mi toglie 'l respiro e opprime il core?

Lidia, che tant' adoro,
Perchè un guardo pietoso, ahimè, mi donò,
Il paterno rigor l'impriggionò.
Tra due mura rinchiusa
Stà la bella innocente,
Dove giunger non può raggio di sole,
E quel che più mi duole
Ed accresc'il mio mal, tormenti
e pene,
È che per mia cagione
Prova male il mio bene.
E voi lumi dolenti, non piangete!
Lagrime mie, à che vi trattenete?

Lidia, ahimè, veggo mancarmi.
L'idol mio, che tanto adoro,
Stà colei tra duri marmi
Per cui spiro e pur non moro.

Se la morte m'è gradita,
Or che son privo di spene,
Dhè, toglietemi la vita
(Ve ne prego) aspre mie pene.

Ma ben m'accorgo, che per tormentarmi
Maggiormente, la sorte
Mi niega anco la morte.
Se dunqu'è vero, o Dio,
Che sol del pianto mio,
Il rio destino ha sete.

My tears, what holds you back,
why don't you give vent to the fierce pain
that takes away my breath and weighs on my heart?

Lidia, whom I adore so much,
because of the pitying glance, alas, that she gave me,
paternal severity has imprisoned her.
Locked up between two walls,
remains the innocent beauty,
where no ray of sun can reach,
and what pains me most
and increases my discomfort, torments,
and anguish,
is that because of me
my beloved suffers.
And you, pained eyes, weep not!
Tears, what holds you back?

Lidia, alas, I feel myself failing.
My idol, whom I adore so much
remains between hard marble walls.
For her I sigh, yet I don't die.

If death suits me,
now that I am deprived of hope,
Oh, take away my life—
I beg you—my bitter suffering.

Still I realize that to torment me
the more, destiny
even denies me death.
It is true then, O God,
that only for my tears
does cruel fate thirst.

In its form, a succession of sections of recitative, arioso, and aria, this work is representative of the solo cantatas of the mid-seventeenth century. The poet may be Giulio Strozzi (of a Florentine noble family but residing in Venice), with whom Barbara Strozzi lived from childhood and who may have been her father. (She set many of his verses.) He founded an academy, the Unisoni, partly to give her an outlet for her performances and compositions.

Except for two stanzas of four eight-syllable lines each, which Strozzi set as a strophic aria (measures 71–87), the text is made up of madrigal-type verse of seven- and eleven-syllable lines without a regular rhyme scheme. She divided this free verse into sections according to content. The first three lines, in which the poet addresses his tears, she made into a lament. The next ten lines, a narration about Lidia, the object of the poet's love, she set as an arioso. When the poet recalled the weeping eyes (measures 49ff.), the composer invoked the conventional emblem of the lament—the descending bass in triple meter. With the return of the opening line, "Lagrime mie, a che vi trattenete?" Strozzi brought back its music as a kind of refrain. After the Aria (so marked in the original), a short recitative leads to a triple-time bel canto section built on a descending fourth bass, which is abandoned for two closing sections, the first ending deceptively on *G* (measure 116), the last on the tonic, E minor.

The dry declamation of theatrical dialogue did not fit such intimate poetic texts, so composers softened, sweetened, and intensified the recitative style in the cantatas meant for chamber performance. In the opening recitative, Strozzi very artfully exploited many of the rhetorical devices that the Roman composers Luigi Rossi (1597–1653) and Giacomo Carissimi (1605–1674) had introduced into cantata recitative. The hesitations on the dissonant *D*♯, *A*, and *F*♯ over the opening E-minor harmony, together with the *C*♮ of the harmonic-minor scale, make a most moving and vivid projection of the lamenting lover's weeping and sobbing. In the Arioso, the tasteful word-inspired runs at "adoro," "pietoso," and "rigor," the delicate chromaticism at "tormenti," and the compelling seventh chords and suspensions—particularly over the descending basses—show Strozzi's mastery in applying the affective vocabulary of this genre.

58 Giovanni Gabrieli (ca. 1557–1612)

Grand Concerto: *In ecclesiis* CD 4

Gabrieli, *Symphoniae sacrae* (Venice, 1615). *Opera omnia*, Vol. 5, ed. Denis Arnold (American Institute of Musicology, 1969), pp. 32–55.

5 al-le-lu-ja. al-le-lu-ja. al-
A
T
B
13 al-le-lu-ja. al-le-lu-ja. al-
14 al-le-lu-ja. al-le-lu-ja. al-
11 al-le-lu-ja. al-le-lu-ja.
12 al-le-lu-ja. al-le-lu-ja. al-

29
le - lu - - ja.
In om - ni
- - le - lu - ja.
- le - lu - ja.
al - - - le - lu - ja.
- le - lu - - ja.
15
lo - - co.
in
om - ni lo - -

co
do - mi-na-ti - o - nis.
do - mi-na-ti - o - nis
be - ne -
20
dic.
be - ne - dic
a - ni-ma me - a Do -
25
30
S
A
T
B
- - - mi - num.
Al - le - lu - ja.
13
Al - le - lu - ja.
al - le -
14
Al - le - lu - ja.
al - le -
11
Al - le - lu - ja.
al - le -
12
Al - le - lu - ja.
al - le -
org

31
30
5
A
T
8
al - le - lu - ja, al - le - lu - ja.
13
lu - ja, al - le - lu - ja.
14
lu - ja, al - le - lu - ja.
11
lu - ja, al - le - lu - ja.
12
lu - ja, al - le - lu - ja.
C
Sinfonia
7
Sinfonia
9
Sinfonia
10
Sinfonia
6
Sinfonia
B
Sinfonia
org.

C
7
9
10
6
B
org.

35

5
A
T
8
C
7
9
10
6
B
org.
In De
o.
In De - - o sa - lu-ta-ri me - o.
in De - o sa - lu-
40

45
ta - ri me - o, in De - o in De - o sa - lu - ta - ri me -
in De - o
o sa lu ta ri me - o et glo - ri - a, glo - ri - a
sa - lu-ta - ri me - o et glo - ri - a, et glo - ri - a

50
me - a. De - us auxi - li - um
me - a. De - us au - xi - li - um me -
me - - - - - um et spes me - a in De - o est.
- - - - - - um et spes me a in De - o

55
in De-o est, et spes me - a in De - o.
est, in De-o est, et spes me - a in De -
60
in De - o, in De - o, in De - - o
- o, in De - o, in De - - - - o

65
5
A
est. Al - le - lu - ja. al - le - lu - ja, al -
T
est. Al - le - lu - ja. al - le - lu - ja, al -
8
13
Al - le - lu - ja, al - le - lu - ja, al -
14
Al - le - lu - ja, al - le - lu - ja, al -
11
Al - le - lu - ja. al - le - lu - ja,
12
Al - le - lu - ja. al - le - lu - ja, al -
C
7
9
10
6
B
org.

32
De - - - - us
- le - lu - - ja.
- le - lu - - ja.
- - le - lu - - ja.
- le - lu - - ja.
al - - - le - lu - ja.
- le - lu - - ja.

70
5
A
T
8
org.
te in - vo-ca - mus. te
De - - us no - - ster te lau - da - mus.
75
in - vo - ca - mus. te a - do - ra - -
te lau - da - mus. te a - do - ra - - - - -
mus. te a - do - ra - mus.
mus. te a - do - ra - - - - mus.

80
Li - be - ra nos
85
vi - vi -
sal - - - - - - - - - - va nos.
90
- fi - ca nos. vi - vi - - - fi - ca
vi - vi - - - - fi - ca nos.

nos, vi - vi - fi - ca. vi - - vi - fi - ca
vi - vi - fi - ca. vi - vi - - - - - fi - ca
95
5
A
T
8
13
14
11
12
org.
nos. Al - le - lu - ja. al - le - lu -
nos. Al - le - lu - ja. al - la - lu -
Al - le - lu - ja. al - le - lu - ja.
Al - le - lu - ja. al - le - lu - ja.
Al - le - lu - ja. al - le - lu - ja.
Al - le - lu - ja. al - le - lu - ja.

33
100
5
ja. al - - le - lu - - ja. De - us.
A
De - us.
T
De - us.
8
ja. al - - le - lu - - ja. De - us.
13
Cantate
al - - le - lu - - ja. De - us.
14
[Cantate]
al - - le - lu - - ja. De - us.
11
Cantate
al - - le - lu - ja. De - us.
12
Cantate
al - - le - lu - - ja. De - us.
C
7
9
10
6
B
org.

105
De - us ad - ju - tor no - - ster. ad - ju -
De - us ad - ju -
De - us ad - ju -
De - us ad - ju - tor no - ster, ad - ju -
De - us ad - ju - tor no - - ster. ad - ju -
De - us ad - ju - - tor no - ster. ad - ju -
De - us ad - ju - - tor no - ster. ad - ju -
De - us ad - ju - - tor no - ster. ad - ju -

tor no - ster. De - us. *De - us*
- tor no - ster. *De - us* ad -
- tor no - ster. De - us ad -
- tor no - ster. De - us. *De - us*
- tor no - ster. De - us. *De - us.*
- tor no - ster. De - us. *De - us.*
- *tor no - ster.* De - us. *De - us.*
- *tor no - ster.* De - us. *De - us.*

110
ad - ju - tor no - -
- ju - - tor no - ster ad - ju - - tor no -
ju - - tor no - ster. ad - ju - tor no - -
ad - ju - - tor no -
De - us ad -
De - us ad -
De - us ad -
De - us ad -

115
ster, ad - ju - tor no - - - ster in æ - ter - -
ster, no - - - ster
ster, no - - - ster in
ster, ad - ju - tor no - - ster in æ -
- ju - tor no - - - ster in æ -
ju - - - tor no - - ster in æ -
ju - - - tor no - - ster in æ - ter - num.
ju - - - tor no - - ster in æ -

in æ - ter
æ - ter
ter
ter - num.
in æ - ter
ter - num. in æ - ter
in æ - ter
ter

120
num.
Al - le - lu - ja.
al - le - lu -
num.
Al - le - lu - ja.
al - le - lu -
num.
Al - le - lu - ja.
al - le - lu -
num.
Al - le - lu - ja.
al - le - lu -
num.
Al - le - lu - ja.
al - le - lu - ja.
num.
Al - le - lu - ja.
al - le - lu - ja.
num.
Al - le - lu - ja.
al - le - lu - ja.
num.
Al - le - lu - ja.
al - le - lu - ja.

125
ja. al - - le - lu - - ja. al -
ja. al - - le - lu - - ja. al -
ja. al - - le - lu - - ja. al -
ja. al - - le - lu - - ja. al -
al - - - le - lu - - - ja. al -
al - - le - lu - - ja. al -
al - - - le - lu - ja.
al - - le - lu - - ja. al -

- le - lu - - ja, al - le - lu - - ja.
- le - lu - - ja, al - le - lu - - ja.
- le - lu - - ja, al - le - lu - - ja.
- le - lu - - ja, al - le - lu - - ja.
- - le - lu - - ja, al - le - lu - - ja.
- le - lu - - ja, al - le - lu - - ja.
al - - le - lu - ja, al - le - lu - - ja.
- le - lu - - ja, al - le - lu - - ja.

In ecclesiis benedicite Domino, Alleluia.
In omni loco dominationis benedic
anima mea Dominum, Alleluia.
In Deo salutari meo et gloria mea,
Deus auxilium meum et spes mea in
Deo est, Alleluia.
Deus noster, te invocamus, te laudamus,
te adoramus;
libera nos, salva nos, vivifica nos,
Alleluia.
Deus adiutor noster in aeternum, Alleulia.

In churches bless the Lord, Alleluia.
In every place of government, bless
the Lord, O my soul, Alleluia.
In God is my salvation and my glory.
God is my help, and my hope is in
God, Alleluia.
Our God, we implore you, we praise you,
we worship you;
free us, save us, enliven us,
Alleluia.
God, our helper in eternity, Alleluia.

This work is a magnificent example of the *grand concerto*, a genre that combines vocal soloists with choral and instrumental ensembles. Gabrieli was a master of the medium in which two or more choirs combined and separated in projecting a sacred text. Antiphonal performance by two half-choirs (*cori spezzati*) of psalms of praise was prescribed at St. Mark's in Venice early in the sixteenth century for certain feasts, and Gabrieli dramatically expanded on this tradition.

The brilliant sonorities commanded by Gabrieli come from three groups: four solo voices, which usually perform as an ensemble, though some sing passages alone; a four-part chorus; a six-part instrumental ensemble; and an organ continuo, which plays throughout. At a time when parts were usually issued without designating the instruments, Gabrieli carefully specified the instrumentation: three cornetti, an alto violin (analogous to the modern viola), and two sackbuts. These forces alternately contrast with each other, join in various combinations, or unite in a massive tutti.

The text is not liturgical, although it borrows phrases from liturgical chants. It combines words of praise to God and a plea for help and salvation. The frequent returns of the refrain "Alleluia," which proclaim a mood of jubilation, illustrate the variety of scoring. In the first Alleluia (measures 6–12), the solo soprano and the chorus exchange short motives, then join in a florid affirmation. The following Alleluias have essentially the same music, but the second (measures 25–31) gives the bass the solo role, the third (measures 62–68) features an alto-tenor duet, joined by the instruments as it answers the chorus, and the next (measures 95–101) pits a soprano-bass duet against the chorus. In the final Alleluia (measures 119–29), the chorus, combined with the instruments, contrasts with the entire solo vocal ensemble. Each of these refrains has the same harmonic plan: a succession of major harmonies in a cycle of fifths from F up to A.

As in the Alleluias, Gabrieli built the rest of the composition around short, crisp motives inspired by the rhythm of the text. Ornamental eighth notes that would normally be grouped over one syllable are set to separate syllables, as in "om-ni" (measure 16), "do-mi-na-tio-nis" (measures 17–19), "De-o est" (measures 54–56), and "in-vo-ca-mus" (measures 72–73). This exaggeration of weak syllables makes the motives stand out and imprints them on the memory.

Gabrieli indulged in some daring harmonies, not so much for the sake of text expression as for their brilliant colors—for example, the cornetto's strident *F* in the Sinfonia (measure 31), and the repeated cross-relations at "in Deo salutari meo" (measures 42, 45), caused by the shift from the major chord on *E* to that on *C*. This same major-third relationship punctuates the entrance of the Alleluias, which break in suddenly with F major after a cadence on *A*.

59 LODOVICO VIADANA (CA. 1560–1627)

Sacred Concerto: *O Domine, Jesu Christe* CD 4

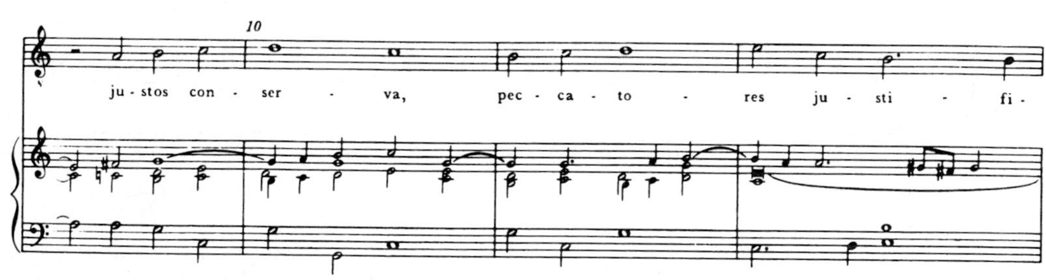

From *Cento concerti ecclesiastici opera duodecima* (Venice, 1602), ed. Claudio Gallico (Kassel, etc., 1964), pp. 64–65. Reprinted by permission of Bärenreiter Music Corporation.

O Domine Jesu Christe,
pastor bone,
justos conserva
peccatores justifica,
omnibus fidelibus miserere,
et propitius esto mihi misero
et indigno peccatori. Amen.

O Lord Jesus Christ,
good shepherd,
preserve the righteous,
do justice to the sinners,
have mercy on all the faithful,
and be gracious toward me, wretched
and unworthy sinner. Amen.

In this concerto from the 1602 collection, Viadana created the illusion of a complex texture in a single voice by having it imitate itself at different pitch levels. This reduction of the polyphonic idiom was of great practical significance: it allowed a work to be performed, if necessary, by one singer or a small number of them. Instead of doubling or replacing vocal parts by instruments, as had been done in the sixteenth century, the thoroughbass and the chords improvised on it took the place of the other parts.

The term *concerto* applies to this work because it concerts (unites) a voice and instrumental accompaniment. Other concertos in Viadana's 1602 collection are for two, three, or four singers with thorough bass. All of them belong to the category of concertos for few voices as opposed to the grand concerto.

In style this piece is closer to the madrigals of Caccini than it is to recitative. The chromatic line at "mihi misero" (measures 29–30) is especially madrigalistic. Like Gabrieli, Viadana used the shift from E major to C major for harmonic color and as a mark of punctuation (measures 6–7, 15–16, 19).

ALESSANDRO GRANDI (CA. 1575/80–1630)

60

Motet: *O quam tu pulchra es* CD 4

Values halved in triple meter. *Ghirlanda sacra. Libro primo . . . per Leonardo Simonetti* (Venice, 1625). Rudolf Ewehart, ed., in *Drei Hohelied Motetten.* Cantio sacra, No. 23 (Cologne: Verlag Edmund Bieler, 1960), pp. 7–9. Reprinted by permission.

36
25
Ve - ni, ve - ni de Li - ba - no, ve - ni, ve - ni de Li - ba - no,
30
ve - ni, a - mi - ca me - a, co - lum - ba me - a, for - mo - sa me - a.
37
35
O quam tu pul - chra es, ve - ni, ve - ni, co - ro - na - be - ris.
40
45
Sur - ge, sur - ge, pro - pe - ra, sur - ge, spon - sa me - a,
50
sur - ge, di - lec - ta me - a, sur - ge, im - ma - cu - la - ta me - a.

sur-ge, ve-ni, ve-ni, ve - ni, sur-ge, ve-ni, ve-ni, ve - ni.
Qui - a a-mo-re lan - - - gue - o,
a-mo-re lan - - - gue - o. Sur-ge,
ve-ni, ve-ni, ve - - ni, sur-ge, ve-ni, ve-ni, ve - - ni, qui -
a a-mo-re, a - mo-re lan - gue - o.

O quam tu pulchra es, amica mea,	O how fair you are, my love,
quam pulchra es, columba mea,	how fair you are, my dove,
o quam tu pulchra es, formosa mea.	how fair you are, my beauty.
Oculi tui columbarum,	Your eyes, the eyes of doves,
capilli tui sicut greges caprarum	your hair, like a flock of goats,
et dentes tui sicut greges tonsarum.	and your teeth like a flock of sheep newly shorn.
O quam tu pulchra es.	O how fair you are.
Veni de Libano, amica mea,	Come with me from Lebanon, my love,
columba mea, formosa mea.	my dove, my beauty.
O quam tu pulchra es,	O how fair you are,
veni, coronaberis.	come, you will make a garland.
Surge, surge, propera, sponsa mea,	Arise, hasten, my bride,
surge, dilecta mea,	arise, my delight,
surge, immaculata mea.	arise, my spotless one.
Quia amore langueo.	For I pine of love. Arise,
Surge, veni, quia amore langueo.	come, for I pine of love.
—*Song of Songs*, 4:1, 4:8	

On a text from the *Song of Songs*, a source popular for musical setting at this time, this solo motet of around 1625 shows how a composer could, without breaking stride, incorporate into a single composition elements from recitative, solo madrigal, and bel canto aria. The first twenty-one measures are clearly recitative, but of a more melodious, rhythmic kind than that used in the theater. Marco Scacchi called it "hybrid recitative" (*recitativo inbastardito*), a mixed style found more appropriate for the church. Then there is a passage in triple-time aria style (measures 22 to 34). It is interrupted by five measures of recitative that recall the opening. After a continuation of the aria, the rest of the motet is in the recitative style. Grandi took advantage of the frequent recurrence of the words "O quam tu pulchra es" to bring back the opening music as a kind of refrain.

61

Giacomo Carissimi (1605–1674)

Historia di Jephte CD 4

a) Filia: *Plorate colles*

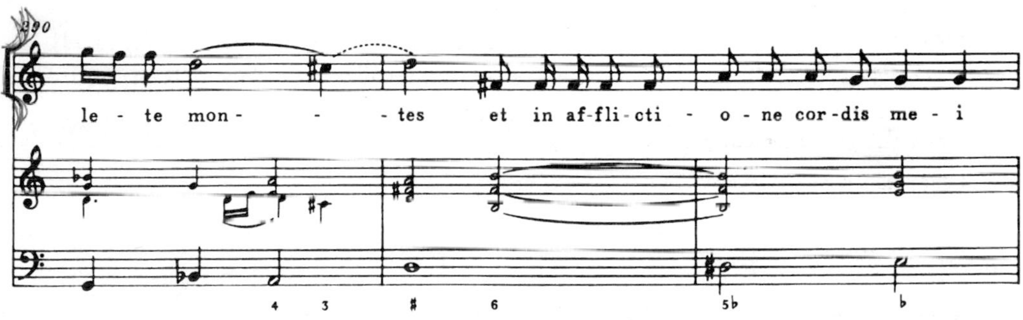

Edited by Gottfried Wolters, figured bass realized by Mathias Siedel (Wolfenbüttel: Möseler Verlag, 1969), pp. 29–39.

297
u - lu - - la - - - te!
Eccho
u - - lu - - la - - te!
u - lu - - la - - - - te!
tasto solo
301
Ec - - ce mo - ri - ar vir - go et non pot - e - ro mor - te
304
me - a me - is fi - li - is con - so - la - - ri, in - ge - mi - sci - te
307
sil - vae, fon - tes et flu - mi - na, in in - te - ri - tu vir - gi - nis

310
la - chri - ma - - - - te, fon-tes et flu - mi-na, in in-
6♭ 4 3 6
313
te - ri-tu vir - gi-nis la - chri - ma - - - - te!
6 5 ♭ 6♭ 6 4 3
316
Heu me do - len-tem, heu
Eccho
la - - chri - ma - te!
la - chri - ma - - - - te!
tasto solo
6♭ 6 6 4 5 3 ♯
320
me do-len - tem in lae-ti - ti-a po - pu-li, in vi-cto-ri-a
♯

323
Is - ra - el et glo - ri - a pa - tris me - i, e - go si - ne
325
fi - li - is vir - go, e - go fi - li - a u - ni - ge - ni - ta
328
mo - ri - ar et non vi - - -
330
vam. Ex - hor - re - sci - te ru - pes, ob - stu - pe - sci - te col - les,
333
val - les et ca - ver - nae in so - ni - tu hor - ri - bi - li re - - so -

335
na - te, val - les et ca - ver - nae in so - ni - tu hor - ri - bi - li, in
338
so - ni - tu hor - ri - bi - li re - - - - - - so - na - te!
340
Plo - ra - te, plo -
Eccho
re - - - - - so - na - te!
re - - - - so - na - te!
tasto solo
343
ra - te fi - li - i Is - ra - el, plo - ra - te vir - gi - ni - ta - tem

346
me - am et Jeph - te fi - li-am u - ni - ge - ni-tam in car - mi-ne do -

349
lo - - ris la - men - ta - - - mi - ni, et

352
Jeph - te fi - li - am u - ni - ge - ni - tam in car - mi - ne do -

354
lo - - ris la - men - ta - - - mi - ni.

Plorate colles, dolete montes
et in afflictione cordis mei ululate!
Ecce moriar virgo
et non potero morte mea
meis filiis consolari,
ingemiscite silvae, fontes et flumina,
in interitu virginis lachrimate,
fontes et flumina.

Heu me dolentem in laetitia populi,
in victoria Israel et gloria patris mei,
ego sine filiis virgo,
ego filia unigenita moriar et non vivam.
Exhorrescite rupes, obstupescite colles,
valles et cavernae in sonitu horribili resonate!
Plorate, filii Israel,
plorate virginitatem meam
et Jephte filiam unigenitam in carmine doloris
lamentamini.

Weep, hills, grieve, mountains
and in the affliction of my heart, wail!
Suddenly I shall die a virgin
and I shall not be able at my death
to be consoled by my children.
Groan, forests, springs, and rivers.
Weep for the death of a virgin,
springs and rivers.

Woe is me, sorrowful, amidst the people's joy
in Israel's victory and my country's glory.
I, without children, a virgin,
I, an only daughter, will die and not live.
Shudder, crags; be stupefied, hills;
valleys and caves, echo the horrible sound.
Weep, sons of Israel,
bewail my virginity
and lament Jephtha's only daughter
in songs of sorrow.

b) Chorus: *Plorate filii Israel*

361/389
ra - te o - mnes vir - - gi- - nes et fi - - li - am
ra - te o - mnes vir - - gi - - nes et fi - li - am
ra - te o - mnes vir - - gi - nes et fi - - li - am
ra - te o - mnes vir - - gi- - nes et fi - - li - am
ra - te o - mnes vir - - gi - - nes et fi - - li - am
ra - te o - mnes vir - - gi - - nes et fi - li - am
6 7 6 ♯ ♭

365/393
Jeph - te u - ni - ge - ni - tam
Jeph - te u - ni - ge - ni - tam
Jeph - te u - ni - ge - ni - tam
Jeph - te u - ni - ge - ni - tam in car - mi - ne do -
Jeph - te u - ni - ge - ni - tam in
Jeph - te u - ni - ge - ni - tam in car - mi - ne do - lo - - -
♯ **) ♯ ♭ 4 2 6 7 6

370/398
in carmi-ne do-lo - - - - - ris, do -
in car-mi-ne do - lo - - -
in car-mi-ne do-lo - - ris, do-lo -
lo - - ris, do - - lo - - - - -
car-mi-ne do - lo - - ris, do - - lo - - - - -
ris, do - - lo - - - - - - - - - -
375/403
lo - ris la-men-ta - mi - ni, la-men - ta - mi - ni, la-men -
ris la-men-ta - mi - ni, la-men - ta - mi - ni, la-men -
- ris la - men - ta - - - mi - ni,
ris la - - men - ta - - - mi - ni,
ris la - men - ta - mi-ni, la-men - ta - mi - ni,
ris la - - - men - ta - mi - ni, la-men -

380/408
Vi -
1.
ta - mi-ni, la-men - ta - mi-ni, la - men - ta - mi - ni.
ta - mi-ni, la-men - ta - mi-ni, la-men - ta - mi - ni. Plo -
la-men - ta - mi-ni, la-men - ta - mi-ni, la-men-ta - mi - ni. Plo-
la-men - ta - mi-ni, la-men - ta - mi-ni, la-men-ta - mi - ni. Plo-
la-men - ta - mi-ni, la-men - ta - mi-ni, la-men-ta - mi - ni.
ta - - mi - ni, la-men - ta - - - - - mi - ni. Plo-
413
2.
ni, la - men - ta - mi- -ni, la - men - ta - mi - ni, la - men -
ni, la - men - ta - mi- - ni,
ni,
ni, la - men - ta - - mi - ni, la - men -
ni, la - men - - ta - - - - mi -
ni, la - - - - men - - ta - - mi -
ergänzt

417

ta- -mi - ni, la-men - ta- -mi - ni, la-men -
la - - - men - ta - mi - ni, la-men -
la - men - ta - mi-ni, la-men - ta - mi - ni, la-men - ta - mi-ni,
ta - -mi - ni, la-men - ta - mi-ni, la-men - ta - mi-ni,
ni, la - - men - ta- -mi - ni, la-men - ta - mi-ni,
ni, la-men - ta - - - -mi - ni, la-men - ta- -mi -

422

-de
ta - mi-ni, la - -men - -ta - -mi - ni, la - men -
ta - mi-ni, la-men - ta - -mi - ni,
la - men - ta - mi-ni, la - men - ta - -mi - ni, la - men
la - men - ta - mi-ni, la - men - ta - -mi - ni,
la - men - ta - mi-ni, la - men - ta - -mi - ni,
ni, la - men - ta - - - -mi - -ni,

CHORUS

Plorate filii Israel, plorate omnes virgines
et filiam Jephte unigenitam in carmine doloris
lamentamini.

Weep, sons of Israel; weep all virgins,
and lament Jephtha's only daughter
in songs of sorrow.

In this scene, based on Judges 11:29–38, Jephtha, the military leader of the Israelites, has just returned victorious from a battle. He owes the victory to a promise he made to the Lord that if allowed to beat the Ammonites, he would on his return home sacrifice the first person who comes out of his house. It is his daughter who runs out to meet him with timbrels and dances.

The daughter's lament, the words of which are not in the biblical account, is a long, affecting recitative, sweetened, as was customary in the sacred hybrid style, with arioso passages built on sequences and with moments of florid song. Two sopranos, representing her companions, echo some of the daughter's cadential phrases.

Carissimi's recitative introduces expressive dissonances in a way that recalls the Florentine style, but they exist in a more harmonically determined environment. For example, the soprano's *D* in measure 295 is not simply a free dissonance but a member of a chord. Even more characteristic is the *F*♯ of measure 302, which is part of a *D* chord over a *G* pedal. Similarly the skip to the seventh in measures 308–09 and the "Neapolitan" lowered sixth at measure 310 and again at measure 314 are harmonic rather than melodic effects. Equally striking are the double suspensions in the chorus (measures 380 ff.). These passages demonstrate how much the emotional intensity of this scene owes to harmonic rather than melodic means.

The excerpt (and the work) closes with a magnificent six-voice chorus of lamentation (b) that employs both polychoral and madrigalistic effects. In what becomes an emblem of lament in the seventeenth century, the choral basses and the basso continuo three times descend a fourth by step (measures 358–70).

62 HEINRICH SCHÜTZ (1585–1672)

Grand Concerto: *Saul, was verfolgst du mich*

SWV 415 CD 4 CD 2

Symphoniarum sacrarum tertia pars, worinnen zubefinden sind deutsche Concerten, Op. 12 (Dresden, 1650), No. 18, ed. Günter Graulich and Paul Horn, Stuttgarter Schützausgabe (Stuttgart: Hänssler-Verlag, 1969), pp. 63–73.

Obligat-Instrumente
Fevorit-Chor
Saul, Saul, Saul,
Saul, Saul, Saul,
Saul, Saul, Saul,
Saul, Saul, Saul,
Saul, Saul, Saul, Saul, was ver-folgst du mich?
Saul, Saul, Saul, Saul, wilt thou in - jure me?
Saul, Saul, Saul, Saul, was ver - folgst du mich?
Saul, Saul, Saul, Saul, wilt thou in - jure me?
mich?
me?
mich?
me?

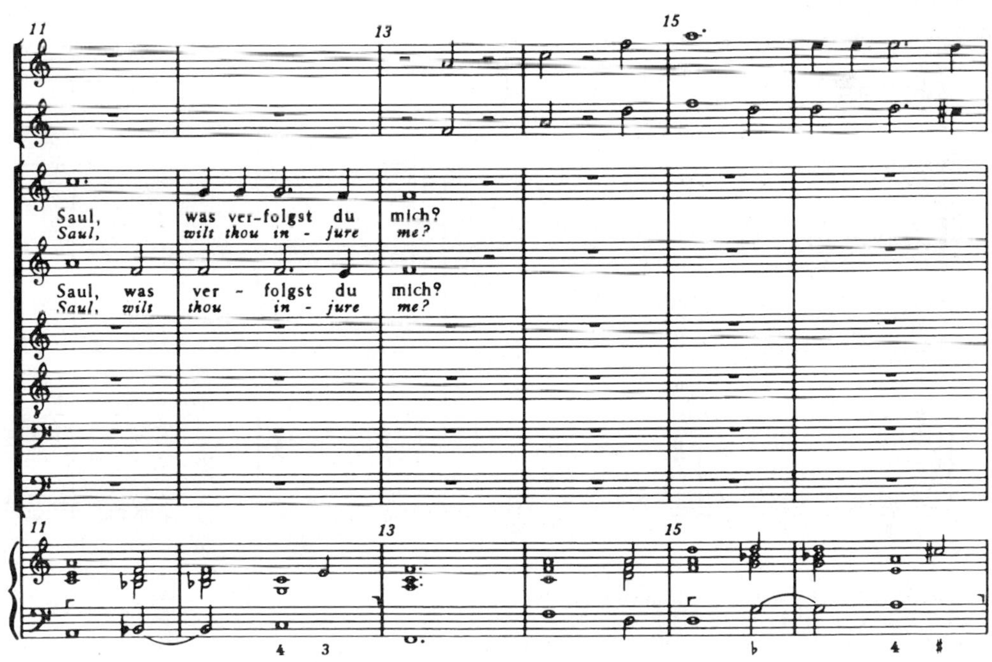
Saul, was ver-folgst du mich?
Saul, wilt thou in - jure me?
Saul, was ver - folgst du mich?
Saul, wilt thou in - jure me?

17
forte
19
21
mezzopiano
pianissimo
23
Obligat-Instrumente
Favorit - Chor
Capell - Chor 1 ad lib.
Capell - Chor 2 ad lib.
Saul, Saul, Saul, Saul, was verfolgst du mich, was verfolgst du mich, was verfolgst du mich?
Saul, Saul, Saul, Saul, wilt thou in - jure me, wilt thou in-jure me, wilt thou in-jure me?
Saul, Saul, Saul, Saul, was ver - folgst du mich?
Saul, Saul, Saul, Saul, wilt thou in - jure me?
Saul, Saul, Saul, Saul, was verfolgst du mich?
Saul, Saul, Saul, Saul, wilt thou in - jure me?

41
28
Obligat-Instrumente
Favoriti-Chor
solus forte
Es wird dir schwer wer - den, wi-der den Sta-chel zu lök - - ken,
It will be hard for thee to kick a - gainst, kick a - gainst the pricks.
Solo
Es wird dir schwer wer - den, wi-der den Sta-chel zu lök - - ken,
It will be hard for thee to kick a - gainst, kick a - gainst the pricks.

34
36
38
forte
mezzopiano
pianissimo
Obligat-Instrumente
Favorit-Chor
Saul, Saul, Saul, Saul, was verfolgst du mich, was verfolgst du mich, was verfolgst du mich?
Saul, Saul, Saul, Saul, wilt thou injure me, wilt thou injure me, wilt thou injure me?
Capell-Chor 1 ad lib.
Saul, Saul, Saul, was verfolgst du mich?
Saul, Saul, Saul, wilt thou injure me?
Capell-Chor 2 ad lib.
Saul, Saul, Saul, was verfolgst du mich?
Saul, Saul, Saul, wilt thou injure me?

Obligat-Instrumente
Favorit-Chor
Solo
Es wird dir schwer wer-den, wi-der den Sta-chel zu lök - - - ken,
It will be hard for thee to kick a - gainst, kick a - gainst the
solus
Es wird dir schwer wer-den, wi-der den Sta-chel zu lök - - - -
It will be hard for thee to kick a - gainst, kick a - gainst the
Solo
pricks,
es wird dir schwer wer - den,
it will be hard for thee,
Es wird dir schwer, es wird dir
It will be hard, it will be
Es wird dir schwer wer - den, es wird dir schwer,
It will be hard for thee, it will be hard,
Es wird dir schwer wer - den, es wird dir schwer
It will be hard for thee, it will be hard
ken, es wird dir schwer wer - den, es wird dir
pricks, it will be hard for thee, it will be
Es wird dir schwer wer - den,
It will be hard for thee,

50
52
54
es wird dir schwer
it will be hard
schwer werden, es wird dir schwer
hard for thee, it will be hard
es wird dir schwer wer - den, es wird dir
it will be hard for thee, it will be
es wird dir schwer wer - den, es wird dir
it will be hard for thee, it will be
schwer wer - den, es wird dir
hard for thee, it will be
es wird dir schwer wer -
it will be hard for
6 5
55
57
59
wer - den,
for thee,
wer - den,
for thee,
schwer wer - den,
hard for thee,
schwer wer - den,
hard for thee,
schwer, schwer wer - den,
hard, hard for thee,
à 3
den, wi-der den Sta-chel zu lök -
thee, to kick a-gainst, kick a-gainst the
4
6

Obligat-Instrumente
Favorit-Chor
Capell-Chor 1 ad lib.
Capell-Chor 2 ad lib.
60
62
64
forte
wi-der den Sta-chel zu lök - - - ken, Saul, Saul, Saul, Saul, was verto kick a - gainst, kick a - gainst the pricks, Saul, Saul, Saul, Saul, wilt thou
Saul, Saul, Saul, Saul, Saul, Saul, Saul, was ver-
Saul, Saul, Saul, Saul, Saul, Saul, Saul, wilt thou
ken, Saul, Saul, Saul, Saul, Saul, Saul, was ver-
pricks, Saul, Saul, Saul, Saul, Saul, Saul, wilt thou

65
mezzopiano
pianissimo
67
forte
mezzopiano
69
pianissimo
folgst du mich, was verfolgst du mich, was verfolgst du mich, was verfolgst du mich, was verfolgst du mich, was ver-
in-jure me, wilt thou in-jure me, wilt thou in-jure me, wilt thou in-jure me, wilt thou in-jure me, wilt thou
folgst du mich, was verfolgst du mich, was verfolgst du mich, was verfolgst du mich, was verfolgst du mich, was ver-
in-jure me, wilt thou in-jure me, wilt thou in-jure me, wilt thou in-jure me, wilt thou in-jure me, wilt thou
folgst du mich, was verfolgst du mich, was verfolgst du mich, was verfolgst du mich, was verfolgst du mich, was ver-
in-jure me, wilt thou in-jure me, wilt thou in-jure me, wilt thou in-jure me, wilt thou in-jure me, wilt thou
forte sempre
folgst du mich, Saul, Saul, Saul, Saul, Saul, Saul, Saul,
in-jure me, Saul, Saul, Saul, Saul, Saul, Saul, Saul,
folgst du mich, was verfolgst du mich, was verfolgst du mich, was verfolgst du mich, was verfolgst du mich, was ver-
in-jure me, wilt thou in-jure me, wilt thou in-jure me, wilt thou in-jure me, wilt thou in-jure me, wilt thou
folgst du mich, was verfolgst du mich, was verfolgst du mich, was verfolgst du mich, was verfolgst du mich, was ver-
in-jure me, wilt thou in-jure me, wilt thou in-jure me, wilt thou in-jure me, wilt thou in-jure me, wilt thou
folgst du mich, was verfolgst du mich,
in-jure me, wilt thou in-jure me,
folgst du mich, was verfolgst du mich,
in-jure me, wilt thou in-jure me,
folgst du mich, was verfolgst du mich,
in-jure me, wilt thou in-jure me,
folgst du mich, was verfolgst du mich,
in-jure me, wilt thou in-jure me,
folgst du mich, was verfolgst du mich,
in-jure me, wilt thou in-jure me,
folgst du mich, was verfolgst du mich,
in-jure me, wilt thou in-jure me,
folgst du mich, was verfolgst du mich,
in-jure me, wilt thou in-jure me,
folgst du mich, was verfolgst du mich,
in-jure me, wilt thou in-jure me,
65
mezzopiano
67
pianissimo
forte
69
mezzopiano
pianissimo

70
forte
mezzopiano
72
pianissimo
74
folgst du mich, was ver- folgst du mich, was ver- folgst du mich, was ver- folgst du mich,
in-jure me, wilt thou in-jure me, wilt thou in-jure me, wilt thou in-jure me,
folgst du mich, was ver- folgst du mich, was ver- folgst du mich, was ver- folgst du mich,
in-jure me, wilt thou in-jure me, wilt thou in-jure me, wilt thou in-jure me,
folgst du mich, was ver- folgst du mich, was ver- folgst du mich, was ver- folgst du mich,
in-jure me, wilt thou in-jure me, wilt thou in-jure me, wilt thou in-jure me,
Saul, Saul, Saul, Saul, was ver- folgst du mich,
Saul, Saul, Saul, Saul, wilt thou in-jure me,
folgst du mich, was ver- folgst du mich, was ver- folgst du mich, was ver- folgst du mich,
in-jure me, wilt thou in-jure me, wilt thou in-jure me, wilt thou in-jure me,
solus
folgst du mich, was ver- folgst du mich, was ver- folgst du mich, was ver- folgst du mich, was ver- folgst du mich,
in-jure me, wilt thou in-jure me, wilt thou in-jure me, wilt thou in-jure me, wilt thou in-jure me,
was ver- folgst du mich,
wilt thou in-jure me,
was ver- folgst du mich,
wilt thou in-jure me,
was ver- folgst du mich,
wilt thou in-jure me,
was ver- folgst du mich,
wilt thou in-jure me,
was ver- folgst du mich,
wilt thou in-jure me,
was ver- folgst du mich,
wilt thou in-jure me,
was ver- folgst du mich,
wilt thou in-jure me,
was ver- folgst du mich,
wilt thou in-jure me,
70
forte
72
mezzopiano
pianissimo
Solo
74

75
forte
mezzopiano
77
pianissimo
79
was ver- folgst du mich, was ver- folgst du mich, was ver- folgst du mich?
wilt thou in-jure me, wilt thou in-jure me, wilt thou in-jure me?
was ver- folgst du mich, was ver- folgst du mich, was ver- folgst du mich, was ver- folgst du mich?
wilt thou in-jure me, wilt thou in-jure me, wilt thou in-jure me, wilt thou in-jure me?
Saul, Saul, Saul, Saul, Saul, was ver- folgst du mich?
Saul, Saul, Saul, Saul, Saul, wilt thou in-jure me?
was ver- folgst du mich?
wilt thou in-jure me?
Solo

For this composition Schütz chose one of the most dramatic episodes in the New Testament, Paul's description of how he was converted to Christianity (Acts 26:12–14, Revised Standard Version):

> Thus I journeyed to Damascus with the authority and commission of the chief priests. At midday, O king, I saw on the way a light from heaven, brighter than the sun, shining round me and those who journeyed with me. And when we had all fallen to the ground, I heard a voice saying to me in the Hebrew language, "Saul, Saul, why do you persecute me? It hurts you to kick against the goads."

Saul, a Jew, had been sent to Damascus to fetch Christian prisoners. The voice he heard in the desert was that of Christ. The experience led to Saul's conversion and to his career (under the name Paul) as a crusader for Christianity.

The concerto is set for six solo voices (the ensemble Schütz called *favoriti*), two violins, two four-voice choirs, and, it may be assumed, an orchestra that doubles the choral parts. Two-note chords from the D-minor triad rise from the depths of the solo basses through the tenors; then the same music is heard shifting to A minor in the sopranos, and finally the violins return it to D minor. Christ's question "Was verfolgst du mich?" (Why do you persecute me?) is a mesh of dissonant anticipations and suspensions.

So far the medium has been that of the concerto for few voices. Now the grand concerto takes over the same music in a bright D major (measure 17), and the choruses and soloists together reverberate with echoes, suggesting the effect of Christ's voice bouncing off rocky projections in the desert. As the voice rings obsessively in Saul's ear, sections in recitative and arioso for solo voices alternate with the "Saul, Saul" grand-concerto music as a refrain.

The idea of the rising chords may have been suggested to Schütz by Monteverdi's famous madrigal *Hor che'l ciel e la terra*, which contains a similar progression. Schütz worked with Monteverdi and Grandi during a visit to Venice in 1628 and 1629. During previous visits, in 1609 and 1612, he had studied with Giovanni Gabrieli, whose polychoral practice is also reflected here.

63 Ennemond Gaultier (ca. 1575–1651)

Gigue: *La Poste* CD 4

a) Lute

42

Special signs pincé (mordent with lower auxiliary); coulé (upward double appoggiatura); , port de voix (appoggiatura starting on lower auxiliary). *Oeuvres du vieux Gaultier*, André Souris, ed. (Paris: Editions du CNRS, 1966). Nos. 63, 85, pp. 83, 111.

b) Arrangement for harpsichord by Jean-Henri D'Anglebert

These two examples illustrate the transfer of the lute idiom to the harpsichord. Although the latter instrument, unlike the lute, is capable of playing chords as simultaneities, the arranger has deferred to the limitations of the lute and distributed the component notes of a chord over several beats in *style brisé* (broken style). The ornaments tend to fall on the same notes and beats in both arrangements, and their function is similar: to mark certain beats as a drum might do, to promote continuity, to play down certain other beats, or to intensify dissonance and thereby the harmonic motion.

This gigue, in duple meter, is in the common binary form, with a close on the dominant in the first part, on the tonic in the second.

64 Johann Jakob Froberger (1616–1667)

Lamentation faite sur la mort très douloureuse de Sa Majesté Impériale Ferdinand le troisième et se joüe lentement avec discretion CD 4

Oeuvres complètes pour clavecin, ed. Howard Schott (Paris: Heugel, HE.33.702), Le Pupitre 58, pp. 160–61.

16
19
22
26
29
32
35

Froberger, in his toccatas, betrayed the influence of his teacher Frescobaldi, but this piece demonstrates his mastery of the French clavecin style. It is in the genre of the *tombeau*, which French lutenists and harpsichordists customarily wrote upon the death of one of their colleagues. Froberger composed this tombeau ("Lamentation on the very sad death of His Imperial Majesty Ferdinand III, to be played slowly, with circumspection") in 1657 to mourn the death of the emperor whose court in Vienna he served as organist. In keeping with the French tradition, this piece is a slow allemande, but its hesitations and impulsive runs remove it from the dance. The *style brisé*, through which Froberger was one of the first to imitate lute music on the harpsichord, dominates the texture. Both the rare key of F minor and the prominent threefold *F*s at the end allude to the emperor's name. Another programmatic touch is the arpeggio in the final two measures from deep in the bass to the treble, representing the ascent of the emperor's soul.

GIROLAMO FRESCOBALDI (1583–1643)

65

Toccata No. 3 (1615, revised 1637) CD 4 CD 2

Toccate d'intavolatura di cimbalo et organo libro 1 (Rome, 1637; first published in *Toccate e partite d' intavolatura di cimbalo . . . Libro primo*, 1615). Ed. Pierre Pidoux, Orgel- und Klavierwerke, Vol. 3 (Kassel: Bärenreiter-Verlag, 1954), pp. 11–13. Reprinted by permission of Bärenreiter Music Corporation.

The restless character of this toccata, meant to be played before a Mass, is typical of Frescobaldi's works. The music is constantly approaching a cadence on either the dominant or tonic, but until the very end the composer evaded or weakened the goal harmonically, rhythmically, or through continued part-movement. Some of the notable points of arrival and immediate departure are measures 5 (dominant), 8 (dominant minor), and 13 (tonic major), and measures 17, 26, and 31 (all tonic minor). The restlessness is also felt in the shifting of styles. At the outset the toccata breathes the spirit of recitative, with jagged lines and nervous rhythms. At measure 5 a short arioso passage, with chains of suspensions over a walking bass, leads to an imitative section (measures 8–11). In the remainder of the piece the two hands alternate, one playing scales and turns while the other has chords, or they toss back and forth short figures that lie easily under the fingers. The emphasis on the dominant and tonic strongly sets the keynote for what is to follow in the music of the Mass.

Alessandro Scarlatti (1660–1725)

66

La Griselda

Act II, Scene 1: *Mi rivedi* CD 4

10
solo
Mi ri - ve - di o sel - va om-bro - sa, ma non più, Re-gi - na e spo - sa, mi ri-
ve - di sven-tu-ra - ta, mi ri - ve-di sven - tu-ra - ta, di-sprez-za-ta, di-sprez-za-ta pa-sto-rel - la, sven-tu-
15
ra - ta, di-sprez-za - - - ta pa-sto-rel - la.
tutti

47
20
p
È pur quel - lo, quel - lo, quel - lo il pa - trio mon - te, que - sta è pur l'a - mi - ca
solo
fon - te, quel - lo è il pra - to e il que - sto è il ri - o; e sol i - o, e sol io non son, no, no, non son più quel -
25
48
p
la no, non son più quel - la no, non son più, no, non son più quel - la. Mi ri -
Dal segno

GRISELDA

Mi rivedi o selva ombrosa, Ma non più Regina e sposa, Sventurata, disprezzata Pastorella. È pur quello il patrio monte, Questa è pur l'amica fonte, Quello è il prato e questo è il rio; E sol io non son più quella. —Based on the libretto by Apostolo Zeno	You see me again, o shady forest, but no longer queen and bride; unfortunate, disdained, a shepherdess. Yet there is my homeland's mountain and here is still the friendly fountain; there is the meadow and this is the river; and only I am not the same.

La Griselda was first performed in Rome in 1721. In this aria, "You see me again, o shady forest," Griselda expresses conflicting reactions to her situation: a queen for fifteen years, she has been repudiated by King Gualtiero of Sicily. She must return to her humble origins and, besides, serve as maid to the new queen, all this to test her virtue. She addresses the familiar surroundings of her native countryside with a mixture of humiliation and nostalgia.

The mood of subjection is summed up in the melody of the first line, out of which the rest of the main (A) section develops through extension, sequence, and combinatorial methods. The subordinate (B) section, linked to the A section rhythmically, presents the bright side for a moment, her pleasure at being home. Only the vocal portion of the A section is then repeated (*da capo dal segno*).

This aria is a concise example of the abbreviated format, popular in the 1720s, in which the opening ritornello is omitted in the da capo. The scheme is:

		𝄋		**Fine**			**Dal segno**
Section:	**Ritornello**	**A**	**Transitional Rit**		**B**		
Key:	**C minor**				**Modulation to E♭**		
Measure:	*1*	*4*	*16*	*18*	*19*	*26*	*(27=)4—18*

The ritornello and the A section occupy 18 measures, all in C minor except for a brief foray into B♭ major. The B section, of 8 measures, modulates from the C-minor cadence at the end of the transitional ritornello by way of G minor to E♭. Then, skipping over the opening ritornello, the singer returns to the A section directly, closing the aria at the fermata that ends the transitional ritornello.

Jean-Baptiste Lully (1632–1687)

67

Le bourgeois gentilhomme: Ballet des nations CD 4

a) L'entrée des Scaramouches Trivelins et Arlequins représente une nuit.
49
6
1.
2.
10
15

Oeuvres complètes de Lully, ed. Henry Prunières, III, *Comédies ballets*, Vol. 3 (Paris: Éditions de la Revue musicale, 1938), pp. 135–39

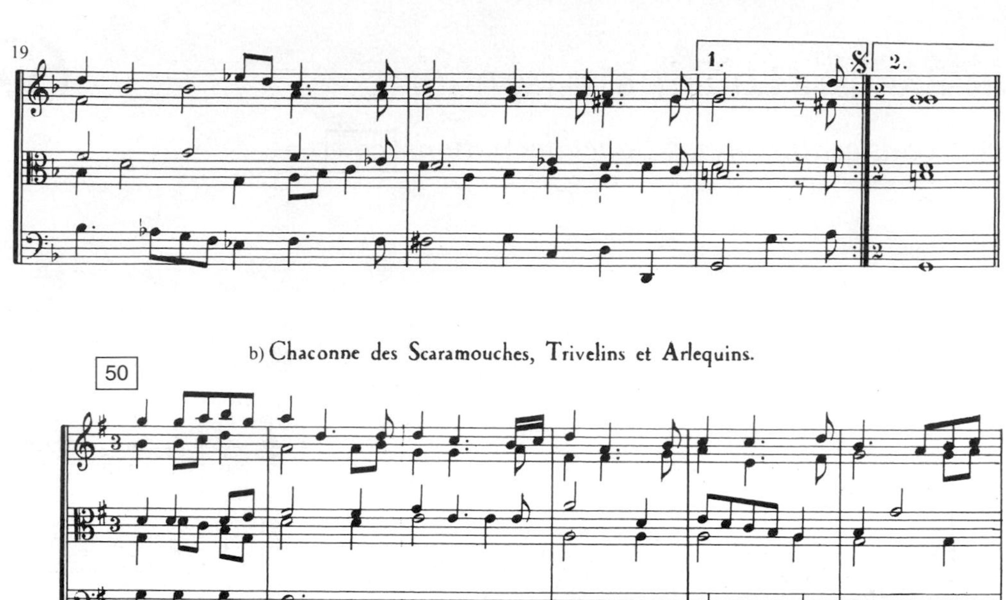
19
1.
2.
b) Chaconne des Scaramouches, Trivelins et Arlequins.
50

7

14

21
28
35
43

The comédie-ballet was a play with dances and songs, a genre devised by the composer and dancing-master Jean-Baptiste Lully and the playwright Jean-Baptiste Molière. This entrée and chaconne are part of the *Ballet des nations*, an independent entertainment that followed the comédie-ballet *Le bourgeois gentilhomme* when it was performed at the court of King Louis XIV in the château at Chambord in October 1670. The music is scored for a five-part string orchestra.

The entrée, as the term suggests, accompanies the entrance of the dancers: Scaramouches (Scaramuccio, a cowardly braggard, is a stock character of the *commedia dell'arte*), the buffoons (Trivelins), and the Harlequins. An allemande in binary form, the entry music modulates to the relative major at the end of the first part, preparing the key for the second part, which modulates back to G minor through its dominant. At measure 17, the proportion three to two (three half notes are now worth two half notes) speeds up the pace while shifting the meter to compound triple, a probable occasion for comedic action by the dancers. The characteristic rhythms of the French overture—dotted notes and figures rushing toward the downbeat—pervade, especially in the first part.

The chaconne, a dance imported to Europe from Latin America, was usually based on a pattern of chords (I-V-IV-V) in major mode. Here a four-measure ground bass descends a fourth under these chords; the ground bass is most evident in measures 10–22 and 44 to the end. For variety's sake, Lully tends to break up the ground with contrasting phrases *en rondeau* and by modulations, as in measures 23–44, in which the bass moves upward.

Both the entrée and chaconne owe their courtly artificiality and grace to consistent four-measure phrases and to the performance convention of doubling the length of the dot and alternating long and short notes in successions of eighth notes.

Jean-Baptiste Lully

68

Armide CD 5

a) Ouverture

Edited by Robert Eitner, *Publikationen älterer praktischer und theoretischer Musikwerke*, 14 (Leipzig: Breitkopf & Härtel, 1885) pp. 1–3, 100–04. Used by permission.

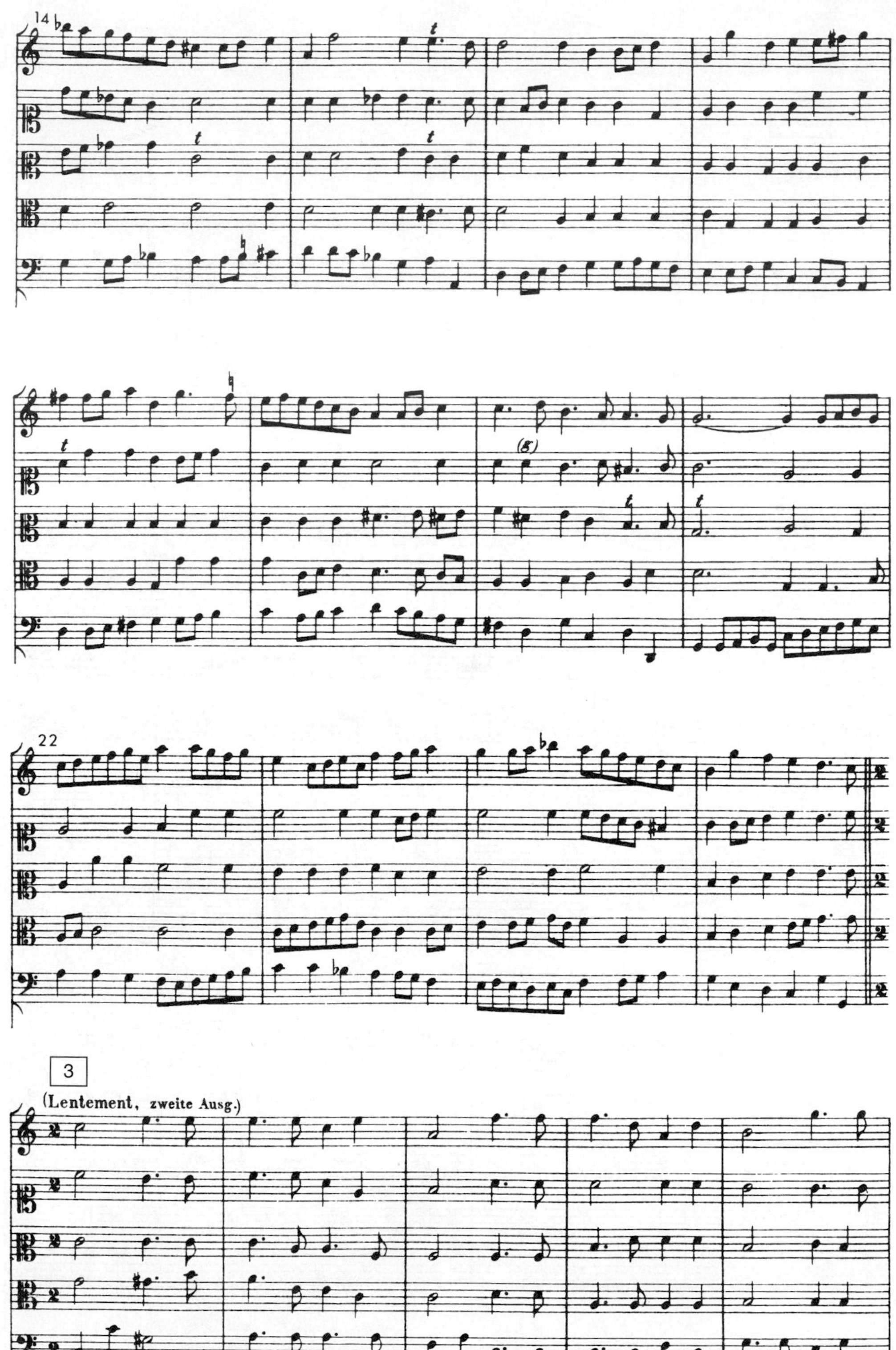
14
22
3
(Lentement, zweite Ausg.)

b) Act II, Scene 5: Armide: *Enfin il est en ma puissance*

4

Violons.

5
Armide. (tenent un dard à la main.)
En - fin il est en ma puis-san-ce. Ce fa-tal en-ne - mi, ce su-per-be vain -

24
queur. La char-me du som - meil-le liv-re à ma ven-gean-ce; je vais per-cer son in-vin-ci-ble

(Armide
coeur. Par lui tous mes cap-tifs sont sor-tis d'es-cla - va-ge; qu'il é-prou-ve tou-te ma ra-ge. Quel

32 va pour frapper Renaud et ne peut exécuter le dessein qu'elle a de lui ôter la vie.)
trou-ble me sai-sit? qui me fait hé-si-ter? qu'est-ce qu'en sa fa-veur la pi-tié me veut
di-re? Frap-pons ciel! qui peut m'ar-ré-ter? A-che vons... je fré-
40
mis! ven-geons-nous... je sou-pi-re! Est-ce ain-si que je dois me ven-ger au-jour-
d'hui! Ma co-lè re s'é-teint quand j'ap-pro-che de lui. Plus je le voi, plus ma ven-geance est
49
vai-ne; mon bras trem-blant se re-fuse á ma hai-ne. Ah! quel-le cru-au-

té de lui ra-vir le jour! A ce jeu-ne hé-ros tout cè-de sur la ter-re. Qui croi-
6 6♯ 6 6

57
rait qu'il fut ne seu-le-ment pour la guer-re? Il sem-ble e-tre fait pour l'a-mour.
6 6 6 6 5♭

Ne puis-je me ven-ger à moins qu'il ne pé-ris-se? Hé! ne suf-fit-il
7♮

64
pas que l'a-mour le pu-nis-se? Puis-qu'il n'a pu trou-ver mes yeux as-sez char-
6 6 6 ♯ 6♯

mants, qu'il m'aime au moins par mes en-chan-te-ments, que s'il se peut, je le ha-
71
6
ïs-se.
78

Ve-nez, ve-
91
nez, se-con - der mes dé - sirs, dé-mons, trans-for-mez vous en d'ai-ma-bles zé - phirs; ve-nez, ve -
1.
2.
phirs. Je cède a ce vain - queur la pi - tié me sur - mon - te, ca - chez ma foi -
103
blesse et ma hon - te dans les plus re-cu-lés dé-serts, vo-lez, vo - lez con-dui-sez-

nous au bout de l'u - ni - vers vo - lez, vo - lez, con - dui - sez nous au bout de l'u - ni - vers.

* On the recording, the music returns to measure 71, continues through measure 90, and again repeats measures 86–90.

ARMIDE

Enfin il est en ma puissance,	Finally he is in my power,
Ce fatal ennemi, ce superbe vainqueur.	this fatal enemy, this superb warrior.
Le charme du sommeille livre à ma vengeance;	The charm of sleep delivers him to my vengeance;
Je vais percer son invincible coeur.	I will pierce his invincible heart.
Par lui tous mes captifs sont sortis d'esclavage;	Through him all my captives have escaped from slavery.
Qu'il éprouve toute ma rage.	Let him feel all my anger.
Quel trouble me saisit? qui me fait hésiter?	What fear grips me? what makes me hesitate?
Qu'est-ce qu'en sa faveur le pitié me veut dire?	What in his favor does pity want to tell me?
Frappons . . . Ciel! qui peut m'arrêter?	Let us strike . . . Heavens! Who can stop me?
Achevons . . . je frémis! vengeons–nous . . . je soupire!	Let us get on with it . . . I tremble! Let us avenge . . . I sigh!
Est-ce ainsi que je dois me venger aujourd'hui?	Is it thus that I must avenge myself today?
Ma colère s'éteint quand j'approche de lui.	My rage is extinguished when I approach him.
Plus je le voi, plus ma vengeance est vaine;	The more I see of him, the more my vengeance is ineffectual.
Mon bras tremblant se refuse à ma haine.	My trembling arm denies my hate.
Ah! quelle cruauté de lui ravir le jour!	Ah! What cruelty, to rob him of the light of day!
A ce jeune héros tout cède sur la terre.	To this young hero everything on earth surrenders.
Qui croirait qu'il fut né seulement pour la guerre?	Who would believe that he was born only for war?
Il semble être fait pour l'Amour.	He seems to be made for love.
Ne puis-je me venger à moins qu'il ne périsse?	Could I not avenge myself unless he dies?
Hé! ne suffit-il pas que l'amour le punisse?	Oh, is it not enough that Love should punish him?
Puisqu'il n'a pu trouver mes yeux assez charmants,	Since he could not find my eyes charming enough,
Qu'il m'aime au moins par mes enchantements.	let him love me at least through my sorcery,
Que, s'il se peut, je le haïsse.	so that, if it's possible, I may hate him.
Venez, venez, seconder mes désirs,	Come, come support my desires,
Démons, transformez-vous en d'aimables zéphirs.	demons; transform yourselves into friendly zephyrs.
Je cède à ce vainqueur, la pitié me surmonte.	I give in to this conqueror; pity overwhelms me.
Cachez ma foiblesse et ma honte	Conceal my weakness and my shame
Dans les plus reculés déserts.	in the most remote desert.
Volez, volez, conduisez-nous au bout de l'univers.	Fly, fly, lead us to the end of the universe.

—Philippe Quinault

Armide, on a libretto by Philippe Quinault, was one of Lully's last operas, produced in Paris in 1686. The Ouverture, in the form and genre known as the *French overture*, is in two parts. The first is homophonic, slow, and majestic, marked by persistent dotted rhythms and by figures rushing toward the downbeats. Moreover, a French performance convention of the time encouraged "double-dotting," the reading of singly dotted quarter notes as if doubly dotted, and performing even eighth notes as if they were dotted eighth notes. The faster second section, in a compound triple measure, starts with a semblance of fugal imitation. Then the slow tempo returns, together with some reminiscences of the opening music. Each of the two sections is marked with a repeat, in keeping with the overture's dance pedigree: it was originally an allemande. Some later opera overtures and other instrumental pieces began in this way, then continued with a number of additional movements. The orchestra consists entirely of strings, divided into five parts rather than the four that became standard later.

The first part of this monologue is one of the most impressive scenes of recitative in all of Lully's work. Armide is an enchantress who captures knights of the Crusades, casts a spell over them, and holds them for her pleasure in her palace. But against her will she has fallen in love with Renaud, who had incited her anger by freeing her captives. In this scene she aims to slay him as he sleeps. Her dagger is ready, but Armide cannot bring herself to kill him because of her deep love for him.

The orchestra introduces the scene with a tense prelude that has the character of the slow section of a French overture. Armide, accompanied by continuo, then sings in an unmetrical rhythm notated in mixed duple and triple measures. This device permits the two accented syllables normally found in each poetic line to fall on downbeats. All the lines, and sometimes caesuras within a line, are marked by rests. Rests are also used dramatically, as in the passage where Armide hesitates: "Let's get it done . . . I tremble . . . let us avenge ourselves . . . I sigh!" (measures 38–42).

Despite the lack of regular meter, Lully's recitative is more melodious than its Italian counterpart, and the line is driven by a more active harmonic background.

The air that follows is accompanied by the orchestra and has the graceful rhythm of a minuet. Armide calls on her demons to transform themselves into zephyrs and transport her and Renaud to some remote desert, where her shame and weakness would not be observed.

Henry Purcell (1659–1695)

69

Dido and Aeneas

Act III, Scene 2

Dido: *Thy hand, Belinda/When I am laid in earth*

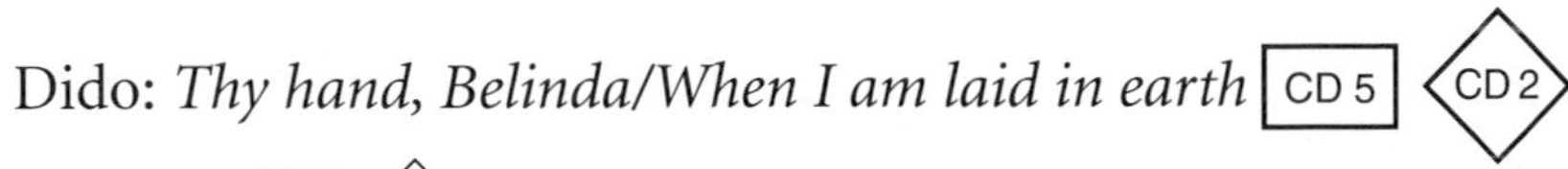

Extract of Purcell's *Dido and Aeneas.* Words by Nahum Tate. Arranged by Margaret Laurie & Thurston Dart.

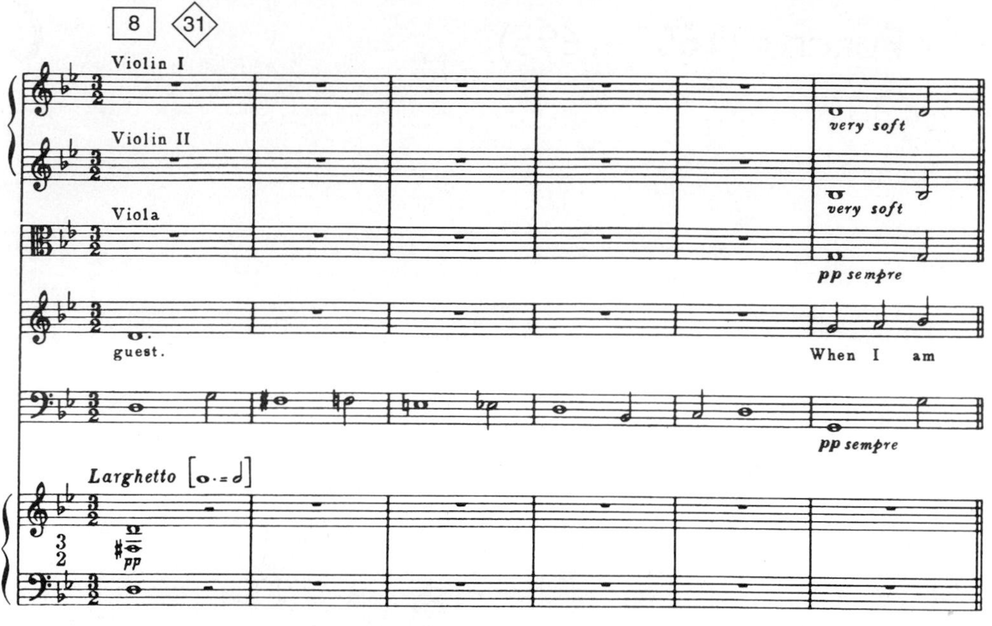
8
31
Violin I
Violin II
Viola
very soft
very soft
pp sempre
guest.
When I am
pp sempre
Larghetto
pp

10
laid, am laid in earth, may my wrongs cre - ate No

2nd time
1st time
1
trou - ble, no trou-ble in thy breast, When I am

9
32
2
20
Re - mem - ber me!
re - mem - ber me!
but
ah!
for - get
my
fate,
re - mem - ber me!
but
ah!
30
for - get
my
fate.
Re - mem - ber me!
re - mem - ber me!
but
ah!
for - get
my
fate,
re - mem - ber me!
but
ah!

Chorus: *With drooping wings* CD 5

10
droop - ing wings, with droop - ing wings ye Cu-pids come, And
Cu - pids come, with droop - ing wings ye Cu - pids come, And
droop-ing wings, with droop-ing wings, with droop-ing wings, with droop-ing wings ye Cu-pids come,
with droop - ing wings ye Cu-pids come, ye Cu-pids come,

scat-ter ro - ses, scat-ter, scat-ter_ ro - ses_ on_ her tomb,
scat-ter ro - ses, scat-ter, scat-ter_ ro - ses on her tomb, Soft, soft ___ and
And scat-ter, scat-ter_ ro - ses on her tomb, Soft, soft,_
And scat-ter_ ro - ses, scat-ter_ ro - ses_ on her tomb,
[pp]

20
Soft,_ soft ___ and gen-tle, soft,_ soft,_ soft,_ soft ___ and
gen-tle as_her heart, gen - tle as her_heart, soft,_ soft ___ and gen-tle,
soft and gen - tle as her heart, soft,_ soft ___ and
Soft,_ soft ___ and gen - tle, soft,_ soft,_ soft,_ soft,_ soft ___ and
#6
#
(6) (7 7 6)
pp

gen-tle as_her heart; Keep here, here your watch, keep here, here, keep here your watch, and
gen-tle_as her heart; Keep here, here_ your watch, keep here, here, keep here your watch, and
gen-tle_as her heart; Keep here, here your watch, keep here, here, keep here your watch, and
gen - tleas her heart; Keep here, here your watch, keep here, here, keep here your watch, and
p
mp
mf
f

Purcell wrote this opera on a libretto by Nahum Tate; it was first performed in 1689 by the pupils at a girl's boarding school in Chelsea, a suburb of London, with a few outsiders probably pressed into service for the men's parts. The plot is distantly descended from the fourth book of Vergil's *Aeneid*. A more immediate antecedent is John Blow's court masque *Venus and Adonis*, with which it shares many musical and dramatic features.

Dido's lament *When I am laid in earth* in the last scene is one of the landmarks of seventeenth-century music, a perfect adaptation of technique to expression. The preceding recitative does more than serve as a vehicle for the text; by its slow stepwise descent of a seventh, it portrays the dying Dido and thus prepares us for the lament. But it does not tell us why she is dying. The reason is that in the midst of an intense love affair with Aeneas she feels abandoned, betrayed, and forlorn when he is called away to fight.

Purcell followed an Italian opera tradition of setting such laments over a *basso ostinato*, or ground bass. The bass itself grows out of the descending fourth common in such pieces, but it is extended by a two-measure cadence formula, adding up to a five-measure pattern, which is heard ten times. Purcell created great tension and forward thrust by re-attacking suspended notes on the strong beat, intensifying the dissonance. We feel a further jolt when, several times, the dissonance is resolved by skip (for example, at the word "trouble," measures 12 and 13). The violins contribute to the grieving effect by adding their own suspensions and other dissonances.

The closing chorus *With drooping wings* was certainly suggested to Purcell by the final chorus of Blow's *Venus and Adonis.* Equally perfect in workmanship, it is on a larger scale and conveys a more profound depth of sorrow. Descending minor-scale figures portray the cupids' "drooping wings," and arresting pauses mark the words "never part."

Henry Purcell

70

The Fairy Queen

Hark! the ech'ing air a triumph sings CD 5

Text by Elkanah Settle (?) from Shakespeare's *A Midsummer Night's Dream*. Reprinted by Broude Bros. (New York, 196–), pp. 179–82.

19
sings, Hark! hark! the ech-'ing air a tri - - - - umph sings
hark! the ech-'ing air a tri - - - - - - - umph sings, a tri - - - - -
27
- - - - - - - umph a tri - - - - - - - umph, tri - umph
sings a tri - - - - umph, tri - umph sings
35
And all a - round, and all a - round pleas'd Cu-pids clap their wings, clap, clap,
clap, clap their wings; pleas'd Cu - pids clap their wings; and all a -
42
- round, and all a - round, pleas'd Cu - pids clap, clap,

clap, clap, clap their wings, clap, clap, clap, clap, clap, clap, clap their wings, pleas'd

40 Trumpet.

1st Violin.

2nd Violin.

Viola.

Cu-pids clap their wings And all a - wings.

CHORUS.

Soprano. Hark! hark! hark! hark! hark!

Alto. Hark! hark! hark! hark! hark!

Tenor. Hark! hark! hark! hark! hark!

Bass. Hark! hark! hark! hark! hark!

Several of the airs that Purcell composed for the masque *The Fairy Queen* (1692), a semi-opera adapted from Shakespeare's *A Midsummer Night's Dream*, are modeled on Italian aria types. The motto aria with trumpet obbligato is called on to evoke the ideas of echo and triumph. The voice echoes the trumpet's triumphant flourish but is interrupted by the bass, which in turn echoes the voice. Then, in the manner of the motto aria, the voice begins again, this time continuing with imitations of trumpet fanfares and trills. The second section introduces new themes to illustrate the words "around," "pleased," and "clap," the last a sound-imitation. It is significant that Purcell did not bring back the first section as in the da capo aria, probably because his aria was modeled on the ABB form popular in Italy earlier in the century.

71

Dieterich Buxtehude (ca. 1637–1707)

Praeludium in E Major, BuxWV 141 CD 5

30
35
40
45
50
trillo longo
trillo longo
55
14
60 Presto

65
70
con discrezione
15
75
80
85
Adagio
16
90
Allegro

This toccata, like most of Buxtehude's, is designated in the manuscripts simply as Praeludium; it contains four fugal sections, each preceded by free figurative exordia or transitions. The longest free section is the first; the internal ones are transitional. The piece begins with a three-measure flourish in the right hand, a grand upbeat to the first E-major chord, which is the goal also of the eight-measure harmonic exploration that follows. The first fugue (measure 13ff.) has two full expositions in the four voices, in Buxtehude's favorite order of soprano, alto, tenor, bass. After an episode built on the tail of the subject that modulates to the dominant, there is a further, incomplete exposition (measure 36ff.). The free section that ensues is full of exuberant runs that take the pitch to the highest point in the piece; it features two "long trills"—so marked in the score—in the pedal part (measures 51 and 53). The second fugal section, marked Presto, breaks up into imitations of a short figure after only two entries; by means of a brief suspenseful transition it reaffirms the tonic for an informal three-voice fugue without pedal in $\frac{12}{8}$ gigue-time (measures 75–86) on a subject that is derived from the first one. A transitional Adagio leads to the final, quite formal exposition of another subject derived from the first. The form of the piece may be summarized as follows:

$\frac{4}{4}$				$\frac{12}{8}$	$\frac{4}{4}$			
Free	**Fugue**	**Free**	**Fugal/Figurative**	**Fugal**	**Trans.**	**Fugue**	**Coda**	
1	*13*	*47*	*60*	*75*	*87*	*91*	*104*	*110*

72 Dieterich Buxtehude

Chorale Prelude: *Danket dem Herrn,* BuxWV 181 CD 5

Dietrich Buxtehudes Werke für Orgel, ed. Phillip Spitta, *Neue Ausgabe* von Max Seiffert, 2 (Leipzig, 1904), pp. 1–2.

This setting of "Thank the Lord, for He is very kind" treats the chorale as a cantus firmus, but in each variation the chorale melody appears in a different voice: in the top part in the first variation, in the pedal as a middle voice in the second, and in the pedal as a bass in the third and last. For each statement of the chorale Buxtehude invented a new, highly individualized subject that was developed initially by imitation, then through free counterpoint.

French Overture

73 FRANÇOIS COUPERIN (1668–1733)

Vingt-cinquième ordre

a) *La Visionaire* CD 5

20

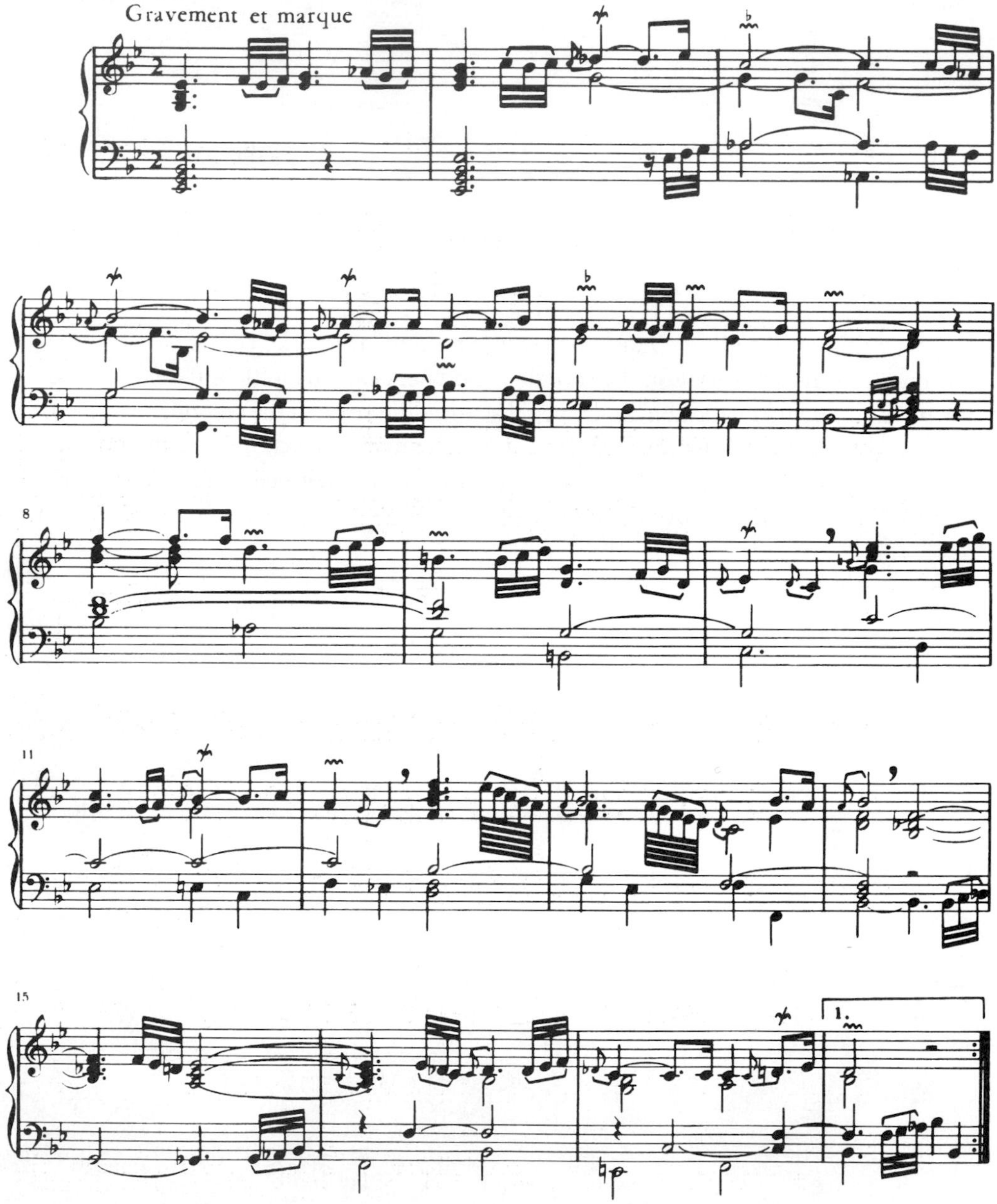
Gravement et marque
8
11
15
1.

For a guide to the realization of Couperin's ornaments, see HWM, 6th ed., p. 355. From *Pièces de clavecin*, Book 4, ed. Kenneth Gilbert. © 1970 Durand S. A. Used by permission of the Publisher.

21
Viste
REPRISE

34
36
38
40
1.
2.
b) La Misterieuse
CD 5
22
Modérement
2

REPRISE

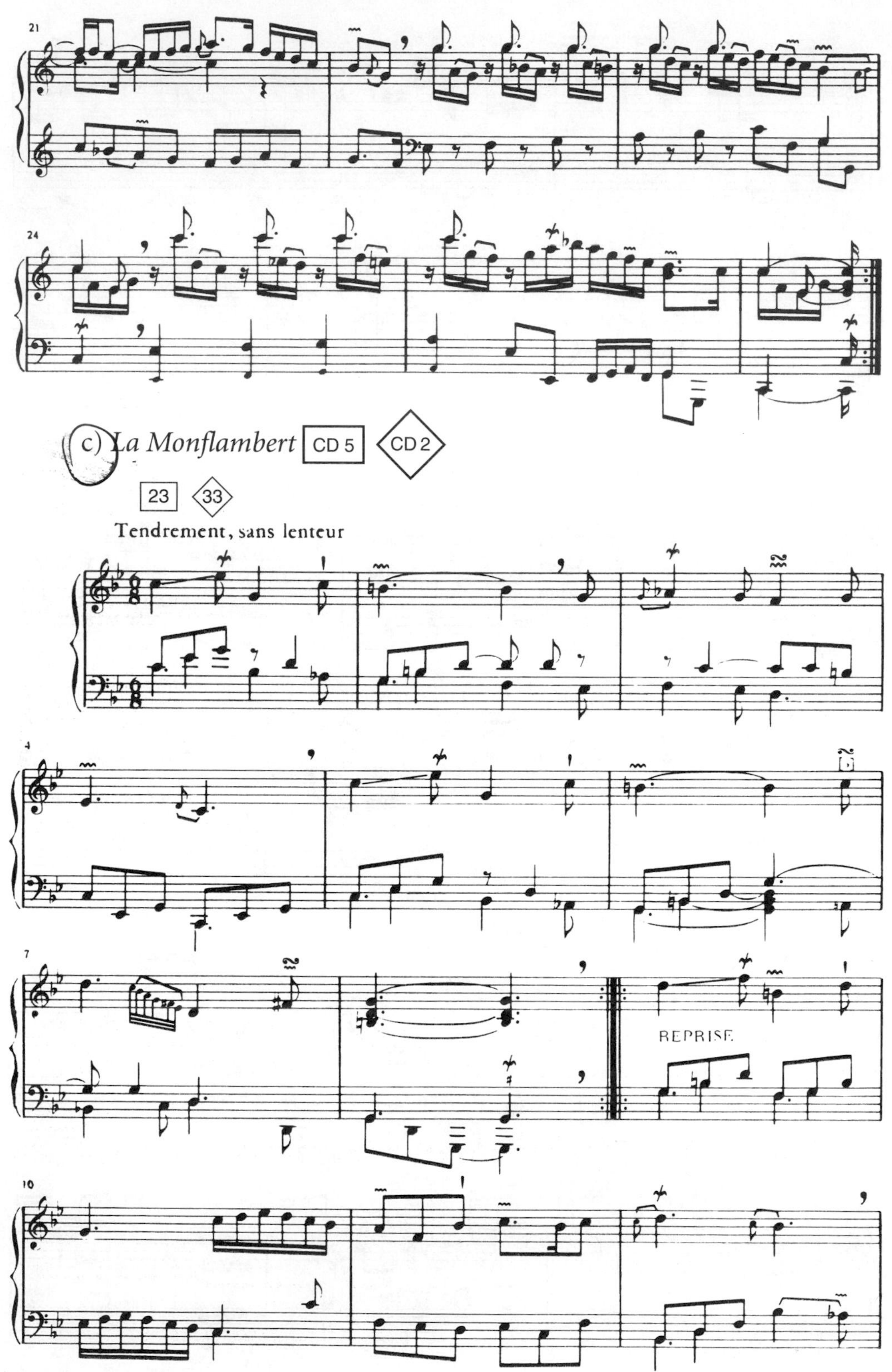
c) La Monflambert
CD 5
CD 2
23
33
Tendrement, sans lenteur
REPRISE

Petitte Reprise
d) La Muse victorieuse CD 5 CD 2
24 34
Audacieusement

13
19
25
31
1.
2.
REPRISE
38
45
52

58
65
71
1.
2.
e) Les Ombres errantes
CD 5
25
Languissamment
3
6

REPRISE

François Couperin published twenty-seven *ordres*, or groups of pieces, for harpsichord between 1713 and 1730. They were intended for amateurs to amuse themselves at the harpsichord. This set, the twenty-fifth, appeared in 1730 in the fourth book, along with seven others. The ordres were made up mostly of stylized dances in binary form, like the suites written by German composers, but the dances did not follow any particular sequence. Couperin gave the numbers fanciful and suggestive titles, such as those in this ordre: *La Visionaire* (The Dreamer), *La Misterieuse* (The Mysterious One), *La Monflambert* (a gigue, probably named after Anne Darboulin, who married Monflambert, the king's wine merchant, in 1726), *La Muse victorieuse* (The Victorious Muse), and *Les Ombres errantes* (The Roving Shadows).

La Visionaire, the first movement of this ordre, is a rather whimsical French overture. After reaching the dominant in measure 13, the first half passes into the dominant minor for a moment's meditation. The second half, after a few imitations between the two hands—a passing bow to the obligatory fugue—lapses into an allemande, haunted by memories of the majestic first half.

La Misterieuse, in C major, is a more proper allemande in $\frac{4}{4}$, mainly with steady sixteenth-note motion. It has the typical binary dance form, the first half modulating to the dominant by way of a pedal point on *D* that imitates the sound of a musette, or French bagpipe, and ending in a full cadence on G major. The second section, somewhat longer than the first, touches on some related keys—E minor and A minor. A return to the dominant occurs in the bass through half steps down a fifth from *A* to *D* (measures 17–19), while the upper voices pass through some strained harmonies that may well have suggested the title.

La Monflambert is a gigue in $\frac{6}{8}$ and, like the final piece of the ordre, in minor. It was probably a favorite of the person after whom it was named. *La Monflambert* consists entirely of four-measure phrases. After the second part is played for the second time, the last four bars are repeated as a coda.

La Muse victorieuse displays a formal device characteristic of binary movements of Couperin and, later, Domenico Scarlatti: the last eleven measures of the first half are paralleled in the close of the second half, except that in the former the progression is to the dominant, while in the latter it is from the dominant to the tonic.

Les Ombres errantes may owe its title to the syncopated middle voice, which seems to shadow the top voice erratically, forming chains of suspensions, some of which resolve upward. Marked *languissamment*, this piece, as well as *La Misterieuse*, combines restrained emotionalism with controlling harmonic and melodic logic, exhibiting the sentimental elegance so appealing to the courtiers and amateurs of this age.

74 GIOVANNI LEGRENZI (1626–1690)

Trio Sonata: *La Raspona* CD 5

Sonate a due, a tre di Giovanni Legrenzi, Libro primo, Opera seconda (Venice, 1665). From *Hortus Musicus* No. 31, Werner Danckert, ed. (Kassel, 1949), pp. 3–7. Reprinted by permission of Bärenreiter Music Corporation.

6
5
6
4
7
3

15
(p)
(p)
6
4
3
5
6

20
(p)
(f)
(p)
(f)
(p)
(f)
(p)
3
4
3

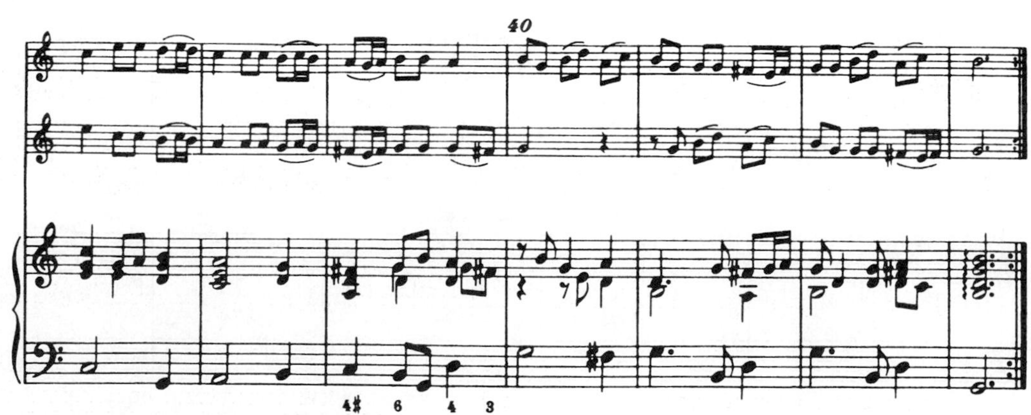

27
ADAGGIO
45
(poco più mosso)
(poco più mosso)
(p)
(p)
(mf)
(p)
(poco più mosso)

50
(mf)
(fp)
(p)
(mf)
(p)

55
(p)

60
(𝆑)
(𝆑)
(𝆑)
6
5
6
5
6
5
6
5

6
6
5
6
5
6
6
5

65

This sonata for two violins and basso continuo (harpsichord and viola da gamba or cello) shows off Legrenzi's renowned aptitude for inventing rhythmically and melodically incisive fugal subjects. The two movements, marked Allegro and "Adaggio," both immediately repeated, have a canzona-like structure in which only the two upper parts are involved in the statements and answers, the bass serving throughout as a foundation.

The Allegro is in two main sections: the first proceeds from G major to C major (measures 1–22); the second returns to G major (measures 22–43). The first section has a series of fugal entries on variants of a single theme. At the outset, the subject is answered at the unison. Then a variation of the subject is heard on the subdominant, answered on the tonic, and again on the dominant, leading to a cadence on the tonic (measure 11). The original subject is now stated in the tonic and answered in the subdominant, followed by an elaboration of the second part of the subject and scalar flourishes that complete the modulation to the subdominant. The second section, in triple time, begins with the two violins exchanging short cantabile motives, but once the dominant of the original key is reached (measure 32), a new fugal subject is briefly exposed.

The Adaggio, after a transitional opening that establishes C major, modulates by means of sequences to the sixth degree (measure 53), when the violins begin to exchange subjects and figurations displaying the verve and agility of the instrument and its player.

75 ARCANGELO CORELLI (1653–1713)

Trio Sonata, Op. 3, No. 2 CD 5 CD 2

From *Sonate a tre* (Bologna, 1689). *Les Oeuvres de Arcangelo Corelli*, J. Joachim and F. Chrysander, eds. (London, n.d.), pp. 130–35.

29
20
Allegro.

24

28

32

35

39

43

47
Adagio.

30
35
Adagio.
9
17
25
33
p
p
p

31
36
Allegro.

5
Viol.
Org

10

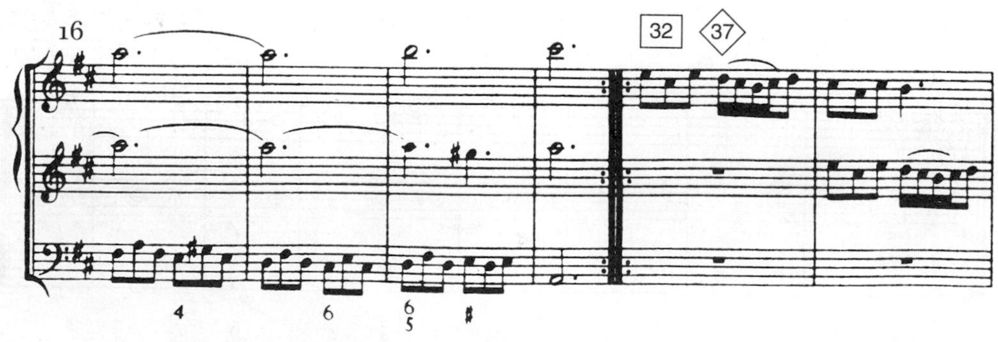
16
32
37

22
6 6 6 7 6 6 6 6 5 ♯ 7 6 5

27
p
p

32
f
f
A
D
G

37
p
p

This sonata da chiesa (church sonata) has the typical slow-fast-slow-fast succession of movements. Although the movements, as befits church music, avoid obvious secular connotations, they betray a kinship with the stylized dances of the suite: the first movement with the allemande, the third with the sarabande, and the fourth with the gigue.

Grave, the marking on the first movement, is not merely a designation of tempo but a description of the music's character: serious, intense, and profound. The intensity is expressed by the determined march of the bass and the deliberate suspended dissonance on nearly every downbeat. That dissonance was by then defined as an alien note against a consonant chord is evident in the leaps within chord tones against the dissonance, as in measure 14. Another indication is the ornamental pattern of leaping from a suspension down to a chord tone, then up to the note of resolution (as in measure 15, and in the first Allegro, measures 47–48). Especially typical of Corelli's slow movements are the chains of suspensions that begin in measure 6 while the violins meet, cross, and separate as the bass walks on.

Unlike Legrenzi, Corelli gave the bass in the fast movements an equal share in the fugal action. Indeed the bass is the first to answer the Allegro movement's subject in direct motion, the second violin having answered by inversion and incompletely. After the first exposition only the second part of the subject reappears (measures 36ff.), both in direct motion and inversion. The three notes that are the head of the subject keep intervening as counterpoints. The key of D major is neatly circumscribed by well-prepared cadences in A major, B minor, and E major, before the return to D. This movement is remarkably taut in its exclusion of non-thematic material.

The Adagio resembles a passionate vocal duet in which two singers alternately imitate each other or proceed in parallel motion. The sigh effects in measures 14–15 are operatic, while syncopations and suspensions on the first and second beats of the triple-time measures emphasize through both resolution and dissonance the second beat of the sarabande rhythm. The dance character is reinforced by the hemiola passages (measures 19–21 and 36–39). A Phrygian cadence at the end of the Adagio makes us expect a return to B minor, but instead an Allegro in D major ensues.

The final movement, although a gigue, is simply labeled Allegro. It again involves all three instrumental parts in a fugue, and the subject of the second half is an inversion of that in the first half, a technique typical of many later gigues for keyboard. There are two sequential episodes of the kind found in later fugues (measures 8–10 and 28–32). Fascination with contrapuntal devices such as inversion, stretto (measures 32–35), and pedal point (measures 15–18) betray the influence of the Bologna school, in which such artifices were cultivated and where Corelli was trained.

Antonio Vivaldi (1678–1741)

76

Concerto Grosso in G Minor, Op. 3, No. 2, RV 578

a) Adagio e spiccato (first movement) CD 5

Vivaldi, *L'estro armonico*, Op. 3 (Amsterdam, 1711), ed. Gian Francesco Malipiero (Milan: Ricordi, 1965), 407:1–33. F. IV, No. 8; Pincherle 326; RV 578. Copyright by CASA RICORDI-BMG RICORDI S.p.A., Milan. Reprinted by permission.

5
p
f
p
f
p
7 5
5 4
♯
6♭ 5
6 4
6 5
3
6♭
♭
7 ♯
7 ♯
7 4
7 5 3♮

10

b) Allegro (second movement) CD 5 CD 2

34 38

6
6
5
5
6
6
5
♯
6♭
♯
6
5
5
6
6
5

20
5 6 6 5 6 5 ♭ ♯
♭ ♮ 4♮ 2 6 ♮ ♯ 4♯ 2

6
4
2
6♭
♭
♮
4
2
♮
♯
4♯
2
6
5
4
♯

35
39

25

36
40
p
p
p
p
p
p
p
p
p
p
6
6
5
5
6
6
5
♯
6
♯
6
5

30
5 6 6 5
5 6 6 5
6 5 ♭
♯
♭ ♮
4♮ 2

37
41
p
p
6
5
4
♯

35

(1 Solo)
f
7

40
7♭
7
7
7
5♭

p
p
p
p
7

f
f
f
f ♯
♯
6
7
♯

45
38
42
tr
(f)
(f)
(f)
(f)
(f)
(f)
(f)
(Tutti)
(f)
(f)
(f)
♯
♯ 6 7 ♯
7

50
5 6 6
5
5 6 6
5
♯ ♮ ♯ 4♯
2

6 ♮ ♯ 4♯ 2 6 6 4 2 6 ♭ ♮ 4♮ 2 6 ♮ ♯ 4♯ 2

39
43
55
6
5
4
♯

6
7

60
♭
7♭
5

6
6
5
♭
6

65
7
5
6
6
5
3

5
4
♯

40
44
70
(f)
(f)
(f)
(f)
(f)
(f)
(f)
(f)
(f)
(f)
6
5
♮
6
♮
6
5
♯
6
♯
6
5

5 6 6 5 5 6 6 5 # 4# 2 6 7 5 5 #

75
(Solo)

tr
tr
tr
p
p
p
p
p
p
6♭
7
5♭
6
5
♯
6

80
tr
f
pp
p
(f)
6
5
♭
♯

Vivaldi's collection of twelve concertos, *L'estro armonico* (The Harmonic Fancy, Op. 3; Amsterdam, 1711), established his European reputation. For the first Allegro of his solo concertos, Vivaldi adopted the alternation of ritornellos and solo episodes that characterized Torelli's fast movements. He also applied this structure, though more loosely, to the concerto grosso, in which the soloists were a group of players known as the *concertino* (little concerto) or small ensemble, as distinguished from the *concerto grosso* (big concerto), or large ensemble. Vivaldi's approach to the first Allegro is illustrated in the second movement of Op. 3, No. 2, RV 578.* Players of the concertino, made up of two violins and a cello, were designated in the score as "concertanti" (concertizing, or solo, players).

In the Adagio e spiccato (a), the soloists play in unison with the orchestra violins and cellos, except for two measures just before the close, when the solo violins are accompanied only by the violas. This movement is a study in chromatic harmony in which suspensions and other dissonances abound. Diminished-seventh chords appear several times, usually prepared by having the dissonant notes sounded in the previous chord, but in some instances (measures 9 and 12) not prepared at all, just as some seventh chords (measures 3 and 9) are not prepared. These previously unsanctioned usages are introduced with a freedom that even today strikes us as refreshing.

In the Allegro (b), the opening ritornello has three motivic sections—measures 14–16, 17–19, and 20–22—the last of which is an inverted counterpoint to the second. The three solo sections contain mostly figurative work, but in the second (measure 38) there is a veiled reference to the opening tutti motive. An unusual feature of this movement occurs in the closing ritornello where the order of motives is reversed. The final seven measures constitute an epilogue composed anew but based on the downward octave skip of the opening motive. This movement is also unusual because only one of four main tutti, the third, is in a foreign key, D minor. Far from following a textbook plan, Vivaldi's Allegro structures show an infinity of invention.

* There are several catalogues of Vivaldi's works. The most recent and reliable is known as "RV," Peter Ryom, *Verzeichnis der Werke Antonio Vivaldis: kleine Ausgabe* (Leipzig, 1974; suppl., Poitiers, 1979).

Antonio Vivaldi

77

Concerto for Violin, Op. 9, No. 2, RV 345 CD 5

Largo (second movement)

Vivaldi, *La Cetra* (Amsterdam, 1728), ed. Gian Francesco Malipiero (Milan: Ricordi, 1952), 126:18–19. F. I, 51; Pincherle 214; RV 345.

120
tr
125

Taken from the collection *La Cetra* (The Kithara, 1728), this slow movement exhibits many features of the early Classic style: balanced phrases, and frequent half-cadences clarifying the structure, trills, triplets, and cadences softened by appoggiaturas. The slow, striking harmonic changes over the long dominant pedal (measures 122–125) intensify suspense after a choppy exposition. Like most of Vivaldi's slow movements, this one is lightly scored; only the solo cello and the continuo play with the solo violin.

78 Jean-Philippe Rameau (1683–1764)

Hippolyte et Aricie

Act IV, Scene 1: *Ah! faut-il* CD 5 CD 2

Rameau, *Oeuvres complètes*, 6, ed. Vincent d'Indy (Paris: Durand, 1900), pp. 262–67.

Fl.
Hb
Bons
Vons
Alt.
B.C.
fort
1re
2e
doux
HIPPOLYTE
Ah! faut-il, en un jour, per - dre
tout ce que j'ai - - me? Mon pè - re pour jamais me bannit de ces lieux Si chéris de Di - a - ne mê - -

Vons
Alt.
H.
-me. Je ne ver-rai plus les beaux yeux Qui fai - saient mon bon-heur su-prê - me.
B.C.

27
Fl.
Hb
doux
Bons
doux
Vons
(doux)
Alt.
H.
Ah! faut-il, en un jour, per - dre tout cequej'ai - me?
B.C.
27

Fl.
Vons
Alt.
H.
Et les maux que je crains, et les biens que je perds, Tout acca - ble mon cœur d'u-ne douleur — ex -
B.C.

37
Vons
Alt.
H.
-trê - - me. Sous le nu_age af_freux dont mes jours sont cou_ - verts, Que deviendra ma gloire aux yeux de l'uni_
B.C.
37
Hb
(doux)
fort
Bons
(doux)
fort
Vons
doux
fort
doux
fort
Alt.
doux
fort
H.
_vers? Ah! faut-il, en un jour, per - dre tout ce que j'ai - me?
B.C.
fort
47
Fl.
doux
Hb
Bons
doux
Vons
doux
(Div.)
doux
Alt.
doux
B.C.
doux
47

Ah! faut-il, en un jour, perdre tout ce que j'aime? Et les maux que je crains, et les biens que je perds, Tout accable mon coeur d'une douleur extrême. Sous le nuage affreux dont mes jours sont couverts, Que deviendra ma gloire aux yeux de l'univers?	Ah, must I, in a day, lose all that I love? And the troubles I fear, and the riches I lose, all overwhelm my heart with extreme pain. Under the terrible cloud that darkens my days, what will become of my glory in the eyes of the world?
Ah! faut-il, en un jour, perdre tout ce que j'aime?	Ah, must I, in a day, lose all that I love?
Mon père pour jamais me bannit de ces lieux Si chéris de Diane même. Je ne verrai plus les beaux yeux Qui faisaient mon bonheur suprême. —Simon-Joseph Pellegrin	My father is banishing me forever from these parts so dear to Diane herself. I shall see no more the beautiful eyes which made me supremely happy.

Abbé S.-J. de Pellegrin drew heavily on Racine's *Phèdre* for the libretto of this *tragédie lyrique*, first performed in Paris in 1733. Hyppolyte, falsely accused of violating his stepmother, complains in this monologue of his banishment and separation from his beloved Aricie.

The music illustrates how Rameau both remained faithful to the Lully tradition and departed from it. Like similar scenes by Lully, this one is a mixture of recitative and an aria-like refrain. After its melody is introduced in the opening orchestral tutti, the tuneful and measured refrain, "Ah! faut-il, en un jour, perdre tout ce que j'aime?" (Ah, must I, in a day, lose all that I love?), appears three times. The rest of the monologue—speechlike, with shorter notes per syllable and frequent changes of meter—lacks the qualities of well-formed melody. Rameau expressed Hippolyte's anguish with harmony highly charged with dissonances that propel it forward, as is evident from the number of sevenths, ninths, diminished fifths, and augmented fourths called for by the bass figures, and the obligatory appoggiaturas and other ornaments notated in the parts. Rameau replaced the five-part string orchestra of Lully with four-part strings, augmented by flutes, oboes, and bassoons.

JOHANN SEBASTIAN BACH (1685–1750)

79

Praeludium et Fuga in A Minor, BWV 543 CD 5 CD 2

From J. S. Bach, *Neue Ausgabe sämtlicher Werke,* Serie IV, *Orgel Werke,* Band 5, ed. Dietrich Kilian (Kassel, 1972), pp. 186–97. Reprinted by permission of Bärenreiter Music Corporation.

21
23
26
29
33
35
38

42
46
50
44
47
Fuga
6
11
16
21

25
30
34
38
43
48
52
57

61
66
71
76
81
85
90
95
100

105
109
113
117
121
126
130
135

During a stay in Weimar (1708–17), when Bach is believed to have composed this work, he copied out many concertos by Italian composers and arranged some of them. Elements of the Italian concerto seep into a number of his toccatas and fugues, particularly in this Prelude and Fugue in A Minor. In the Prelude violinistic figuration resembling that of concerto solos alternates with toccata-like sections, including a pedal solo (measures 25–28) and chains of suspensions in the manner of Corelli (measures 37–38).

The structure of the fugue is analogous to that of a concerto Allegro. The opening exposition gives each of four "voices" a chance to state the violinistic subject on either the tonic minor or the dominant minor. The episode that follows, as well as others later on, has the character of solo sections, while the returns of the subject in related keys (E minor, C major, D minor) and in the tonic function like tuttis. Following the last statement of the subject (measures 131–36) there is an elaborate cadenza.

80 Johann Sebastian Bach

Durch Adams Fall, BWV 637 CD 5

a) Chorale melody

Durch A-dams Fall ist ganz ver-derbt Mensch-lich Na-tur und We-sen;
Das-selb Gift ist auf uns ge-erbt, Dass wir nicht moch-ten g'ne-sen
Ohn Got-tes Trost, der uns er-löst Hat von dem gros-sen Scha-den
Dar-ein die Schlang' Hie-nam be-zwang, Gotts Zorn auf sich zu la-den.

b) Organ chorale

45

4
1.
2.

a) Text by Lazarus Spengler, *Geistliche Lieder auffs new gebessert* (Wittemberg: Joseph Klug, 1535), after Johannes Zahn, *Die Melodien der deutschen evangelischen Kirchenlieder* (Gütersloh, 1892), 4, No. 7549.

Durch Adams Fall is ganz verderbt	Through Adam's fall are entirely spoiled
Menschlich Natur und Wesen;	both human nature and character.
Dasselb Gift ist auf uns geerbt,	The same venom was by us inherited,
Daß wir nicht mochten g'nesen	so that we could not recover from it
Ohn Gottes Trost, der uns erlöst	without God's solace, which saved us
Hat von dem grossen Schaden,	from great harm;
Darein die Schlang' hienam bezwang	for the serpent somehow managed
Gotts Zorn auf sich zu laden.	to take unto itself God's anger.
—Lazarus Spengler	

As in the other chorale preludes of the *Orgelbüchlein* (Little Organ Book), which Bach compiled mostly in Weimar (1716–17) but never finished, the chorale melody of *Durch Adams Fall* (Through Adam's fall) is heard once, in complete, continuous, and readily recognizable form. The tune itself (a) is in Bar form, consisting of a repeated section (two *Stollen*, each with two lines of text) and a closing section (*Abgesang* of four lines).

Bach's arrangement of the chorale *Durch Adams Fall* is one of his most graphic representations. A jagged series of dissonant leaps in the pedals depicts the idea of "fall," departing from a consonant chord and falling into a dissonant one—as if from innocence into sin—while the twisting chromatic lines in the inner voices suggest at once temptation, sorrow, and the sinuous writhing of the serpent.

81 Johann Sebastian Bach

1731

Cantata: *Wachet auf, ruft uns die Stimme,* BWV 140

1. Chorus: *Wachet auf* CD 6 CD 2

Norton Critical Scores, from J. S. Bach, *Neue Ausgabe sämtlicher Werke*, Serie I, Band 27: *Kantaten zum 24. bis 27. Sonntag nach Trinitatis*, ed. Alfred Dürr (Kassel: Bärenreiter-Verlag, 1968). Reprinted by permission of Bärenreiter Music Corporation.

6

11

2
49
16
p
f
tr
Wa - chet
auf,
ruft
uns
Wa - chet
auf, wa - chet
auf, ruft
Wa - chet
auf, wa - chet
Wa - chet

22
tr
die
Stim - me
uns die
Stim - me, ruft
uns die
Stim - me
auf, ruft
uns die
Stim - me, die
Stim - me
auf, wa - chet
auf, ruft
uns die
Stim - me

27
der
Wäch - - ter
sehr
der Wäch-ter sehr
hoch
der Wäch-ter sehr
hoch
der Wäch-ter sehr

33
hoch
auf
der
Zin - - - - -
auf der
Zin - ne,
hoch
auf der Zin -
- ne,
hoch
auf der
auf der
Zin - - ne,
der Wäch-ter sehr
hoch auf der
hoch
auf der Zin - ne, der Wäch-ter
sehr
hoch auf der

38
ne
Zin - ne,
Zin - ne,
Zin - ne,

43
wach
auf,
du
Stadt
Je
wach auf,
wach auf,
wach auf, du
Stadt Je-ru - sa -
lem, wach auf
wach auf,
wach auf,
wach auf,
du Stadt Je
ru - sa - lem,
wach auf,
wach auf,
wach auf, du Stadt
Je - ru - sa - lem,
wach auf,

48
ru - sa - lem
—, du Stadt Je - ru - sa - lem, wach auf, du Stadt Je - ru - sa -
du Stadt Je - ru - sa - lem, wach auf, du Stadt Je - ru - sa - lem, Je - ru - sa -
du Stadt Je - ru - sa - lem, wach auf, du Stadt Je - ru - sa -

3 50

53
—!
lem!
lem!
lem!

59

64
tr

69
Mit - ter - nacht heißt die -
Mit - ter - nacht, Mit - ter - nacht heißt
Mit - ter - nacht, Mit - ter -
Mit - ter -

74
tr
se Stun - - - - - de;
die - se Stun - de, heißt die - - se Stun - de,
nacht heißt die - se Stun - de, die-se Stun - de;
nacht, Mit - ter - nacht heißt die - se Stun - de;

79
sie
ru - - -
fen
sie ru-fen uns mit
sie ru-fen uns mit
hel - - -

84
uns
mit
hel - -
lem
Mun - -
hel - - - lem
Mun - de, sie
ru-fen uns
mit hel -
- - - - lem
Mun - de, sie ru-fen
uns,
sie ru-fen uns mit
sie ru-fen uns mit
hel - - - lem Mun - de, sie ru-fen uns, sie ru-fen

89
de
lem Mun - de:
hel - lem Mun - de:
uns mit hel - lem Mun - de:

94
wo seid ihr klu -
wo, wo, wo, wo, wo seid ihr klu - gen Jung -
wo, wo, wo, wo, wo seid ihr klu - gen Jung -
wo, wo, wo, wo, wo seid ihr, wo, wo, wo seid

99
gen Jung - - - frau - - - en
frau-en, wo , wo seid ihr klu - gen Jung - frau - en, wo
frau - en, wo seid ihr, wo seid ihr klu-gen Jung - frau - en, wo seid
ihr, wo seid ihr klu - gen Jung - frau - - - - en, wo seid ihr

4
51
103
seid ihr klu - gen Jung- frau - en, wo, wo?
ihr, ihr klu - gen Jung-frau - en, wo, wo?
klu - gen Jung - frau - en, wo, wo?

108
Viol. picc.
Viol. I

5 52

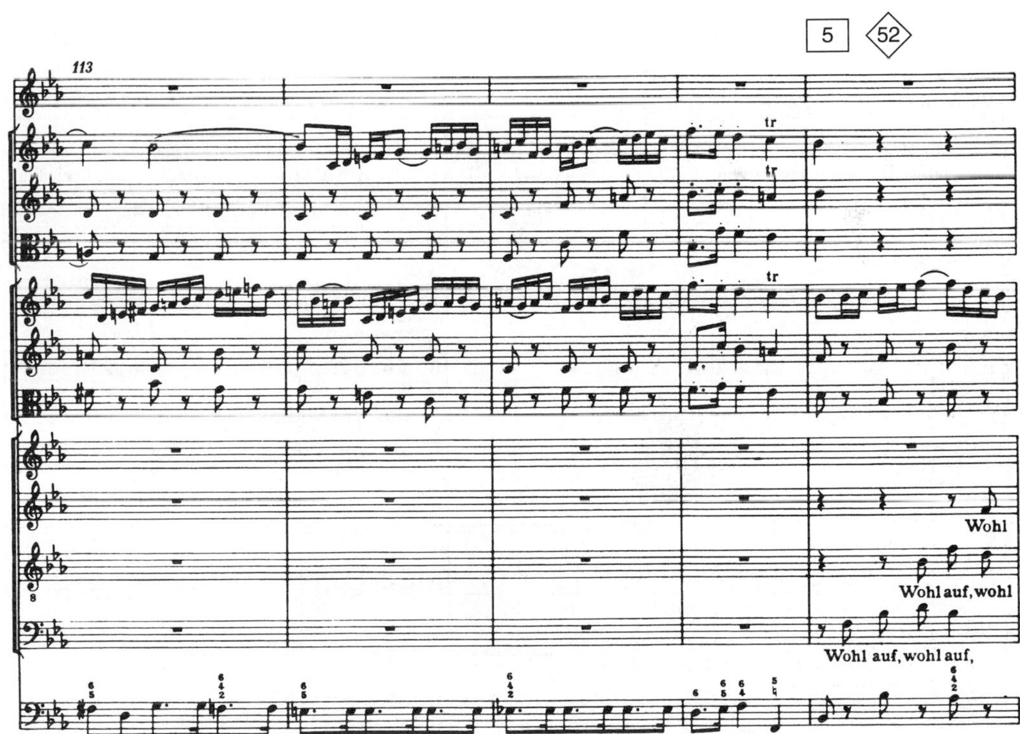
113
tr
Wohl
Wohl auf, wohl
Wohl auf, wohl auf,

118
Wohl
auf,
der
Bräut - - -
auf, wohl auf,
der Bräut - gam
kömmt, wohl auf,
wohl
auf,
wohl auf,
auf,
wohl
auf,
wohl
auf,
wohl auf,
der Bräut - gam
der Bräut - gam
kömmt, wohl auf,
der Bräut - gam
kömmt, wohl auf,

122
gam
kömmt
der Bräut - gam
kömmt, wohl auf,
wohl
auf,
kömmt, wohl auf,
wohl
auf,
wohl auf, wohl
auf,
der Bräut - gam
kömmt, wohl auf,
wohl
auf,

127
steht auf, die
steht auf, steht auf, die Lam - pen nehmt, steht auf, steht
steht auf, steht auf, steht auf, steht auf, steht auf,
steht auf, steht auf, die Lam - pen nehmt, steht auf, die Lam - pen

131
Lam pen nehmt !
auf, steht auf, die Lam - pen nehmt, steht auf, steht auf!
die Lam - pen nehmt, steht auf, steht auf, steht auf, steht auf!
nehmt, steht auf, die Lam - pen nehmt, steht auf, steht auf!

135
Al - - - - - le - lu - ja, al - le - lu - ja
Al -

140
, al - le - lu - ja, al - le - lu - ja,
- - - - le - lu - ja, al - le - lu - ja
Al -

145
tr
al - le - lu - ja , al - le - lu - ja
, al - le - lu - ja , al - le - lu - ja ,
- - le - lu - ja , al - le - lu - ja , al - le - lu -

149
Al - - le - - lu - - -
, al - le - lu - ja
tr
al - le - lu - ja , al - le - lu - ja, al - le - lu -
ja , al - le - lu - ja, al - le - lu -

153
ja !
, al - le - lu - ja, al - le - lu - ja!
ja , al - le - lu - ja!
ja, al - le - lu - ja, al - le - lu - ja!

158
Macht euch
Macht euch be - reit, macht
Macht euch be - reit, macht euch be - reit,
Macht euch be - reit, macht euch be -

163
be - - reit
euch be-reit, be - reit, be - reit, macht euch be - reit,
macht euch be - reit, be - reit, macht euch be - reit,
reit, macht euch be - reit, be - reit, macht euch be - reit,

168
zu der Hoch -
macht euch be - reit, macht euch be -
macht euch be - reit, macht euch be -
macht euch be - reit zu der

173
zeit
reit, macht euch be - reit zu der Hoch - zeit, macht euch be - reit zu der Hoch - zeit,
reit, macht euch be - reit zu der Hoch - zeit, macht euch be - reit zu der Hoch - zeit,
Hoch - zeit, macht euch be - reit zu der Hoch - zeit, macht euch be - reit zu der Hoch - zeit,

178
ihr müs - set ihm
ihr, ihr, ihr müs - set ihm ent - ge - gen
ihr, ihr, ihr müs - set ihm ent -
ihr, ihr, ihr müs - set ihm ent - ge - gen

183
ent - - - ge - - - gen gehn
gehn, ihr müs - - set ihm ent - ge - gen, ent - ge - gen gehn, ihr
ge - - gen gehn, ihm ent - ge - gen gehn, ihr müs - set
gehn, ihr müs - set ihm ent - ge - gen gehn, ihr müs -

187
müs - set ihm ent - ge - - gen gehn!
ihm ent - ge - gen - gehn, ent - ge - gen gehn!
set ihm ent - ge - - gen gehn!

191

196

201

Wachet auf, ruft uns die Stimme	"Wake up," calls the voice
Der Wächter sehr hoch auf der Zinne,	of the watchmen, high up in the tower,
Wach auf, du Stadt Jerusalem!	"wake up, O city of Jerusalem!"
Mitternacht heißt diese Stunde;	Midnight is this hour;
Sie rufen uns mit hellem Munde:	they call us with loud mouths:
Wo seid ihr klugen Jungfrauen?	"Where are you, wise virgins?
Wohl auf, der Bräutgam kömmt,	Cheer up, the bridegroom comes;
Steht auf, die Lampen nehmt!	get up, take your lamps!
Alleluja!	Alleluia!
Macht euch bereit	Make yourselves ready
Zu der Hochzeit,	for the wedding.
Ihr müsset ihm entgegen gehn!	You must go to meet him."
—Philipp Nicolai	

2. Tenor Recitative: *Er kommt*

6
Tenore
Er kommt, er kommt, der Bräut-gam kommt! Ihr Töch-ter Zi-ons, kommt her-aus, sein Aus-gang
Fagotto
Continuo
Organo (bez.)
Org.
4
ei - let aus der Hö - he in eu - er Mut - ter Haus.
Der Bräut-gam kommt, der ei - nem

Re - he und jun-gen Hir-sche gleich auf de-nen Hü-geln springt und euch das Mahl der Hoch-zeit bringt.
Wacht auf, er-mun-tert euch! den Bräut-gam zu emp-fan-gen! Dort, se-het, kommt er her-ge - gan-gen.

Er kommt, er kommt, der Bräutgam kommt!
Ihr Töchter Zions, kommt heraus,
Sein Ausgang eilet aus der Höhe
In euer Mutter Haus.

Der Bräutgam kommt, der einem Rehe
Und jungem Hirsche gleich
Auf denen Hügeln springt
Und euch das Mahl der Hochzeit bringt.

Wacht auf, ermuntert euch!
Den Bräutgam zu empfangen!
Dort, sehet, kommt er hergegangen.

He comes, he comes, the bridegroom comes!
You, daughters of Zion, come out.
He is hurrying from on high
into your mother's house.

The bridegroom comes; like a roe
and a young hart
leaping on the hills,
he brings you the wedding feast.

Wake up, get yourselves up
to receive the bridegroom.
There, see, he approaches.

3. Aria (Duet): *Wann kommst du, mein Heil?*

7
Adagio
Violino piccolo
Soprano
Basso
Fagotto
Continuo
Organo (bez.)
Org.

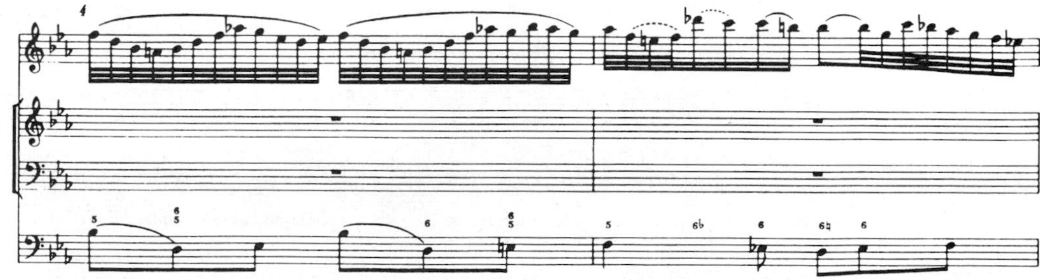

Wenn kömmst du, mein Heil, wenn
Wann kommst
Ich kom - me, dein Teil,
p

kömmst du, mein Heil, wenn kömmst du, mein
ich kom-me, dein Teil, ich kom-me,

Heil, mein Heil? Ich war - te, ich war - te mit
dein Teil, dein Teil, ich kom-me, ich kom-me,

18
bren - nen-dem Ö - le; wenn kömmst du, mein Heil, wenn
ich kom-me, ich kom - me, dein Teil,

21
kömmst du, mein Heil? Ich war - - - - - te, ich
ich kom-me, dein Teil, ich kom - me,

24
war-
ich kom - me, ich kom - me, dein

26
te mit bren - nen - dem Ö - le, mit
tr
Teil, ich kom - me, dein Teil, ich

28
bren - nen - dem Ö - le; wenn kömmst du, mein Heil ? Ich
kom - me, dein Teil, ich kom - me, dein Teil,

31
war - - te mit bren - nen - dem Ö - le.
ich kom - me.

35
Er -
Ich öff - ne den Saal

38
öff - ne den Saal, er - öff - ne den Saal
, ich öff - ne den Saal zum

41
zum himm-li-schen Mahl, komm, Je - su, komm,
himm-li-schen Mahl, zum himm - li-schen Mahl, ich kom - me,

44
Je - su, komm, Je - - - - su!
ich kom-me, ich kom - me; komm, lieb - li - che See - le!

47

49
Er -
Ich öff - ne den Saal

52
öff - ne den Saal, er - öff - ne den Saal
, ich öff - ne den Saal zum
55
zum himm-li - schen Mahl, komm, Je - su, komm,
himm-li - schen Mahl, zum himm - li - schen Mahl, ich kom - me,
58
Je - su, komm, Je - - - su!
ich kom-me, ich kom - me; komm, lieb - li - che See - le!
61
Wenn kömmst du, mein Heil,
Ich

64
wenn
kömmst du, mein Heil,
wenn
kom - me, dein Teil,
ich
kom - me, dein Teil,

67
kömmst du,
mein
Heil,
mein
Heil?
Ich
ich kom-me,
dein Teil,
dein Teil,

70
war - - - te, ich
war - - - - - - - - - - te, ich
ich kom - me, dein
Teil,
ich
kom - me,

72
war -
ich
kom - me,
ich kom - me, dein

74
- - - - - - - - -te mit bren - nen - dem Ö - le, mit
Teil, ich kom - me, dein Teil, ich

76
bren - nen - dem Ö - le; wenn kömmst du, mein Heil ? Ich
kom - me, dein Teil, ich kom - me, dein Teil,

79
war- - - -te mit bren-nen - dem Ö - le.
ich kom - me.

83

SEELE: Wenn kömmst du, mein Heil?
JESUS: Ich komme, dein Teil.
SEELE: Ich warte mit brennendem Öle;
Eröffne den Saal,
Zum himmlischen Mahl,
JESUS: Ich öffne den Saal,
Zum himmlischen Mahl,
SEELE: Komm, Jesu!
JESUS: Komm, liebliche Seele!

SOUL: When will you come, my salvation?
JESUS: I come, a part of yourself.
SOUL: I wait with burning oil.
Open the hall
to the heavenly feast!
JESUS: I am opening the hall
to the heavenly feast.
SOUL: Come, Jesus!
JESUS: Come, lovely Soul!

4. Chorale: *Zion hört die Wächter singen*

9
13
Zi - on hört die Wäch - ter sin - - gen, das
più p
17
Herz tut ihr vor Freu - den sprin - - gen, sie wa - chet
21
und steht ei - lend auf.
26
30

Ihr Freund kommt vom Him - mel präch - - tig, von
Gna - den stark, von Wahr - heit mäch - - tig,
ihr Licht wird
hell, ihr — Stern geht auf.
Nun komm, du wer - te Kron,
Herr Je - su,
Got - tes Sohn!
Ho - si - an - - na!

Zion Hört die Wächter singen,	Zion hears the watchmen singing;
Das Herz tut ihr vor Freuden springen,	her heart jumps for joy,
Sie wachet und steht eilend auf.	she wakes and gets up quickly.
Ihr Freund kommt vom Himmel prächtig,	Her friend comes from heaven proudly,
Von Gnaden stark, von Wahrheit mächtig,	sturdy in grace, mighty in truth;
Ihr Licht wird hell, ihr Stern geht auf.	her light shines bright, her star is rising.
Nun komm, du werte Kron,	Now come, you worthy crown,
Herr Jesu, Gottes Sohn!	Lord Jesus, God's son.
Hosianna!	Hosanna!
Wir folgen all zum Freudensaal	We all follow to the hall of joy
Und halten mit das Abendmahl.	and join in the evening meal.
—Philipp Nicolai	

5. Recitative: *So geh herein zu mir*

So geh herein zu mir,	So come in with me,
Du mir erwählte Braut!	My chosen bride!
Ich habe mich mit dir	I have bound myself
Von Ewigkeit vertraut.	to you for eternity!
Dich will ich auf mein Herz,	I will set you on my heart
Auf meinen Arm gleich wie ein Siegel setzen	and also on my arm as a seal
Und dein betrübtes Aug ergötzen.	and delight your sorry eye.
Vergiß, o Seele, nun	Forget now, O soul,
Die Angst, den Schmerz,	the anxiety, the pain
Den du erdulden müssen;	that you had to endure.
Auf meiner Linken sollst du ruhn,	On my left will you rest,
Und meine Rechte soll dich küssen.	and my right will kiss you.

6. Aria (Duet): *Mein Freund ist mein!*

13
p
mein

17
p
p sem-
Freund ist mein, die Lie - be soll nichts schei - - den; mein
und ich bin sein, die Lie - be soll nichts schei-den, nichts schei-den;

21
pre
Freund ist mein, mein Freund ist mein, mein Freund ist mein
und ich bin sein, und ich bin sein, und ich bin

25
, die Lie- - - be soll nichts schei- - - den; mein Freund ist
sein, die Lie- - be soll nichts schei- - - den; und

28
mein, die Lie-be soll nichts schei-den__; mein Freund ist__ mein, die Lie - be soll nichts
ich bin sein, und ich bin sein, und ich bin sein, und

31
schei- den__, die Lie - be soll nichts schei - - - - - den, die Lie - be
ich bin sein, die Lie - - be soll nichts schei - - - den__, die Lie - - -

34
soll nichts schei - den; mein Freund ist mein, die Lie - - -
tr
- be soll nichts schei - den; und ich bin sein, die Lie - be

38
f
tr
- be soll nichts schei - den.
tr
soll nichts schei - - den.

43
11
Ich

47
p
will mit dir, ich will mit dir in Him - mels Ro - - sen
Du sollst mit mir, du sollst mit mir in Him - mels Ro -

50
wei - - den, ich will mit dir, ich will mit dir in
- sen wei - - - - den, du sollst mit mir, du sollst mit

53
Him - mels Ro - sen wei - - - - - - - - - - - -
mir in Him - mels Ro - - sen wei - - den, du

56
- den _, ich will _ mit dir in Him - mels Ro - sen
sollst mit mir in Him - mels Ro - sen wei - - - -
60
wei - - - - - - - - - - - den _, da Freu - de die Fül - le _, da
- - - - - - - - - - - den _, da Freu - de die Fül - le, da

63
Won - ne _ wird sein, da Freu - de _ die Fül - le, da
Won - ne _ wird sein, da Won - ne _ wird sein, da

66
Freu - de die Fül - le, da Won - ne _ wird sein, da Freu - de _ die Fül - le, da
Freu - de die Fül - le _, da Won - ne _ wird sein, da

70
Won-ne_wird sein, da Won- - - - - - - - - -ne, Won-ne_wird sein.
Freu-de_ die Fül-le, da Won-ne_ wird sein, da Won- - - - - - - - - -ne wird sein.
Da capo *dal segno*

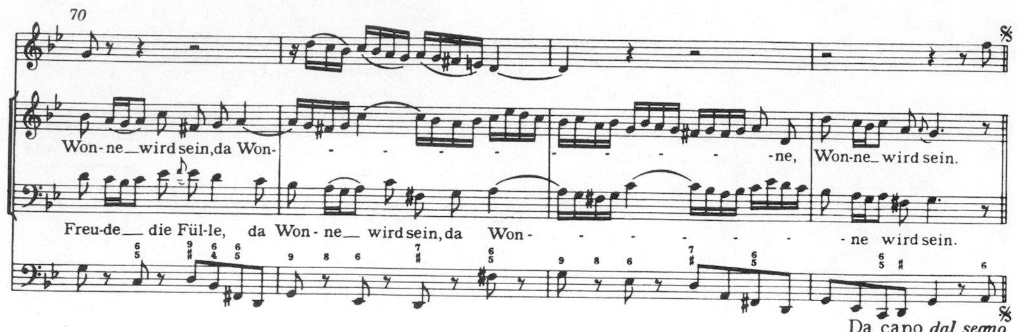

SEELE: Mein Freund ist mein,
JESUS: Und ich bin sein,
BEIDE: Die Liebe soll nichts scheiden;
SEELE: Ich will mit dir in Himmels Rosen weiden,
JESUS: Du sollst mit mir in Himmels Rosen weiden,
BEIDE: Da Freude die Fülle, da Wonne wird sein.

SOUL: My friend is mine!
JESUS: And I am his!
BOTH: Nothing shall keep love apart;
SOUL: I want to graze with with you in heaven's roses;
JESUS: You shall graze with me in heaven's roses;
BOTH: there fullness of joy, there bliss will reign.

7. Chorale: *Gloria sei dir gesungen*

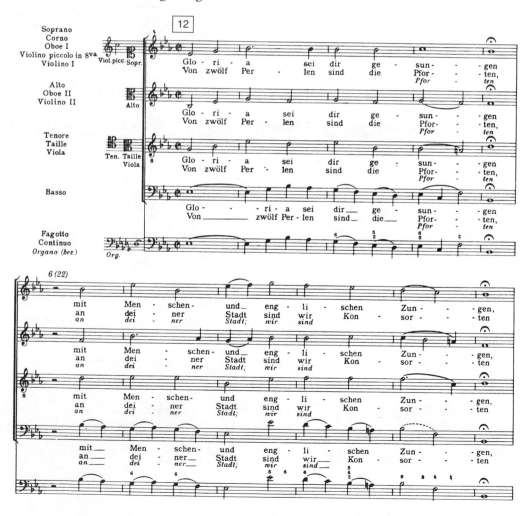

12
Soprano
Corno
Oboe I
Violino piccolo in 8va
Violino I
Viol. picc. Sopr.
Alto
Oboe II
Violino II
Alto
Tenore
Taille
Viola
Ten. Taille Viola
Basso
Fagotto
Continuo
Organo (bez.)
Org.
Glo - ri - a sei dir ge - sun- - gen
Von zwölf Per - len sind die Pfor- - ten,
Pfor - ten

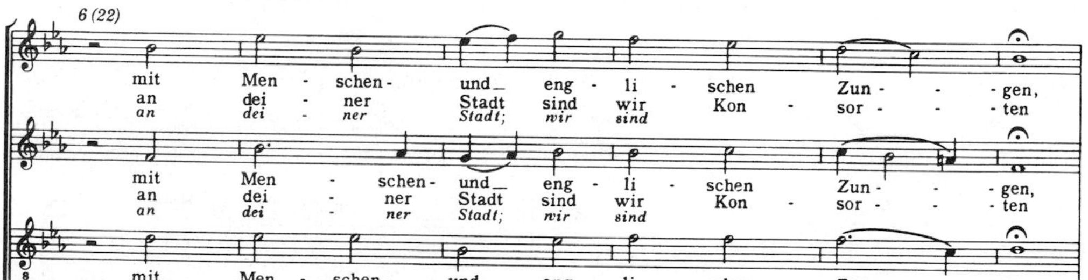

6 (22)
mit Men - schen- und eng - li - schen Zun- - gen,
an dei - ner Stadt sind wir Kon - sor- - ten
an dei - ner Stadt; wir sind

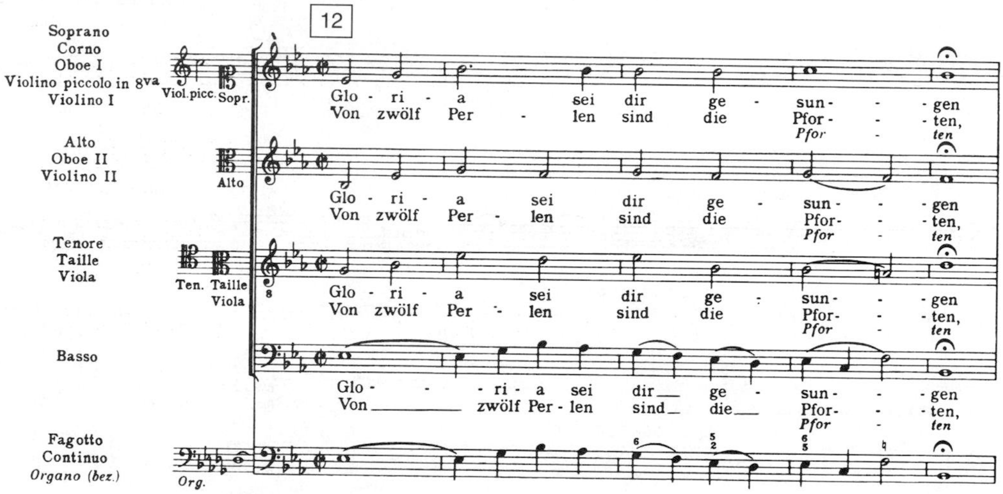

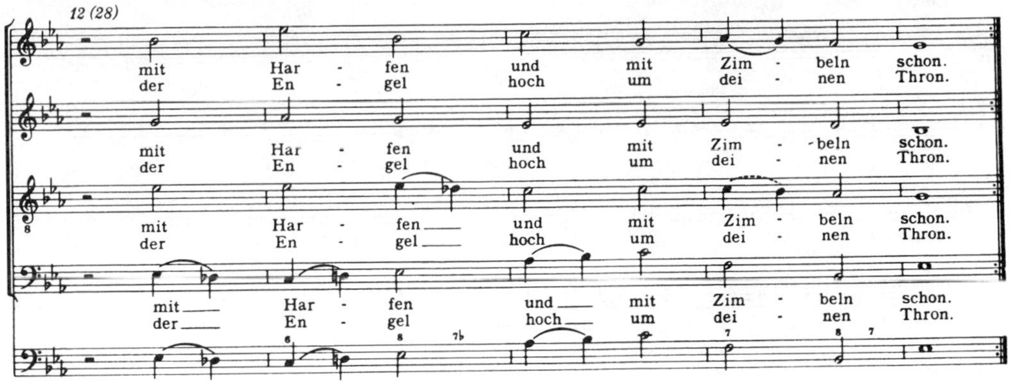
12 (28)
mit Har - fen und mit Zim - beln schon.
der En - gel hoch um dei - nen Thron.
mit Har - fen und mit Zim - beln schon.
der En - gel hoch um dei - nen Thron.
mit Har - fen und mit Zim - beln schon.
der En - gel hoch um dei - nen Thron.
mit Har - fen und mit Zim - beln schon.
der En - gel hoch um dei - nen Thron.

33
Kein Aug hat je ge - spürt, kein Ohr hat
Kein Aug hat je ge - spürt, kein Ohr hat
Kein Aug hat je ge - spürt, kein Ohr hat
Kein Aug hat je ge - spürt, kein Ohr hat

39
je ge - hört sol - che Freu - de. Des sind wir
je ge - hört sol - che Freu - de. Des sind wir
je ge - hört sol - che Freu - de. Des sind wir
je ge - hört sol - che Freu - de. Des sind wir

Gloria sei dir gesungen	May the Gloria be sung to you
Mit Menschen- und englischen Zungen,	with people's and angels' tongues,
Mit Harfen und mit Zimbeln schon.	with harps and with cymbals too.
Von zwölf Perlen sind die Pforten	Of twelve pearls are the gates
An deiner Stadt; wir sind Konsorten	to your city; we are consorts
Der Engel hoch um deinen Thron.	of the angels high around your throne.
Kein Aug hat je gespürt,	No eye has ever seen
Kein Ohr hat je gehört	nor ear has ever heard
Solche Freude.	such joy.
Des sind wir froh,	Of this we are happy,
Io io,	Oho, oho!
Ewig in dulci jubilo.	Forever *in dulci jubilo.*
—Philipp Nicolai	

Wachet auf, first performed November 25, 1731, is one of the few cantatas of J. S. Bach that can be dated precisely. It was composed for the 27th Sunday after Trinity, which occurred only twice in Bach's Leipzig period—1731 and 1742—and various circumstances exclude 1742. The Gospel read at the Sunday service was Matthew 25:1–13, which tells of the ten virgins who watch by night for the arrival of the bridegroom. Some of the virgins are wise, because they brought oil for their lamps; the foolish ones, who are compelled to fetch some oil, miss his arrival and are locked out of the wedding hall. Three stanzas of Philipp Nicolai's chorale that dwell upon this parable serve as texts for the opening chorus, a chorale movement for the tenors, and the final chorus. The remaining poetry by an unknown author, for the recitatives and arias, is based on the same Gospel account. As he often did, Bach arranged the seven movements in a symmetrical fashion: the middle tenor-chorale stanza is flanked by a recitative and aria on each side, and chorale-choruses begin and end the cantata.

The opening chorus, the weightiest movement in Bach's chorale cantatas, is one of the most magnificent of them all. Its form is modeled on the ritornello structure of the instrumental concerto. The full sixteen-measure ritornello returns twice: between the two *Stollen* (lines 1–3 and 4–6) of the chorale and at the end. An abridged ritornello (omitting the first four bars) precedes the *Abgesang* (lines 7–12). As in many Vivaldi concertos, the ritornello is divisible into four-bar phrases based on several distinct motives. The first three notes of the chorale together with its verbal message inspired the musical motives of the ritornello. The twelve dotted-chord patterns of the first phrase (motive a) suggest a church bell striking midnight. The rising motive (b) in the violins and oboe (measures 4–7), which hesitates at the third and fifth of the triad, alludes to the first three notes of the chorale as well as to the anxiety and expectancy of the virgins. The rushing, rising figure in the first violins (measure 9, motive c) suggests the vigilance and impatience of the wise virgins. The last four measures of the ritornello combine motives a (in the continuo), b (in the oboes), and c (in the first violins). The instrumental accompaniment of the chorale phrases rework these motives, while the chorale melody, sung only by the sopranos, supplies subjects for the imitative counterpoint of the three other voices. Only on the word "Alleluja" (measures 135ff.) do the voices pick up one of the instrumental motives, c, which is forged into a fugue subject.

The first recitative (Number 2), accompanied by continuo only, typifies Bach's approach in its triadic and often wide leaps, their tension heightened by the dissonant chords they outline. The second recitative (Number 5), sung by the bridegroom who represents Christ, is accompanied by strings, as are the speeches of Jesus in Bach's Passions.

Both arias are duets. Number 3, *Wann kommst du, mein Heil?* (When will you come, my salvation?), is a conversation between the Soul and Jesus written as a love duet. The arabesques woven around the voices by the violino piccolo (a three-quarter size violin specially tuned to make playing high notes easier) brings to mind the improvisatory passage work that embellished the simple lines of Corelli's slow movements (see facsimile in HWM, p. 361). At the end of the aria, performers repeat only the opening ritornello instead of a full da capo.

The other aria-duet, *Mein Freund ist mein* (My friend is mine, Number 6), by contrast, is a full-blown da capo form. It is also more conventional: the ritornello announces the melody that the voices then elaborate. This melody is in the galant style of the 1730s and consists of balanced two-measure phrases. The contentment of a love union is heard in the parallel phrases sung by the two voices and in their parallel motion in thirds (for example, measures 8–12). In the middle section, which reworks the same material, this oneness is symbolized by quasi-canonic writing. The runs that had been the preserve of the oboe are commandeered by the singers to portray the grazing in heaven's roses. The da capo ends at the fermata (measure 46).

The central chorale (Number 4) is one of the best-known pieces of Bach, who must have been fond of it too because he transcribed it for organ (BWV 645), and Johann Georg Schübler published it as the first of *Sechs Choräle von verschiedener Art* (Six Chorales of Diverse Sorts, ca. 1748–49). As in the aria just discussed, Bach composed the obbligato line (here played by strings) in the modern style. We hear an opening two-measure phrase that is immediately repeated and is then followed by another pair of two-measure phrases, the second of which joins even shorter segments. All of these phrases end—in comic-opera fashion—on a weak beat. But despite the stops and starts, a remarkable continuity rules, and the violins project a single affection of quiet joy against the disparate lines of the chorale's second stanza sung by the tenor section.

Compared to the chorale in Number 4, the note values of the tune are doubled in the final chorus (Number 7), permitting Bach to energize the hymn with driving quarter notes in the bass and elsewhere. The entire orchestra joins in this number, playing *colla parte*—that is, doubling the vocal parts.

82

Johann Sebastian

Mass in B Minor, BWV

Credo: *Symbolum Nicen*

a) Et in Spiritum sanctum Dominum

From J. S. Bach, *Neue Ausgabe sämtlicher Werke*, ed. Friedrich Smend (Kassel, 1954), pp. 190–215. Reprinted by permission of Bärenreiter Music Corporation.

24
tr
tr
piano
piano
et in Spi-ri-tum san-ctum Do - mi-num et vi - vi - fi - can - tem, vi-vi-fi-
30
can-tem, Spi-ri-tum san-ctum, Spi-ri-tum san-ctum vi-vi-fi - can - tem, vi-vi-fi - can-tem Do - mi-
36
num, qui ex Pa-tre Fi - li - o - - - - que pro-ce - - - - - - - - -
42
tr
tr
- - - - dit, ex Pa - tre Fi - li - o-que pro - ce - dit, qui ex Pa - - - tre Fi - li - o - -
14
48
tr
tr
forte
forte
- que pro-ce - - dit;

54
tr
60
tr
piano
piano
qui cum Pa - - - - tre et Fi - li - o si-mul a - do - ra - tur, a - do-
66
ra - - - - - - - - - - - - - - - - - tur et con - glo - ri - fi - ca - -
72
forte
forte
tr
- - - - tur, et con - glo - ri - fi - ca - - tur;
78
tr
piano
piano
qui lo - cu-tus est per Pro - phe - - tas, lo - cu-tus est per Pro - phe-tas, per Pro -

84
phe-tas lo-cu-tus est, lo-co-tus est per Pro-phe- - -tas, lo-cu-tus est per Pro-
90
forte
forte
phe- - -tas, per Pro-phe- -tas. Et u-nam san-ctam ca-tho-li-cam et a-po-sto-li-
96
cam ec-cle- - - -si-am,
102
tr
tr
tr
tr
piano
piano
et u-nam san-ctam ca-tho-li-cam et a-po-sto-li-
108
cam ec-cle-si-am, et u-nam san-ctam ca-tho- - - - - - - - -

114
- li - cam et a - po - sto - li - cam ec - cle -
120
si - am, u - nam san - ctam ca-tho-li-cam et a-po-sto - li - cam ec-cle -
126
- si - am, u-nam san - ctam ca - tho-li cam et a - po - sto - li - cam ec-cle-si-
132
forte
forte
am.
138
tr
tr

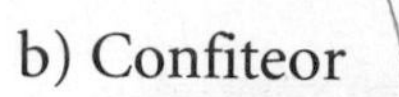

b) Confiteor

15
Soprano I
Soprano II
Alto
Tenore
Basso
Continuo
1
3
4
6
Con - fi - te - or, con - fi - - te - or u - - num ba - pti - - -
Con - fi - - te - or, con - fi - - te - or u - - num ba -
Con - fi - te - or, con - fi - - te
Con - fi - te - or, con - fi -
Con -

8
sma, u - num ba - pti - - - sma, u - - num ba - pti-sma, u - - num ba - pti - - -
pti - - sma, con - fi - te - or u - - num ba - pti-sma, u - num ba - pti - - -
or u - num ba - pti - - - sma, u - num, u - num ba - pti - - - -
- te - or u - num ba - pti - sma, u - num ba - pti - - sma, u - num ba - pti -
fi - te - or, con - fi - - te - or u - num ba - pti - - - sma, u - num ba - pti - - -

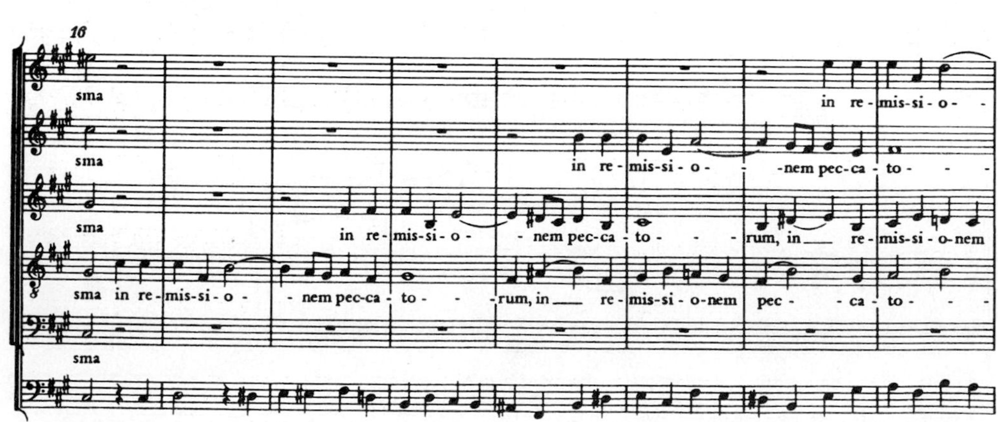
16
sma in re - mis - si - o -
sma in re - mis - si - o - - nem pec - ca - to - - -
sma in re - mis - si - o - nem pec - ca - to - - rum, in re - mis - si - o - nem
sma in re - mis - si - o - nem pec - ca - to - - rum, in re - mis - si - o - nem pec - ca - to - - -
sma

24
- - nem pecca - to - - - rum, in re - mis - si - o - nem pec - - ca - to - - - rum, con -
rum, in re - mis - si - o - nem pec - - ca - to - - - - - - - - - - rum, in re -
pec - - ca - to - - - rum, in re - mis - si - o - nem pecca - to - - - rum, pec - - ca - to - -
rum, in re - mis - si - o - nem pec - ca - to - - - - - - - rum, pec - ca - to - -
in re - mis - si - o - - nem pecca - to - - - rum, in re - mis - si - o - nem pec - - ca - to - -

32
fi - - te - or, con - fi - - te - or u - num ba - pti - - sma in re - mis - si - o - - nem pec - ca -
mis - si - o - - nem pecca - to - - rum, con - fi - - te - or, con - fi - -
rum, in re - mis - si - o - - nem pec - ca - to - - rum, con - fi - te - or u - num ba -
rum, con fi - - te - or, con - fi - - te - or u - num ba - pti - sma, u -
rum,

40
to - - - - - rum, pecca - to - - rum, in re - mis - si - o - - nem pec - ca -
- te - or u - num ba - pti - sma, con - fi - - te - or u - num ba - pti - sma, con - fi - - te -
pti - - sma, u - num ba - pti - sma in re - missi - o - nem pec - ca - to - rum, con - fi - - te - or u - num ba -
num ba - pti - sma, con - fi - - te - or, con - fi - - te - or u - num ba - pti - sma,
con - fi - - te - or, con - fi - - te - or u - - num ba - pti - - - sma in re -

48
to - rum, con - fi - - te - or, con - fi - - te - or, con - fi - - te - or u - -
or u-num ba - pti - sma, con - fi - - te - or, con-fi-te - or u - num ba - pti - sma, con -
pti-sma in re - mis-si - o - - nem pec-ca - to - - - rum, pec-ca - to - - rum, con - fi - - te-
con - fi - - te - or, con - fi - - te - or u - num ba - pti - - sma,
mis - si - o - - - nem pec-ca - to - - - rum, in re - mis - si - o - - nem pec-ca - to - - rum,

56
- num ba - pti - - - sma, con - fi - - te - or u-num ba - pti-sma in re -
fi - - te - or, con - fi - - te - or, con - fi - - te - or u - - - num ba - pti - sma
or, con - ti - - - te - or in re - mis-si - o - - nem pec-ca - to - - rum, in re-mis-si -
con - fi - - te - or, con - fi - - te - or u-num ba - pti-sma in re -
con - fi - - te - or, con-fi - - te - or u-num ba-pti-sma in re - mis-si-o - -

64
mis - si - o - - - - nem pec-ca-to - - - rum, in re - mis-si - o - - nem pec-ca -
in re - mis-si - o - - nem pec-ca - to-rum, pec-ca - to - - rum, in re-mis-si - o - - nem
o - - - - nem pec - ca - to-rum, pec-ca - to - - rum, in re - mis-si - o - - nem pec- -
mis-si - o - - nem pec-ca - to-rum, pec - ca - to - - - rum, in re - mis-si - o-nem pec-ca -
- - nem pec-ca - to - - - - - - - - - - rum,

72
16
to - - - rum, in re - mis-si - o - - nem pec-ca - to - - - rum, pec - - ca - to - - - - -
pec - ca - to - - rum, con - fi - - te - or u - num ba - pti - sma, con - fi - - te -
- - ca - to - - rum, con - - fi - te - or u - num ba - pti - - -
to - - - rum, in re - mis - si - o - - nem pec-ca - to - rum, in
con - - fi - te - or u - num ba - pti - - sma

80
rum, con - fi - - te - or, con-fi - - te - - or u - num ba - pti-sma
or u-num ba - pti - sma, con-fi - - te - or, con - fi - te - - or u - - num ba - pti - - -
sma in re - mis - si - - o - nem pec - ca - to - - -
re - mis - - si - o-nem pec - ca - - to - - - rum, in re - mis-si - o - - nem pec-ca - to - - -
in re - mis - si - - o - nem pec - ca- - to - - - rum,

88
in re-mis-si - o - - - nem pec - - ca - to - rum, in re - mis-si - o - - nem pecca-
sma, con - fi - - te - or, in re - mis-si - o - nem pec - - - ca - to-rum, con -
rum, con - fi - - te - or u - num ba - pti - - - sma in re - mis-si - o - - nem pecca - to - rum,
rum, con - - - fi - - - te - - -
in re-mis-si - o - - - nem pec-ca - to - - - rum,

96
to - - rum, con - fi - te - or, con-fi - - te - or, in re-
fi - te - or, con- fi - - te - or u - - num ba - pti - - sma, con - fi - - te - or, con-fi- -
con - fi - te - or, con- fi - - te - or, in re - mis-si - o - - nem pecca - to - -
or u - - num ba - - pti - - sma
in re-mis-si-o - - nem pecca - to - rum, con - fi - - te - or, con-fi- -

105
mis- si - o - - nem pecca - to - - rum, con- - fi - - te - or, con-fi- -
- - - te - or, in re - mis-si - o - - nem pecca - to - - rum, con - fi - - te- -
rum, in re - mis-si - o - - nem pec-ca - to - - rum, pec - ca - to - - - rum, u- -
in re - - mis - - si - - o - - nem
- te - or u - - num ba - pti - - sma in re-mis-si-o - - nem pecca - to - - -

113
- te - or u - num ba - pti - sma in re-mis - - si - o - - nem pec-ca-
or u - num ba - pti - - sma in re-mis - - si - o - - nem pec-ca-
num ba-pti-sma in re-mis-si - o - - nem pec-ca - to - - - rum, in re - mis- si - o-nem
pec - - ca - - to - - rum, in re - mis-si - o - - nem
rum, con-fi - - te - or u - num ba - pti-sma in re-mis-si - o - - - nem pec - ca- -

17
121
Adagio
to - - - rum. Et ex - pe - - - cto, ex - pe - - cto
to - - - rum. Et ex - pe - - - cto, ex - pe - - cto re -
pec - ca - to - rum. Et ex - pe - - - cto, ex - pe-cto re-sur - re - cti -
pec - ca - to - - rum. Et ex - pe - - - cto, ex - pe-cto re-sur - re - cti -
to - - rum. Et ex - pe - - - cto, ex - pe -

130
re-sur-re-cti - o-nem mor-tu o - - - - rum, ex -
- sur-re-cti - o - nem mor - tu - o - - - rum,
o - nem mor - tu - - o - rum, mor - tu - o - rum, mor - tu - - o - - rum,
o - nem mor - tu - - o - - rum, re-sur-re-cti - o-nem mor-tu - o - - rum,
- cto re-sur-re-cti - o-nem mor-tu o - - rum,

138
pe - - cto re-sur - re - - cti - o - nem mor - - tu - o -
ex - pe - - cto, ex-pe - cto re - - sur - re-cti - o - - nem mor-tu - o -
ex - pe - - cto re-sur - re-cti - o - - nem mor-tu - o -
ex - pe - - cto re-sur - re-cti - o-nem mor - tu - o -
ex - pe - - cto re-sur - re - - cti - o-nem mor-tu - o -

c) Et expecto resurrectionem

6
re - cti - o-nem mor-tu - o - rum.
- - cti - o - nem mor-tu - o - rum.
re - cti - o - nem mor-tu-o - rum.
re - cti - o-nem mor-tu - o - rum.
- - cti - o - nem mor tu - o - rum.

13
Ex - pe - -
Ex - pe - - - - - -
Ex - pe - - - - - cto re -
Ex -

21
Ex - pe - cto re - sur-re-cti - o - nem mor-tu - o -
cto, ex - pe - cto re-sur-re-cti - o - nem mor-tu - o -
cto re - sur-re-cti - o - nem mor - tu - o - rum, re-sur-re-cti -
sur-re-cti - o - nem mor-tu - o - rum, re-sur-re-cti - o - nem mor-tu -
pe - cto re-sur - re - cti - o - nem mor-tu - o -

29
rum, re - sur - re - cti - o - - - - nem mor-tu - o - - rum, et ex - pe - - cto, ex-
- - - - - - - rum, re-sur - re - cti - o - - - - nem, et ex - pe -
o - - - - nem mor-tu o - - - - rum, et ex - pe - - cto, ex - pe - cto, ex-
o - - - - - - - - - - - - - rum, et ex - pe - - cto, ex - pe -
- - - - - - - - - - - - - - - rum, et ex - pe - - -

19
36
pe - cto, ex - pe-cto re-sur - re - cti - o-nem mor-tu - o - - - rum, re - sur-
- cto, ex - pe-cto re - sur - re - cti - o-nem mor-tu - o - - - rum,
pe - - - cto re-sur - re - cti - o nem, re - sur - re-cti - o - - - -
cto, ex - pe - cto re-sur re cti - o-nem mor-tu - o - - - rum,
cto, ex - pe - cto re - sur - re-cti - o - nem mor-tu - o - - - rum,

43
re - cti - o - - - - - - nem mor - tu - o - - - - rum, re - sur - re - - -
re - sur - re - cti - o - - - - - nem, re - sur-
- - nem mor - tu - o - - - - rum, re - sur - re - cti - o - nem mor - tu - o -
re - sur - re - cti - o - - - - - - - nem mor - tu - o - - -
re - sur - re - cti - o - - - - - -

50
- - cti - o - - - nem mor - tu - o - - rum
re - - - - cti - o - nem mor - tu - o - rum
- rum, re - sur - re - cti - o - nem mor - tu - o - rum
rum, re - sur - re - cti o nem mor tu o rum
- - nem, re - sur - re - cti - o - nem mor - tu - o - rum

57
et
vi - - - - tam ven -
et
vi - - -
et

64
et vi - - - tam ven - tu - - ri___ se - - - - cu -
et vi - - - - tam ven - tu - - ri se - - cu - li, ven - tu - ri
tu - ri se - cu - li, vi - - tam ven - tu - - ri se - - - - - - - - cu-li,
- tam ven - tu - ri se - cu - li, vi - - tam ven - tu - - ri se - - - - -
vi - - - - tam ven - tu - ri___ se - cu - li, ven - tu - ri___ se - - - - - - -

71
li, ven - tu - ri se - - - - cu-li, a - - - - - men, a -
se - - - cu-li, a - - - - - - - men,
a - - - - - - - - men, a - - -
- - cu - li, ven - tu - ri se - - - - cu-li, a - - - - - men,
- - - - - - - - cu - li, ven - tu - ri se - - - - cu-li, a - - -

78
men, et vi-tam ven-tu-ri se - cu-
a - men, a - men, et vi-tam ven - tu - ri se- cu-
- men, a - men, et vi-tam ven - tu - ri se- cu-
a - men, a - men, et vi-tam ven - tu-ri se - cu-
men, ven-tu-ri se - cu-

85
li, ven - tu-ri se - cu-li, a-men, a -
li, ven - tu-ri se - cu-li, a-men, a -
li, ven - tu-ri se - cu-li, a-men, a - men,
li, ven - tu - ri se - cu-li, a-men, a - men, a - men,
li, ven - tu-ri se - cu-li, a-men,

92
- men, a - - men, a - - men, a - men, a - - men,
men, a - men, a - - men, a -
a - men, a men, a -
a - men, a -
a - - men, a - - men,

For a translation of the Credo, see NAWM 3.

Bach assembled the Mass in B Minor between around 1747 and 1749, mostly from previously composed music. Several of the movements were choruses from cantatas, in which the German text was replaced by the Latin words of the Mass and the music sometimes reworked. One of these is the *Et expecto* (c), taken from Cantata No. 120 (*Gott, man lobet dich in der Stille*, 1728–29). The Et in Spiritum (a) and Confiteor (b) date from 1747–49. The entire work was apparently never performed in Bach's lifetime.

Et in Spiritum sanctum (a), for bass solo with two oboi d'amore, like a number of other late works of Bach, shows traces of the popular galant style—repeated phrases, parallel thirds, and slow harmonic rhythm. Another modern trait is the great care Bach took to subordinate the instrumental parts to the voice, indicating *piano* for the obbligato instruments when the voice is singing and *forte* when it is not. This aria is singularly monothematic, with the instrumental ritornello and vocal elaboration sharing the same material. The pillars of the structure are three full statements of the twelve-measure ritornello, in A major, E major, then again in A major. The sometimes awkward text-setting suggests that the music may originally have been composed for other words.

The Confiteor (b), on the other hand, must have been expressly set to this text. As in the opening of the Credo, Bach here took the appropriate segment from the Gregorian Credo II (*Liber usualis*, p. 67) as a cantus firmus (it is heard in the tenor part starting at measure 73). He wrote the choral parts in *stile antico*, marked by the *alla breve* time signature and fugal procedures of that style. But in the continuo accompaniment he added a modern touch: a quasi-ostinato bass. At the words "Et expecto resurrectionem mortuorum" (And I await the resurrection of the dead), Bach dropped the cantus firmus and inserted a transitional Adagio, intensely chromatic and dissonant, symbolizing the death that will be defied by the resurrection.

The brilliant Vivace e Allegro that follows, triumphantly reiterating the words "Et expecto resurrectionem mortuorum" (c), is a reworking of the chorus *Jauchzet, ihr erfreuten Stimmen* (Shout, you joyful voices), from Cantata No. 120. Some of the purely instrumental music of the cantata chorus is ingeniously made to accompany a choral fugue (measures 61–87).

83 George Frideric Handel (1685–1759)

Giulio Cesare: Act II, Scene 2

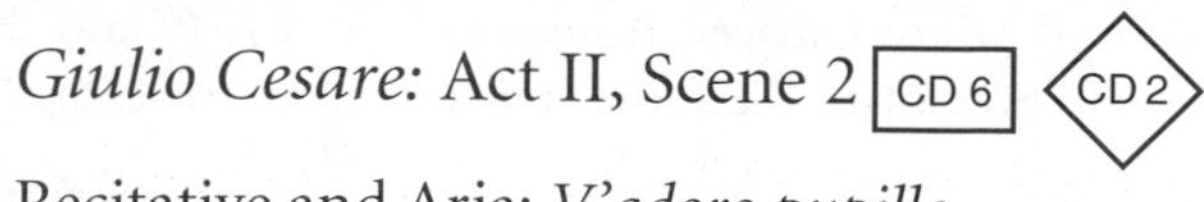

Recitative and Aria: *V'adoro pupille*

20 53

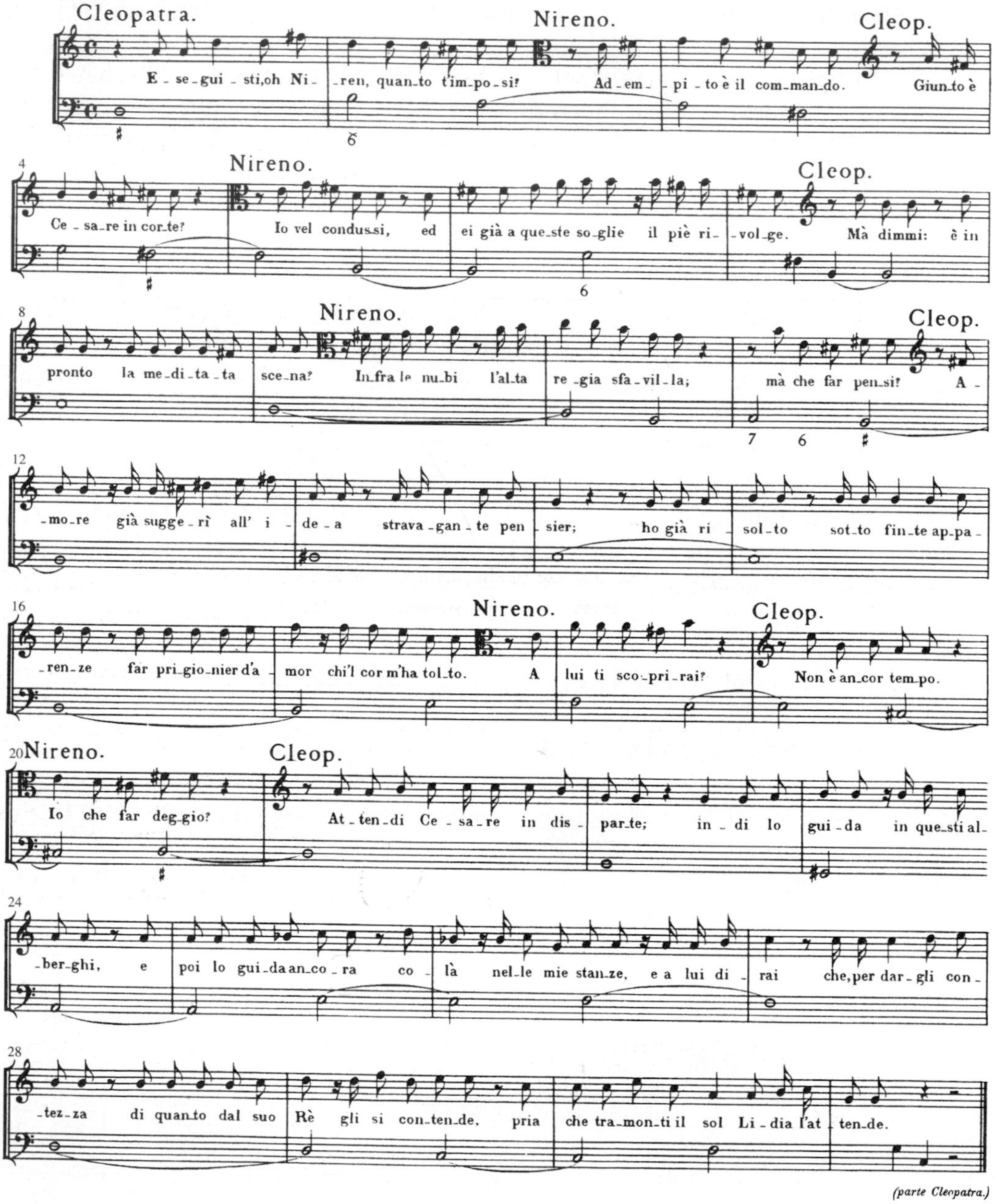

Cleopatra. E - se-gui - sti, oh Ni - ren, quan-to t'im-po - si?

Nireno. Ad - em - pi - to è il com-man-do.

Cleop. Giun-to è Ce - sa-re in cor-te?

Nireno. Io vel condus-si, ed ei già a que-ste so-glie il piè ri - vol-ge.

Cleop. Mà dimmi: è in pronto la me-di-ta - ta sce-na?

Nireno. In-fra le nu-bi l'al-ta re - gia sfa - vil - la; mà che far pen-si?

Cleop. A - mo-re già sugge - rì all' i - de - a strava - gan - te pen - sier; ho già ri - sol-to sot-to fin-te ap-pa - ren-ze far pri-gio-nier d'a - mor chi'l cor m'ha tol-to.

Nireno. A lui ti sco - pri - rai?

Cleop. Non è an-cor tem-po.

Nireno. Io che far deg-gio?

Cleop. At - ten - di Ce - sa - re in dis - par-te; in - di lo gui - da in que-sti al - ber-ghi, e poi lo gui-da an-co - ra co - là nel-le mie stan-ze, e a lui di - rai che, per dar - gli con - tez-za di quan-to dal suo Rè gli si con-ten-de, pria che tra-mon-ti il sol Li - dia l'at - ten-de.

(parte Cleopatra.)

Handel Gesellschaft, Vol. 68, pp. 51–58. Reprinted by permission of Bärenreiter Music Corporation.

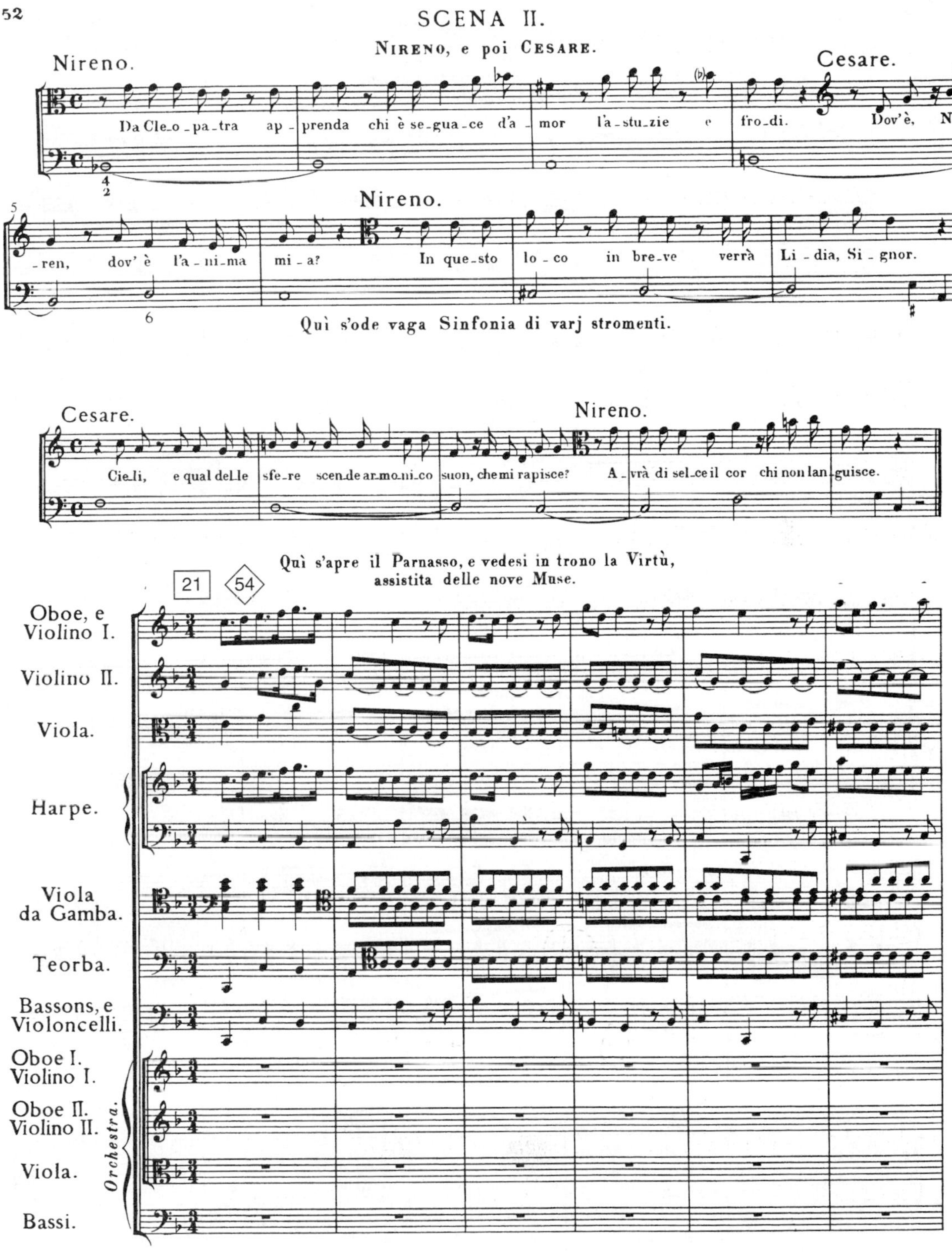

52
SCENA II.
NIRENO, e poi CESARE.
Nireno.
Da Cle-o-pa-tra ap-prenda chi è se-gua-ce d'a-mor l'a-stu-zie e fro-di.
Cesare.
Dov'è, Ni-ren, dov' è l'a-ni-ma mi-a?
Nireno.
In que-sto lo-co in bre-ve verrà Li-dia, Si-gnor.
Quì s'ode vaga Sinfonia di varj stromenti.
Cesare.
Cie-li, e qual del-le sfe-re scen-de ar-mo-ni-co suon, che mi rapisce?
Nireno.
A-vrà di sel-ce il cor chi non lan-guisce.
Quì s'apre il Parnasso, e vedesi in trono la Virtù, assistita delle nove Muse.
21
54
Oboe, e Violino I.
Violino II.
Viola.
Harpe.
Viola da Gamba.
Teorba.
Bassons, e Violoncelli.
Oboe I. Violino I.
Oboe II. Violino II.
Viola.
Bassi.
Orchestra.

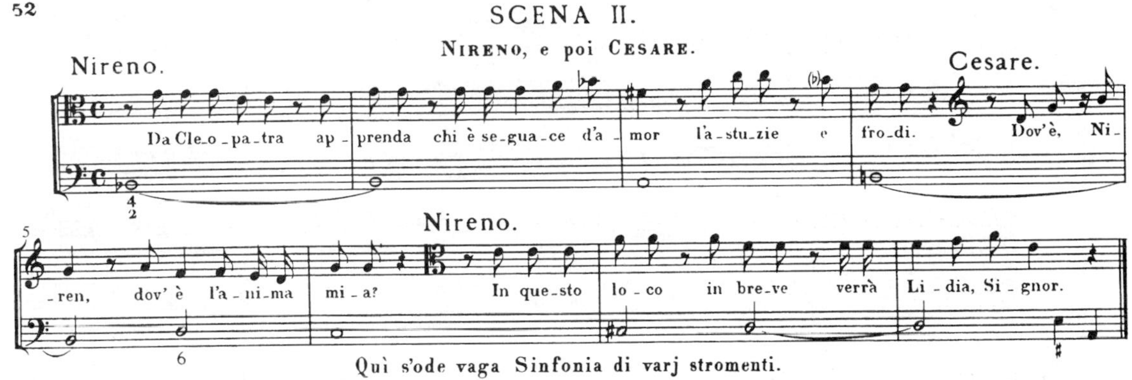

7
tr
12
5
6
6
6

Cesare.
Giu_lio, che mi_ri? e quando con a_bis_so di lu_ce sce_se_ro i Nu_mi in ter_ra?
22
55
Largo.
Oboe.
unis.
Oboe, e Violino I.
Sordini.
Viol.
Violino II.
Viola.
Viola da Gamba.
Teorba, Harpe, Bassons e Violoncelli.
Cleopatra.
V'a_do_ro, pu_pil_le, sa_et_te d'A_mo_re, le vo_stre fa_vil_le son
Violino I.
Sordini.
Violino II.
Viola.
Bassi.
Orchestra.
8
tr
gra_te nel sen; v'a_do_ro, pu_pil_le, le vo_stre fa_vil_le son gra_te, son

16
gra - te nel sen, v'a - do - ro, pu - pil - le, sa - et - te d'A - mo - re, le vo - stre fa -
24
- vil - le son gra - te nel sen, le vo - stre fa - vil - le son gra - te nel sen.

B
23
56
32
Pie - to - se vi bra - ma il me - sto mio co - re, ch'ogn'
(Fine.)
41
o - ra vi chia - ma l'a - ma - to suo ben, ch'ogn' o - ra vi chia - ma l'a - ma - to suo ben.
CESARE.
Non ha in cie - lo il To - nante me - lo - dia, che pa - reggi un si bel can - to.
50
52
24
57
Aria da Capo.

	CLEOPATRA
Eseguisti, oh Niren, quanto t'imposi?	Did you carry out, Nireno, what I commanded?
	NIRENO
Adempito è il commando.	The order has been executed.
	CLEOPATRA
Giunto è Cesare in corte?	Has Caesar arrived in the court?
	NIRENO
Io vel condussi, ed ei Già a queste soglie il piè rivolge.	I led him here, and he is already directing his steps toward this threshold.
	CLEOPATRA
Ma dimmi: è in pronto La meditata scena?	But tell me, is the projected stage-set ready?
	NIRENO
Infra le nubi l'alta regia sfavilla; Ma che far pensi?	Among the clouds the lofty kingdom sparkles, but what are you thinking of doing?
	CLEOPATRA
Amore Già suggerì all'idea Stravagante pensier; ho già risolto Sotto finte apparenze Far prigionier d'amor chi 'l cor m'ha tolto	Cupid gave me the idea— an extravagant thought; I have resolved in disguise to make prisoner of love him who has stolen my heart.
	NIRENO
A lui ti scoprirai?	Will you reveal yourself to him?
	CLEOPATRA
Non è ancor tempo.	It's not time yet.
	NIRENO
Io che far deggio?	What must I do?
	CLEOPATRA
Attendi Cesare in disparte: indi lo guida In questi alberghi, e poi lo guida ancora Colà nelle mie stanze, e a lui dirai Che, per dargli contezza Di quanto dal suo Rè gli si contende, Pria che tramonti il sol Lidia l'attende. *(Cleopatra exits)*	Wait for Caesar aside, then lead him to these quarters, and afterwards show him to my chambers, and I will tell him that—to give him an account of the nature of the dispute with his king— before the sun sets Lidia will be waiting for him.

NIRENO

Da Cleopatra apprenda chi è seguace D'amor l'astuzie e frodi.	From Cleopatra, who pursues love, you may learn cunning tricks and deception.

CESARE

Dov'è, Niren, dov'è l'anima mia?	Where is she, Niren, where is my soul?

NIRENO

In questo loco in breve verrà Lidia, Signor	Here in this place you will shortly see Lidia, Sir.

CESARE

Cieli! E qual delle sfere scende armonico suon, che mi rapisce?	Heavens! And from which of the spheres descends the harmonious sound that enchants me?

NIRENO

Avrà di selce il cor chi non languisce.	He has a heart of stone who does not surrender.

Parnassus opens and we see Virtue in her throne, accompanied by the nine Muses

CESARE

Giulio, che mira? E quando con abisso di luce scesero i Numi in terra?	Julius, what do you see? When, in a blaze of light, did the gods descend to earth?

CLEOPATRA (*in costume as Virtue*)

V'adoro pupille, Saette d'Amore, Le vostre faville Son grate nel sen; Pietose vi brama Il mesto mio core, Ch'ogn'ora vi chiama L'amato suo ben.	I adore you, pupils, Cupid's darts. Your sparks are welcome to the heart. Pitiable, for you longs my gloomy heart, which every hour calls you, its beloved treasure.

CESARE

Non ha in cielo il Tonante melodia, Che pareggi un si bel canto.	Jupiter in heaven has no melody that matches such beautiful song.

CLEOPATRA

V'adoro pupille, etc.	I adore you, pupils, etc.

—Nicola Haym

Handel composed about forty operas for London between 1711 and 1741. Produced in 1724 while Handel was enjoying his greatest success as an opera composer, *Giulio Cesare* has a libretto by Nicola Haym (1679–1729), a cellist and composer as well as a producer and poet.

In her official capacity as co-ruler of Egypt with her brother Ptolemy, Cleopatra welcomes Caesar to Egypt and immediately falls in love with him. Not wishing to reveal her weakness, she hopes to seduce him disguised as Lidia. In this scene Nireno, Cleopatra's confidant, leads Caesar to an enchanted grove where a woman is singing; it is Cleopatra taking the part of Virtue, surrounded by the nine Muses.

Both the symphony and the accompaniment to her aria are scored in the manner of a concerto grosso. The concertino demands solo players: one oboe, two muted violins, viola, harp, viola da gamba, theorbo, bassoon, and cello. Handel scored the tutti orchestra for strings, with oboes doubling the muted violins. In the symphony all play in unison, but in the aria the concertino continually accompanies the voice, while the tutti orchestra punctuates and complements this accompaniment, except in the B section of the aria, when it is silent. Handel rarely used such a division of the orchestra into soli and tutti, which Alessandro Stradella had pioneered in his oratorios performed in Rome.

The vocal line grows from a four-note motive into paired antecedent-consequent four-measure phrases. The word "saetta"—Cupid's arrow—probably inspired the flirting, darting motive. The A section has the rhythmic characer of a sarabande, with emphasis on the second of three beats. By contrast, the B section, in the relative minor, features perpetual eighth-note motion in the accompaniment, but the vocal line still leans on the second beat. Rather than reaching a cadence at the end of the aria, Handel delays it for Ceasar's reaction to Cleopatra's song, thus integrating the aria with the action of the drama, after which we hear the conventional da capo, usually sung with embellishments.

George Frideric Handel

84

Saul: Act II, Scene 10 CD 6

a) No. 66, Accompagnato, Saul: *The Time at length is come*

Hallische Händel-Ausgabe (Kassel, 1962), pp. 213–40. Reprinted by permission of Bärenreiter Music Corporation.

b) No. 67, Recitative, Saul and Jonathan: *Where is the Son of Jesse?*

26

SAUL
Where is the Son of Jes - se? Comes he not to grace our Feast?
JONATHAN
He earn - est - ly ask'd

Continuo (Violoncello, Cembalo)

4
Leave To go to Beth - lem, where his Fa - ther's House At sol - emn Rites of an - nual Sac - ri - fice Re - quir'd his

7
Pres - ence.
SAUL
O Per - verse! Re - bel - lious! Thinkst thou, I do not know, that thou hast chose The Son of

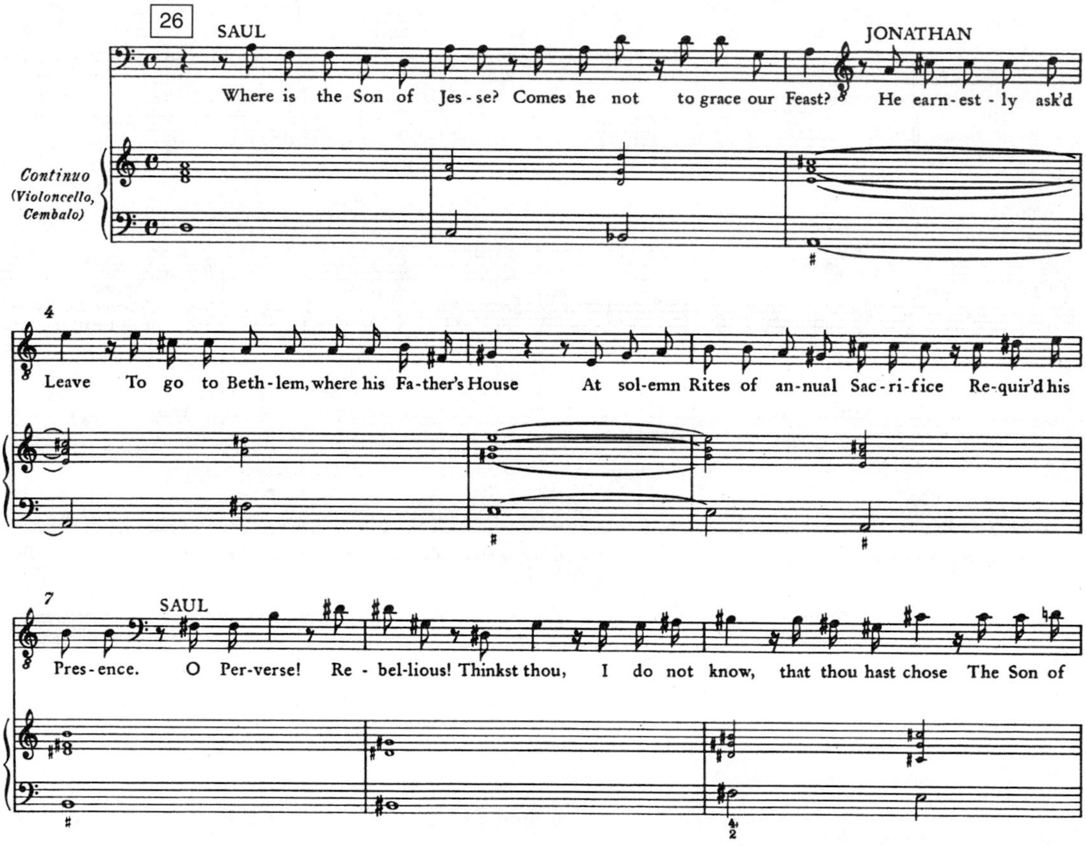

10
Jes - se to thy own Con-fu - sion? The World will say, thou art no Son of mine, Who thus canst
13
love the Man I hate; the Man, Who, if he lives, will rob thee of thy Crown.
16
Send, fetch him hith - er; for the Wretch must die.
JONATHAN
What has he done? And where-fore must he
19
SAUL
die? Dar'st thou op - pose my Will? Die then thy self.
(Throws his Javelin. Exit Jonathan, then Saul.)

c) No. 68, Chorus: *O fatal Consequence of Rage*

7
O fa - tal
Con - se-quence of
Rage,
O fa - tal
Con - se-quence of
Rage, by Rea - son
O fa - tal
Con - se-quence of
O fa - tal
Org.
Vc.
Tutti

13
O fa - tal Con - se-quence of Rage, by Rea - son un - - con - troll'd! With ev' - ry
un - con - troll'd! Of Rage, by Rea - son un - con - troll'd! With ev' - ry
Rage, un - con - troll'd——! Of Rage, by Rea - son un - con - troll'd! With ev' - ry
con - se-quence of Rage, Of Rage, by Rea - son un - - con - troll'd! With ev' - ry
6 4 2 6 7 6 6 3

18
Law he can dis - pense; No Ties the fu - rious Mon-ster hold, No Ties the fu - rious Mon-ster
Law he can dis - pense; No Ties the fu - rious Mon-ster hold, No Ties the fu - rious Mon-ster
Law he can dis - pense; No Ties the fu - rious Mon-ster hold, No Ties the fu - rious Mon-ster
Law he can dis - pense; No Ties the fu - rious Mon-ster hold, No Ties the fu - rious Mon-ster

22
hold: With ev' - ry Law he can dis - pense; No Ties the fu - rious Mon - ster hold, No
hold: With ev' - ry Law he can dis - pense; No Ties the fu - rious Mon - ster hold, No
hold: With ev' - ry Law he can dis - pense; No Ties the fu - rious Mon - ster hold, No
hold: With ev' - ry Law he can dis - pense; No Ties the fu - rious Mon - ster hold, No

26
Ties the fu-rious Mon-ster hold: O fa - tal Con - se-quence of Rage, by Rea - son
Ties the fu rious Mon-ster hold: O fa - tal Con - se-quence of
Ties the fu-rious Mon-ster hold: O fa - tal
Ties the fu-rious Mon-ster hold:
7 6 5 3
senza Violone

31
un - - - con- troll'd, un - con - troll'd!
O fa - tal
Rage, by Rea - son un - - - con- troll'd!
Con - se-quence of Rage, un - con - troll'd!
O fa - tal Con - se-quence of Rage.
Tutti
Org.
Vc.

37
Con - se-quence of Rage, O fa - tal Con - se-quence of
O fa - tal Con - se-quence of Rage, by Rea - son un - con - troll'd! Of
O fa - tal Con - se-quence of Rage, un - con - troll'd! Of
O fa - tal Con - se-quence of Rage, of
Tutti

42
Rage, by Rea - son un - - - con - troll'd! With ev' - ry Law he can dis - pense; No Ties the
Rage, by Rea - son un - con - troll'd! With ev' - ry Law he can dis - pense; No Ties the
Rage, by Rea - son un - con - troll'd! With ev' - ry Law he can dis - pense; No Ties the
Rage, by Rea - son un - - - con - troll'd! With ev' - ry Law he can dis - pense; No Ties the

47
fu-rious Mon-ster hold, No Ties the fu-rious Mon-ster hold: With ev' - ry Law he can dis -
fu-rious Mon-ster hold, No Ties the fu-rious Mon-ster hold: With ev' - ry Law he can dis -
fu-rious Mon-ster hold, No Ties the fu-rious Mon-ster hold: With ev' - ry Law he can dis -
fu-rious Mon-ster hold, No Ties the fu-rious Mon-ster hold: With ev' - ry Law he can dis -

51
pense; No Ties the fu-rious Mon-ster hold, no Ties the fu-rious Mon-ster hold:
pense; No Ties the fu-rious Mon-ster hold, no Ties the fu-rious Mon-ster hold:
pense; No Ties the fu-rious Mon-ster hold, no Ties the fu-rious Mon-ster hold:
pense; No Ties the fu-rious Mon-ster hold, no Ties the fu-rious Mon-ster hold:

28
Andante larghetto
56
blind - ly, blind - ly, blind - ly he goes, from Crime to Crime he
From Crime to Crime he blind - ly goes, he blind - ly goes, blind - ly,
blind - ly, blind - ly, from Crime to Crime he
Org.
col Vc.

64
— blind - ly goes, he blind - - ly, blind - ly goes, blind - ly,
blind - ly, he — blind - - ly goes, he blind - ly goes, he blind - ly, blind - ly
blind - - - ly goes, blind - ly, blind - ly, he — blind - ly
From Crime to Crime he — blind - ly goes, he
Tutti

72
blind - ly, he blind - ly goes, from Crime to Crime he blind - ly goes, from Crime to
goes, he blind - ly goes, he blind - ly goes,
—, blind - ly goes, he blind - ly goes, from Crime to
blind - ly goes, from Crime to Crime, from Crime to Crime he blind - ly

80
Crime,
blind - ly,
blind - ly, he
blind - ly
goes,
he
blind - ly
goes,
he
he
blind - ly,
blind - ly
goes,
he
blind - ly
Crime
he
blind - ly
goes,
he
blind - ly
goes,
blind - ly,
blind - ly,
he
blind - ly
goes, blind - ly,
blind - ly,
he
blind - ly
goes,
blind - ly,
blind - ly
goes,
senza Violone

88
29
p
blind - ly goes, from Crime to Crime he blind - ly goes, Nor End, but with his own De-struc-tion,
goes, from Crime to Crime he blind - ly, blind - ly goes,
goes, blind - ly, blind - ly, he blind - ly, blind - ly goes,
from Crime to Crime he blind - ly, blind - ly goes,
Tutti
p

96
p
p
knows ____, but with his own De-struc - tion, knows ____, but with his own
Nor End, but with his own De-struc-tion, knows ____
Nor End, but with his
senza Violone

103
De - struc-tion, knows, Nor End, but with his
und stürmt zum Un - ter-
Nor End, but with his own De-struc - tion, knows, but with his
own De-struc-tion, knows, but with his own
Nor End, but with his own De - struc-tion, knows, but with his own
Tutti

109
own De-struc-tion, knows, he blind-ly goes, blind-ly, blind-ly, he blind-ly
own De-struc-tion, knows, he blind-ly goes, he blind-ly, blind-ly goes,
De-struc-tion, knows, blind-ly, blind-ly, he blind-ly, blind-ly goes,
De-struc-tion, knows, From Crime to Crime he blind-ly goes, he blind-ly goes, from

117
goes, from Crime to Crime he blind - ly' goes, from Crime to Crime
he blind - ly goes, he blind - ly goes,
he blind - ly goes, from Crime to Crime he blind - ly
Crime to Crime, from Crime to Crime he blind - ly goes, blind - ly, blind - ly, he

125
blind - ly, blind - ly, he blind - ly goes, he blind - ly goes, he blind - ly goes, From
he blind - ly, blind - ly goes, he blind - ly goes, From Crime to
goes, he blind - ly goes, blind - ly, blind - ly, he blind - ly goes, blind - ly,
blind - ly goes, blind - ly, blind - ly goes, From Crime to
senza Violone
Tutti

133
p
Crime to Crime he blind - ly goes, Nor End, but with his own De - struc - tion, knows
Crime he blind - ly, blind - ly goes,
blind - ly, he blind - ly, blind - ly goes,
Crime he blind - ly, blind - ly goes,
4 2 6 4 # p 6

140
p
p
, but with his
own De-struc - tion,
knows
, but
with his own
De - struc-tion,
in ih - rem
Nor
End, but with his
own De-struc-tion,
knows
Nor
End, but with his
own De-struc-tion,
senza Violone

147
p
p
p
p
p
p
knows, nor End, but with his own De-struc-tion,
, nor End, but with his own De-struc - tion, knows, but with his own De-struc-tion,
knows, but with his own De - struc-tion,
Nor End, but with his own De - struc-tion, knows, but with his own De - struc-tion,
p Tutti

153
f
knows, Nor End, but with his own De-struc-tion, knows, nor
knows, Nor End, but with his own De-struc-tion, knows, nor
knows, Nor End, but with his own De-struc-tion, knows, but with his own De-struc-tion, knows, nor
knows, Nor End, but with his own De-struc-tion, knows, but with his own De-struc-tion, knows, nor

End of the Second Act

Saul (1739) was one of Handel's first English oratorios, preceded only by *Esther* in 1732, and *Deborah* and *Athalia* in 1733. Charles Jennens, who also wrote librettos for *Messiah* and other oratorios, here dramatized the Bible's First Book of Samuel, Chapters 16 to 20, 24, 28, and 31, and Chapters 1 and 2 of the Second Book.

David, who played the harp to calm Saul during his fits of anger, becomes a military hero, defending the Israelites against Goliath and other enemies. In Act I (No. 22) at a victory celebration for David, a chorus of women praises him for having slain "ten thousands," compared to Saul's "thousands." This and similar incidents arouse Saul's jealousy. At a banquet in which Saul plans his revenge against David, who wisely does not attend, Saul is so angry that he throws the javelin meant for David at his own son Jonathan, who dares make excuses for David's absence.

In Saul's obbligato recitative (No. 66), in which he expresses his resolve to have David killed, the violins and violas simulate bellicose trumpet fanfares between the lines of rhymed poetry.

In the continuo recitative (No. 67), Saul's fury intensifies as he listens to the excuses Jonathan makes for David's absence. The accompaniment, en route from the initial D minor to its dominant, passes through alien chords of G♯ minor, C♯ major, F♯ major, and E major, sometimes progressing through a chordal seventh in the bass. Finally Saul orders Jonathan to capture David, to face his death. But when Jonathan again pleads David's innocence, Saul threatens: "Dar'st thou oppose my Will? Die then thy self"; he throws the javelin at Jonathan, who manages to dodge it and escape.

The chorus, "O fatal Consequence of Rage" (No. 68), which Jennens modeled on those from Greek tragedy, reflects on the morality of the situation. The chorus is a succession of three fugues, each of which ends with majestic homorhythmic passages. The first fugue is based on "Quos pretioso sanguine" of the Te Deum by Antonio Francesco Urio (ca. 1631–ca. 1719), one of six occasions in *Saul* that Handel borrowed from Urio's Te Deum.

Like Urio's fugue, Handel's begins with a stretto, a device usually saved for the final climactic effect. The similarity between Handel's and Urio's fugues ends at the first exposition; Handel develops the subject much more exhaustively. The second fugue aptly describes the furious assailant, who goes blindly "from Crime to Crime," with a subject that, after a rising second, leaps a minor seventh, and an episode that meanders over a chromatic bass. The last fugue is a picture of Saul's headstrong drive to self-destruction, bringing back the chromatic episode of the previous fugue to delay the final denoument.

INSTRUMENT NAMES AND ABBREVIATIONS

The following tables set forth the English, Italian, German, and French names used for the various musical instruments in these scores, and their respective abbreviations.

WOODWINDS

English	*Italian*	*German*	*French*
Piccolo (Picc.)	Flauto piccolo (Fl. Picc.)	Kleine Flöte (Kl. Fl.)	Petite flûte
Flute (Fl.)	Flauto (Fl.); Flauto grande (Fl. gr.)	Große Flöte (Fl. gr.)	Flûte (Fl.)
Alto flute	Flauto contralto (fl.c-alto)	Altflöte	Flûte en sol
Oboe (Ob.)	Oboe (Ob.)	Hoboe (Hb.); Oboe (Ob.)	Hautbois (Hb.)
English horn (E.H.)	Corno inglese (C. or Cor. ingl., C.i.)	Englisches Horn	Cor anglais (C.A.)
Sopranino clarinet	Clarinetto piccolo (clar. picc.)		
Clarinet (C., Cl., Clt., Clar.)	Clarinetto (Cl., Clar.)	Klarinette (Kl.)	Clarinette (Cl.)
Bass clarinet (B. Cl.)	Clarinetto basso (Cl. b., Cl. basso, Clar. basso)	Bass Klarinette (Bkl.)	Clarinette basse (Cl. bs.)
Bassoon (Bsn., Bssn.)	Fagotto (Fag,. Fg.)	Fagott (Fag., Fg.)	Basson (Bssn.)
Contrabassoon (C. Bsn.)	Contrafagotto (Cfg., C. Fag., Cont. F.)	Kontrafagott (Kfg.)	Contrebasson (C. bssn.)

BRASS

English	*Italian*	*German*	*French*
French horn (Hr., Hn.)	Corno (Cor., C.)	Horn (Hr.) [*pl.* Hörner (Hrn.)]	Cor; Cor à pistons
Trumpet (Tpt., Trpt., Trp., Tr.)	Tromba (Tr.)	Trompete (Tr., Trp.)	Trompette (Tr.)
Trumpet in D	Tromba piccola (Tr. picc.)		
Cornet	Cornetta	Kornett	Cornet à pistons (C. à p., Pist.)
Trombone (Tr., Tbe., Trb., Trm., Trbe.)	Trombone [*pl.* Tromboni (Tbni., Trni.)]	Posaune (Ps., Pos.)	Trombone (Tr.)
Tuba (Tb.)	Tuba (Tb., Tba.)	Tuba (Tb.)	Tuba (Tb.)

PERCUSSION

English	*Italian*	*German*	*French*
Percussion (Perc.)	Percussione	Schlagzeug (Schlag.)	Batterie (Batt.)
Kettledrums (K. D.)	Timpani (Timp., Tp.)	Pauken (Pk.)	Timbales (Timb.)
Snare drum (S. D.)	Tamburo piccolo (Tamb. picc.) Tamburo militare (Tamb. milit.)	Kleine Trommel (Kl. Tr.)	Caisse claire (C. cl.), Caisse roulante Tambour militaire (Tamb. milit.)
Bass drum (B. drum)	Gran cassa (Gr. Cassa, Gr. C., G. C.)	Große Trommel (Gr. Tr.)	Grosse caisse (Gr. c.)
Cymbals (Cym., Cymb.)	Piatti (P., Ptti., Piat.)	Becken (Beck.)	Cymbales (Cym.)
Tam-Tam (Tam-T.)			
Tambourine (Tamb.)	Tamburino (Tamb.)	Schellentrommel, Tamburin	Tambour de Basque (T. de B., Tamb. de Basque)
Triangle (Trgl., Tri.)	Triangolo (Trgl.)	Triangel	Triangle (Triang.)
Glockenspiel (Glocken.)	Campanelli (Cmp.)	Glockenspiel	Carillon
Bells (Chimes)	Campane (Cmp.)	Glocken	Cloches
Antique Cymbals	Crotali, Piatti antichi	Antiken Zimbeln	Cymbales antiques
Sleigh Bells	Sonagli (Son.)	Schellen	Grelots
Xylophone (Xyl.)	Xilofono	Xylophon	Xylophone

STRINGS

English	*Italian*	*German*	*French*
Violin (V., Vl., Vn., Vln., Vi.)	Violino (V., Vl., Vln.)	Violine (V., Vl., Vln.) Geige (Gg.)	Violon (V., Vl., Vln.)
Viola (Va., Vl., *pl.* Vas.)	Viola (Va., Vla.) *pl.* Viole (Vle.)	Bratsche (Br.)	Alto (A.)
Violoncello, Cello (Vcl., Vc.)	Violoncello (Vc., Vlc., Vcllo.)	Violoncell (Vc., Vlc.)	Violoncelle (Vc.)
Double bass (D. Bs.)	Contrabasso (Cb., C. B.) *pl.* Contrabassi or Bassi (C. Bassi, Bi.)	Kontrabass (Kb.)	Contrebasse (C. B.)

OTHER INSTRUMENTS

English	*Italian*	*German*	*French*
Harp (Hp., Hrp.)	Arpa (A., Arp.)	Harfe (Hrf.)	Harpe (Hp.)
Piano	Pianoforte (P.-f., Pft.)	Klavier	Piano
Celesta (Cel.)			
Harpsichord	Cembalo	Cembalo	Clavecin
Harmonium (Harmon.)			
Organ (Org.)	Organo	Orgel	Orgue
Guitar		Gitarre (Git.)	
Mandoline (Mand.)			

GLOSSARY OF SCORE AND PERFORMANCE INDICATIONS

(For a glossary of general music terms, see *A History of Western Music,* 6th ed.)

a The phrases *a 2, a 3* (etc.) indicate that the part is to be played in unison by 2, 3 (etc.) players; when a simple number (1., 2., etc.) is placed over a part, it indicates that only the first (second, etc.) player in that group should play.
abdämpfen To mute.
aber But.
accelerando (acc.) Growing faster.
accompagnato (accomp.) In a continuo part, this indicates that the chord-playing instrument resumes (*cf. tasto solo*).
adagio Slow, leisurely.
a demi-jeu Half-organ; i.e., softer registration.
ad libitum (ad lib.) An indication giving the performer liberty to: (1) vary from strict tempo; (2) include or omit the part of some voice or instrument; (3) include a cadenza of one's own invention.
agitato Agitated, excited.
alla breve A time signature (¢) indicating, in the sixteenth century, a single breve per two-beat measure; in later music, the half note rather than the quarter is the unit of beat.
allargando (allarg.) Growing broader.
alle, alles All, every, each.
allegretto A moderately fast tempo (between allegro and andante).
allegro A rapid tempo (between allegretto and presto).
alto, altus (A.) The deeper of the two main divisions of women's (or boys') voices.
am Frosch At the heel (of a bow).
am Griffbrett Play near, or above, the fingerboard of a string instrument.
amoroso Loving, amorous.
am Steg On the bridge (of an instrument).
ancora Again.
andante A moderately slow tempo (between adagio and allegretto).
animato, animé Animated.
a piacere The execution of the passage is left to the performer's discretion.
arco Played with the bow.
arpeggiando, arpeggiato (arpeg.) Played in harp style, i.e., the notes of the chord played in quick succession rather than simultaneously.
assai Very.
a tempo At the (basic) tempo.
attacca Begin what follows without pausing.
auf dem On the (as in *auf dem G*, on the G string).
Auftritt Scene.
Ausdruck Expression.
ausdrucksvoll With expression.
Auszug Arrangement.

baguettes Drumsticks (*baguettes de bois, baguettes timbales de bois*, wooden drumsticks or kettledrum sticks; *baguettes d'éponge*, sponge-headed drumsticks; *baguettes midures*, semi-hard drumsticks; *baguettes dures,* hard drumsticks; *baguettes timbales en feutre*, felt-headed kettledrum sticks).
bariton Brass instrument.
bass, basso, bassus (B.) The lowest male voice.
Begleitung Accompaniment.
belebt Animated.
beruhigen To calm, to quiet.
bewegt Agitated.
bewegter More agitated.
bien Very.
breit Broadly.
breiter More broadly.
Bühne Stage.

cadenza An extended passage for solo instrument in free, improvisatory style.
calando Diminishing in volume and speed.
cambiare To change.
cantabile (cant.) In a singing style.
cantando In a singing manner.
canto Voice (as in *col canto*, a direction for the accompaniment to follow the solo part in tempo and expression).

cantus An older designation for the highest part in a vocal work.
chiuso Stopped, in horn playing.
col, colla, coll' With the.
come prima, come sopra As at first; as previously.
comme Like, as.
comodo Comfortable, easy.
con With
Continuo (Con.) A method of indicating an accompanying part by the bass notes only, together with figures designating the chords to be played above them. In general practice, the chords are played on a lute, harpsichord, or organ, while, often, a viola da gamba or cello doubles the bass notes.
contratenor In earlier music, the name given to the third voice part that was added to the basic two-voice texture of discant and tenor, having the same range as the tenor, which it frequently crosses.
corda String; for example, *seconda* (2*a*) *corda* is the second string (the A string on the violin).
coro Chorus.
coryphée Leader of a ballet or chorus.
countertenor Male alto, derived from *contratenor altus.*
crescendo (cresc.) Increasing in volume.

da capo (D.C.) Repeat from the beginning, usually up to the indication *Fine* (end).
daher From there.
dal segno Repeat from the sign.
Dämpfer (Dpf.) Mute.
decrescendo (decresc., decr.) Decreasing in volume.
delicato Delicate, soft.
dessus Treble.
détaché With a broad, vigorous bow stroke, each note bowed singly.
deutlich Distinctly.
diminuendo, diminuer (dim., dimin.) Decreasing in volume.
discantus Improvised counterpoint to an existing melody.
divisés, divisi (div.) Divided; indicates that the instrumental group should be divided into two or more parts to play the passage in question.
dolce Sweet and soft.
dolcemente Sweetly.
dolcissimo (dolciss.) Very sweet.
Doppelgriff Double stop.
doppelt Twice.
doppio movimento Twice as fast.
doux Sweet.
duplum In medieval polyphonic music, the first voice composed over the tenor.
drängend Pressing on.

e And.
Echoton Like an echo.
éclatant Sparkling, brilliant.
einleiten To lead into.
Encore Again.
en dehors Emphasized.
en fusée Dissolving in.
erschütterung A violent shaking, deep emotion.
espressione intensa Intense expression.
espressivo (espress., espr.) Expressive.
et And.
etwas Somewhat, rather.
expressif (express.) Expressive.

falsetto Male singing voice in which notes above the ordinary range are obtained artificially.
falsobordone Four-part harmonization of psalm tones with mainly root-position chords.
fauxbourdon (faulx bourdon) Three-part harmony in which the chant melody in the treble is accompanied by two lower voices, one in parallel sixths, and the other improvised a fourth below the melody.
fermer brusquement To close abruptly.
fine End, close.
flatterzunge, flutter-tongue A special tonguing technique for wind intruments, producing a rapid trill-like sound.
flüchtig Fleeting, transient.
fois Time (as in *premier fois*, first time).
forte (f) Loud.
fortissimo (ff) Very loud (*fff* indicates a still louder dynamic).
fortsetzend Continuing.
forza Force.
frei Free.
fugato A section of a composition fugally treated.
funebre Funereal, mournful.
fuoco Fire, spirit.
furioso Furious.

ganz Entirely, altogether.
gebrochen Broken.
gedehnt Held back.
gemächlich Comfortable.
Generalpause (G.P.) Rest for the complete orchestra.
geschlagen Struck.

geschwinder More rapid, swift.
gesprochen Spoken.
gesteigert Intensified.
gestopft (chiuso) Stopped; for the notes of a horn obtained by placing the hand in the bell.
gestrichen (gestr.) Bowed.
gesungen Sung.
geteilt (get.) Divided; indicates that the instrumental group should be divided into two parts to play the passage in question.
gewöhnlich (gew., gewöhnl.) Usual, customary.
giusto Moderate.
gleichmässig Equal, symmetrical.
gli altri The others.
glissando (gliss.) Rapidly gliding over strings or keys, producing a scale run.
grande Large, great.
grave Slow, solemn; deep, low.
gravement Gravely, solemnly.
grazioso Graceful.
groß, großes, großer, etc. Large, big.

H⌐ *Hauptstimme*, the most important voice in the texture.
Halbe Half.
Halt Stop, hold.
harmonic (harm.) A flute-like sound produced on a string instrument by lightly touching the string with the finger instead of pressing down on the string.
Hauptzeitmass Original tempo.
heftiger More passionate, violent.
hervortretend Prominently.
Holz Woodwinds.
hörbar Audible.

immer Always.
impetuoso Impetuous, violent.
istesso tempo The same tempo, as when the duration of the beat remains unaltered despite meter change.

klagend Lamenting.
klangvoll Sonorous, full-sounding.
klingen lassen Allow to sound.
kräftig Stong, forceful.
kurz Short.
kurzer Shorter.

laissez vibrer Let vibrate; an indication to the player of a harp, cymbal, etc., that the sound must not be damped.
langsam Slow.
langsamer Slower.
largamente Broadly.
larghetto Slightly faster than largo.
largo A very slow tempo.
lebhaft Lively.
legato Performed without any perceptible interruption between notes.
leggéro, leggiero (legg.) Light and graceful.
legno The wood of the bow (*col legno tratto*, bowed with the wood; *col legno battuto*, tapped with the wood; *col legno gestrich*, played with the wood).
leidenschaftlich Passionate, vehement.
lent Slow.
lentamente Slowly.
lento A slow tempo (between andante and largo).
l.h. Abbreviation for "left hand."
lié Tied.

ma But.
maestoso Majestic.
maggiore Major key.
main Hand (*droite*, right; *gauche*, left).
marcatissimo (marcatiss.) With very marked emphasis.
marcato (mar.) Marked, with emphasis.
marcia March.
marqué Marked, with emphasis.
mässig Moderate.
mean Middle part of a polyphonic composition.
meno Less.
mezza voce With half the voice power.
mezzo forte (mf) Moderately loud.
mezzo piano (mp) Moderately soft.
minore In the minor mode.
minuetto Minuet.
mit With.
M.M. Metronome; followed by an indication of the setting for the correct tempo.
moderato, modéré At a moderate tempo.
molto Very, much.
mosso Rapid.
motetus In medieval polyphonic music, a texted voice part above the tenor.
moto Motion.
muta, mutano Change the tuning of the instrument as specified.

N⌐ *Nebenstimme*, the second most important voice in the texture.
Nachslag Auxiliary note (at end of trill).

nehmen (nimmt) To take.
neue New.
nicht, non Not.
noch Still, yet.

octava (okt., 8va) Octave; if not otherwise qualified, means the notes marked should be played an octave higher than written.
ohne (o.) Without.
open In brass instruments, the opposite of muted. In string instruments, refers to the unstopped string (i.e., sounding at its full length).
ordinario, ordinairement (ordin., ord.) In the usual way (generally cancelling an instruction to play using some special technique).
ôtez les sourdines Remove the mutes.

parlando A singing style with the voice approximating speech.
parte Part (*colla parte*, the accompaniment is to follow the voice parts).
passione Passion.
pause Rest.
pedal (ped., P.) In piano music, indicates that the damper pedal should be depressed; an asterisk indicates the point of release (brackets below the music are also used to indicate pedalling). On an organ, the pedals are a keyboard played with the feet.
perdendosi Gradually dying away.
peu Little, a little.
pianissimo (pp) Very soft (*ppp* indicates a still softer dynamic).
piano (p) Soft.
più More.
pizzicato (pizz.) The string plucked with the finger.
plötzlich Suddenly, immediately.
plus More.
pochissimo (pochiss.) Very little.
poco Little, a little.
poco a poco Little by little.
ponticello (pont.) The bridge (of a string instrument).
portato Performance manner between legato and staccato.
prenez Take up.
près de la table On the harp, the plucking of the strings near the soundboard.
prestissimo Very fast.
presto A very quick tempo (faster than allegro).
prima First.
principale (pr.) Principal, solo.

quasi Almost, as if.
quasi niente Almost nothing, i.e., as softly as possible.
quintus An older disignation for the fifth part in a vocal work.

rallentando (rall., rallent.) Growing slower.
rasch Quick.
recitative (recit.) A vocal style designed to imitate and emphasize the natural inflections of speech.
rinforzando (rinf.) Sudden accent on a single note or chord.
ritardando (rit., ritard.) Gradually slackening in speed.
ritmico Rhythmical.
rubato A certain elasticity and flexibility of tempo, speeding up and slowing down the performance of written music.
ruhig Calm.
ruhiger More calmly.

saltando (salt.) An indication to the string player to bounce the bow off the string by playing with short, quick bow-strokes.
sans Without.
scherzando (scherz.) Playfully.
schleppend Dragging.
schnell Fast.
schneller Faster.
schon Already.
schwerer Heavier, more difficult.
schwermütig Dejected, sad.
sec., secco Dry, simple.
segno Sign in form of 𝄋 indicating the beginning and end of a section to be repeated.
segue (1) Continue to the next movement without pausing; (2) continue in the same manner.
sehr Very.
semplice Simple, in a simple manner.
sempre Always, continually.
senza Without.
senza mis[ura] Free of regular meter.
serpent Bass of the cornett family.
seulement Only.
sforzando, sforzato (sfz, sf) With sudden emphasis.
simile In a similar manner.
sino al . . . Up to the . . . (usually followed by a new tempo marking, or by a dotted line indicating a terminal point).

sombre Dark, somber.
son Sound.
sonore Sonorous, with full tone.
sopra Above; in piano music, used to indicate that one hand must pass above the other.
soprano (Sop., S.) The voice with the highest range.
sordino (sord.) Mute.
sostenendo, sostenuto (sost.) Sustained.
sotto voce In an undertone, subdued, under the breath.
sourdine Mute.
soutenu Sustained.
spiccato With a light bouncing motion of the bow.
spirito Spirited, lively.
spiritoso Humorous.
sprechstimme (sprechst.) Speaking voice.
staccato (stacc.) Detached, separated, abruptly disconnected.
stentando, stentato (stent.) Hesitating, retarding.
Stimme Voice.
strepitoso, strepito Noisy, boisterous.
stretto In a nonfugal composition, indicates a concluding section at an increased speed.
stringendo (string.) Quickening.
subito (sub.) Suddenly, immediately.
sul On the (as in *sul G*. on the G string).
suono Sound, tone.
superius The uppermost part.
sur On.

Takt Bar, beat.
tasto solo In a continuo part, this indicates that only the string instrument plays; the chord-playing instrument is silent.
temp primo (temp I) At the original tempo.
tendrement Tenderly.
tenerezza Tenderness.
tenor, tenore (T., ten.) High male voice or part.
tenuto (ten.) Held, sustained.
touche Fingerboard or fret (of a string instrument).
tranquillo Quiet, calm.
trauernd Mournfully.
treble Soprano voice or range.
tremolo (trem) On string instruments, a quick reiteration of the same tone, produced by a rapid up-and-down movement of the bow; also a rapid alternation between two different notes.
très Very.
trill (tr.) The rapid alternation of a given note with the note above it. In a drum part it indicates rapid alternating strokes with two drumsticks.
triplum In medieval polyphonic music, a voice part above the tenor and duplum.
tristement Sadly.
troppo Too much.
tutti Literally, "all"; usually means all the instruments in a given category as distinct from a solo part.

übertönend Drowning out.
unison (unis.) The same notes or melody played by several instruments at the same pitch. Often used to emphasize that a phrase is not to be divided among several players.
Unterbrechung Interruption, suspension.

veloce Fast.
verhalten Restrained, held back.
verklingen lassen To let the sound die away.
Verwandlung Change of scene.
verzweiflungsvoll Full of despair.
vibrato Slight fluctuation of pitch around a sustained tone.
vif Lively.
vigoroso Vigorous, strong.
vivace Quick, lively.
voce Voice.
volti Turn over (the page).
Vorhang auf Curtain up.
Vorhang fällt, Vorhang zu Curtain down.
voriges Preceding.
vorwärts Forward, onward.

weg Away, beyond.
wieder Again.
wie oben As above, as before.

zart Tenderly, delicately.
ziemlich Suitable, fit.
zurückhaltend Slackening in speed.
zurückkehrend zum Return to, go back to.

INDEX OF COMPOSERS

INDEX OF TITLES

INDEX OF FORMS AND GENRES